I0883225

SAXON® ALGEBRA 2

Practice Workbook

SAXON®
HOUGHTON MIFFLIN HARCOURT
Supplemental Publishers

www.SaxonPublishers.com
800-531-5015

ISBN 13: 978-1-6027-7529-9
ISBN 10: 1-6027-7529-x

© 2009 Saxon®, an imprint of HMH Supplemental Publishers Inc.

All rights reserved. No part of this material protected by this copyright may be reproduced or utilized in any form or by any means, in whole or in part, without permission in writing from the copyright owner. Requests for permission should be mailed to: Paralegal Department, 6277 Sea Harbor Drive, Orlando, FL 32887.

Saxon® is a registered trademark of HMH Supplemental Publishers Inc.

Printed in the United States of America

If you have received these materials as examination copies free of charge, HMH Supplemental Publishers Inc. retains title to the materials and they may not be resold. Resale of examination copies is strictly prohibited and is illegal.

Possession of this publication in print format does not entitle users to convert this publication, or any portion of it, into electronic format.

2 2026
4500939738

Table of Contents

© Saxon. All rights reserved.

Table of Contents

© Saxon. All rights reserved.

Table of Contents

© Saxon. All rights reserved.

Name ______________________________ Date ____________ Class ____________

Using Properties of Real Numbers

LESSON 1

Simplify each expression.

1. (SB) $-3 - 6 + 1$

2. (SB) $-4 + 6 - 8 =$

Simplify each expression using the properties of real numbers.

***3.** (1) $-2[(5 - 7 - 2) - (-2 - 7) - 2]$

***4.** (1) $4[3 - (-2)] + 5(-2 + 1)$

Simplify each expression.

5. (SB) $14.6 - 9.03$

6. (SB) $39.75 + 49.2$

Order the given numbers from least to greatest.

7. (SB) 2.1, 2.3, 2.09

8. (SB) $\frac{3}{5}, \frac{4}{7}, \frac{1}{2}$

Find the distance traveled given the rate and time below.

9. (SB) rate = 40 miles per hour, time = $3\frac{1}{2}$ hours

10. (SB) rate = 55 miles per hour, time = 0.5 hours

***11.** (1) **Write** Explain the steps you would use to simplify $-2(28 - 19) + 6$. Then find the value.

***12.** (1) **Justify** Simplify $2 \cdot 3 \cdot 6$. Justify your answer by identifying which property you used for each step.

13. (SB) **Geography** The following graph represents the elevations of mountains located in the United States.

Which mountain has the lowest elevation?

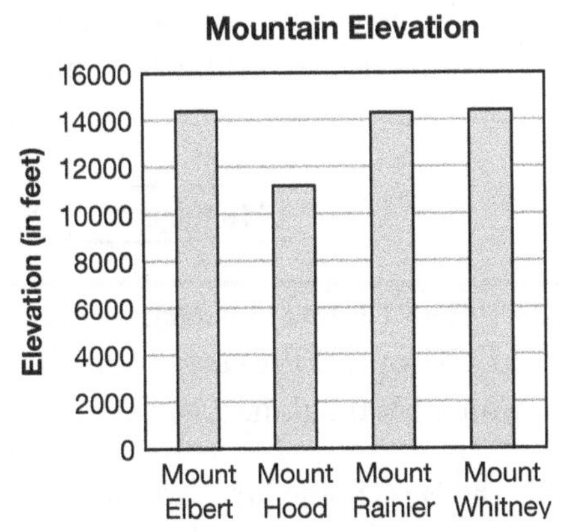

14. (SB) **Sports** A football field is 120 yards long and 160 feet wide. What is the area in square yards?

***15.** (1) **Verify** Simplify the expression $(6 \cdot 5) \cdot 2$ using only one property of real numbers. Identify the property that you used. Verify your result using two properties of real numbers.

© Saxon. All rights reserved.

*16. (1) **Multiple Choice** Identify the subset of real numbers of which 7 is not a member.

A irrational number **B** integer

C whole number **D** real number

17. (SB) **Multi-Step** Suzy can read 12 pages in four minutes. Jonas can read 9 pages in three minutes.

a. Find the number of pages Suzy and Jonas can read per minute.

b. Compare the rates.

*18. (1) **Multiple Choice** Identify which property or properties of real numbers are being demonstrated.

$$27 \cdot 3 = (20 \cdot 3) + (7 \cdot 3) = 60 + 21 = 81$$

A Commutative Property of Addition

B Associative Property of Addition

C Both A and B

D Distributive Property

19. (SB) **Sports** The specified circumference of an official professional baseball is from 9 to 9.25 inches.

a. Find the approximate radius of the smallest official baseball.

b. Find the approximate surface area of the smallest official baseball.

*20. (1) **Statistics** The table below shows the number of homeruns hit by a softball player over a three-year period. Use properties of real numbers to mentally calculate the average annual homeruns that she hit during this period.

	Year 1	Year 2	Year 3
Homeruns	6	13	14

*21. (1) **Interest Rates** The average credit card annual interest rate is around 19%. Use the Distributive Property to mentally calculate the amount of interest paid annually on a $500 balance.

22. (SB) **Biology** Some large species of bamboo plants can grow at a rate of 1 meter per day.

a. If a 2-meter tall bamboo plant grows at this rate, how tall will it be after 2 weeks?

b. How long will it take for the bamboo plant to reach a height of 50 meters?

*23. (1) **Geometry** The base of a triangle equals $\frac{1}{m}$ and the height equals m. The area of the triangle can be calculated as shown below. Which properties of real numbers are demonstrated?

$$A = \frac{1}{2}(bh) = \frac{1}{2}\left(\frac{1}{m} \cdot m\right) = \frac{1}{2} \cdot 1 = \frac{1}{2}$$

© Saxon. All rights reserved.

24. Carlos measures an angle x. He then finds that the complement of the angle is 35°.
(SB)

a. What is the measure of angle x?

b. What is the supplement of angle x?

*25. **Error Analysis** Explain the error in the statement that follows and correct the statement. "−7 is a real number, a rational number, and a whole number."
(1)

26. **Estimate** The chart below shows the total amount of hybrid vehicles sold by a manufacturer over a 4-year time span. Round to the nearest ten-thousand to estimate:
(SB)

a. the total number of hybrid vehicles sold from 2003 to 2006.

b. the sales increase from 2003 to 2006.

Year	2003	2004	2005	2006
Cars Sold	47,525	83,153	209,711	246,642

*27. **Graphing Calculator** Use the Distributive Property to mentally calculate 12(18). Check using a graphing calculator.
(1)

28. **Error Analysis** Two students calculated the total cost for 3 CDs. Each CD cost $14.95. Which student has the correct answer? Explain the other student's error.
(SB)

Student A	Student B
3(15 − 0.05) 3(15) − (0.05) 45 − 0.05 44.95	3(15 − 0.05) 3(15) − 3(0.05) 45 − 0.15 44.85

29. A cube has a side length of 5 centimeters.
(SB)

a. Find the surface area of the cube.

b. Find the volume of the cube.

30. **Analyze** John asked 100 people to choose their favorite pet. Use the chart to determine how many people chose dogs as their favorite pet.
(SB)

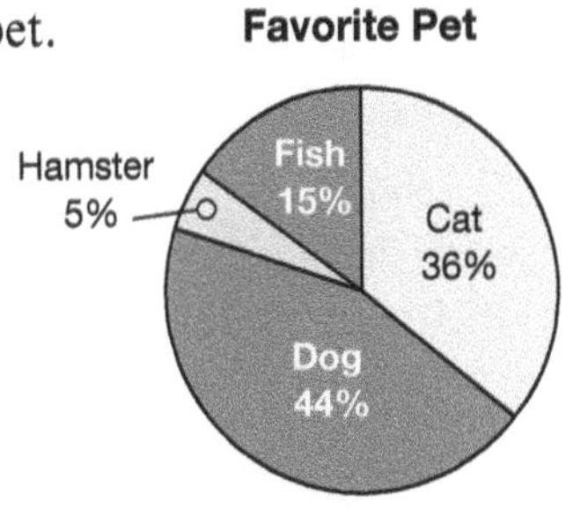

© Saxon. All rights reserved.

Name ________________________ Date __________ Class __________

Evaluating Expressions and Combining Like Terms

LESSON 2

Find the volume of the rectangular prisms with the given dimensions.

1. (SB) $l = 2$ inches, $w = 4$ inches, $h = 9$ inches

2. (SB) $l = 0.5$ cm, $w = 1.2$ cm, $h = 6$ cm

3. (1) **(Golf)** Tiger Woods obtained an average score of 68 during the four rounds of golf at the PGA Championship in 2007. Use the Distributive Property to mentally calculate his total score for the four rounds of golf.

***4.** (2) **(Amusement Parks)** An amusement park in Atlanta, Georgia offers a child's ticket for \$29.99 and an adult ticket for \$39.99.

a. Round individual ticket prices to the nearest dollar and write an expression for the total ticket cost for a family with A adults and C children.

b. Which would pay more, a family with one adult and four children, or a family with three adults and one child? Explain.

Evaluate each expression for the given values of x and y.

***5.** (2) $x - xy^2 - xy$ if $x = -2$ and $y = -3$

***6.** (2) $(x - y) - x(-y)$ if $x = -5$ and $y = 3$

***7.** (2) $x^2(x - xy)$ if $x = -2$ and $y = 3$

***8.** (2) $x^2 - y(x - y)$ if $x = -\frac{1}{2}$ and $y = \frac{1}{4}$

***9.** (2) $xy(1 - y)$ if $x = \frac{1}{5}$ and $y = -10$

***10.** (2) $xy - (x^2 - y)$ if $x = -\frac{1}{3}$ and $y = \frac{1}{2}$

Identify the subsets of real numbers of which each number is a member.

11. (1) $\sqrt{8}$

12. (1) -3

13. (1) $\frac{2}{3}$

***14.** (2) **(Budgets)** Van budgets \$12 a day for groceries for weekdays and \$15 a day for weekends. Write an expression in simplest form to show his grocery budget for w weeks.

***15.** (2) **Multi-Step** For the expression $2qr(3 + r)$

a. evaluate if $q = 2$ and $r = -1$.

b. explain how the result would be affected if q was doubled.

c. show this is true by evaluating the expression if $q = 4$ and $r = -1$.

***16.** (2) **(Sports)** A football is kicked from ground level. The height h in feet of the ball after t seconds can be modeled by the expression $-16t^2 + 48t$. Find the height of the ball after 2 seconds.

Measurement Find the measure of the complementary angle given the measures of the angles below.

17. (SB) 35°

18. (SB) 68°

19. (SB) 5°

20. (SB) 89°

© Saxon. All rights reserved.

*21. (2) **Multiple Choice** Evaluate $4x^2 + 7y$ if $x = 3$ and $y = -2$.
A 10 **B** 41 **C** 50 **D** 22

22. (1) **Error Analysis** Two students multiplied $-13 \cdot 18$ using the Distributive Property. Which student is correct? Find and explain the other student's error.

Student A	Student B
$-13 \cdot 18 = -13(20 - 2)$ $= -13(20) + 13(2)$ $= -260 + 26$ $= -234$	$-13 \cdot 18 = -13(20 - 2)$ $= -13(20) - 13(2)$ $= -260 - 26$ $= -286$

*23. (2) **Geometry** A rectangle has length c and width $2d$. Another rectangle has length 4 and width $(5 - c)$. Write a simplified expression of their combined area.

*24. (2) **Verify** Is $a^2 + b^2 = (a + b)^2$? Support your answer with an example.

*25. (2) **Consumer** A local sandwich shop has \$6 lunches, and you receive a \$5 discount on the tenth lunch. Calculate your total cost for ten lunches at this shop.

26. (1) **Write** Does zero have a multiplicative inverse? Explain your answer.

*27. (2) **Graphing Calculator** Use a calculator to evaluate the expression $fg^2 - (2f - g^2)$ if $f = 1$ and $g = -2$. Then, verify the answer by simplifying and solving.

Simplify by combining like terms.

*28. (2) $5ab + 7a - 3ab + 4b$ *29. (2) $y - 9x^2y + 4 + 3x^2y + 12$ *30. (2) $2(x + 3) - x$

© Saxon. All rights reserved.

Name ______________________ Date __________ Class __________

Using Rules of Exponents

LESSON 3

Evaluate each expression for the given values of *a* and *b*.

1. (2) $-b^2 - b(a - b^2)$ if $a = 4$ and $b = -3$

2. (2) $a^2 - b^3(a - b)$ if $a = -2$ and $b = -3$

State the properties illustrated below.

3. (1) $a + b + c = b + a + c$

4. (1) $a(b + c) = ab + ac$

Use the rules of exponents to simplify the expressions below.

***5.** (3) $\dfrac{(2x^2)^{-3}(xy^0)^{-2}}{2xx^0x^1xxy^2}$

***6.** (3) $\dfrac{a^0bc^0(a^{-1}b^{-1})^2}{ab(ab^0)abc}$

***7.** (3) $\dfrac{(2x^2y^3)^{-3}y}{(4xy)^{-2}(x^{-2}y)^3y}$

***8.** (3) $\dfrac{xx^{-2}y(x^{-3})^2xy^0}{(2xy)^{-2}x^2(y^{-3})^2}$

9. (SB) What is the area of a circle with radius 3 meters? Give your answer in terms of π.

10. (SB) Angles *a* and *b* are vertical angles. If angle *b* measures 74°, what is the measure of angle *a*?

***11.** (3) **Write** In 2002, the average height of a 10-year old girl was 1.4×10^{-3} km. Approximately 3×10^7 10-year old girls lying head-to-toe would equal the circumference of the earth at the equator. Explain how you could use properties of real numbers to mentally estimate the circumference.

12. (1) **Consumer** Your dinner total at your favorite restaurant is $18.

a. Use the Distributive Property to mentally calculate 10% of your dinner bill.

b. Explain how the result in part **a** would be helpful to mentally calculate a 15% tip.

13. (1) **Error Analysis** A student is asked to simplify an expression and identify which property was used for each step. His answer is shown below. Identify and explain the error(s).

$(8 + 4) \cdot 9$	
$(8 \cdot 9) + (4 \cdot 9)$	Associative Property of Addition
$72 + 36$	Distributive Property
108	Add.

14. (2) **a.** Evaluate the expression $1 - (3x^2 - 2y)$ if $x = 2$ and $y = 3$.

b. Explain how the result would be affected if *y* was doubled

c. Show that this is true by evaluating the expression if $x = 2$ and $y = 6$.

15. (2) **Nutrition** The U.S. recommended daily amount of calcium for most adults is 1000 mg per day. Milana's breakfast consists of cereal that contains 33 mg calcium in $\frac{1}{4}$-cup and milk that contains 75 mg calcium per $\frac{1}{4}$-cup. Calculate the total amount of calcium in milligrams in Milana's breakfast of $\frac{3}{4}$-cup cereal with $\frac{1}{2}$-cup milk.

© Saxon. All rights reserved.

16. **Justify** A square drawn on a coordinate grid has adjacent vertices at points $(u, 1)$ and $(5u, 1)$. Another square has adjacent vertices at points $(2u, 1)$ and $(4u, 1)$. Write a simplified expression of their combined area. Explain how you obtained your answer.
(2)

17. **Coordinate Geometry** A figure on a coordinate graph is translated 2 units to the right and 5 units up. Its new coordinates can be written with the expressions $(x + 2, y + 5)$. A point is translated to $(19, 19)$, what are the coordinates of the original point?
(2)

18. **Verify** Evaluate the expression $3g - 2f + fg^2 - 5g + 4fg^2 + 6f$ if $f = 1$ and $g = -1$ by inserting the variable values into the expression as written. Verify your answer by simplifying the expression first, then inserting the variable values.
(2)

*19. **Multiple Choice** Simplify $\frac{y^{-3}xy^2x^{-4}x^5}{x^3y^{-1}}$.
(3)

A $\frac{1}{x}$ B $\frac{1}{x^2y^5}$ C $\frac{x^5}{y^2}$ D $\frac{x^3}{y}$

20. **Write** Why is $1^{10000000} = 1$?
(SB)

*21. **Error Analysis** Two students incorrectly simplified the expression $\frac{2^3(2^{-2})^3}{2(2^2+2)}$. Their steps are shown below. Explain the error of each student.
(3)

Student A	Student B
$\frac{2^3(2^{-2})^3}{2(2^2+2)} = \frac{2^3(2^{-6})}{2(4+2)}$	$\frac{2^3(2^{-2})^3}{2(2^2+2)} = \frac{2^3(2^{-6})}{2(2^3)}$
$= \frac{2^{-3}}{12} = \frac{1}{12(-2)^3} = -\frac{1}{96}$	$= \frac{2^{-3}}{2^4} = \frac{1}{2^7} = \frac{1}{128}$

22. **Volcanos** Vailulu'u is an underwater volcano in the Pacific Ocean. The volcano has a height of about 4,200 m off the sea floor. If the top of the volcano is at a depth of 590 m below sea level, what is the depth of the sea floor in this area?
(SB)

*23. **Verify** The Atlantic Ocean is 3.93×10^3 m deep and has 8.24×10^{13} m^2 of surface area. Calculate the total volume of the Atlantic Ocean. Write your answer in scientific notation. Verify your answer if you know that the Pacific Ocean has approximately two times the volume and approximately the same depth of the Atlantic Ocean, and a surface area of about 1.66×10^{14} m^2.
(3)

24. **Geography** The Danube River is Europe's second longest river. It flows through 9 countries and has a length of 1,770 miles. About how many feet long is the Danube?
(SB)

*25. **Geometry** A box has a volume of $\frac{x^3y^2x^{-2}}{y^{-3}x^2y}$. The area resulting from length times width is $\frac{x^{-2}y^3x^{-1}}{y^{-4}x^{-2}y^2}$. Find an expression for the height of the box.
(3)

© Saxon. All rights reserved.

26. (2) **Analyze** Rita can choose to rent movies from one of two movie stores. The first store charges \$5 per movie, and she can rent her 8th movie for free. The second store charges \$7 per movie, and she can rent her 4th movie for free. Rita assumes that the second shop has a better deal because she must only rent 3 movies before receiving a free movie rental. Explain why she should not make this assumption.

***27.** (3) **Graphing Calculator** Simplify $\frac{2^{-3}}{8^{-2}}$. Use a calculator to check your answer.

28. (2) **Error Analysis** The EPA lists the greenest hybrid car as getting 61 miles per gallon on the highway and 50 miles per gallon in the city. Assuming the fuel tank holds 15 gallons of gas, one owner decided to calculate the total miles that he could drive one tank of gas if 4 gallons were used in the city. Explain and correct his error.

$$61(4) + 50(15 - 4) = 244 + 75 - 200 = 119 \text{ miles}$$

29. (1) **Analyze** Identify which property of real numbers is being demonstrated. Explain why this property might be helpful in solving this problem without a calculator.

$$(9 \cdot 3) \cdot 3 = 9 \cdot (3 \cdot 3) = 9 \cdot 9 = 81$$

***30.** (2) **Multi-Step** Shane spent \$2.24 on breakfast and x dollars on lunch.

a. Write an expression for the amount of money Shane spent on breakfast and lunch.

b. If Shane spent \$5.97 on lunch, how much money did he spend in all?

© Saxon. All rights reserved.

Name ______________________ Date __________ Class __________

Identifying Functions and Using Function Notation

LESSON 4

Find the additive inverse for each of the following.

1. $-3p$ (1)

2. 50 (1)

Evaluate each expression for the given values of *m* and *n*.

3. $2m - 4n(3m - 4)$ if $m = 1$ and $n = -3$ (2)

4. $-m^3 + mn^2(n - m)$ if $m = -2$ and $n = -3$ (2)

Use the rules of exponents to simplify the expressions below.

5. $\dfrac{(m^3n^{-1})^{-4}}{(3mn)^{-2}}$ (3)

6. $\dfrac{-a^3(a^3b^{-2})^3}{ab(ab)^{-4}}$ (3)

Identify whether each of the following represent a function. If so, state the domain and range.

*7. $y^2 = x$ (4)

*8. $y = 3x^2 - 2$ (4)

9. **Error Analysis** Two students simplified $\frac{x^{-2}(y^2)^3}{y(x^{-1})^2}$. Their steps are shown below. Who is correct? Explain the error in the other student's work. (3)

Student A	Student B
$\dfrac{x^{-2}(y^2)^3}{y(x^{-1})^2} = \dfrac{x^{-2}y^6}{yx^{-2}} = y^5$	$\dfrac{x^{-2}(y^2)^3}{y(x^{-1})^2} = \dfrac{x^{-2}y^5}{yx} = \dfrac{y^4}{x^3}$

10. What is the radius of a circle with circumference 16π feet? (SB)

*11. Use the table to answer the following questions. (4)

a. What is the domain?

b. What is the range?

c. Does this data represent a function? Explain.

x	y
2	9
5	7
3	4
2	11
7	7

*12. **Multiple Choice** Which set of x- and y-values makes the equation $y = 3x^2 + 4$ true? (4)

A $x = 1, y = 10$ **B** $x = 3, y = 31$ **C** $x = 5, y = 229$ **D** $x = 2, y = 24$

13. **Write** Alyson saves \$75 each month. Use the distributive property to mentally calculate the amount of money that she will save in 12 months. Explain. (1)

*14. **Geometry** Explain whether the relationship from a circle's radius to its area is a function. (4)

© Saxon. All rights reserved.

15. **Hawaii** Mauna Kea in Hawaii is about 1.02×10^4 meters from its base to its peak.
(3) The speed of light is about 3×10^8 meters/second. About how many seconds would it take light to reach the base from the peak? Write your answers in scientific notation.

16. **Verify** Evaluate the expression $ab + 3b - a - 5ab + 2b$ if $a = -3$ and $b = 2$ by
(2) inserting the variable values into the expression as written. Verify your answer by simplifying the expression first, then inserting the variable values.

17. **Multiple Choice** Simplify $\frac{a^3b^{-2}c^{-3}b^6c^{-1}a^{-1}}{b^2c^4b^{-1}a^{-5}}$.
(3)

A $\frac{b^5c^8}{a^3}$ **B** a^3b^5 **C** $\frac{a^7b^3}{c^8}$ **D** $\frac{b^6}{a^2c}$

18. **Baseball** The table shows the number of homeruns hit by Ryan Howard of the Philadelphia Phillies over a three-year period. Which property of real numbers would be useful to mentally calculate as quickly as possible the total homeruns that he hit over this period? Explain.
(1)

	2004	2005	2006
Homeruns	2	22	58

19. **Multi-Step** A computer sales representative makes a base salary of $9/hr.
(2) She can also earn an additional $30 for every computer that she sells and $20 for every printer that she sells.

a. Write an expression to represent the total amount the representative will make in an 8-hour day.

b. How much will she make if she sells 10 computers and 4 printers in an 8-hour day?

20. **Generalize** The product of a number and its multiplicative inverse is one. What is the
(1) product of a number and its additive inverse?

21. **Hybrids** The EPA lists the greenest hybrid car as getting 61 miles per gallon on
(2) the highway and 50 miles per gallon in the city. Write and simplify an expression for the total number of miles the car will travel if the fuel tank holds 15 gallons of gas.

*22. **Error Analysis** PC Haven sells computers at a 15% discount on the original price plus a
(4) $200 rebate. Which function correctly represents the final price of a computer at PC Haven? Explain the error.

$$f(r) = 0.85r - 200 \qquad g(r) = 0.15r + 200$$

*23. **Analyze** What values of a and b would make the relation
(4) not a function?
Explain your reasoning.

x	2	3	a
y	5	b	8

© Saxon. All rights reserved.

Identifying Functions and Using Function Notation

24. (3) **Precipitation** New York City gets an average of 1.14×10^2 cm of rainfall each year. The area of New York City is 8.02×10^8 m^2. Calculate the average annual volume in cubic meters of precipitation in New York City. Write your answer in scientific notation.

For the function $f(x) = 3x^2 + x$, evaluate:

*25. (4) $f(-1)$ *26. (4) $f(0)$ *27. (4) $f\left(\frac{3}{2}\right)$

*28. (4) **Justify** Simplify the expression, $-36 + (36 + 17)$, using properties of real numbers. Justify your answer by identifying which property you used for each step.

*29. (4) **Graphing Calculator** For the function $f(x) = x^2$, use a calculator to find $f(-2.8)$ and $f(2.8)$. Did you use the same key strokes to evaluate both? Explain.

30. (3) **Probability** In a year, lightning strikes one person out of every 2.8×10^5 people. Calculate the number of people in the United States that will likely be struck by lightning this year if the population is 2.8×10^8. Write your answer in standard notation.

© Saxon. All rights reserved.

Name ______________________ Date __________ Class __________

Using Matrices to Organize Data and to Solve Problems

LESSON 5

Find the multiplicative inverse for each of the following.

1. (1) $-\frac{2}{3}$

2. (1) 6

3. (2) Evaluate $x^2y(x + 3y)$ for $x = 0$ and $y = -6$.

4. (3) Simplify: $4x^2(x^{-2}y^{-4})^{-1}$

5. (4) Determine whether the graph represents a function. Explain.

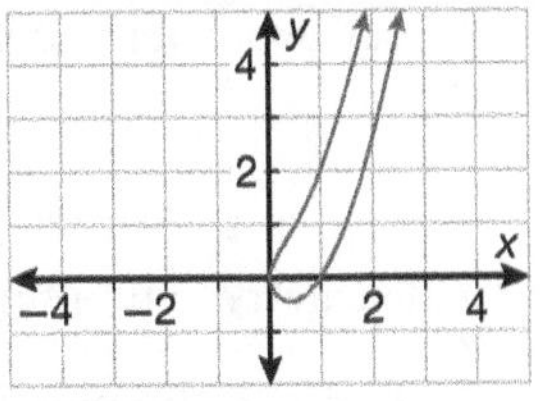

Graphing Calculator **Simplify the following matrices. Check using a graphing calculator.**

***6.** (5) $4\begin{bmatrix}2 & 1\\ -6 & 3.5\end{bmatrix} - 3\begin{bmatrix}0 & 0.4\\ 8 & -2\end{bmatrix}$

***7.** (5) $\frac{1}{4}\begin{bmatrix}2 & 4\\ 6 & 8\end{bmatrix} + \begin{bmatrix}-2 & 1\\ -\frac{1}{2} & 5\end{bmatrix}$

Find the area of each triangle.

8. (SB) $h = 2$ cm, $b = 10$ cm

9. (SB) $h = \frac{1}{3}$ feet, $b = 18$ feet

10. (SB) Angles x and y are alternate interior angles formed by a transversal and 2 parallel lines. What is the measure of x if y measures 32°?

11. (1) **(Golf)** Tiger Woods obtained an average score of 72 during the four rounds of golf at the Player's Championship in 2007. Explain how you can use the distributive property to mentally calculate his total score for the four rounds of golf.

12. (1) **Multi-Step** Classify each statement as sometimes, always, or never true. Use properties of real numbers to support your answer.

a. $a \cdot \left(-\frac{1}{b}\right) = b \cdot \left(-\frac{1}{a}\right)$

b. if a and b are rational numbers, then $a + b$ is a real number.

13. (2) **(Museums)** The Bob Bullock Texas State History Museum offers student tickets for 3 dollars to view the exhibits. Tickets to view the IMAX theatre cost 5 dollars. The table below shows expressions for the number of students that visited the exhibits and theater over a 2-day period. Write an expression for the total cost of student tickets to view the exhibits during the 2 days.

Number of Students

	Exhibits	IMAX Theater
Day 1	$9v$	$7v$
Day 2	$7v$	$6v$

© Saxon. All rights reserved.

Using Matrices to Organize Data and to Solve Problems

14. (3) **Solar System** The average distance between Jupiter and the Sun is approximately 7.786×10^{11} m.

a. Estimate the distance in kilometers that Jupiter travels around the Sun in one rotation. Write your answer in scientific notation. Round to the nearest hundredth.

b. Estimate the average speed at which Jupiter rotates around the Sun in km/s. Jupiter makes one rotation in 4,333 Earth days.

15. (4) Tell whether the given ordered pairs satisfy a function.

$$\{(2, 5), (2, 4), (2, 3), (2, 2), (2, 1)\}$$

***16.** (5) **Geometry** The matrix $R = \begin{pmatrix} 3 & 3.5 \\ 4 & 4.5 \end{pmatrix}$ shows the radii of four circles.

a. Write the matrix operation that gives the related circumferences.

b. Is there an addition or scalar-multiplication matrix operation that could show the related areas of the circles? Explain.

17. (4) **Precipitation** The mass of a large raindrop is equivalent to 1×10^{22} water molecules. The mass of a snowflake is equivalent to 1×10^{20} water molecules. Write a function to represent the mass of a raindrop in snowflakes.

***18.** (5) **Error Analysis** Find and explain the error the student made below.

$$\begin{bmatrix} 14 \\ 0 \\ 7 \end{bmatrix} + [23 \quad -8 \quad -6] = [37 \quad -8 \quad 1]$$

***19.** (4) **Write** Explain why the vertical line test works.

20. (SB) The length of the side of a square is given by the expression $2x + 5$. Use the Distributive Property to write an expression for the perimeter of the square.

***21.** (5) **Estimate** Estimate $4.8P$ given that $P = \begin{bmatrix} 2\frac{2}{3} & \pi \\ -\frac{1}{8} & 0.4\overline{5} \end{bmatrix}$.

22. (2) **Multiple Choice** Evaluate $x(xy + 2y^2)$ if $x = 4$ and $y = -1$.

A -24 **B** -12 **C** -8 **D** -2

***23.** (5) **a.** Create matrix A such that $a_{11} = 4$, $a_{12} = 6$, $a_{21} = 0$, and $a_{22} = -1$.

b. What is the additive inverse of A?

24. (1) **Error Analysis** Explain the error in the statement that follows and correct the statement.

"$\sqrt{48}$ is a real number and a rational number."

© Saxon. All rights reserved.

25. **Verify** Evaluate the expression $uv + 8v - u - 4uv + 7u$ if $u = -1$ and $v = -1$ by
(2) inserting the variable values into the expression as written. Verify your answer by simplifying the expression first, then inserting the variable values.

*26. $f(x) = x + 2$. Find $f(16)$.
(4)

*27. **Formulate** Write a function that represents the data set $(-4, 9)$, $(0, 1)$, $(1, -1)$,
(4) $(3, -5)$, $(4, -7)$.

28. **Model** One day the value of one US dollar was equivalent to 0.49 British pounds. On
(4) the same day, one US dollar was equivalent to 115.84 Japanese yen. Write a function to represent the value of yen in pounds.

*29. **Justify** Does the Commutative Property hold true for Matrix Subtraction? Justify
(5) your answer.

30. **Skyscrapers** One cubic foot of pennies contains approximately 4.9×10^4 pennies.
(3) If the Sears Tower in Chicago were filled with pennies, it would hold about 2.6×10^{12} pennies. What is the approximate volume of the Sears Tower? Write your answer in scientific notation rounded to the nearest tenth.

© Saxon. All rights reserved.

Name ______________________________ Date ____________ Class ____________

Finding Percent of Change

LESSON 6

Determine whether the following numbers are rational numbers.

1. $\sqrt{225}$ *(1)*

2. π *(1)*

3. Evaluate $\frac{xy(x^2)}{2x}$ for $x = -1$ and $y = 4$. *(2)*

4. Simplify $x^5y(2x^{-5}y^4)^3$. *(3)*

5. **Graphing Calculator** Find $\begin{bmatrix} 1 & 5 \\ 2 & -3.2 \end{bmatrix} + 2\begin{bmatrix} 1 & 0 \\ -1 & 4 \end{bmatrix}$. Check using the calculator. *(5)*

6. What solid figure is described by the net? *(SB)*

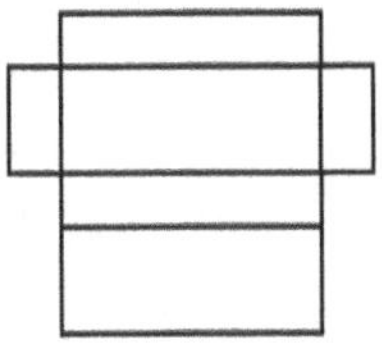

Find the percent change.

***7.** from 3 to 4.5 *(6)*

***8.** from 0.8 to 2.74 *(6)*

Identify whether each of the following represent a function. If so, state the domain and range.

9. $y^2 = x + 1$ *(4)*

10. $y = x^2 - 2$ *(4)*

11. **Error Analysis** Two students are asked to simplify an expression and identify which property was used for each step. Their answers are shown below. Identify which student has an error in the procedure and correct the error. Simplify $(4 + 2) \cdot 10$. *(1)*

Student A	
$(4 \cdot 10) + (2 \cdot 10)$	Associative Property
$40 + 20$	Distributive Property
60	Add.

Student B	
$6 \cdot 10$	Add
60	Multiply

***12.** A student bought a \$3.20 notebook for 30% off and a \$78 calculator for 10% off. *(6)*

a. How much did the student spend?

b. **Verify** Show that it is not correct to add the prices of the items and then take 40% off their total.

13. **Multiple Choice** Evaluate $-x^2 + 6y$ if $x = 2$ and $y = 0$. *(2)*

A -10 **B** -4 **C** 4 **D** 10

14. Ty uses the function $g(x) = 0.5 + 0.2(x - 1)$ to calculate the cost in dollars of using a calling card to make a long distance call lasting x minutes. The variable x must be a whole number. Determine the cost of a 10-minute call. *(4)*

© Saxon. All rights reserved.

*15. (6) **Population** The population of Indiana in 1990 was reported to be 5,544,159 and in 2000 was reported to be 6,080,485. Find the percent increase. Round to the nearest hundredth of a percent.

16. (1) **Multiple Choice** Identify the subset of real numbers of which -5 is not a member.
A integer **B** real number **C** whole number **D** rational number

17. (5) **Sports** The table shows results from the first three track meets last year and this year.

Last Year

	1st	2nd	3rd
Meet 1	27	33	51
Meet 2	29	42	41
Meet 3	25	29	60

This Year

	1st	2nd	3rd
Meet 1	18	45	47
Meet 2	34	33	62
Meet 3	35	31	54

a. Create a matrix for each year.

b. Use matrix subtraction to subtract last year's matrix from this year's matrix.

18. (2) **Multi-Step a.** Evaluate the expression $-5vw(-2 + w)$ if $v = 3$ and $w = -4$.

b. Explain how the result would be affected if v was tripled.

c. Show that this is true by evaluating the expression if $v = 9$ and $w = -4$.

*19. (6) **Analyze** What is the percent decrease when the original amount is 75 and the new amount is 0? Explain.

20. (2) **Planets** The speed of light is about 3×10^8 meters/second.

a. About how many seconds would it take light to reach Pluto from the Sun at their minimum distance apart of about 4.437×10^{12} meters?

b. About how many seconds would it take light to reach Pluto from the Sun at their maximum distance apart of about 7.376×10^{12} meters? Round your answers to the nearest second.

*21. (6) **Write** Compare and contrast markups and discounts.

*22. (6) **Geometry** Every side of a 2 by 7 rectangle is tripled to form a new rectangle. By what percent did the area of the rectangle increase?

23. (1) **Verify** Simplify the expression $(2 + 3) + 1$ using only one property of real numbers. Identify the property that you used. Verify your result using two properties of real numbers.

© Saxon. All rights reserved.

24. **Currency** On the first day of 2007, the value of one US dollar was equivalent to
(4) 119 Japanese yen. On the same day, one euro was equivalent to 157 Japanese yen.

a. Write a function to represent the value of US dollars in euros.

b. What is the value of the function for an input of 5 rounded to the nearest cent, and what does it represent?

*25. Evaluate $a^2b^3 - (5a - b^2)$ if $a = 1$ and $b = 3$.
(2)

26. For the expression $\frac{-4x}{7}$
(1)

a. find the additive inverse.

b. find the multiplicative inverse.

27. **Coordinate Geometry** The coordinates of points in the coordinate plane
(5) can be written in matrices where the x-coordinates are listed in the first row and the corresponding y-coordinates are listed in the second row.

a. Graph $A = \begin{bmatrix} -1 & 0 & 5 \\ 4 & -2 & 2 \end{bmatrix}$.

b. Graph $A + B$ where $B = \begin{bmatrix} 3 & 4 & 9 \\ 6 & 0 & 4 \end{bmatrix}$. What happened?

*28. Find the additive inverse matrix of $\begin{bmatrix} 2 \\ 4 \\ -5 \end{bmatrix}$.
(5)

29. **Estimate** One cubic foot of pennies contains approximately 4.9×10^4 pennies. The
(3) Giants Stadium in New Jersey has an approximate volume of 6.45×10^7 cubic feet. About how many pennies would fit in the Giants Stadium?

30. **Write** Explain how Scalar Multiplication is similar to the Distributive Property and
(5) how it is different.

© Saxon. All rights reserved.

Name ______________________ Date __________ Class __________

Solving Linear Equations

LESSON 7

Find the measure of the angles that are supplementary to the angles given.

1. 65° (SB)

2. 138° (SB)

3. Evaluate $3xy^3 + x - y$ for $x = -2$ and $y = -2$. (2)

***4.** **Graphing Calculator** Find $\frac{3}{4}\begin{bmatrix} 8 & -4 \\ 2 & 0 \end{bmatrix} - \begin{bmatrix} 1 & -6 \\ -7 & -2 \end{bmatrix}$. Check using a graphing calculator. (5)

Find the area of each rectangle given the dimensions below.

5. $l = 2$ inches, $w = 1.3$ inches (SB)

6. $l = 4$ cm, $w = 3$ cm (SB)

7. Find the percent change from 5 to 6.1. (6)

Solve each equation.

***8.** $3(x + 2) = 2x - 1$ (7)

***9.** $\frac{1}{2}x + 8 = 24$ (7)

10. Use the table to answer the following questions. (4)

x	0	1	2	3
y	9	7	5	3

a. What is the domain?

b. What is the range?

c. Does this data represent a function? Explain.

11. **Astronomy** Saturn's smallest moon, Tethys, has a diameter of about 6.5×10^2 miles. The diameter of Jupiter's largest moon, Ganymede, is 5 times that of Tethys. Determine the diameter of Ganymede. Write your answer in standard form. (3)

12. **Justify** Simplify the expression using properties of real numbers. Justify your answer by identifying which property you used for each step. (1)

$$3 \cdot 5 \cdot \frac{1}{3}$$

13. **Diving** The pressure on a diver is given by $P(d) = \frac{1}{33}d + 1$ where the pressure is in atmospheres and d is the diver's depth in feet. What is the pressure of the diver at 50 feet under water? (4)

14. Which is less expensive: an \$85 pair of shoes with a 40% discount or a \$68 pair of shoes with a 15% discount? How much less expensive is it? (6)

© Saxon. All rights reserved.

*15. (7) Sandra's brother is 6 years older than her, her sister is 2 years younger than her, and her mother is 3 times her age. Her brother, sister, and mother's combined age is 64.

a. Write an equation to solve for Sandra's age.

b. Solve your equation.

16. (3) **Speed of Sound** Mauna Kea in Hawaii is about 1.02×10^4 meters from its base to its peak. Assume that the speed of sound is about 3.44×10^2 meters/second. Use this information to solve the following questions. Write your answers in scientific notation.

a. About how many seconds would it take sound to reach the base from the peak? Round your answer to the nearest second.

b. Approximately 5.96×10^3 meters of Mauna Kea is below sea level. About how many seconds would it take sound to reach sea level from the peak? Write your answers in scientific notation.

*17. (7) **Verify** Is $x = \frac{1}{14}$ the solution to the equation $9x - \frac{2}{7} = 8x + \frac{11}{14}$?

18. (4) **Coordinate Geometry** Explain whether a circle drawn on a coordinate grid represents a function.

19. (6) **Economics** The median income for US females with a doctorate degree rose from \$40,172 in 1990 to \$60,733 in 2000. The median income for US males with a doctorate degree rose from \$54,626 to in 1990 to \$78,092 in 2000. Which group had the greater percent increase? How much greater? (Round to the nearest percent.)

20. (5) **Error Analysis** Find and explain the error the student made below.

$$6\begin{bmatrix} 2 & 5 \\ 9 & -2 \end{bmatrix} = \begin{bmatrix} 8 & 11 \\ 15 & 4 \end{bmatrix}$$

21. (5) Given that $A = \begin{bmatrix} 4 & 5 & -6 \\ -9 & 0 & 3 \\ 8 & 2 & -1 \end{bmatrix}$ and $B = \begin{bmatrix} 1 & 7 \\ 8 & -14 \\ 5 & -9 \end{bmatrix}$, what is $a_{13} + b_{21}$?

*22. (6) **Error Analysis** A student said that a change from 15 to 30 is a 50% increase because 15 is 50% of 30. Explain the error in the student's thinking.

*23. (7) **Coffee** On Sunday a coffee shop sold 115 lb of coffee. The amount of regular coffee sold was 5 lb more than the amount of decaffeinated coffee sold. There were twice as many pounds of flavored coffee sold than there was regular coffee sold.

a. Write an equation to solve for the amount of regular coffee sold.

b. Solve the equation from part a.

*24. (6) **Multiple Choice** What is the discount when a \$14 shirt is on sale for 20% off?

A \$2.80 B \$7.00 C \$11.20 D \$16.80

© Saxon. All rights reserved.

25. (2) **Multiple Choice** Evaluate $-5x^2 + 2y$ if $x = 1$ and $y = -1$.

A -7 **B** -3 **C** 3 **D** 7

26. (4) **Formulate** Write a function that represents the data set $(-19, -12)$, $(-12, -5)$, $(-5, 2)$, $(2, 9)$, $(9, 16)$.

27. (6) **Verify** Show how to check that 28 increased by 80% is 50.4.

***28.** (7) **Geometry** Janice wants to find the value of y for the triangle shown. The perimeter of the triangle is $8y$. Write and solve an equation to find the value of y.

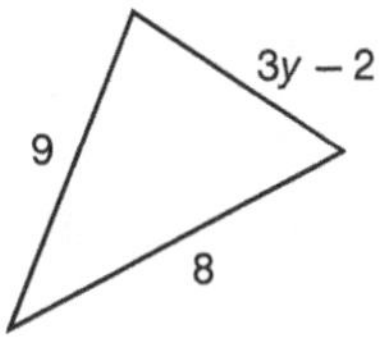

29. (2) **Multi-Step** **a.** Evaluate the expression $6st(6 + t)$ if $s = 6$ and $t = -2$.

b. Explain how the result would be affected if s was doubled.

c. Show that this is true by evaluating the expression if $s = 12$ and $t = -2$.

***30.** (7) **Sales Tax** The state sales tax for Colorado, Louisiana, and Nevada total to 13.4%. The sales tax in Colorado is 1.1% less than that of Louisiana and 3.6% less than that of Nevada. Find the state sales tax rate for Colorado.

© Saxon. All rights reserved.

Name ______________________ Date __________ Class __________

Finding Direct Variation

LESSON 8

1. (1) Simplify the expression using the properties of real numbers.

$$(-7 + 3) - |-2 + 9| - 2[1 - (-5)]$$

2. (2) Simplify $\frac{3x}{y} - 7x^2x^{-1}y^{-1} + 2y^2y^{-1}x^{-1}$.

3. (3) Simplify $\frac{xy^2}{x^0x^{-3}}\left(\frac{xy^{-2}}{x(y^2)^0} - \frac{3y^{-2}}{x^4}\right)$.

4. (SB) Find the area of a circle with radius 1.5 inches.

5. (6) Find the percent change from 10 to 12.8.

Solve each equation.

***6.** (7) $15(4 - 5b) = 16(4 - 6b) + 10$

***7.** (7) $-2(2x - 3) - 2^3 - 3 = -x - (-4)$

For the following problems, *x* varies directly with *y*. Find the constant of variation.

***8.** (8) $x = 12, y = 3$

***9.** (8) $x = 4, y = 16$

10. (2) Simplify the expression $5x^2 - 2(x - 3x^2)$.

***11.** (1) **Graphing Calculator** The average credit card annual interest rate is around 19%. Use the distributive property to mentally calculate the amount of interest paid annually on a $600 balance. Use a graphing calculator to verify your answer.

12. (6) **Multi-Step** Admission to the museum is $12. Students receive a 15% discount.

a. How much is the discount?

b. How much do students pay?

13. (5) **(Education)** The table shows the number of men and women who attended a university and if they were attending on a full or part-time basis.

University Enrollment

	2000		2005	
	Men	Women	Men	Women
Full-time	315	484	511	562
Part-time	631	709	826	914

a. Create a matrix to show the number of men attending the university in both years.

b. Create another matrix to show the number of women attending the university in a way that it could be added to the matrix in part a.

c. Add the matrices.

***14.** (8) **Multiple Choice** In a peanut butter cookie recipe, the amount of sugar used varies directly with the amount of peanut butter used. For 2 c of peanut butter, $1\frac{1}{2}$ c of sugar is needed. Circle the letter that best represents the constant of variation.

A 1 **B** $\frac{1}{4}$ **C** $\frac{3}{4}$ **D** 2

© Saxon. All rights reserved.

15. **Analyze** A quarter is about 6.89×10^{-2} inches thick. A quarter has a diameter that is about 13.9 times its thickness. Estimate the diameter of a quarter in inches. Write your answer in scientific notation. Explain whether you think the magnitude of your answer seems reasonable.
(3)

16. **Statistics** The first time a teacher tested her students, the scores were 75, 82, 93, 81, 64, 78, and 80. The second time she tested them, the scores were 65, 72, 100, 83, 68, 55, and 40. What was the percent change in the average score from the first to the second testing? Round to the nearest whole percent.
(6)

*17. **Bowling** The number of pounds varies directly with the number of ounces. A bowling ball that weighs 12 pounds weighs 192 ounces. What is the constant of variation? Find the weight, in pounds, of a bowling ball that weighs 240 ounces.
(8)

18. **Multi-Step** Solve for x, y, and z: $\begin{bmatrix} 1 & x^2 \\ y+4 & \frac{y}{2} \end{bmatrix} = \begin{bmatrix} z+2 & 25 \\ 16 & x+1 \end{bmatrix}$.
(5)

*19. **Geometry** The area of a triangle varies directly with the product of the base and height of the triangle. If the area of a triangle is 6 cm^2 then the product of the base and height is 12 cm^2, find the area of a triangle whose product of base and height is 27 cm^2.
(8)

20. **Consumer** A ticket service marks up prices on concerts and other events by 150%. Use a scalar product to find the marked up prices.
(5)

Concert Ticket Prices

Day	Floor	Balcony
Friday	\$60	\$35
Saturday	\$80	\$45

*21. **Verify** Is $x = 2$ the solution to the equation $-10x + 6 = 4x + 34$?
(7)

22. Solve the equation $6x + 3 - 8x = 13$.
(7)

23. **Marketing** If you buy one quarter page ad, the cost is \$400 per week. This can be expressed as the ordered pair (1, 400). There is a special if you buy one ad at the regular price, each additional week is \$300. Find the total cost if you buy 2, 3, and 4 ads. Express the answer as ordered pairs in set notation.
(4)

24. **Write** Does $(x^2)^3 = (x^3)^2$? Explain.
(3)

25. **Analyze** When will a percent change equal 0%? Give an example.
(6)

© Saxon. All rights reserved.

*26. (8) **Verify** The volume of a sphere varies directly with the cube of the radius. The table shows the volume and radius of three different spheres. Verify the constant of variation is 4.189.

Volume	Radius
2,144.768 in^3	8 in.
20,580.557 in^3	17 in.
65,453.125 in^3	25 in.

27. (5) **Multiple Choice** What are the dimensions of matrix $C = [\,9\ 1\ 7\ 0\,]$?

A 1×3 **B** 1×4 **C** 3×1 **D** 4×1

*28. (7) **Exports** The total exports of goods and services, in millions of dollars, for the U.S. in 2004, 2005, and 2006 was 3,886,023. The exports in 2005 were 125,820 more than in 2004 and 162,633 less than in 2006. What were the exports in millions of dollars in 2005?

29. (4) If $a(x) = 12 + 9x$ and $v(x) = 5x + 2x^2$, find $v(4)$.

30. (1) **Error Analysis** Explain the error in the statement that follows and correct the statement. "3 is an irrational number and an integer."

© Saxon. All rights reserved.

Name ______________________ Date __________ Class __________

Multiplying Matrices

LESSON 9

Write each decimal as a fraction in lowest terms.

1. (SB) 0.24 2. (SB) 0.82 3. (SB) 0.32

4. (SB) What is the measure of an interior angle of a regular pentagon?

5. (4) Determine whether $y^2 = 8x$ is a function. If so, state the domain and range.

6. (5) Find the sum: $2\begin{bmatrix} 1 & 0 \\ 0 & 1 \end{bmatrix} + \begin{bmatrix} -3 & -2 \\ -4 & 0 \end{bmatrix}$

*7. (8) If m varies directly with n, and $m = 8$ when $n = 2$, what is the value of the constant of variation?

Graphing Calculator **Find each product. Check using the graphing calculator.**

*8. (9) $\begin{bmatrix} 2 & -1 \\ 3 & 0 \\ 1 & 4 \end{bmatrix} \times \begin{bmatrix} 1 & 1 & -3 \\ 6 & -5 & 0 \end{bmatrix}$

*9. (9) $\begin{bmatrix} -1 & -1 & -1 \\ 2 & 5 & 3 \\ -5 & 4 & -2 \end{bmatrix} \times \begin{bmatrix} 0 \\ 1 \\ 0 \end{bmatrix}$

10. (5) **Verify** Use the matrices A and B below to verify that $A + B = B + A$.

$$A = \begin{bmatrix} -3 & 7 \\ 12 & -1 \end{bmatrix} \quad B = \begin{bmatrix} 9 & 17 \\ 3 & -1 \end{bmatrix}$$

11. (1) **Baseball** The table shows the number of home runs hit by Orlando Hernandez of the New York Yankees over a three-year period. Which property of real numbers would be useful to mentally calculate as quickly as possible the total home runs that he hit over this period? Explain.

	2004	2005	2006
Home Runs	9	18	22

12. (3) **Earth** The surface area of the land on Earth is approximately 1.488×10^{14} m^2. The state of New York has a surface area of approximately 1.272×10^{11} m^2. Approximately how many times could the state of New York fit on the land of the Earth? Write your answer in scientific notation.

*13. (9) **Multiple Choice** Circle the letter that best represents the product matrix AB.

$$A = \begin{bmatrix} -3 & 1 & -1 \\ -4 & 6 & 2 \\ -1 & -1 & 4 \end{bmatrix} \quad B = \begin{bmatrix} -7 & 0 & 1 \\ -8 & -2 & -1 \\ 0 & 3 & -3 \end{bmatrix}$$

A $\begin{bmatrix} 20 & -8 & 11 \\ 33 & -19 & 0 \\ -9 & 21 & -6 \end{bmatrix}$ **B** $\begin{bmatrix} 13 & -5 & -1 \\ -20 & -6 & -16 \\ 15 & 14 & -12 \end{bmatrix}$

C $\begin{bmatrix} 21 & 0 & -1 \\ 32 & -12 & -2 \\ 0 & -3 & -12 \end{bmatrix}$ **D** $\begin{bmatrix} -10 & 1 & 0 \\ -12 & 4 & 1 \\ -1 & 2 & 1 \end{bmatrix}$

© Saxon. All rights reserved.

14. (5) **Scores** Create matrices to represent the following: Juan's high scores on three arcade games in one year are 34,950, 7800, and 12,300. His low scores on the same games are 6400, 2100, and 970. Tatia's high scores on the same games are 28,900, 10,450, and 11,950. Her low scores are 7200, 3600, and 4860.

15. (3) **Write** Is $a^{-1} < 1$, for all $a > 1$? Explain why or why not.

16. (6) **Population** The population of Alaska in 1990 was reported to be 550,043 and in 2000 was reported to be 626,932. Find the percent increase. Round to the nearest hundredth of a percent.

17. (5) **Property Management** The table shows the cost of renting three different apartment styles in an apartment complex.

	Monthly Rental Cost
One bedroom	$650
Two bedrooms	$890
Three bedrooms	$940

a. Convert the table into a 3×1 matrix.

b. All rents at an apartment complex will be increased by 10%. What scalar can be used to make a matrix with the updated prices? Create this matrix.

18. (5) **Verify** Verify that $D = \begin{bmatrix} -14 & -6 \\ -6 & -1 \end{bmatrix}$ if $\begin{bmatrix} 1 & -6 \\ -6 & 4 \end{bmatrix} = D + \begin{bmatrix} 15 & 0 \\ 0 & 5 \end{bmatrix}$.

19. (1) Identify which property of real numbers is being demonstrated.

$$5(2 + 9) = 5 \cdot 2 + 5 \cdot 9$$

***20.** (8) **Planets** The weight of an object on Saturn varies directly with the weight of that object on Earth. An object that weighs 2 kg on Earth, weighs 1.86 kg on Saturn. Find the weight of an object on Saturn that weighs 85 kg on Earth.

21. (4) **Error Analysis** Two students were asked to determine which of the following sets of ordered pairs are functions. Set 1: (9, 4), (7, 9), (8, 2) and Set 2: (3, −1), (4, −1), (7, 9). Their answers are below. What is the correct answer? Explain the error(s).

Britan's Answer: Set 2 because the 9's are paired with different values.

Sara's Answer: Set 1 because the −1's are paired with different values.

22. (6) **Economics** In 2002, San Jose, California topped the list for the US metropolitan areas with the highest average annual salaries with an average salary of $76,252. Find the approximate average annual salary in 2001 if the percent change from 2002 to 2001 was a percent decrease of about 13.5%.

© Saxon. All rights reserved.

Name ______________________ Date __________ Class __________

Multiplying Matrices

LESSON 9

23. (1) Classify each statement as sometimes, always, or never true. Give examples to support your answer.

a. $a \cdot \left(\frac{1}{b}\right) = b \cdot \left(\frac{1}{a}\right)$

b. if a and b are irrational numbers, then $a \cdot b$ is an irrational number.

***24.** (9) **Geometry** Create a matrix representing the three triangles below.

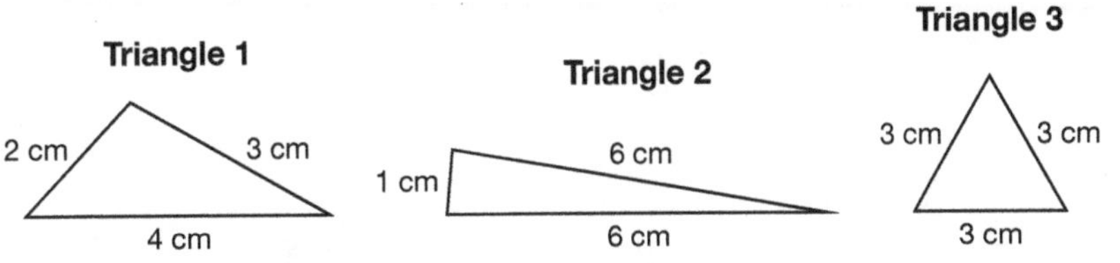

Use matrix multiplication to double side 1 (left), triple side 2 (bottom) and half side 3 (right) of each triangle and find the new perimeter of each triangle. Which triangle has the greatest perimeter?

25. (6) **Multi-Step** A mechanic bought a part for \$4.25 and marked the price up by 200% to sell to a customer. How much did the customer pay for the part? How much would the customer have paid if she had used a 5% off coupon?

Solve for x.

26. (7) $3x - 5 = 2 - 4x$

***27.** (7) $\frac{3}{4}x - \frac{1}{5}x = 2\frac{3}{4}$

28. (7) $5x - 2 = 7 + 2x$

29. (5) **Coordinate Geometry** The coordinates for a triangle are A (−3, 7), B (6, 8), and C (2, −3).

a. Write the coordinates as a matrix such that row one is x-values, row two is y-values, and each column is a coordinate.

b. Add the transformation matrix $\begin{bmatrix} -2 & -2 & -2 \\ 3 & 3 & 3 \end{bmatrix}$.

c. What are the coordinates of the transformation?

***30.** (8) Juanita is conducting an experiment where the temperature of a liquid varies directly with time. Her observations are recorded in the table below.

Temperature	80 degrees	120 degrees	? degrees
Time	120 seconds	180 seconds	240 seconds

a. Using the values in the table, identify the constant of variation.

b. Find the missing temperature in the table.

c. Determine an accurate prediction for the temperature of the liquid after 360 seconds.

© Saxon. All rights reserved.

Name ________________________________ Date ____________ Class ____________

Solving and Graphing Inequalities

LESSON 10

1. *(SB)* What solid figure is described by the net shown?

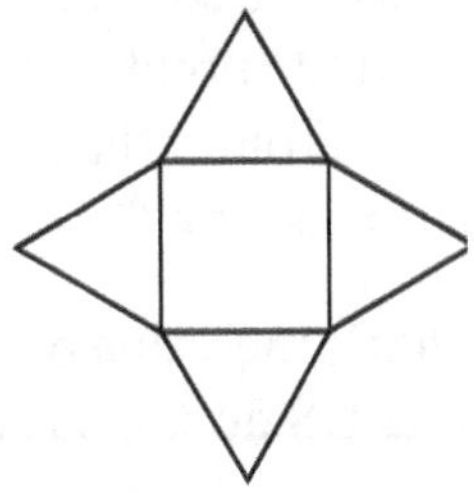

2. *(4)* Determine whether $y = -2x^2$ is a function. If so, state the domain and range.

Simplify.

3. *(3)* $\dfrac{(2x^{-2}y^0)^{-2}yx^{-2}}{xxxy^2(y^{-2})^2}$

4. *(3)* $\dfrac{(m^2n^{-5})^{-2}m(n^0)^2}{(m^2n^{-2})^{-3}m^2}$

Solve each equation.

5. *(7)* $0.003x + 0.02x - 0.03 = 0.177$

6. *(7)* $4\frac{1}{3}x - \frac{1}{2} = 3\frac{2}{5}$

Solve and graph each inequality.

***7.** *(10)* $3(x - 4) > 6$

***8.** *(10)* $2x + 3 \geq 4x - 5$

9. *(8)* **Multi-Step** The amount of water added to a dry mortar mix varies directly with the amount of dry mortar. 100 lb of dry mortar requires 11.25 pt of water.

a. Find the constant of variation for the dry mortar mix.

b. Find how many pints of water are needed for 240 lb of dry mortar mix.

10. *(2)* Simplify $4[3(x + 9) + 2]$.

Graphing Calculator **Find each product. Check using the graphing calculator.**

***11.** *(9)* $\begin{bmatrix} 1 & 0 \\ 0 & 1 \end{bmatrix} \times \begin{bmatrix} -1 & 2 \\ 3 & -2 \end{bmatrix}$

***12.** *(9)* $\begin{bmatrix} 0 & -1 \\ -1 & 0 \end{bmatrix} \times \begin{bmatrix} 4 & -1 \\ -2 & -6 \end{bmatrix}$

Find each percent change. Tell whether it is a percent increase or decrease.

13. *(6)* 265 to 318

14. *(6)* 17 to 14.45

15. *(3)* **Estimate** One cubic foot of pennies contains approximately 4.9×10^4 pennies. Think about covering the entire earth with two layers of pennies. The total number of pennies needed could be stacked in a cube that measures 2.73×10^4 ft on each side. Approximately how many pennies are in this cube?

© Saxon. All rights reserved.

*16. **Error Analysis** Look at the explanation given for graphing the solution of two
(10)
inequalities. To draw the graph of the solution $x \leq 2$ or $x > 5$ you draw a number line. Draw an open circle around the point 2 and a line through all the values less than 2. Next draw an open circle around the point 5 and a line through all values greater than 5. Is this explanation correct?

17. **Currency** On the first day of 2007, the value of one US dollar was equivalent to
(4)
0.76 euro. On the same day, one US dollar was equivalent to 1.22 Swiss francs.

a. Write a function to represent the value of francs in euros.

b. What is the value of the function for an input of 5 rounded to the nearest euro, and what does it represent?

c. How can you tell from the given data that your answer makes sense?

18. **a.** Which is the greater percent change: from 50 to 60 or from 60 to 50?
(6)

b. Analyze How can the answer to part a be found without actually finding the percents?

19. **Error Analysis** Find and explain the error in solving the equation below. Correct
(7)
the error and solve:

$$7x - 14 = -9 + 12x$$
$$7x = -23 + 12x$$
$$-5x = -23$$
$$x = \frac{23}{5}$$

20. **Geometry** The length of a rectangle equals $x + 4$ and the width equals 5 inches. The
(1)
perimeter of the rectangle can be calculated as shown below. Which properties of real numbers are demonstrated?

$$P = 2(x + 4) + 2(5) = 2(x + 4 + 5) = 2(x + 9) = 2x + 18.$$

21. **Statistics** The mean for the list of numbers below is 11.8. Use the formula for mean to
(7)
create a linear equation to solve for the missing data point.

12, 15, 8, ?, 20

22. **Predict** The weight of an object on Neptune varies directly with the weight of
(8)
that object on Earth. An object that weighs 5 g on Earth, weighs 6 g on Neptune. Without doing any calculations, predict the weight of an object on Neptune that weighs 10 g on Earth. Explain your prediction.

23. In 2002, the average height of a 15-year old boy was 1.737×10^3 mm. About how
(3)
many 15-year old boys lying head-to-toe would it take to equal the circumference of the earth at the equator, if its circumference measures about 4.0076×10^4 km? Write the answer in scientific notation rounded to the nearest ten thousandth.

© Saxon. All rights reserved.

*24. **Verify** The circumference of a circle varies directly with the radius. The table below (8) shows the circumference and radius of three different circles. Verify that the constant of variation is 6.283.

Circumference	Radius
12.566 cm	2 cm
94.245 cm	15 cm
232.471 cm	37 cm

*25. **Football** The first table below show the scoring plays made in three games by the (9) Philadelphia Eagles. The second table shows the point value of each play. Use matrix multiplication to find out in which game the team scored the most points. Use your graphing calculator to verify your answer.

Plays Made

Game	Touchdown	Field Goal	Extra Point
# 4	4	1	4
# 9	3	2	3
# 12	5	0	5

Point Value

Touchdown	6
Field Goal	3
Extra Point	1

*26. **Multiple Choice** A school is holding an International dinner as a fundraiser to raise (10) money for a local charity. The budget for the food is \$300. It will cost \$2.25 to prepare the food and beverages for one meal. Which inequality represents the number of meals that can be prepared?

A $x \le 134$ **B** $x \ge 134$ **C** $x \le 133$ **D** $x \ge 133$

27. **Bulk Foods** The table shows the cost of three sizes of bottles of water. (5)

Cost of Water Bottles

16 oz	24 oz	32 oz
\$0.75	\$1.20	\$1.60

a. Create two different matrices with different dimensions for the table.

b. Choose one of the matrices in part **a** and multiply it by a scalar to show the cost of purchasing 200 bottles of each size.

c. When a total of 500 bottles or more are purchased, a discount of 5% off each bottle is given. Use scalar multiplication to show the cost of each bottle when 500 or more of each size are purchased.

28. **Multiple Choice** What is the percent change from 35 to 31.5? (6)

A 10% **B** 90% **C** 100% **D** 900%

© Saxon. All rights reserved.

*29. (9) $A = \begin{bmatrix} 6 & -3 \\ 1 & 4 \end{bmatrix}$ and $B = \begin{bmatrix} 0 & 4 \\ -2 & 6 \end{bmatrix}$.

a. Find AB. **b.** Find BA. **c.** Is $AB = BA$?

*30. (9) **Write** If the number of columns of matrix A is not the same as the number of rows of matrix B, explain why the product AB is not defined.

© Saxon. All rights reserved.

Name ______________________ Date __________ Class __________

Understanding Polynomials

LESSON 11

*1. (7) **Geography** The table shows the relationship of the annual estimated population for three cities in the year 2005. The population in Oklahoma City, Oklahoma, is represented by the variable x.

2005 City Population

City	Population
Oklahoma City	x
Chicago	$5.354x$
Arlington	$0.683x$
Total of 3 cities	3,736,275

a. **Formulate** Write a linear equation to approximate the population in Oklahoma City in 2005.

b. **Estimate** Find the approximate population in Oklahoma City in 2005. Round to the nearest hundred.

2. (7) **Multi-Step** Twice a number is decreased by 9, and then multiplied by 4. The result is 8 less than 10 times the number. What is the number?

Simplify the expressions.

3. (3) $x^6(2x^2)$ 4. (3) $2(2x^2)^6$ 5. (3) $\frac{x^2}{2x^6}$

6. (7) **Geometry** Let x represent the first angle in a triangle. The second angle is twice the measure of the first. The third angle is triple the measure of the first. Write and solve a linear equation to find the measure of all three angles.

Solve the inequalities.

*7. (10) $-7 \leq -2x + 3 < 9$ *8. (10) $\frac{3}{2}x + 2 < \frac{1}{2}x + 5$

Evaluate.

9. (2) $(a - b) - a(-b)$ if $a = -5$ and $b = 3$

10. (2) $(a - x)(x - a)$ if $a = -2$ and $x = 4$

11. (2) $a^2 - y^3(a - y^2)y$ if $a = -2$ and $y = -3$

Write each fraction or decimal as a percent.

12. (6) 0.05 13. (6) $\frac{3}{10}$ 14. (6) $\frac{4}{5}$ 15. (6) 0.37

© Saxon. All rights reserved.

***16.** (8) **Error Analysis** Two scientists solved the following problem:

Sulfur is mixed with other chemicals to make sulfuric acid. If it takes 16 tons of sulfur to make 49 tons of sulfuric acid, how many tons of other constituents are needed to make 294 tons of acid? (Hint: Sulfuric acid is the total.) Which scientist solved the problem using the correct steps? Explain your reasoning.

Scientist A	Scientist B
$\frac{16}{49} = \frac{x}{294}$ $(16)(294) = 49x$ $x = 96$ tons	$\frac{33}{49} = \frac{x}{294}$ $(33)(294) = 49x$ $x = 198$ tons

17. (8) **Chemistry** A formula requires that 20 kilograms (kg) of carbon be used to produce 160 kg of a compound. How many kilograms of other components are needed to make 640 kg of the compound?

Justify Determine if these statements are a tautology, a contradiction, or neither. Justify your answer by constructing truth tables.

18. (Inv. 1) $\neg p \rightarrow q$

19. (Inv. 1) $\neg p \vee q$

20. (10) **Consumer** Nerissa's car can travel between 380 and 410 miles on a full tank of gas. She filled her gas tank and drove 45 miles. How many miles m can she drive without running out of gas?

21. (3) **Astronomy** The speed of light is about 3×10^8 meters/second. If Saturn's distance from Earth is about 1.321×10^{12} meters, about how many seconds would it take light to reach Saturn from Earth? Round the answer to the nearest second.

22. (3) **Earth Science** The garter snake is a small snake that is typically no more than 6×10^{-4} km in length. About how many garter snakes would it take to equal the circumference of the earth at the equator, if its circumference measures about 4.0076×10^4 km? Write the answer in scientific notation rounded to the nearest ten thousandth.

Analyze Determine if the expressions are polynomials. If the expression is a polynomial, rewrite it in standard form. If the expression is not a polynomial, explain why.

***23.** (11) $5x^2 + 3x^4 + 2$

***24.** (11) $\sqrt{3x + 5x^3}$

Classify the polynomial expressions by their degree and by the number of terms.

***25.** (11) $7x^3 + 3x^2 + 5x$

***26.** (11) $x^1 + 5x^0$

© Saxon. All rights reserved.

Simplify the expression.

***27.** $(7x^3 + 3x^2 + 5x) - (3x^3 + x)$
(11)

28. **Multiple Choice** Choose a letter that represents a set of x- and y-values that makes the equation $y = \frac{1}{2}x + 4$ true.
(4)

A $x = 2,\ y = 4$ **B** $x = 6, y = 6$

C $x = 4, y = 6$ **D** $x = 4, y = 8$

Graphing Calculator **Multiply the matrices. Check using a graphing calculator.**

***29.** $\begin{bmatrix} 2 & -3 & 4 \\ 5 & 8 & -1 \\ 7 & 0 & 9 \end{bmatrix} \cdot \begin{bmatrix} -4 & 7 \\ 0 & 1 \\ 3 & 6 \end{bmatrix}$
(9)

***30.** $\begin{bmatrix} 4 & -1 \\ 6 & -2 \end{bmatrix} \cdot \begin{bmatrix} -1 & \frac{1}{2} & 0 \\ -2 & 4 & -3 \end{bmatrix}$
(9)

© Saxon. All rights reserved.

Name ______________________ Date ____________ Class ____________

Solving Inverse Variation Problems

LESSON 12

Analyze Determine if each expression is a polynomial. If the expression is a polynomial, write it in standard form. If the expression is not a polynomial, explain why not.

***1.** (11) $\frac{3x + 7x^2}{10x^5}$

***2.** (11) $28x^2 - x^9 + 12x^7$

***3.** (8) **Data Analysis** Two scientists solved the following problem:

It takes 900 kg of acetylene to make 2400 kg of a compound. How many kilograms of other components will be required to make 3600 kg of the compound? Which scientist solved the problem using the correct steps? Explain your reasoning.

Scientist A	Scientist B
$\frac{1500}{2400} = \frac{x}{3600}$	$\frac{900}{2400} = \frac{x}{3600}$
$\frac{5}{8} = \frac{x}{3600}$	$\frac{3}{8} = \frac{x}{3600}$
$8x = 5(3600)$	$8x = 3(3600)$
$x = 2250$ kg	$x = 1350$ kg

***4.** (7) **Geometry** An isosceles triangle has two angles that each measure $x°$. The third angle is 1.75 times the measure of either angle. Write and solve a linear equation to find the measure of each angle.

Determine the constant k, then solve the problem.

***5.** (12) The number of revolutions per minute (RPM) varies inversely as the number of teeth in the gear. If 40 teeth result in 120 RPM, what would the RPM be if the gear had 30 teeth?

***6.** (12) The number of students in every class varies directly with the number of basketballs. For one class there are 8 students and 2 basketballs. If in another class there are 7 basketballs, how many students are in this class?

***7.** (12) The number of runners varies jointly as bicyclists and walkers. If 100 runners went with 4 bicyclists and 5 walkers, how many bicyclists would go with 20 runners and 2 walkers?

Simplify the expressions.

8. (3) $5x^7(3^3xy^2)$

9. (3) $\left(\frac{5xy^3}{2x^3y^2z^{-4}}\right)^2$

10. (3) $\frac{2^{-2}}{x^{-6}}$

11. (3) **Earth Science** The typical length of a green frog is about 5 to 10 cm. If a green frog is about 7.5×10^{-5} km, about how many green frogs would it take to equal the diameter of the Earth? The diameter is about 1.2753×10^4 km. Round the answer to the nearest ten thousandth.

Evaluate.

12. (1) $-8 - 3^2 - (-2)^2 - 3(-2) + 2$

13. (1) $-\{-[-5(-3 + 2)\ 7]\}$

© Saxon. All rights reserved.

14. (2) $-p^2 - p(a - p^2)$ if $a = 4$ and $p = -3$

Solve the inequalities.

15. (10) $-9 \leq 2x - 5 < 9$

16. (10) $-\frac{1}{2}x + 7 \geq 15$

*17. (7) **Geography** The table shows the relationship of the annual estimated population for three cities in the year 2005. The population in Phoenix, Arizona, is represented by the variable x.

2005 City Population

City	Population
Albuquerque	$0.151x$
Madison	$0.336x$
Phoenix	x
Total of 3 cities	2,185,816

a. **Formulate** Write a linear equation to approximate the population in Phoenix in 2005.

b. **Estimate** Find the approximate population of Phoenix in 2005. Round to the nearest thousand.

18. (7) **Multi-Step** The number of ducks on the pond tripled when the new flock landed. Then, 11 more ducks came. The resulting number of ducks was 13 less than 4 times the original number. How many ducks were there to begin with?

Write each fraction or decimal as a percent.

19. (6) 1.3

20. (6) $\frac{5}{8}$

21. (6) $\frac{13}{20}$

22. (6) 0.4

23. (8) **Chemistry** A formula required that 500 kilograms (kg) of sulfur be used to produce 3000 kg of a compound. How many kilograms of other materials are needed to make 6000 kg of the new compound?

24. (4) **Multiple Choice** Which set of x- and y-values would make the equation $y = \frac{3}{4}x - 1$ true?

A $x = 8, y = -5$

B $x = -8, y = -7$

C $x = 4, y = 2$

D $x = -8, y = 7$

Graphing Calculator **Multiply the matrices. Check using a graphing calculator.**

*25. (9) $\begin{bmatrix} -2 & 3 & -4 \\ 0 & -3 & -1 \\ 5 & 0 & 2 \end{bmatrix} \cdot \begin{bmatrix} 4 & 7 \\ -6 & 1 \\ 3 & 6 \end{bmatrix}$

*26. (9) $\begin{bmatrix} -2 & -1 \\ 6 & 4 \end{bmatrix} \cdot \begin{bmatrix} -1 & 0 & 1 \\ 0 & 1 & 0 \end{bmatrix}$

27. (3) **Astronomy** The speed of light is about 3×10^8 meters/second. If Saturn is about 1.35×10^{12} meters from the sun, how many seconds would it take light to reach Saturn from the Sun? Round the answer to the nearest hundredth of a second.

Justify **Determine if these statements are a tautology, a contradiction, or neither. Justify your answer by constructing truth tables.**

28. (Inv. 1) $(p \wedge q) \rightarrow \neg p$

29. (Inv. 1) $(p \vee q) \vee q$

30. (5) **Justify** Does the Commutative Property hold true for matrix subtraction? Justify your answer.

© Saxon. All rights reserved.

Name ______________________ Date __________ Class __________

Graphing Linear Equations I

LESSON 13

Determine the constant k, and solve the problem.

***1.** (12) **Multi-Step** The number of elk varied inversely as the number of deer and directly as the number of antelope. When there were 75 elk, there were 85 deer and 15 antelope. How many deer were there when there were 20 elk and 30 antelope? Round the answer down to the nearest whole number.

***2.** (12) **Formulate** The number of daisies varied inversely as the number of sunflowers and directly as the number of roses. When there were 65 daisies, there were 15 roses and 3 sunflowers. How many sunflowers were there when there were 5 daisies and 100 roses?

***3.** (13) Graph the equation $y = -\frac{3}{4}x + 1$ by constructing a table of values.

***4.** (13) Graph $-2x - y = 3$ using the intercepts.

***5.** (8) **Error Analysis** Two farmers solved the following problem:

Strawberries varied jointly as plums and tomatoes. If 500 strawberries went with 4 plums and 25 tomatoes, how many plums would go with 40 strawberries and 2 tomatoes?

Farmer A	Farmer B
$500 = k(4)(25)$ $k = 5$ $40 = 5(p)(2)$ $p = 4$ plums	$500 = k\frac{(25)}{(4)}$ $k = 80$ $40 = 80\frac{(25)}{(p)}$ $p = 50$ plums

Which farmer solved the problem using the correct steps? Explain your reasoning.

Calculate the slope of the lines that contain the following pairs of points. Tell whether the line rises, falls, is horizontal, or is vertical.

***6.** (13) $(-2, 0), (7, -5)$

7. (13) $(0, 4), (-2, 0)$

***8.** (13) Identify the slope and y-intercept of the line $y = -\frac{5}{4}x + 2$.

Analyze Determine whether each expression is a polynomial. If the expression is a polynomial, rewrite it in standard form. If the expression is not a polynomial, explain why.

***9.** (11) $25x^3 + x^{-7} + 2xy$

10. (11) $0.25x^4 + 5x^{\frac{4}{2}}$

© Saxon. All rights reserved.

11. *(7)* **Geography** The table shows the relationship of the annual estimated population for three cities in the year 2005. The population in Modesto, California, is represented by the variable x.

a. Formulate Write a linear equation to approximate the population in Modesto in 2005.

b. Estimate Find the approximate population of Modesto in 2005. Round to the nearest thousand.

2005 City Population

City	Population
Dallas	$5.879x$
St. Louis	$1.704x$
Modesto	x
Total of 3 cities	1,775,721

Evaluate.

12. *(1)* $-2 - 3(-2 - 2) - 5(-5 + 7)$

13. *(1)* $-[-2(-5 + 2) - (-2 - 3)]$

14. *(2)* $a^2 - y^3(a - y^2)y^2$ if $a = -2$ and $y = 3$

15. *(7)* **Geometry** Find x and y.

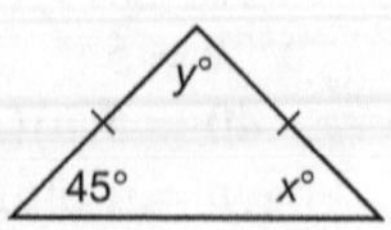

16. *(10)* **Justify** Explain why the inequality has no solution. $3x - 5 \geq 3(x + 7)$

17. *(10)* Solve the inequality, and graph its solution. $7x - 5 < 7(x + 5) + 2$

18. *(10)* **Civil Engineering** One cubic foot of pennies contains approximately 4.9×10^4 pennies. If approximately 1.8×10^{12} pennies would fit in the Empire State Building in New York City, what is the building's approximate volume in cubic feet? Write your answer in scientific notation. Round to the nearest tenth.

Solve for *p*.

19. *(7)* $(7p - 6) + 3p - (-2 - p) = 73$

20. *(7)* $\frac{7(p + 3)}{2} = 21$

21. *(7)* $4p + (p - 4)(2) = 8p - 7$

Use the matrices to find the products. Check the answer on a graphing calculator.

$$A = \begin{bmatrix} -1 & 2 \end{bmatrix}, B = \begin{bmatrix} 4 & 0 & 2 \\ -3 & 5 & 1 \end{bmatrix}, C = \begin{bmatrix} 7 & 1 \\ -2 & 0 \\ 0 & -3 \end{bmatrix}$$

22. *(9)* Find AB.

23. *(9)* Find ABC.

© Saxon. All rights reserved.

24. (11) **Citrus Production** The production of oranges and grapefruit (in millions of tons) in the U.S. for the years 2000 through 2006 is modeled by the polynomial functions below. The variable x represents the number of years since 2000.

Oranges $f(x) = -0.044x^3 + 0.258x^2 - 0.657x + 12.883$

Grapefruit $g(x) = 0.004x^3 - 0.065x^2 - 0.040x + 2.695$

What polynomial function is a model for the combined production of oranges and grapefruit in the United States for the years 2000–2006?

Write each fraction or decimal as a percent.

25. (6) 0.005 **26.** (6) $\frac{1}{6}$ **27.** (6) $\frac{5}{16}$

***28.** (12) **Meteorology** According to the Saffir-Simpson scale, hurricanes fall into five categories based on wind speed. The table below shows the relationship between category, wind speed, and storm surge (the height of waves). Analyze the data to determine the relationship between wind speed and storm surge. Is it a direct, joint, or inverse variation?

Category	Minimum Wind Speed (mph)	Minimum Storm Surge (ft)
1	74	4
2	96	6
3	111	9
4	131	13
5	155	19

29. (4) **Multiple Choice** Which of the following sets of ordered pairs are functions?

A (−7, 6), (−7, 3), (4, 3) **B** (−2, 5), (5, −2), (−2, 7)

C (1, −1), (−1, 1), (2, 1) **D** (0, 1), (0, 2), (0, 3)

***30.** (13) **Geography** A section of the Uncanoonuc Mountains, called the West Side Trail, is located in New Hampshire. The trail has a vertical change of about 268 feet vertically for every 1000 feet it changes horizontally. What is the slope of the trail?

© Saxon. All rights reserved.

Name ______________________ Date __________ Class __________

Finding Determinants

LESSON 14

***1.** (6) **Multi-Step** The regular price of a cell phone was $89.99. The price was reduced by 25%.

a. Find the amount saved. Then find the new price of the cell phone. Round to the nearest hundredth.

b. If the new price is later reduced by $15, find the percent change from the original price to the lowest price at which the cell phone is sold. Round to the nearest percent.

***2.** (12) **Error Analysis** Two students analyzed the data table shown at right. One student determined that the relationship between the variables is an inverse variation, while the other determined that it is a direct variation. Which student is correct? What error did the other student make?

Beads

Quantity	Price
1000	$90
900	$100
750	$120
600	$150
500	$180

Student A

Quantity	Price	$Q \times P$
1000	$90	90,000
900	$100	90,000
750	$120	90,000
600	$150	90,000
500	$180	90,000

Student B

Quantity	Price	$Q \div P$
1000	$90	90,000
900	$100	90,000
750	$120	90,000
600	$150	90,000
500	$180	90,000

Identify which equations are direct variations and which are inverse variations.

3. (8, 12) $y = 3x$

4. (8, 12) $y = \frac{1}{2}x$

5. (8, 12) $y = \frac{20}{x}$

Model **Graph the equation by using the stated method.**

6. (13) Graph the equation $y = -\frac{2}{3}x + 4$ using a table of values.

***7.** (13) Graph the equation $y = \frac{5}{4}x + 1$ using its intercepts.

Calculate the slope of the lines that contain the following pairs of points. Tell whether the line rises, falls, is horizontal, or is vertical.

8. (13) $(-8, 2), (3, -1)$

9. (13) $(6, 4), (-5, -2)$

10. (13) $(6, 2), (-5, 2)$

***11.** (14) Evaluate $\begin{vmatrix} -1 & 2 \\ 3 & 5 \end{vmatrix}$.

***12.** (14) Find x. $\begin{vmatrix} 3 & 5 \\ -2x + 1 & -7 \end{vmatrix} = 24$

© Saxon. All rights reserved.

*13. (14) **Verify** Evaluate $\begin{vmatrix} 7 & -1 & 2 \\ -3 & 0 & -2 \\ 4 & 3 & 5 \end{vmatrix}$. Show the steps of the method specified.

a. Use expansion by minors.

b. Set up diagonals. Find the difference of products.

*14. (14) **Graphing Calculator** Use a graphing calculator to find $\begin{vmatrix} 7 & 3 & 8 \\ 0 & -5 & 6 \\ -1 & 2 & -4 \end{vmatrix}$.

*15. (14) **Geometry** Find the area of the triangle with coordinates (−2, 5), (7, 3), (−4, −3).

16. (5) **Meteorology** The average temperatures were calculated, in degrees Fahrenheit, for the city of Hilo, Hawaii, and for the city of Lihue, Hawaii, from the year 1971 to 2000.

City	Jan	Feb	Mar	Apr	May	Jun
Hilo	71.4	71.5	72.0	72.5	73.7	75.1
Lihue	71.7	71.1	72.7	73.9	75.4	77.7

a. Model Record this information in a matrix and name it matrix A.

b. Let $B = \begin{bmatrix} -32 & -32 & -32 & -32 & -32 & -32 \\ -32 & -32 & -32 & -32 & -32 & -32 \end{bmatrix}$. Convert the temperatures from Fahrenheit to Celsius by applying the operations on matrix A. Round each element to the nearest tenth.

$$C = \frac{5}{9}([A] + [B])$$

17. (8) **Measurement** The number of feet varies directly with the number of yards. If a rope measures 18 feet, it measures 6 yards. Josh is asked to write a proportion to find the number of yards in a rope that measures 33 feet. Josh wrote the proportion $\frac{18}{6} = \frac{x}{33}$. Identify Josh's error and solve the problem correctly.

18. (10) **Formulate** A friend is trying to earn at least $500 this month by delivering newspapers. If she earns $0.25 per delivery, how many papers will she have to deliver? Write an inequality and solve it.

Solve the inequalities.

19. (10) $-1.9 < 2(x - 0.25) \leq 2.5$

*20. (10) $-2 < \frac{2(x-7)}{3} \leq 5$

© Saxon. All rights reserved.

(Basketball) In basketball, points are determined by throwing the ball into the basket, also called making a shot. Use the tables to answer the problems.

Player	Behind the 3-Point Line	Inside the 3-Point Line	Foul
Lan	2	1	1
Stacey	1	1	1
Robert	2	3	0

Type of Shot	Points
Behind the 3-Point Line	3
Inside the 3-Point Line	2
Foul	1

21. (5) Record Lan's, Stacey's, and Robert's points into a matrix. Name it matrix A. Record the point system into a matrix and name it matrix B.

***22.** (9) Find the total points for each player by finding the product $A \cdot B$.

Determine the kind of variation, if any, for each equation.

23. (8, 12) $y = mx + b$, for $m \neq 0$, $b \neq 0$

24. (8, 12) $y = mx + b$, for $m \neq 0$ and $b = 0$.

Identify the subsets of real numbers of which each number is a member.

25. (1) 0.33

26. (1) 0

27. (1) $\sqrt{5}$

28. (12) **(Meteorology)** According to the Saffir-Simpson scale, hurricanes fall into five categories based on wind speed. The table at right shows the relationship between category, wind speed, and storm surge (the height of waves). Analyze the data to determine the relationship between wind speed and storm surge. Is it a direct, joint, or inverse variation?

Category	Maximum Wind Speed (mph)	Maximum Storm Surge (ft)
1	95	5
2	100	8
3	130	12
4	155	18
5	155+	19+

29. (11) **Multiple Choice** Which polynomial is in standard form?

A $\frac{1}{2}x^3 - x$

B $\frac{1}{3} - \frac{1}{3}x^3$

C $4x^2 + 3x^3 + 2x^4$

D $x^4 + x^5$

© Saxon. All rights reserved.

30. (11) **Simple Interest** Al's grandfather deposited the amounts shown in Bank A as gifts on Al's birthday during the years 2002 through 2005. His aunt deposited the amounts shown in Bank B. The value of the accounts on 7/2/06 is represented by these polynomials, where $x = 1 + r$, and r is the interest rate for both accounts:

Date	Bank A	Bank B
7/2/02	$500	$1000
7/2/03	$1000	$200
7/2/04	$600	$200
7/2/05	$500	$200

Bank A $500x^4 + 1000x^3 + 600x^2 + 500x$

Bank B $1000x^4 + 200x^3 + 200x^2 + 200x$

a. Write the polynomial that represents the total value of both accounts on 7/2/06.

b. What is the total value of both accounts on 7/2/06 if the interest rate is 5%?

© Saxon. All rights reserved.

Name ______________________ Date __________ Class __________

Solving Systems of Equations by Graphing

LESSON 15

Given $h(x) = 6x + 3$ and $p(x) = 2x^2 - x$, find each of the following.

*1. (4) $p(-5)$

2. (4) $h\left(\frac{1}{2}\right)$

Identify whether the equation is a direct, inverse, or joint variation.

3. (12) $\frac{1}{3}y = x$

*4. (12) $y = \frac{1}{2}xz$

5. (12) $xy = 10$

Geometry **For each equation identify the kind of variation it represents.**

6. (12) Circumference $= 2\pi \times$ Radius

7. (12) Area of a circle $= \pi(\text{Radius})^2$

*8. (6) **Multi-Step** A jacket is on sale for 75% off the original price of $39.99. Find the amount of the price reduction. Then find the new price, which includes a sales tax of 5%.

9. (14) **Multiple Choice** Evaluate $\begin{vmatrix} -1 & 3 \\ 2 & 3 \\ 7 & -4 \end{vmatrix}$.

A 0

B −9

C −29

D This matrix does not have a determinant.

10. (13) Given the equation $8x - 2y = -10$,

a. identify the slope and the y-intercept.

b. graph the line.

Use the slope formula to find the missing coordinate.

*11. (13) The slope of a line is $\frac{4}{9}$. The points (3, 8) and $(-6, y)$ lie on the line. Find y.

12. (13) The slope of a line is $-\frac{7}{3}$. The points (4, −4) and $(x, 3)$ lie on the line. Find x.

*13. (6) **Error Analysis** The price of a product decreased from $9 to $6. A student incorrectly computed the percent of decrease to be 50%. What was the student's error?

14. (14) Evaluate $\begin{vmatrix} -5 & 2 \\ 1 & -3 \end{vmatrix}$.

15. (14) Find x. $\begin{vmatrix} 2x & 3 \\ -x-4 & -1 \end{vmatrix} = 10$

*16. (15) **Graphing Calculator** Graph to solve the system. Then classify the system.

$2x - y = -2$

$2y = 4x - 4$.

© Saxon. All rights reserved.

*17. (11) **Woodworking** A lathe operator has a piece of wood in the shape of a square prism with dimensions $2x$, $2x$, and h. He wants to make the largest possible cylinder by turning the wood on the lathe and cutting it down. The cylinder will have radius x and height h. Write a polynomial that represents the volume of wood he will cut off to make the cylinder. (The formula for the volume of a cylinder is $V = \pi r^2 h$.)

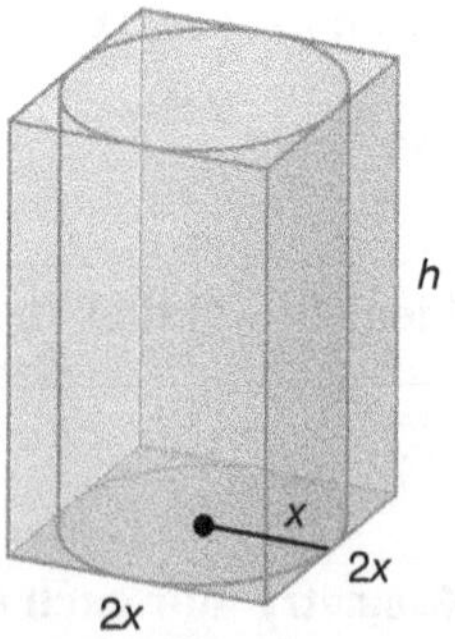

18. (12) **Physics** According to Ohm's Law, a direct current flowing in a wire is inversely proportional to the resistance of the wire. If the current in a wire is 0.01 amperes (A) and the resistance is 1200 ohms (Ω), what resistance will result in a current of 0.1 A?

19. (7) **Travel** Aaron is traveling 955 miles from Phoenix, Arizona, to Jackson, Wyoming. He leaves Phoenix, driving 410 miles before stopping for gas in Cortez, Colorado. He makes one last stop in Rock Springs, Wyoming, before traveling the final 180 miles to his destination. Write and solve an equation to find the number of miles Aaron drove between Cortez and Rock Springs.

*20. (4) **Formulate** Write a function that represents the data set $(-4, 16)$, $(1, 1)$, $(3, 9)$, $(4, 16)$, $(7, 49)$.

21. (10) **Business** A snow cone vendor wants to make at least \$2,500 the first month. If he charges \$1.25 per snow cone, how many snow cones will he have to sell? Write and solve an inequality to find how many snow cones he will have to sell.

22. (10) **Verify** Solve $-2(7x + 1) \leq -8x - 9$. Check the answer by substituting an integer that makes the inequality true.

23. (9) **Scoring** Andrew, Max, and Gracie are all taking a test where each type of question is given a certain point value. Use matrix multiplication to find out who scored the greatest number of points on the test.

Questions answered correctly

	Type 1	Type 2	Type 3
Andrew	7	5	4
Max	6	7	3
Gracie	7	4	5

Point Value	
Type 1	3
Type 2	5
Type 3	10

© Saxon. All rights reserved.

Use the matrices to find the products, if possible.

$$A = \begin{bmatrix} -1 \\ 5 \\ 3 \end{bmatrix} \qquad B = \begin{bmatrix} -2 & 0 & 2 \end{bmatrix}$$

24. (9) AB

25. (9) BA

26. (15) **Multiple Choice** Which is a solution to the system below?

$$-x + 2y = 6$$
$$-3x + 4y = 4$$

A (7, 5) **B** (8, 7) **C** (0, 0) **D** (−16, −11)

***27.** (15) **Graphing Calculator** Use a graphing calculator to determine the solution of the system.

$-2x - y = 2$

$3x + 2y = 1$

***28.** (15) **Write** The solution of a system is a single point. Classify the system and describe the graph.

29. (8) **Meaurement** In a certain recipe, the amount of sugar is directly proportional to the amount of flour. If 3 cups of sugar are used with 8 cups of flour, how many cups of sugar are used with 12 cups of flour?

30. (3) **Population** The U.S. population is approximately 2.99×10^8. In one year, the United States produced 4.78×10^{11} pounds of garbage. Approximately how much garbage did the average American produce that year?

© Saxon. All rights reserved.

Name ______________________________ Date ____________ Class ____________

Using Cramer's Rule

LESSON 16

1. **Multi-Step** One T-shirt costs \$15.50. This can be expressed as the ordered pair (1, 15.5). *(4)* The store is having a buy-one-get-one-free sale on T-shirts. Find the total cost if 2, 3, 4, 5, and 6 T-shirts are purchased. Express the answers as ordered pairs in set notation. Identify the domain and range. Determine if the set of ordered pairs represents a function. Explain.

*2. **Error Analysis** After examining the two function tables below, a student concluded that *(15)* the two equations were inconsistent.

$y = -\frac{7}{3}x + 3$

x	−2	−1	0	1
y	$-\frac{5}{2}$	−1	2	5

$y = \frac{1}{3}x - 1$

x	−2	−1	0	1
y	$-\frac{5}{3}$	$-\frac{4}{3}$	−1	$-\frac{2}{3}$

a. Describe the student's error.

b. How can this error be avoided?

c. Solve the system.

3. **Model** One day the value of one U.S. dollar was equivalent to 0.77 euro. On the same *(4)* day, one U.S. dollar was equivalent to 1.24 Canadian dollars. Write a function to represent the value of Canadian dollars in euros.

*4. **Graphing Calculator** Solve the system: $\begin{matrix} x - 2y = 6 \\ -6x + 3y = 1 \end{matrix}$. Round to the nearest tenth. *(5)*

5. The number of students attending a certain sports event decreased from 2080 to 1575 *(6)* from one school year to the next.

a. Estimate Estimate the percent of change.

b. Find the actual percent of change. Round to the nearest percent.

Which of the following depict functions? Identify the domain and the range.

6. *(4)*

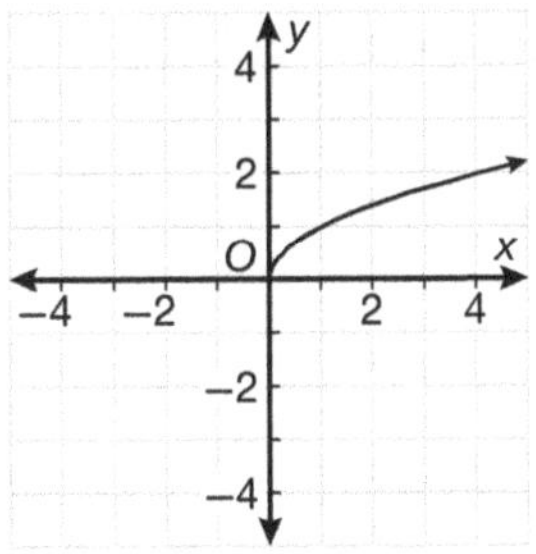

7. *(4)*

x	y
−2	−1
−2	3
−2	7

© Saxon. All rights reserved.

8. (11) **Measurement** This figure consists of a cylinder with a hemisphere on top. Write a polynomial in x that represents the total surface area of the figure. For reference, formulas for surface area are given below.

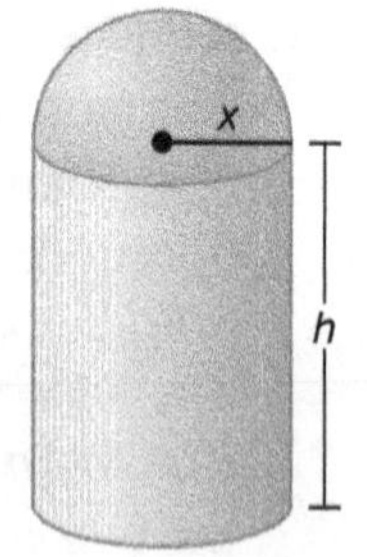

Cylinder: $SA = 2\pi r^2 + 2\pi rh$
Sphere: $SA = 4\pi r^2$

(Hint: The figure has only one circular base.)

Given matrices A, B, and C, multiply, if possible.

$$A = \begin{bmatrix} 1 & 1 \\ 2 & 3 \end{bmatrix} \quad B = \begin{bmatrix} 3 & 2 \\ -1 & 1 \end{bmatrix} \quad C = \begin{bmatrix} 0 & 2 & 0 \\ 3 & 1 & 4 \end{bmatrix}$$

9. (9) CA **10.** (9) AB **11.** (9) BC

Solve.

12. (7) $\frac{4}{7} + \frac{x+2}{3} = \frac{5}{3}$ **13.** (7) $\frac{5}{3} - \frac{x-4}{2} = \frac{1}{2}$

14. (7) $x - 7 + \frac{x}{4} = -\frac{1}{3}$

***15.** (15) **Demography** The population of Sacramento, California, in 2005 was 451,743 and increased by 2038 people by 2006. The population of Miami, Florida, in 2005 was 386,619 and increased by 17,429 people by 2006. If the population of these cities continued to grow at these rates, then the following equations would represent the population of the cities, where x is the number of years after 2005 and y is the population.

$y = 2038x + 451{,}743$ Sacramento's Population
$y = 17{,}429x + 386{,}619$ Miami's Population.

a. In what year would the populations of Sacramento and Miami be equal?

b. About how many people are in each city when the populations are equal?

16. (14) Find x. $\begin{vmatrix} x & 2 & 1 \\ -1 & 1 & 0 \\ 0 & 0 & 1 \end{vmatrix} = 5$

17. (11) **Aquarium Design** The aquariums shown each require the same-sized shelf, but they hold different amounts of water. Write a polynomial that represents how much more water the cube-shaped aquarium holds than the cylindrical aquarium. (Hint: The formula for the volume of a cylinder is $V = \pi r^2 h$.)

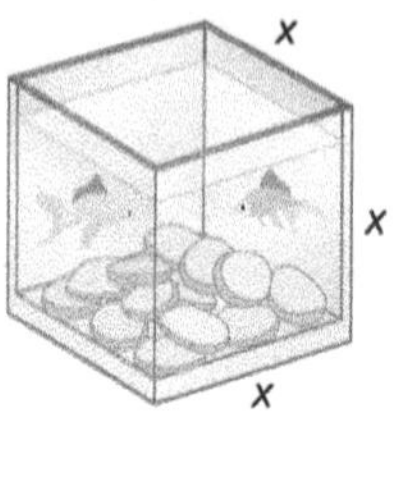

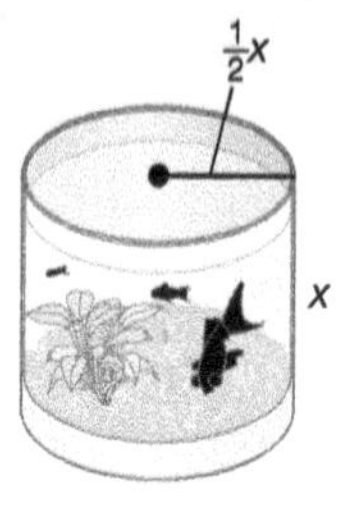

© Saxon. All rights reserved.

18. (10) **Explain** Why is there no solution for the compound inequality $-10 > n > -1$?

Solve the inequalities.

19. (10) $3x + 1 > -2$ or $6 < 2x - 4$

20. (10) $\frac{1}{3}x + 5 \leq 6$ or $-8 \leq \frac{1}{2}x - 7$

***21.** (16) **Construction** A contractor is replacing the tile in two bathrooms. For one bathroom, she purchased 416 large tiles and 256 small tiles at a cost of \$233.60. For the other bathroom, she purchased 400 large tiles and 512 small tiles at a cost of \$251.20. How much does each size tile cost?

Use Cramer's rule to solve each system.

***22.** (16) $\begin{aligned} -3x + 4y &= 8 \\ x + 4y &= 4 \end{aligned}$

***23.** (16) $\begin{aligned} -3x + 5y &= 8 \\ -3x + 5y &= 4 \end{aligned}$

***24.** (16) $\begin{aligned} 2x + 4y &= 10 \\ -5x - 10y &= -25 \end{aligned}$

***25.** (16) **Multiple Choice** Match the solution with the system of equations.

$$x = \frac{\begin{vmatrix} 8 & 2 \\ 1 & -1 \end{vmatrix}}{\begin{vmatrix} 5 & 2 \\ 3 & -1 \end{vmatrix}} \qquad y = \frac{\begin{vmatrix} 5 & 8 \\ 3 & 1 \end{vmatrix}}{\begin{vmatrix} 5 & 2 \\ 3 & -1 \end{vmatrix}}$$

A $\begin{aligned} 8x + 2y &= 5 \\ x - y &= 3 \end{aligned}$

B $\begin{aligned} 5x + 8y &= 2 \\ 3x + y &= -1 \end{aligned}$

C $\begin{aligned} 5x + 2y &= 8 \\ 3x - y &= 1 \end{aligned}$

D $\begin{aligned} 8x + y &= 5 \\ 2x - y &= 2 \end{aligned}$

***26.** (16) **Write** When using Cramer's rule to solve systems of equations, what types of systems could exist if the determinant of the coefficient matrix equals zero? Describe the graphs of the lines.

***27.** (14) **Geometry** A quadrilateral with vertices (x_1, y_1), (x_2, y_2), (x_3, y_3), and (x_4, y_4) has an area equal to the absolute value of

$$\frac{1}{4}\begin{vmatrix} x_1 & x_2 & x_3 & x_4 \\ y_1 & y_2 & y_3 & y_4 \\ 1 & 1 & 1 & 1 \\ -1 & 1 & -1 & 1 \end{vmatrix}.$$ Find the area of the quadrilateral.

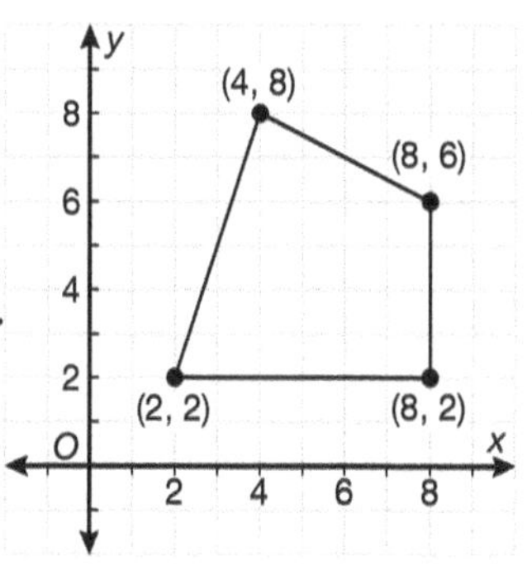

© Saxon. All rights reserved.

28. Find the x- and y-intercepts of the line with equation $3x - \frac{1}{2}y = 6$.
(13)

29. **Meteorology** The average temperatures were calculated, in degrees Fahrenheit, for the city of Kodiak, Alaska, and for the city of Valdez, Alaska, from the year 1971 to 2000.
(5)

City	Jan	Feb	Mar	Apr	May	Jun
Kodiak	29.7	29.9	32.6	37.3	43.5	49.2
Valdez	21.9	24.8	29.8	37.7	45.8	52.2

a. Model Record this information in a matrix and name it Matrix A.

b. Let $B = \begin{bmatrix} -32 & -32 & -32 & -32 & -32 & -32 \\ -32 & -32 & -32 & -32 & -32 & -32 \end{bmatrix}$. Convert the temperatures from Fahrenheit to Celsius by applying the operations on Matrix A. Round each element to the nearest tenth.

$$C = \frac{5}{9}([A] + [B])$$

30. **Geography** Christine is hiking a trail to the summit of a mountain. The mountain has a vertical change of 15 feet upward for every 25 feet of horizontal distance.
(13)

a. What is the slope of the mountain?

b. If the trail has changed vertically by 450 feet, how much has it changed horizontally?

© Saxon. All rights reserved.

Name ________________________________ Date __________ Class __________

Solving Equations and Inequalities with Absolute Value

LESSON 17

*1. (17) **Construction Engineering** A company's safety regulations require the wire rope used to suspend a 100-ton load to have a thickness that is within $\frac{3}{8}$ inch of $1\frac{3}{4}$ inches. Write and solve an absolute value equation to find the minimum safe thickness of rope.

2. (13) **Explain** Two points, $(3, -7)$ and $(3, 5)$, lie on a line. Using the slope formula, explain why the slope does not exist. What kind of line do these points lie on?

*3. (17) **Generalize** Will the inequality $3|x - 7| > -12$ have a solution?

Use Cramer's rule to solve each system.

*4. (16) $\begin{aligned} 4x - 2y &= 6 \\ 10x - 5y &= 15 \end{aligned}$

5. (16) $\begin{aligned} -5x + 2y &= 7 \\ 10x - 4y &= 3 \end{aligned}$

6. (16) $\begin{aligned} -3x + 2y &= 4 \\ x + 2y &= 10 \end{aligned}$

*7. (15) **Multiple Choice** Which is *not* a solution to the system below?

$$\begin{aligned} 2x - 5y &= -3 \\ -10x + 25y &= 15 \end{aligned}$$

A (1, 1) **B** (0, 0)

C (6, 3) **D** All of these are solutions.

Find the product.

8. (9) $\begin{bmatrix} 1 & 0 & -2 \\ 0 & 3 & -1 \\ 2 & 0 & 4 \end{bmatrix} \cdot \begin{bmatrix} 4 & -3 \\ 1 & 2 \\ 0 & -1 \end{bmatrix}$

9. (9) $\begin{bmatrix} 2 & -3 & 1 & -2 \end{bmatrix} \cdot \begin{bmatrix} 0 & 1 \\ -3 & 2 \\ 1 & 0 \\ 4 & 6 \end{bmatrix}$

10. (8) **Temperature** Juanita is conducting an experiment where the temperature of a liquid varies directly with time. Her observations are recorded in the table below.

Temperature	80 degrees	120 degrees	? degrees
Time	120 seconds	180 seconds	240 seconds

a. Using the values in the table, identify the constant of variation.

b. Find the missing temperature in the table.

c. Determine an accurate prediction for the temperature of the liquid after 360 seconds.

11. (13) **Multiple Choice** Identify the slope of the line with the equation $2x + 9y = 18$.

A 2 B $\frac{2}{9}$ C $-\frac{9}{2}$ D $-\frac{2}{9}$

© Saxon. All rights reserved.

Solving Equations and Inequalities with Absolute Value

12. (8) **Baseball** When a baseball pitcher throws a baseball, the ball is slowed down by wind resistance. The relationship between the force (F) of wind resistance and velocity (v) of the baseball is a direct variation of the form $F = kv^2$. The data tables below represent sample pitches from two ball games.

Pitcher A

Ball Speed (mph)	Force
90	1620
91	1656
92	1693
93	1730
94	1767
95	1805

Pitcher B

Ball Speed (mph)	Force
90	2025
91	2070
92	2116
93	2162
94	2209
95	2256

a. Find the constant of variation for each pitcher.

b. Based on your results, which pitcher was throwing the ball harder?

c. What could account for the difference in the force of wind resistance?

13. (16) **Multi-Step** Use Cramer's Rule to solve the system. Check your solution by graphing.

$$-2x + 3y = 0$$
$$x + 3y = 6$$

14. (11) **Error Analysis** A student says that the polynomial $ab^4 + a^2b^2 - 3$ is of higher degree than the polynomial $a^2b^3 + ab + 2$. What is the error? Explain.

Solve the equation or inequality.

15. (7) $\frac{y-2}{4} = 7y - 2 - 6(y + 1)$

16. (10) $2 + \frac{1}{3}x \leq 1\frac{2}{3}$ and $-2x - 5 \leq 7$

17. (10) $-\frac{1}{3} - \frac{2x}{3} > \frac{1}{3}$ and $-7x - \frac{1}{2} < 6\frac{1}{2}$

***18.** (17) $|-2x + 7| - 3 = 10.$

***19.** (17) **Verify** Solve $|8x - 3| = 16x$. Check for extraneous solutions by substituting the solution into the equation.

***20.** (17) Solve $|3x + 2| \leq 14$. Graph the solution.

21. (15) **Geometry**

a. Graph the system below. Describe the shape that the lines form.

$$3x - 2y = 2$$
$$-3x - 2y = -34$$
$$x - 2y = 6$$

b. Find the vertices of the shape.

© Saxon. All rights reserved.

22. (14) A triangle has vertices (1, 2), (1, −4), and (4, −4). Find the area of the triangle by writing and solving a determinant.

Use a table to graph the equation. (Hint: Choose x-values that are multiples of the slope's denominator.)

23. (13) $y = -\frac{5}{3}x - 2$

24. (13) $y = -\frac{1}{2}x + 5$

***25.** (14) **Graphing Calculator** Use a graphing calculator to evaluate

$$2\begin{vmatrix} -2 & 1 & 4 \\ -5 & 7 & 0 \\ 8 & -3 & 1 \end{vmatrix} - 3\begin{vmatrix} 0 & 1 & 4 \\ 1 & 7 & 0 \\ -6 & -3 & 1 \end{vmatrix} - 1\begin{vmatrix} 0 & -2 & 4 \\ 1 & -5 & 0 \\ -6 & 8 & 1 \end{vmatrix} - 5\begin{vmatrix} 0 & -2 & 1 \\ 1 & -5 & 7 \\ -6 & 8 & -3 \end{vmatrix}.$$

26. (3) **Solar System** The average distance between the earth and sun is approximately 1.495×10^{11} m. Earth's orbit around the sun is nearly circular. For estimation purposes, assume that Earth's orbit is circular.

a. Estimate the distance in kilometers that the earth travels around the sun in one year. Write your answer in scientific notation. Round to the nearest hundredth.

b. Estimate the average speed at which the earth travels around the sun in km/s. Use 365.25 days per year.

***27.** (13) Find the slope of the line between (−2, −7) and (2, 1). Determine if the line rises, falls, or is horizontal or vertical.

***28.** (8) **Landscaping** When mixing concentrated fertilizer for a garden, the amount of fertilizer varies directly with the amount of water. If 2 cups of fertilizer are used in 16 gallons of water, how much fertilizer is used in 48 gallons of water?

Determine the kind of variation, if any, for each equation.

29. (12) $y = ax^2 + bx + c$, for $a, b, c \neq 0$

30. (12) $y = ax^2 + bx + c$, for any values of a, b, and c.

© Saxon. All rights reserved.

Name ______________________ Date ____________ Class ____________

Calculating with Units of Measure

LESSON 18

Use Cramer's rule to solve each system.

*1. (16) $x = y + 1$
$3x + 2y = 8$

2. (16) $3x - y = 22$
$2x + 3y = -11$

3. (16) $x + y = 20$
$5x + 10y = 200$

Solve.

*4. (17) $-5|2x - 7| - 4 = -34$

5. (17) $\left|\frac{1}{2}x + 1\right| \le -\frac{1}{2}$

6. (17) $|8 - 3x| > 9$

Identify whether the equation is a direct, inverse, or joint variation. Find the constant of variation.

7. (12) $\frac{y}{x} = \sqrt{2}$

8. (12) $y = \frac{15}{x}$

*9. (15) **Chemical Mixture** A chemist has one solution that is 10% iodine and another that is 50% iodine. How many milliliters of each should the chemist use to make 100 mL of a mixture that is 20% iodine?

a. **Formulate** Set up a system of equations that models the problem.

b. **Graphing Calculator** Use a graphing calculator to solve the system.

10. (12) **Multiple Choice** In the data set at right, what is the relationship between x and y?

A joint variation **B** direct variation

C inverse variation **D** none of the above

x	1	2	3	4
y	4	2	$1\frac{1}{3}$	1

11. (15) **Sports** Suppose you and a friend are practicing basketball. To make practice more interesting, you invent a game. Every time you make a basket, you will gain 2 points. Every time your friend makes a basket, you will lose 1 point. Likewise, every time your friend makes a basket, he will gain 2 points, and every time you make a basket, he will lose 1 point. Both of you start with 0 points. At the end of the game, you have 16 points and your friend has 10.

a. **Formulate** Write a system of equations to represent this situation.

b. How many baskets did each of you make?

12. (12) **Geometry** As the diameter (d) of a circle increases in size, the circumference (C) increases. Likewise, as the diameter decreases in size, so does the circumference. The constant of variation between C and d is π. Describe the kind of variation between circumference and diameter. Write the equation.

© Saxon. All rights reserved.

13. **Error Analysis** Explain the error in the work below. Then find the correct determinant.
(14)

$$\begin{vmatrix} -2 & 6 \\ 3 & -1 \end{vmatrix} = (6)(3) - (-2)(-1) = 18 - 2 = 16$$

Convert the units and unit rates.

*14. Change 0.075 hours to seconds.
(18)

*15. Convert 1224 in^2 to yd^2.
(18)

*16. Convert 0.26 miles per hour to feet per minute.
(18)

*17. **Space Travel** The Endeavor, a space shuttle, has speeds of about 27,404 feet per second. Convert the speed into kilometers per hour and miles per hour.
(18)

18. **Verify** Show that $|2x + 3| = 16x$ has two solutions, one of which is extraneous.
(17)

*19. **Analyze** Write the four resulting inequalities that are used to solve $|-3x + 5| \geq |x|$.
(17)

20. **Chemical Elements** For oxygen to be a liquid, it must be within 35.845° of −332.925°F.
(17)

a. Write an absolute value equation to determine the least and greatest temperatures at which oxygen will remain a liquid.

b. Solve the equation.

21. **Explain** Give a written explanation on how to graph an equation using intercepts.
(13)

22. **Analyze** Give an example of two trinomials whose sum has 6 terms.
(11)

Solve for x.

*23. $\begin{vmatrix} \frac{x}{2} & 4 \\ 3 & -10 \end{vmatrix} = -(-x + 7)$
(7, 14)

24. $\begin{vmatrix} -3 & 2 \\ 4x - 1 & 2x - \frac{1}{3} \end{vmatrix} = -16x + 7$
(7, 14)

Multi-Step Given the slope and a point of the line, graph the line. Determine the y-intercept of the line.

25. $m = \frac{5}{3}$ $(-3, 1)$
(13)

26. $m = -\frac{4}{5}$ $(5, -5)$
(13)

*27. **Solar System** The earth revolves about the sun at about 29.8 kilometers per second. Convert the rate into meters per hour. Write the answer in scientific notation rounded to the thousandths.
(3, 18)

$A = \begin{bmatrix} 6 & -3 \\ 1 & 4 \end{bmatrix}$ **and** $B = \begin{bmatrix} 0 & 4 \\ -2 & 6 \end{bmatrix}$. **Find each product.**

28. Find AB.
(9)

29. Find BA.
(9)

30. Find A^2.
(9)

© Saxon. All rights reserved.

Name ________________ Date ________ Class ________

Multiplying Polynomials

LESSON 19

Simplify each expression.

1. (18) 2.25 yd + 7.6 yd + 0.58 yd

2. (18) 2.08 ft × 0.033 ft × 15.5 ft

3. (8, 12) **Geometry** Which type of variation is represented by the equation Area = length × width, if the Area = 25 ft^2? Find the constant of variation.

4. (8, 12) **Analyze** Which type of variation is represented by the equation $d = r \times t$ if d is held constant? r is held constant? t is held constant?

5. (18) Kellie's last three walks were 2.25 mi, 3.2 mi, and 2.31 mi. What is the sum of the distances Kellie walked?

6. (17) **Multiple Choice** Solve $|2x + 1| < 4$.

A $-\frac{5}{2} < x < \frac{3}{2}$

B $\frac{3}{2} < x < -\frac{5}{2}$

C $x < -\frac{5}{2}$ or $x > \frac{3}{2}$

D $x < \frac{3}{2}$

***7.** (11, 19) **Packaging Technology** An engineer has a box in the shape of a cube. She wants to know how the volume is affected if she adds 1 unit to each base edge and subtracts 2 units from the height. Does the volume increase, decrease, or remain the same? Explain your answer.

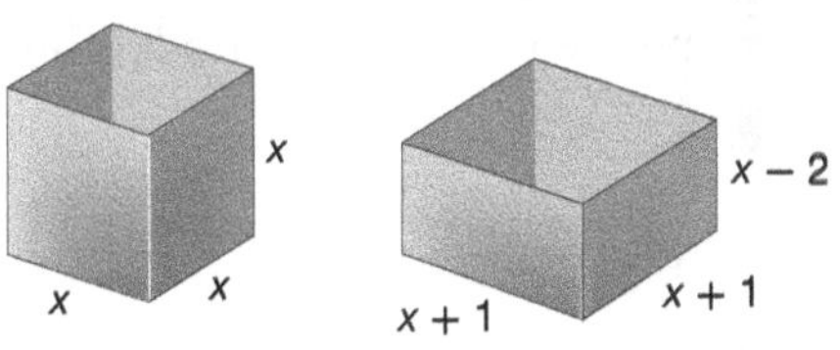

8. (13) Graph to determine the solution of $\begin{aligned} x + 2y &= 2 \\ y &= -\frac{1}{2}x - 3 \end{aligned}$.

9. (18) **Explain** How can feet per second be converted to miles per hour?

***10.** (15) **Chemical Mixture** Ocean water is about 3.5% salt. A chemist has a solution that is 25% salt and 75% water. If the chemist needs to make 1600 mL of a solution that is 15% salt, about how much ocean water should the chemist use? Round the answer to the nearest whole number.

a. Set up a system of equations that models the problem.

b. Graphing Calculator Use a graphing calculator to solve the system.

© Saxon. All rights reserved.

11. (12) **Data Analysis** Each of the data sets shown is either a direct or an inverse variation. For each data set, find the constant of variation.

a.

x	y
1	1.5
2	3
3	4.5
4	6
5	7.5

b.

x	y
1	4
2	2
3	$\frac{4}{3}$
4	1
5	$\frac{4}{5}$

c.

x	y
2	$\frac{4}{3}$
3	2
4	$\frac{8}{3}$
5	$\frac{10}{3}$

***12.** (12) **Generalize** In the diagram, there is a volume (V) of air in a cylinder with a movable pressure device that applies pressure (P) on the column of air. When downward pressure is applied, the volume of air decreases. When pressure is released by moving the pressure device up, the volume of air increases. What would need to be true for the relationship between P and V to be an inverse variation? What would be the equation to model this situation?

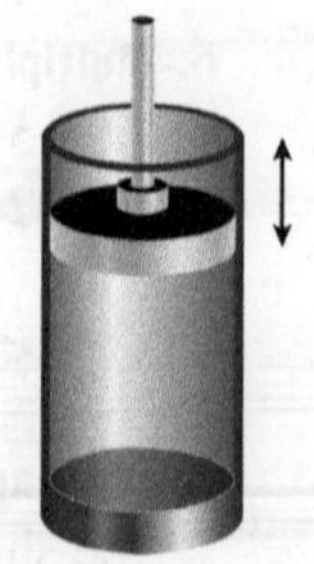

Multiply.

***13.** (19) $(8x + 6)(7x - 9)$

***14.** (19) $(y - 3)(y^2 + 2y - 5)$

15. (18) **Error Analysis** Two students converted 200 feet per second to miles per hour. Which student is correct? Explain the error in the other student's work.

Student A

$$\frac{200 \text{ ft}}{1 \text{ s}} \times \frac{1 \text{ mi}}{5280 \text{ ft}} \times \frac{360 \text{ s}}{1 \text{ hr}} = \frac{(200)(360)}{5280} \frac{\text{mi}}{\text{hr}}$$

Using a calculator, this simplifies to about 13.6 miles per hour.

Student B

$$\frac{200 \text{ ft}}{1 \text{ s}} \times \frac{1 \text{ mi}}{5280 \text{ ft}} \times \frac{3600 \text{ s}}{1 \text{ hr}} = \frac{(200)(3600)}{5280} \frac{\text{mi}}{\text{hr}}$$

Using a calculator, this simplifies to about 136 miles per hour.

Convert each of the following measurements.

16. (18) 8 yd^2 to in^2

© Saxon. All rights reserved.

17. (18) 72 hours to seconds

18. (15) **Multiple Representations** The ordered pairs $(-1, -\frac{5}{2})$, $(0, -1)$, $(2, 2)$, and $(4, 5)$ are values in one function of a system that is consistent and dependent. Complete the table to represent ordered pairs of the other function in the same system.

x	0	2	4	6
y				

19. (18) **Multi-Step** While bicycling one weekend, Jess recorded the total distance and time he traveled each time that he stopped. The table shows his records.

Time (hours)	Distance Traveled (miles)
0.5	6
1	12
1.5	18
3	36

a. What was Jess's average speed, in miles per hour, for the total trip?

b. Convert Jess's speed in miles per hour to feet per second.

c. How long, in seconds, would it take Jess to travel 500 feet?

Simplify.

20. (3) $\dfrac{5x^2y}{7y^5} \cdot \dfrac{28z}{115x^{-2}y^{-3}}$

21. (3) $\dfrac{3x^2yz^{-4}}{18xy^{-2}} \div \dfrac{9y^4}{54x^6z^8}$

***22.** (17) **Chemical Elements** For helium to be a liquid, it must be within 3.0935° of −454.9065°F.

a. Formulate Write an absolute value equation to determine the least and greatest temperatures at which helium will remain a liquid.

b. Solve the equation.

***23.** (17) **Analyze** Write the distance from each point to the origin as an absolute value expression. Then simplify the expression.

a. $(5, 0)$ **b.** $(-7, 0)$ **c.** $(0, 9)$ **d.** $(0, -8)$

Simplify the expressions.

***24.** (19) $(-3y + 7)^2$

***25.** (19) $(4a + 6b)(4a - 6b)$

© Saxon. All rights reserved.

26. (11) **Generalize** Consider the following polynomials: $P_1 = 2x^5 + x^3$, $P_2 = -2x^5 - x^3 + x$, $P_3 = x^2$, and $P_4 = x^5$. Find the number of terms in each of these sums: $P_1 + P_2$, $P_1 + P_3$, and $P_1 + P_4$. Use the results to make a generalization about the number of terms in the sum of two polynomials compared to the number of terms in the polynomials that make up that sum.

27. (3) **Solar System** The mass of the moon is 7.3477×10^{22} kg. If the mass of Earth is 5.9736×10^{24} kg, how many times larger is Earth than the moon?

***28.** (19) **Exterior Design** The diagram at the right shows the area in Lucy's backyard that she is preparing for planting.

a. Write an expression for the area of the garden.

b. Simplify the expression using multiplication.

c. Find the area of the garden if $x = 3$ feet.

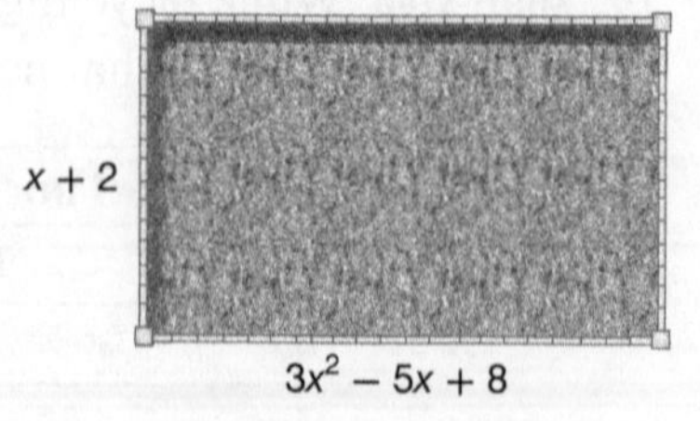

Calculate the slope of the lines that contain the following pairs of points. Tell whether the line rises, falls, is horizontal, or is vertical.

29. (13) $\left(-\frac{1}{2}, \frac{1}{2}\right)$ and $\left(-\frac{1}{2}, \frac{3}{4}\right)$

30. (13) $\left(-1, \frac{1}{2}\right)$ and $\left(3, \frac{1}{2}\right)$

© Saxon. All rights reserved.

Name ______________________________ Date ____________ Class ____________

Performing Operations with Functions

LESSON **20**

1. **Write** Explain how to simplify this problem: 12.65 in. + 30.1 in. + 15.843 in.
(18)

2. **Multi-Step** The solution to the system of equations $\begin{matrix} x + y = 5 \\ px + qy = -4 \end{matrix}$ is (3, 2).
(16)

   a. Use Cramer's rule to set up equations for x and y.

   b. Set $x = 3$ and $y = 2$. Simplify to write an equation with variables p and q.

   c. Graph the line from part **b.**

   d. Choose a point (p, q) along the line in part **c.** Substitute those values for p and q into the original system to write a system of equations with variables x and y.

   e. Graph your system from part **d** to check your answer. How can you tell if your answer is correct?

Solve the equations.

3. $3(5r - 10) = 8(2r - 4) + 5r$
(7)

4. $\frac{3}{4}\left(\frac{1}{2}x - 4\right) = (x - 7)$
(7)

*5. **Graphing Calculator** Solve the system using Cramer's Rule. Verify the solution by using a graphing calculator.
(16)

6. **Geometry** Write an expression for the area of the triangle and simplify.
(19)

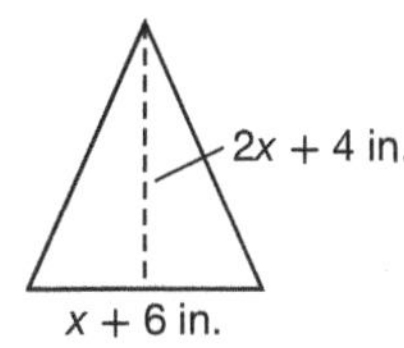

*7. **Transportation** The rate of one knot equals one nautical mile per hour. One nautical mile is 1852 meters. What is the speed in meters per second of a ship traveling at 20 knots?
(18)

*8. **Bird Flight** The peregrine falcon is perhaps the fastest animal on earth. In a stoop, or dive, the peregrine has been clocked at speeds of over 180 miles per hour. Convert this to feet per seconds.
(18)

9. A scientist has one solution that is 10% iodine and another that is 40% iodine. How much of each should the scientist use to produce 100 mL of a mixture that is 25% iodine?
(15)

Multiply the polynomials.

10. $(x + 7)(x - 9)$
(19)

11. $(x + 3)^2 (x - 2)$
(19)

12. **Write** Explain how to multiply $(2x + 8)(3x - 6)$ using the FOIL method.
(19)

13. **Justify** Is the equation $xyz = 0$ a joint variation? Why or why not?
(12)

© Saxon. All rights reserved.

***14.** **Graphing Calculator** The population of Tulsa, Oklahoma, in 2005 was 381,479 and increased by 1393 people by 2006. The population of Tampa, Florida, in 2005 was 325,800 and increased by 7088 people by 2006. If the population of these cities continued to grow at these rates, then the following equations would represent the population of the cities, where x is the number of years after 2005 and y is the population.
(16)

$$y = 1393x + 381{,}479 \quad \text{Tulsa's Population}$$
$$y = 7088x + 325{,}800 \quad \text{Tampa's Population}$$

a. In what year would the populations of Tulsa and Tampa be equal?

b. About how many people would be in each city when the populations are equal?

***15.** **Architecture** A concrete support for a highway bridge consists of (from the bottom up) a rectangular prism, a trapezoidal prism, and another rectangular prism, with the dimensions shown. Write a polynomial in standard form to represent the total volume. (Hint: The formula for the area of a trapezoid is $A = \frac{1}{2}(b_1 + b_2)h$.)
(11)

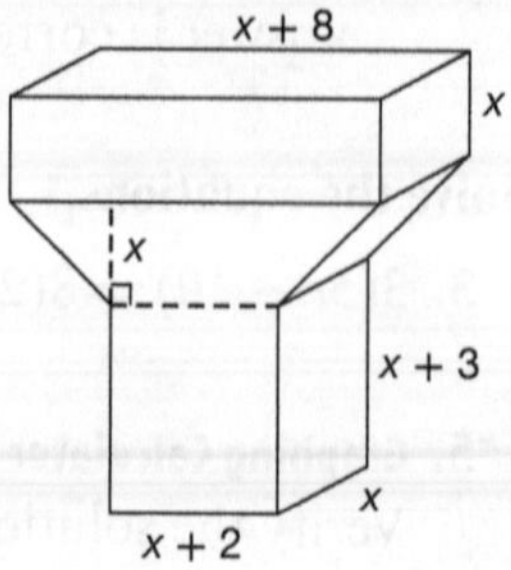

Find the percent of change in each situation. Round to the nearest tenth.

16. The population changes from 135,000 people to 150,000 people.
(6)

17. A price changes from \$2.49 for a cup of tea to \$2.59.
(6)

18. The energy usage changes from 25,500 trillion Btu to 22,500 trillion Btu.
(6)

Determine the kind of variation, if any, for each equation.

19. $y = \frac{1}{x}$, for $x \neq 0$
(12)

20. $z = \frac{1}{xy + a}$, for $x, y \neq 0$ and any value of a
(12)

21. Write the determinant as an equation, and then solve the equation.
(14)

$$\begin{bmatrix} -x & 2 & -2 \\ 0 & -3 & 1 \\ 2x & 8 & -3 \end{bmatrix} = -4x + 10$$

***22.** **Error Analysis** Two students were evaluating $(f - g)(3)$, given $f(x) = 5x - 2$ and $g(x) = 9x + 20$. Who is correct? Explain the error.
(20)

Student A	Student B
$(f - g)(3) = 5(3) - 2 - (9(3) + 20)$ $= 15 - 2 - 27 - 20$ $= -34$	$(f - g)(3) = 5(3) - 2 - (9(3) + 20)$ $= 15 - 2 - 27 + 20$ $= 6$

© Saxon. All rights reserved.

23. (11, 19) **Geometry** Write a polynomial in standard form that represents the shaded area formed by the two rectangles.

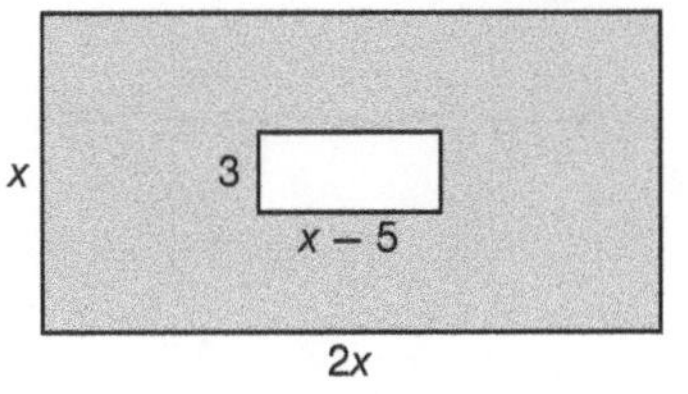

24. (20) **Spending and Saving** The amount of money Hannah has saved is given by the function $f(x) = 20x + 100$. Jess, Hannah's sister, has started spending her money and this is given by the function $g(x) = -10x + 400$. The number of weeks the girls are spending and saving is represented by x.

a. **Formulate** Find the function representing the amount of money that the girls have combined, $h(x)$.

b. Find the amount of money that the girls would have together in 3 weeks.

c. Who will have more money in 15 weeks?

***25.** (20) Given $f(x) = 6x + 13$ and $g(x) = 7x - 15$, find $(f + g)(x)$.

***26.** (20) Explain how to find $(f \cdot g)(x)$, given $f(x) = 5x - 9$ and $g(x) = 9x + 8$.

***27.** (20) **Multiple Choice** Given $f(x) = -2x + 11$ and $g(x) = 6x - 1$, find $(f + g)(8)$.

A 42 B 52 C 74 D 76

28. (17) Solve $|-3x - 4| \geq 2$, then graph the solution. Is $x = 4$ a solution to the inequality?

29. (17) **Multiple Representations** Write the absolute value function shown in the graph.

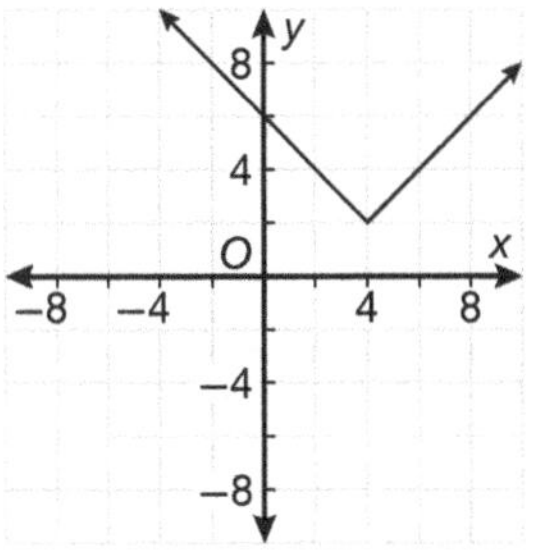

***30.** (17) **Chemical Elements** For neon to be a liquid, it must be within 1.2715° of −247.1755°C.

a. **Formulate** Write an absolute value inequality to determine the least and greatest temperatures at which neon will remain a liquid.

b. Solve the equation.

© Saxon. All rights reserved.

Name ______________________ Date __________ Class __________

Solving Systems of Equations Using the Substitution Method

LESSON 21

Use substitution to solve each system of linear equations.

***1.** (21) $\begin{aligned} 3x + y &= 10 \\ -2x - 5y &= -11 \end{aligned}$

***2.** (21) $\begin{aligned} -x + 3y &= 10 \\ 3x + 4y &= -4 \end{aligned}$

3. (17) Graph $|-2x - 1| \geq 3$.

***4.** (20) Find $(f + g)(3)$ if $f(x) = -2x + 4$ and $g(x) = -(x^2)$.

5. (9) Find the product. $\begin{bmatrix} 2 & -1 \\ 3 & 1 \\ 1 & 5 \end{bmatrix} \times \begin{bmatrix} 2 & 0 & -1 \\ 1 & 5 & 3 \end{bmatrix}$

***6.** (21) **Verify** Use the system of equations: $\begin{aligned} 2y - 4x &= 6 \\ y + 5x &= -10 \end{aligned}$.

a. Solve the system of equations by solving the first equation for y, then substituting.

b. Verify your answer by solving the second equation for y, then substituting. Show your work.

Solve each equation.

7. (17) $|x + 3| = 16$

8. (17) $|2x + 3| = 2 - x$

9. (17) $2|x + 6| = 8x$

***10.** (20) **Error Analysis** Two students evaluated $(f - g)(2)$, given $f(x) = 5x - 2$ and $g(x) = 8x + 10$. Who is correct? Explain the error.

Student A	Student B
$(f - g)(2) = 5(2) - 2 - (8(2) + 10)$ $= 10 - 2 - 16 - 10$ $= -18$	$(f - g)(2) = 5(2) - 2 - (8(2) + 10)$ $= 10 - 2 - 16 + 10$ $= 2$

***11.** (19) **Geometry** Write an expression for the area of the triangle.

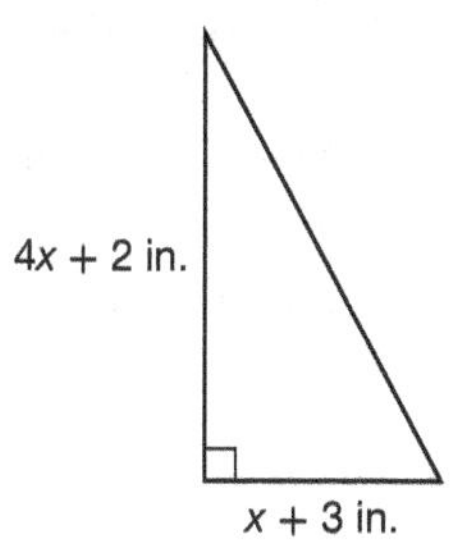

12. (14) Evaluate the determinant: $\begin{vmatrix} -2 & 6 \\ 1 & 5 \end{vmatrix}$

© Saxon. All rights reserved.

***13.** (16) **Multiple Choice** Phyllis collects silver dollars and half-dollars. She has 5 times as many half-dollars as silver dollar coins. She has 192 coins. Which solution gives the number of silver dollars Phyllis has?

A $\dfrac{\begin{vmatrix} 192 & 1 \\ 0 & -5 \end{vmatrix}}{6}$ **B** $\dfrac{\begin{vmatrix} 1 & 192 \\ -5 & 0 \end{vmatrix}}{-6}$ **C** $\dfrac{\begin{vmatrix} 1 & 192 \\ -1 & 0 \end{vmatrix}}{6}$ **D** $\dfrac{\begin{vmatrix} 192 & 1 \\ 0 & 1 \end{vmatrix}}{-6}$

14. (10) **Multiple Choice** Tickets to the community theatre cost $20. It is also possible to purchase a season pass for $170. Use an inequality to determine how many productions you can attend at the $20 price before spending more than it costs for the season pass.

A 7 **B** 8 **C** 9 **D** 10

15. (20) Given $f(x) = 4x - 1$ and $g(x) = 2x - 1$, find the sum $(f + g)(x)$.

16. (6) **Estimate** Estimate the new amount when 14.082 is increased by 9.68%. Explain your reasoning.

***17.** (21) **Formulate** Bill leaves his house for Makayla's house riding his bicycle at 8 miles per hour. At the same time, Makayla leaves her house heading toward Bill's house walking at 3 miles per hour. Write a system of equations that could be used to determine how long it takes for them to be the same distance d from Makayla's house in h hours. They live 8.25 miles apart.

18. (14) **Computer Graphics** A computer programmer wants a shape to move and expand on the screen. The programmer decides to multiply the coordinates of each vertex of the shape by the matrix $\begin{bmatrix} 4 & 6 \\ 2 & 3 \end{bmatrix}$. The area of the shape is multiplied by a factor that equals the determinant of this matrix. By what factor is the area multiplied? Explain.

19. (11) Write the polynomial $3x + 6x^5 - 3x^2 + 43 - 5x^3$ in standard form.

20. (11) **Measurement** This figure consists of a cylinder with a hemisphere on top. Write a polynomial in terms of x that represents the total volume of the figure. Formulas for volume are given below.

Cylinder: $V = \pi r^2 h$

Sphere: $V = \dfrac{4}{3}\pi r^3$

(Hint: The figure has only one circular base.)

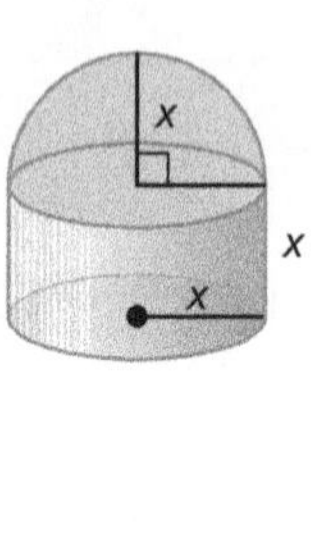

21. (12) **Justify** Is the equation $abc = 0$ a joint variation? Why or why not?

© Saxon. All rights reserved.

22. *(9)* **(Basketball)** The table shows the types of shots made in a game by the three top scoring L.A. Lakers and the point value of each type of shot. Use matrix multiplication to find out which player scored the most points in the game.

Shots Made

Player	3 Point	2 Point	1 Point
K. Bryant	1	5	6
M. Evans	2	5	5
L. Walton	1	7	1

23. *(13)* **(Pyramids)** The Great Pyramid of Giza has a height of 138 m and a horizontal distance from the side to the center of about 115 m. What is the slope of the pyramid to the nearest tenth?

24. *(19)* Simplify the product: $\frac{a^{-3}x}{y^{-3}}\left(\frac{xxx^{-2}}{y^{-2}yy} - 3\right)$

25. *(8)* **(Planets)** The weight of an object on Mercury varies directly with the weight of that object on Earth. An object that weighs 150 lb on Earth weighs 57 lb on Mercury. Find the weight of an object on Mercury that weighs 25 lb on Earth.

26. *(7)* Margaret wants to determine her average speed on her way to work. She knows she drives for about 10 minutes through her neighborhood, then $\frac{1}{2}$ hour on the highway, and finally 10 minutes to her office. Her odometer tells her the total distance from her home to her work is 40 miles. Write and solve an equation to find her average speed in miles per hour.

27. *(1)* Your dinner total at your favorite restaurant is $24. Use the distributive property to mentally calculate a 15% tip

***28.** *(9)* **Graphing Calculator** Find the product. Check using the graphing calculator.

$$\begin{bmatrix} 1 & 0 \\ 0 & 1 \\ 1 & 0 \end{bmatrix} \times \begin{bmatrix} -2 & 3 & -4 \\ 0 & -1 & 1 \end{bmatrix}$$

***29.** *(19)* **Multi-Step** The length of a regulation basketball court is represented by the expression $(x + 12)$ feet. The width of a regulation basketball court is represented by the expression $(x - 32)$ feet.

a. Write an expression that represents the area of a regulation NBA basketball court.

b. Evaluate the area of the court if $x = 82$.

30. *(10)* Solve and graph the inequality: $-2(x + 3) \leq 4$.

© Saxon. All rights reserved.

Name ________________________________ Date ____________ Class ____________

Analyzing Continuous, Discontinuous, and Discrete Functions

LESSON 22

1. (7) **Population** According to the 2000 census the three largest states by population in the U.S. are California, Texas, and New York. The total population of the three states is 73,699,925. The population of California is 13,019,828 more than the population of Texas and the population of New York is 1,875,363 less than the population of Texas. Find the population of Texas.

Graph and state the domain and range of each function. State whether the function is discrete or continuous.

***2.** (22) $\{(1, -2), (3, 0), (-6, 5), (6, 3)\}$

***3.** (22) $f(x) = 3x$

***4.** (20) Find $(f)(g)(-2)$ if $f(x) = 3x + 1$ and $g(x) = x + 6$.

5. (16) Use Cramer's Rule to solve the system of equations.
$$\begin{aligned} 3x + 7y &= -18 \\ -4x + 11y &= -37 \end{aligned}$$

6. (Inv 2) **Rocket** A physics class is about to test their first rocket out on the football field. The teacher fires the rocket at a 75° angle. At ignition, the rocket travels 38 feet per second horizontally and 110 feet per second vertically.
In t seconds, the rocket will travel x and y feet. The parametric equations that the rocket will travel are
$$x = 38t$$
$$y = -16t^2 + 110t$$

a. How many seconds does it take the rocket to hit the ground? Round your answer to the nearest thousandth of a second.

b. How far does the rocket travel?

c. Approximately how far has the rocket traveled when it has reached its highest point in flight? Round your answer to the nearest foot.

State the degree of each polynomial.

7. (11) $x^4 + 2x - x^7$

8. (11) $5x^2 + 2x^5 - 3$

***9.** (19) The Temple of Kukulcan, located in the ancient Mayan city of Chichen Itza, was built on a square base. If the expression $(4x + 12)$ represents one side of the base, write an expression that represents the area of the base.

10. (13) **Mountains** Mt. McKinley in Alaska is the highest mountain in North America with an elevation of 20,320 ft. From its center the mountain runs horizontally approximately 119,727 ft. Find the approximate slope of Mt. McKinley. Round your answer to the thousandths place.

Simplify the expressions. Use negative exponents when necessary.

11. (3) $\dfrac{(4x)^{-2}y^0(y^{-2})^2y}{32^{-1}x^2(yx^0)^{-3}}$

12. (3) $\dfrac{9x^{-4}(y^3x^2)^{-2}}{2^{-3}x^2y^3x(x^{-4}y^2)}$

© Saxon. All rights reserved.

*13. (22) James examines the graph below and states that the domain of the function is all real numbers. Identify the error in his decision.

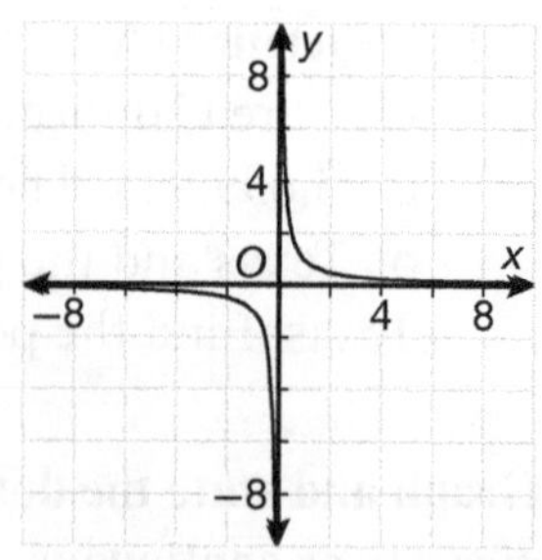

14. (17) **Error Analysis** Two students solve the inequality $32 + \frac{|x-7|}{13} < 7$ and their answers are below.

Which student is correct? Explain how you know.

Ben: No solution.

Ralph: $x = 332$ or $x = 318$.

Calculate the percent of change.

15. (6) from 5 to 8.2

16. (6) from 5 to 9.4

17. (Inv 2) **Rugby** Jonny Wilkinson, the fly half of the England rugby team, is at the 41 meter line on the rugby pitch. He runs up to kick the ball for a field goal. The ball moves at a horizontal speed of 11 meters per second and a vertical speed of 23 meters per second.

In t seconds, the rugby ball will travel x and y meters. The parametric equations that the ball will travel are

$$x = 11t$$
$$y = -4.9t^2 + 23t$$

a. How many seconds does it take for the ball to get to the field goal post? Round to the nearest hundredth of a second.

b. The field goal posts are 1.2 meters tall. Assume Jonny kicks the ball directly center of the field goal. Will the ball travel through the goal posts? Explain why or why not.

*18. (21) **Multi-Step** Kate and Riley are reading the same book. Kate reads $\frac{1}{3}$ page per minute, and Riley reads $\frac{3}{4}$ page per minute. Kate has already read 70 pages, while Riley has read 30 pages. If they both resume reading together, eventually Riley will catch up to Kate.

a. On what page will that occur?

b. How many minutes have they read when Riley catches up?

© Saxon. All rights reserved.

19. (8) **Engines** Two-stroke engines require a pre-mix of gas and oil. The amount of gas used varies directly with the amount of oil used. In most two-stroke engines 3 gal of gas requires 19.2 oz of oil.

a. Write the proportion that can be used to find how many ounces of oil to use with 5 gal of gas.

b. Solve the proportion in part **a.**

c. Check the answer from part **b.** with the proportion from part **a.**

20. (8) Convert 420 inches to feet.

21. (14) **Geometry** If one corner of a parallelepiped is at the origin, then all the vertices of the shape can be determined by knowing that the three other vertices with edges to the origin are at (1, 3, 4), (−3, 2, 1), and (4, −2, 3). The volume of the parallelepiped is the determinant of the matrix with these coordinates as rows. Find the volume of the parallelepiped.

22. (9) **Multiple Choice** The following matrix is the product of which two matrices? [19]

A $\begin{bmatrix} 6 & -1 \end{bmatrix}\begin{bmatrix} 3 \\ 1 \end{bmatrix}$ **B** $\begin{bmatrix} 3 \\ 1 \end{bmatrix}\begin{bmatrix} 6 & -1 \end{bmatrix}$ **C** $\begin{bmatrix} 1 & 0 & 3 \end{bmatrix}\begin{bmatrix} 4 \\ -2 \\ 5 \end{bmatrix}$ **D** $\begin{bmatrix} 4 \\ -2 \\ 5 \end{bmatrix}\begin{bmatrix} 1 & 0 & 3 \end{bmatrix}$

23. (12) **Justify** Is the equation $xy = 0$ an inverse variation? Why or why not?

Use substitution to solve the system of equations.

***24.** (21) $\begin{aligned} -x + y &= -2 \\ x + y &= 8 \end{aligned}$

***25.** (21) $\begin{aligned} 3x + y &= 4 \\ -3x + y &= 8 \end{aligned}$

26. (10) **Write** Write a compound inequality using *and* and a compound inequality using *or*. Explain the difference when you connect two inequalities with *and* and when you connect two inequalities with *or*.

27. (8) Find the constant of variation if x varies directly with y and $x = 28$ when $y = 7$.

***28.** (6) **Graphing Calculator** The US minimum wage increased from \$0.75 in 1950 to \$5.15 in 2000. Use your calculator to find the percent increase to the nearest percent.

29. (1) **Justify** Simplify: $3 \cdot 4 \cdot 7$. Justify your answer by identifying which property you used for each step.

30. (13) **Multi-Step** Use Point 1 (−8, −3) and Point 2 (1, −8).

a. Find the slope of the line that goes through Point 1 and Point 2.

b. Based on the slope, is the line rising or falling?

c. Sketch a graph of the line that goes through Point 1 and Point 2.

d. Based on the graph, is the line rising or falling?

© Saxon. All rights reserved.

Name ______________________ Date __________ Class __________

Factoring Polynomials

LESSON 23

Evaluate each expression.

1. (2) $-a(a - b)$ if $a = -\frac{1}{2}$ and $b = \frac{1}{3}$

2. (2) $-xy(-x^2 - y)$ if $x = -\frac{1}{2}$ and $y = \frac{1}{4}$

3. (4) Determine whether $f(x) = 3x + x^2$ is a function.

4. (18) Convert 120 inches per second to feet per minute.

5. (19) Find the product: $\frac{-3^{-2}x}{y}\left(\frac{9y^0x}{-x} - \frac{3x}{y}\right)$.

Solve each equation for x.

6. (7) $0.003x + 0.02x - 0.03 = 0.177$

7. (7) $2\frac{1}{3}x + 1\frac{3}{5} = 7\frac{2}{5}$

8. (7) $\frac{1}{2}x + 4 = 6\frac{1}{5}$

***9.** (22) Graph and state the domain and range of the discrete function: $\{(-2, -2), (4, 1), (-1, 6), (0, 2)\}$.

Factor each polynomial.

***10.** (23) $-3x^3 + 6x^2 + 3x$

***11.** (23) $-2x^2 + 5x + 3$

***12.** (23) $x^2 - 5x + 6$

***13.** (23) **Analyze** Is $x^2 - 25$ a Basic Quadratic Polynomial, a Perfect Square Trinomial, or a Difference of Two Squares? Explain how you can tell by looking at the polynomial.

14. (20) **Geometry** In the diagram of a rectangle, $f(x) = 2x + 5$ and $g(x) = 5x + 4$. Find the perimeter of the rectangle in terms of x.

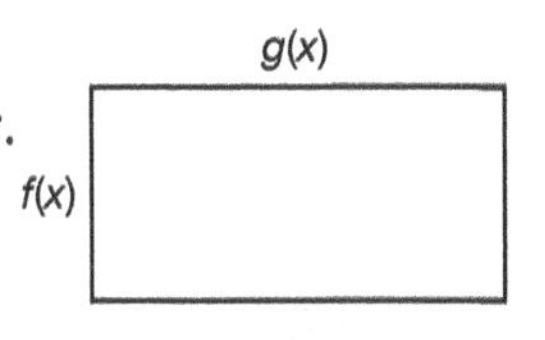

15. (7) **Verify** Is $x = -1$ the solution to the equation $5(4x - 1) = -7(9 + 4x) + 8 - 2x$?

16. (13) **Write** Give a written explanation on how to graph a linear equation using intercepts.

17. (17) **Multi-Step** At a sugar plantation processing plant, a machine fills a bag with 5 pounds of white sugar. For quality control, another machine weighs each bag in ounces and rejects bags that differ from 5 pounds by more than y ounces.

a. Write an absolute-value function to show the minimum and maximum weight of sugar that could be in each bag.

b. Graph the solution of the function.

18. (16) **Verify** **a.** Use Cramer's Rule to solve the system.
$$\begin{aligned} x + 2y &= 0 \\ x + 3y &= 6 \end{aligned}$$

b. Check your solution by graphing.

© Saxon. All rights reserved.

*19. **Graphing Calculator** Find the product. Check using the graphing calculator.
(9)

$$\begin{bmatrix} 1 & 0 \\ 0 & 1 \\ 1 & 0 \end{bmatrix} \times \begin{bmatrix} -1 & 4 & -8 \\ 0 & -3 & 1 \end{bmatrix}$$

20. **Multiple Choice** What is the degree of the polynomial $3x + 2x + 1$?
(11)
A 0 **B** 1 **C** 2 **D** 3

*21. For the system of equations below, find values of b and c so that the system is characterized as follows.
(21)

$$x - 3y = 12$$
$$3x + by = c$$

a. consistent and dependent

b. inconsistent

c. consistent and independent

22. **Error Analysis** Describe and correct the error.
(10)

$$4x - 3 > x - 2$$
$$4x > x - 5$$
$$x > -5$$

23. **Justify** Show and explain each step in finding the product AB.
(9)

$$A = \begin{bmatrix} 5 & 2 & 14 \\ 9 & 11 & 18 \\ 3 & 7 & 6 \end{bmatrix} \quad B = \begin{bmatrix} 15 & 6 \\ 7 & 13 \\ 10 & 16 \end{bmatrix}$$

24. **Planets** The weight of an object on the Sun varies directly with the weight of that object on Earth. An object that weighs 12 oz on Earth weighs 336 oz on the Sun. Find the weight of an object on the Sun that weighs 7 oz on Earth.
(8)

*25. **Data Analysis** Death Valley has the lowest elevation in North America. Below is a table of the temperature over the course of one day in the desert.
(22)

Time	1 a.m.	6 a.m.	10 a.m.	2 p.m.	4 p.m.	8 p.m.	11 p.m.
Temperature	83°	75°	90°	101°	105°	99°	90°

a. Graph the time and temperature data. Connect the points with line segments.

b. Explain why the temperature data creates a continuous relation.

c. Determine if the graph is a function. Explain.

© Saxon. All rights reserved.

26. (15) **Nutrition** Nutritionists recommend a daily diet consisting of at least 85 g of carbohydrate and at least 50 g of protein. A cup of fried rice contains 48.7 g of carbohydrate and 9.1 g of protein. A cup of sweet and sour prawn contains 28.6 g of carbohydrate and 16.5 g of protein. How many cups of each dish will give the minimum daily allowance of carbohydrate and protein? Let r represent the number of cups of fried rice and p the number of cups of prawn.

*27. (23) **Envelopes** The United States Postal Service will mail an envelope that is no greater than $2x + 1.5$ inches long and no greater than $x + 1$ inches high. The total area of an envelope with the maximum dimensions is approximately 69 in^2. Calculate the approximate maximum dimensions of an envelope that can be mailed through the USPS.

28. (13) **Population** The table below lists the population estimates in millions for Hawaii from 2000 to 2002.

Year	2000	2001	2002
Population	1.21	1.22	1.23

a. Write the data above as ordered pairs where x is the number of years after 2000 and y is the population in millions.

b. Use slope and y-intercept to find the equation of the line representing this data.

Factor each expression.

*29. (23) $4x^2 - 25$

*30. (23) $x^2 + 3x - 18$

© Saxon. All rights reserved.

Name ______________________ Date __________ Class __________

Solving Systems of Equations Using the Elimination Method

LESSON 24

Solve for *x*.

1. (14) $\begin{vmatrix} -2 & 1 \\ 1 & x \end{vmatrix} = 16$

2. (14) $\begin{vmatrix} -3 + x & x \\ 1 & 6 \end{vmatrix} = 5$

3. (14) $\begin{vmatrix} 4 & -5 \\ 2 & x \end{vmatrix} = 8$

4. (18) Convert 120 inches per second to feet per minute.

5. (13) Calculate the slope of the line that passes through the points (2, 1) and (0, 5).

Find each product.

6. (9) $\begin{bmatrix} -5 & 2 \\ 0 & 1 \end{bmatrix} \times \begin{bmatrix} 3 & 4 \\ 1 & 8 \end{bmatrix}$

7. (9) $\begin{bmatrix} -1 & 5 \end{bmatrix} \times \begin{bmatrix} 6 \\ 8 \end{bmatrix}$

8. (9) $\begin{bmatrix} -3 & 4 \end{bmatrix} \times \begin{bmatrix} 1 \\ 7 \end{bmatrix}$

***9.** (23) Factor the polynomial: $x^4 - 16$.

Solve each system of equations using elimination.

***10.** (24) $\begin{aligned} 2x - 5y &= 5 \\ -5x + y &= -1 \end{aligned}$

***11.** (24) $\begin{aligned} -4x + 7y &= -47 \\ 3x - 5y &= 34 \end{aligned}$

***12.** (24) $\begin{aligned} 5x + y &= 14 \\ -3x - 4y &= -5 \end{aligned}$

***13.** (24) $\begin{aligned} 2x - 5y &= -3 \\ -10x + 25y &= 15 \end{aligned}$

***14.** (23) **Geometry** Find the possible value(s) of x if Volume = 104.

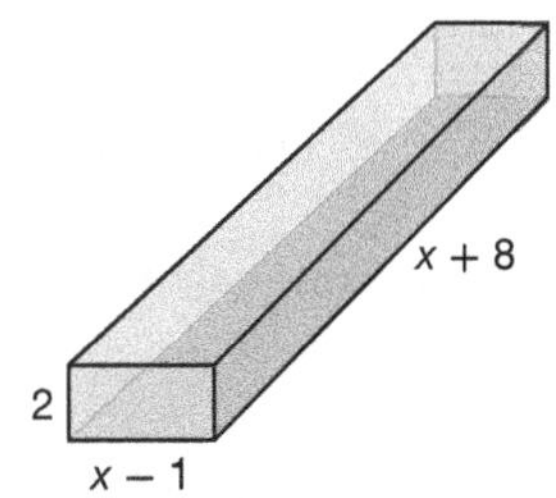

15. (21) Solve $\begin{aligned} 2x + y &= -4 \\ x + y &= 7 \end{aligned}$ by substitution.

16. (19) **Model** Model FOIL for the multiplication of any two binomials in the form $(a + b)(c + d)$.

17. (9) **Multi-Step** Use $A = \begin{bmatrix} 5 & 3 \\ 6 & 5 \end{bmatrix}$ $B = \begin{bmatrix} 7 & 4 \\ 8 & 7 \end{bmatrix}$.

a. Find AB.

b. Find BA.

c. Is $AB = BA$?

***18.** (24) **Sightseeing** The cost of tickets to the observatory on the 86th floor of the Empire State Building in 2007 were such that 5 adult tickets and 4 senior citizen tickets cost \$154 and 3 adult tickets and 8 senior citizen tickets cost \$182. Find the cost of each type of ticket.

© Saxon. All rights reserved.

19. Justify (11) If polynomial P_1 has a greater degree than polynomial P_2, does P_1 have a greater value than P_2? Explain your answer and justify it by giving examples.

20. (20) If $f(x) = 3x - 9$ and $g(x) = x - 3$, find $(fg)(x)$.

21. Coordinate Geometry (14) A quadrilateral with vertices (x_1, y_1), (x_2, y_2), (x_3, y_3),

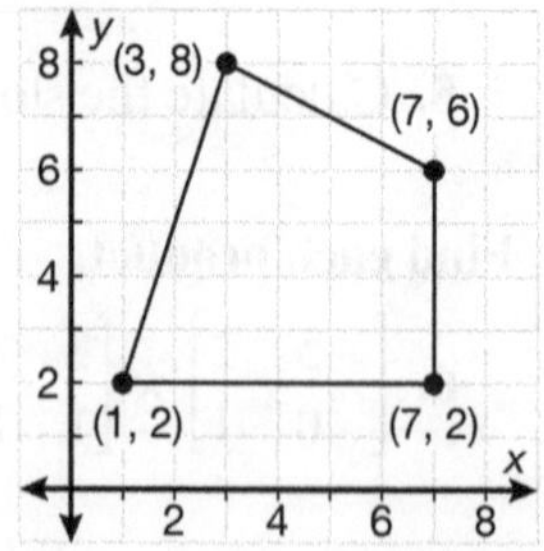

and (x_4, y_4) has an area equal to the absolute value of $\frac{1}{4}$

$$\begin{vmatrix} x_1 & x_2 & x_3 & x_4 \\ y_1 & y_2 & y_3 & y_4 \\ 1 & 1 & 1 & 1 \\ -1 & 1 & -1 & 1 \end{vmatrix}.$$

Find the area of the quadrilateral.

***22. Graphing Calculator** (13) The table shows the total number of birdhouses Sal made, y, after x amount of days.

Number of Days	2	3	7
Birdhouses	$5\frac{1}{3}$	8	$18\frac{2}{3}$

a. Plot the data on your graphing calculator.

b. Find the line that best fits the data using linear regression and graph the line on your graphing calculator.

c. Use the line to predict the number of birdhouses Sal can make in 10 days.

***23. Error Analysis** (24) Find and correct the error a student made below.

$$\begin{matrix} 4x + y = 9 \\ 4x - 3y = 5 \end{matrix} \rightarrow \begin{matrix} 4x + y = 9 \\ -4x + 3y = 5 \end{matrix}$$

$$\begin{array}{r} 4x + y = 9 \\ + -4x + 3y = 5 \\ \hline 4y = 14 \\ y = 3.5 \end{array} \longrightarrow \begin{array}{r} 4x + y = 9 \\ 4x + 3.5 = 9 \\ 4x = 5.5 \\ x = 1.375 \end{array} \quad \text{The solution is } (1.375, 3.5).$$

24. Multi-Step (10) At the local bowling alley there is a tournament underway. One of the bowlers has played two games and has a total score of 530. To win the tournament, a total score of 750 for three games is needed. Use the information given to write an inequality describing the possible number of points the bowler can score and win the tournament. What is the minimum score possible in order to win the tournament?

25. Estimate (18) A cheetah runs at a speed of 70 miles per hour. Estimate a cheetah's speed in feet per second.

© Saxon. All rights reserved.

26. (17) (**Grizzly Bears**) The table below shows amounts of three foods that a 200-lb grizzly bear can eat in a day. Which term, *disjunction* or *conjunction*, would represent the amount of these foods required for a 200-lb grizzly bear? Explain.

Type	Deer	Salmon	Vegetation
Amount (lb)	24	30	67

27. (8) **Multiple Choice** The amount of water added to a dry concrete mix varies directly with the amount of dry concrete. If 80 lb of dry concrete requires 6 pt of water, how much water is needed for 200 lb of dry concrete? Circle the letter that best represents the amount of water needed.

A 15 pt **B** 10 pt **C** 8 pt **D** 6.5 pt

State whether the function is discrete or continuous.

***28.** (22) (1, 5), (0, 9), (2, 7), (−5, 4)

***29.** (22) (2, 5), (4, 8), (6, 9), (−9, −6)

30. (22) (**Sports**) A baseball when hit travels in a parabolic path. If time is represented by the x-values and the height of the ball is represented by the y-values, the graph at right can be drawn. Does this example represent a continuous, discontinuous, and/or discrete function? Justify your answer.

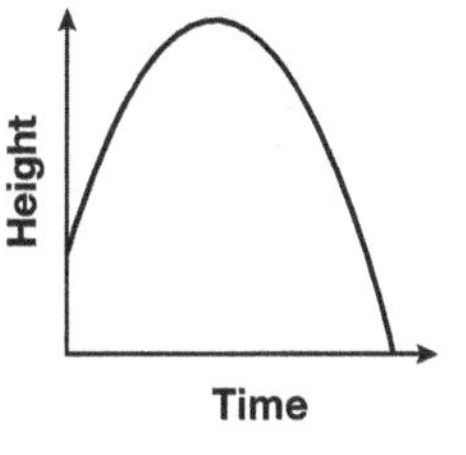

© Saxon. All rights reserved.

Name ______________________ Date __________ Class __________

Finding Measures of Central Tendency and Dispersion

LESSON 25

Simplify each expression using the properties of real numbers.

1. (1) $-5[(2 - 1 - 3) - (5 - 8) - 6]$

2. (1) $2(2 - 6) - (-1 - 1) - 3$

3. (3) Simplify: $-3x^6(x^{-1}y^{-8})^{-3}$

4. (10) Solve for x and graph the solution. $3x + 1 > x + 13$

5. (9) Find the product $\begin{bmatrix} -2 & 10 \\ 3 & 2 \end{bmatrix} \times \begin{bmatrix} -1 & 0 \\ 0 & 1 \end{bmatrix}$.

6. (19) Simplify the product: $3x^2(2x^2 - 3x)$.

***7.** (23) Factor the polynomial: $2x^2 + 9x - 5$.

Solve each system of linear equations using substitution.

8. (21) $\begin{array}{l} 4x + y = -11 \\ -x + y = 9 \end{array}$

9. (21) $\begin{array}{l} x + y = 4 \\ x - y = 6 \end{array}$

Find the mean and median for each data set.

***10.** (25) {2, 2, 3, 10, 11, 13, 15}

***11.** (25) {1, 2, 3, 3}

***12.** (25) {1, 1, 13, 15, 14}

***13.** (23) **Geometry** The area of a new window is $x^2 - 24x + 144$ in^2. What are the dimensions of the new window?

14. (20) **Multiple Choice** Given $f(x) = -3x + 11$ and $g(x) = 4x - 10$, find $(f + g)(12)$.

A −9 **B** 13 **C** 85 **D** 105

Solve each system using elimination.

***15.** (24) $\begin{cases} 5x + y = 19 \\ -2x - y = -7 \end{cases}$

***16.** (24) $\begin{cases} -x + 3y = 12 \\ 6x - y = -21 \end{cases}$

***17.** (24) $\begin{cases} 2x + y = 8 \\ x - y = 10 \end{cases}$

18. (11) **Write** Describe how the graph of polynomial function $P_1 + P_2$ compares to the graph of polynomial function P_1 if P_2 does not equal 0, but has degree 0. Explain.

19. (18) **Drumming** Mike "Da Man" Mangini holds the title as the world's fastest drummer. At the 2005 Summer NAMM Session, Mike drummed out 1,247 singles in 60 seconds.

a. How many singles could Mike drum in one hour?

b. Not only does Mike have fast hands, he has fast feet, pounding down a toe-stomping 13,222 singles with his feet in 15 minutes. How many singles could Mike drum with his feet in one hour?

c. How much faster does Mike drum with his hands than with his feet?

© Saxon. All rights reserved.

20. (23) **Quilting** Kylie is making a rectangular quilt out of 4 inch squares. So far, her quilt is 36 inches by 56 inches. She wants to add a border around her quilt that is the same number of squares on each side. A standard twin comforter covers approximately 4800 square inches.

a. How many squares should she add to each side if she wants her quilt to cover the same area?

b. Verify that her quilt will cover the same area.

21. (9) **Data Analysis** Alea, Cory, and Troy had lunch together. Alea bought 1 drink, 2 sandwiches, and 2 snacks. Cory bought 2 drinks, 2 sandwiches, and 1 snack. Troy bought 2 drinks, 1 sandwich, and 3 snacks. The cost of a drink is $1.50, a sandwich is $4.00, and a snack is $1.00.

a. Organize the information into the tables below.

Lunch

Person	Drink	Sandwich	Snack

Cost	

b. Create two matrices to represent the tables in part a.

c. Who spent the most money?

***22.** (14) **Graphing Calculator** **a.** Write the determinant as an equation.

$$\begin{vmatrix} -x & 2 & -2 \\ 0 & -3 & 1 \\ 8 & 2x & 0 \end{vmatrix} = 0$$

b. Solve for x.

c. Check your answer by substituting for x and finding the determinant with a graphing calculator.

23. (7) **Multi-Step** A cell phone plan costs $29.95 a month and $0.40 per minute used over 250 minutes. There is a one time only activation fee of $25.00. The first month's bill is $114.95.

a. Write an equation to solve for the minutes over 250 used.

b. Solve the equation from part a.

c. Show the work to check the answer to part b.

d. How many total minutes were used?

© Saxon. All rights reserved.

***24.** (24) **Formulate** Create a linear system that requires that both equations be multiplied by a constant before they are added together. Tell which constants should be used and why.

25. (19) **Write** The length of one side of a square patio is represented by the expression $(2x - 5)$. Write an expression that represents the area of the patio.

26. (17) **(Exercise)** For a 30-year-old to work out within her cardio range, her heart rate should be within 24 beats per minute of 147 bpm.

a. Write an absolute-value equation to determine the lowest and highest heart rate at which she will be in her cardio range.

b. Solve the equation.

27. (13) **Error Analysis** Ani is asked find the slope of the line through the points (11, 6) and (7, 4), and then to tell whether the line rises or falls. Her solution is shown below. Identify whether there is an error in her solution. If so, give the correct solution.

Ani's solution:

$\frac{4-6}{7-11} = \frac{-2}{-4} = \frac{1}{2}$, so $m = \frac{1}{2}$. Because the slope is a fraction, the line falls.

28. (22) Determine if each graph is continuous, discontinuous, and/or discrete. Determine if each graph is a function or a relation. Determine the domain and range of each.

a.

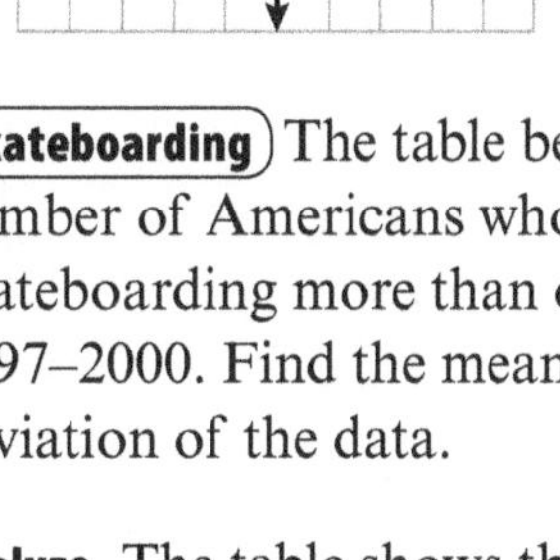

b.

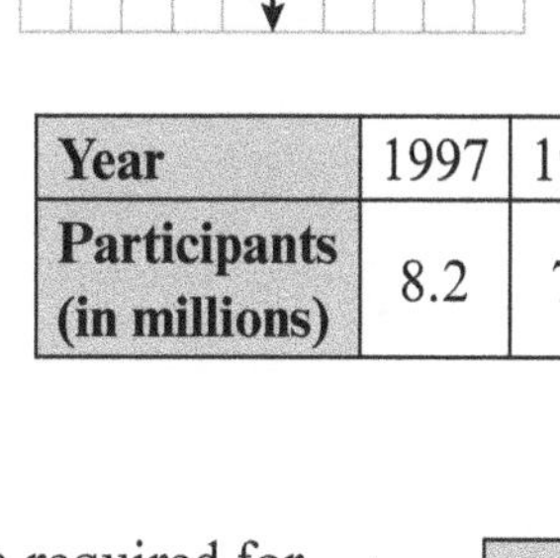

***29.** (25) **(Skateboarding)** The table below shows the number of Americans who participated in skateboarding more than once during 1997–2000. Find the mean and standard deviation of the data.

Year	1997	1998	1999	2000
Participants (in millions)	8.2	7.2	7.8	11.6

30. (8) **Analyze** The table shows the amount of pasta required for each number of servings. Is this a direct variation relationship? If so, what is the constant of variation? If not, explain why.

Servings	Pasta
4	8 oz
13	26 oz
17	34 oz
29	58 oz

© Saxon. All rights reserved.

Name ______________________ Date ____________ Class ____________

Writing the Equation of a Line

LESSON 26

Classify each polynomial by degree and number of terms.

1. $3x^4$ (11)

2. $-x^3 + 5x$ (11)

3. $2x^2 - 5x + 1$ (11)

4. Find the sum: $\begin{bmatrix} 0 & 1 \\ 1 & 0 \end{bmatrix} + 6\begin{bmatrix} 2 & -2 \\ -3 & 1 \end{bmatrix}$ (5)

5. Convert 450 feet to yards. (18)

Factor each polynomial.

***6.** $-15x^2 + 5x$ (23)

***7.** $4x^2 - 9$ (23)

***8.** $6x^2 + 19x - 7$ (23)

***9.** Find the mode of the data set: {100, 120, 128, 128, 129, 130, 130}. (25)

Find the equation of the line that passes through the two points given.

***10.** (0, 3) and (4, −4) (26)

***11.** (1, 5) and (4, 2) (26)

***12.** (−3, 2), (5, 0) (26)

13. **Analyze** Identify which property of real numbers is being demonstrated. Explain why this property might be helpful in solving this problem without a calculator. (1)

$$(4 \cdot 6) \cdot 5 = 4 \cdot (6 \cdot 5) = 4 \cdot 30 = 120$$

14. **Multi-Step** **a.** Graph $y = x^2 + 2$. (22)

b. Is this relation a function?

c. Determine if the graph is continuous, discontinuous, and/or discrete.

15. **Multiple Choice** Choose the letter that best represents the solution to the equation: $\frac{2}{5}c + 3 = -5c + \frac{3}{4}$. (7)

A $-2\frac{2}{5}$ **B** $\frac{12}{13}$ **C** $\frac{1}{11}$ **D** $-\frac{5}{12}$

16. **Geometry** Write a compound inequality using the fact that the sum of the lengths of any two sides of a triangle is greater than the length of the third side (Triangle Inequality) using the diagram. (*Hint*: Remember that length cannot be negative.) (10)

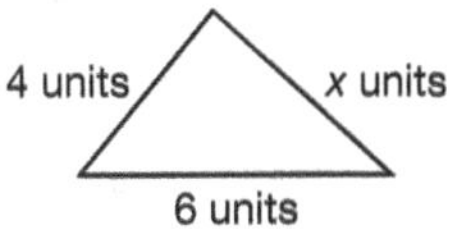

***17.** **Multi-Step** A homeowner painted her bathroom. She has a mirror that is 30 inches high and 20 inches wide. She decides to decrease both mirror dimensions by the same amount, and she will now have to paint the newly exposed wall. She only has enough paint to cover 225 square inches. (23)

a. Calculate the new area of the mirror.

b. Write and solve an equation to find out how much she should decrease each dimension.

© Saxon. All rights reserved.

18. (Inv 2) **Soccer** Mia Hamm is running with the ball and is about to make a chip shot aiming to kick the ball above the goalie's head. Mia is 31 feet from the goal and kicks the ball at a horizontal speed of 14 feet per second and a vertical speed of 37 feet per second.

In t seconds, the soccer ball will travel x and y feet. The parametric equations that the ball will travel are

$$x = 14t$$
$$y = -16t^2 + 37t$$

a. How many seconds does it take the ball to travel to the goal? Round your answer to the nearest hundredth of a second.

b. The goalie is 5.5 feet tall and the goal is 8 feet tall. If the ball lands below the goalie's head, it is assumed that the goal has been blocked. Will Mia make the goal? Explain why or why not.

19. (20) **Multi-Step** Given $f(x) = -4x + 3$ and $g(x) = -x + 2$.

a. Graph $f(x)$ and $g(x)$ on the same grid.

b. Graph the difference $(f - g)(x)$.

c. Use algebra to verify the difference $(f - g)(x)$.

20. (13) **Error Analysis** The work below uses the slope-intercept form of a linear equation to graph the equation $3x - 2y = 9$. Inspect the work. Is it correct? If not, explain the error and find the correct solution. If it is correct, explain in words each step of the work.

$$3x - 2y = 9$$
$$2y = -3x + 9$$
$$y = -\frac{3}{2}x + 4\frac{1}{2}$$

slope $= -\frac{3}{2}$; y-intercept $= \left(0, 4\frac{1}{2}\right)$

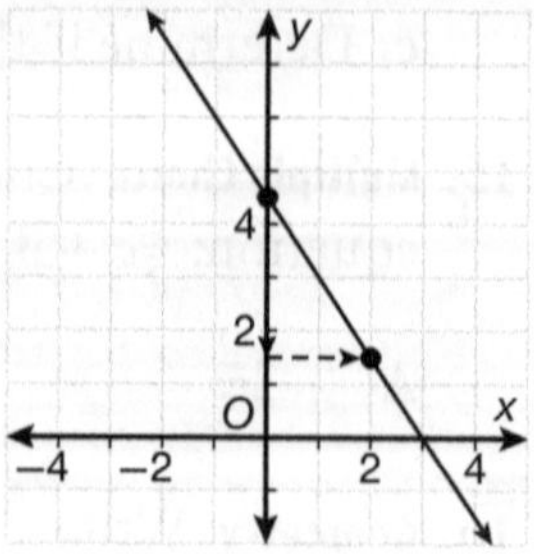

21. (17) **Fitness** An adult is considered to be in a healthy weight range if his or her BMI is within 3.2 of 21.7.

a. Write an absolute value inequality to determine the minimum and maximum BMI range that is considered healthy.

b. Solve the inequality.

22. (18) **Running** The record for the fastest mile ever run by a human belongs to Hicham El Guerrouj of Morocco. He ran one mile in 3.719 minutes. Determine El Guerrouj's speed in miles per hour.

23. (21) **Coffee** A coffee blend contains Sumatra beans, which cost \$12/lb, and Kona Hawaiian beans, which cost \$45/lb. If the blend costs \$30/lb, how much of each type of coffee is in 50 lb of the blend?

© Saxon. All rights reserved.

*24. **Write** Explain how using the elimination methods to solve systems with infinitely many solutions is similar to and different from using the elimination method to solve systems with no solutions.
(24)

25. **Verify** Find the determinant using expansion by minors. Verify the solution using a graphing calculator.
(14)

$$\begin{vmatrix} -1 & 2 & -2 \\ 2 & 4 & 1 \\ -1 & 1 & -3 \end{vmatrix}$$

*26. **Justify** Is the equation $2\pi x + 3y = 20$ in standard form? Explain your reasoning.
(26)

27. **Data Analysis** Amara, Kate, and Ava are all taking a test where each type of question is given a certain point value. Use matrix multiplication to find out who scored the greatest number of points on the test.
(9)

Questions Answered Correctly

	Type 1	Type 2	Type 3
Amara	2	3	7
Kate	5	5	4
Ava	9	6	3

Point Value

Type 1	4
Type 2	6
Type 3	8

28. **Medicine** A 7% saline (salt) solution can help people with cystic fibrosis, but it must be mixed by hand from commercially available solutions of 0.9% and 10% solutions. How much of each commercial solution is needed to make 6 mL of the 7% solution?
(16)

a. Set up equations relating the number of mL of each solution to the saline concentrations. Let a represent the number of mL of the 0.9% solution and b the number of mL of the other solution.

b. Use Cramer's Rule to solve the system of equations.

*29. **Graphing Calculator** When you step on the brakes to stop a car, the car still continues forward. The distance traveled is called the "stopping distance." The faster a car is moving, the longer the stopping distance. The table shows the stopping distance at three different speeds for a passenger car traveling on dry pavement. Use the linear regression capabilities of your graphing calculator to write an equation in slope-intercept form for the stopping distance.
(26)

Initial Traveling Speed (mile/hour)	Stopping Distance (feet)
35	46.430
49	91.097
62	142.364

30. **Write** Explain how to multiply $(x + 2)(2x - 1)$ using the FOIL method.
(19)

© Saxon. All rights reserved.

Name ______________________ Date __________ Class __________

Connecting the Parabola with the Quadratic Function

LESSON 27

Convert each function to standard form.

*1. (27) $f(x) = (2x + 3)^2$

*2. (27) $f(x) = 2(x + 5) + x^2$

*3. (27) $f(x) = (x - 5)^2$

Graph each function.

*4. (27) $f(x) = (-x + 1)^2$

*5. (27) $f(x) = x^2 - 3$

Factor each polynomial.

6. (23) $2x^2 - 4x - 30$

7. (23) $-4x^3 + 20x^2 + 12x$

8. (18) Convert 3 liters per minute to milliliters per second.

9. (13) Identify the y-intercept given the linear equation $y - 4 = 2(x - 2)$.

Find the constant of variation for the given values of x and y given that x varies inversely with y.

10. (12) $x = 3, y = 12$

11. (12) $x = 10, y = 5$

12. (12) $x = 4, y = 9$

*13. (24) **Multi-Step** Shirley has 47 coins in a jar. The jar contains only dimes and nickels and the value of the coins is $3.20.

a. Using d for dimes and n for nickels, write an equation representing the number of coins.

b. Write an equation to show that the value of the dimes plus the value of the nickels is $3.20 in all.

c. Write and solve a linear system to find the number of dimes and number of nickels in Shirley's jar.

14. (7) Solve the equation for r: $3(5r - 10) = 8(2r - 4) + 5r$.

A $r = \frac{1}{4}$ **B** $r = \frac{1}{3}$ **C** $r = 2$ **D** $r = 3$

*15. (27) **Justify** Tell why the range of a quadratic function will never be the set of all real numbers.

16. (21) **Write** Without solving the system, can you tell how many solutions this system of equations has? Explain.

$$y + 1 = 3x$$
$$2y - 6x = -2$$

17. (12) **Geometry** Identify the kind of variation each equation represents.

a. Volume of a rectangular prism = length × width × height

b. Volume of a cube = $(\text{length})^3$

© Saxon. All rights reserved.

Connecting the Parabola with the Quadratic Function

LESSON 27

18. *(13)* **Multiple Choice** Choose the letter that best represents the graph of $y = -4x + 2$.

A

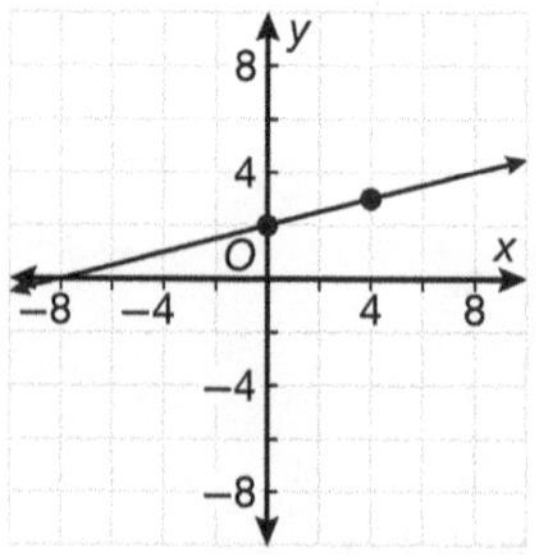

B

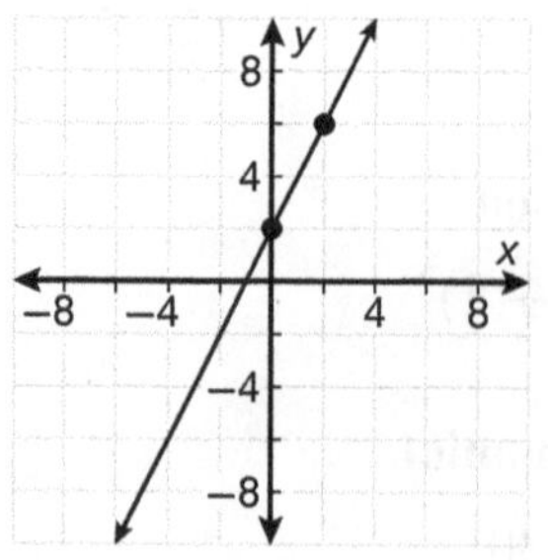

C

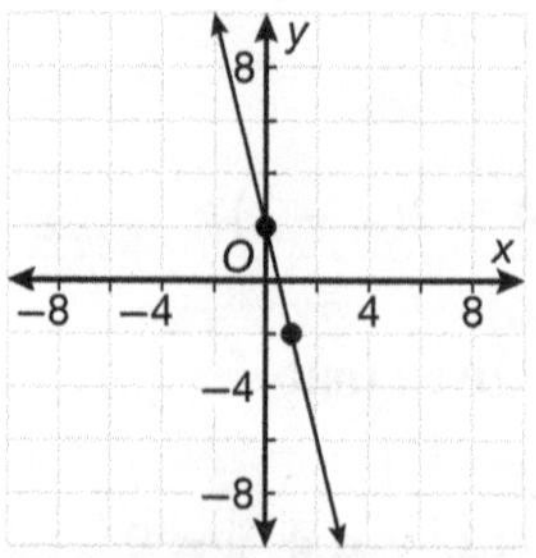

D

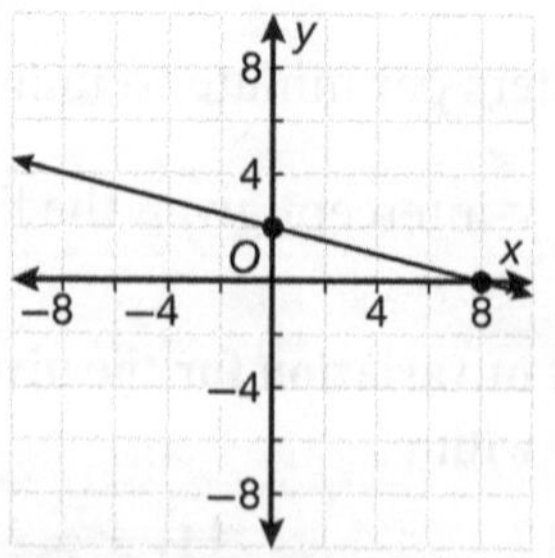

***19.** *(23)* **Multi-Step** A rectangular wooden deck is 40 feet long and 30 feet wide. The owner wants to increase the width and length to double the area of the deck. He also wants the increase in length to be twice as much as the increase in width.

a. Calculate the new area of the deck.

b. Write and solve an equation to find out how much the owner should increase each dimension.

***20.** *(21)* **Error Analysis** Two students were asked which of these lines coincide. Their answers are below. Which student is correct? What is the relationship between the lines of the incorrect answer?

Equation 1: $y + 3x = 7$ Equation 2: $y = -3x + 5$ Equation 3: $10 - 2y = 6x$

Becky: Equations 1 and 3 coincide.

Randy: Equations 2 and 3 coincide.

21. *(14)* **Justify** Justify the claim that the determinant of the product of matrices $\begin{bmatrix} 3.1 & -2.2 \\ 0.6 & 4.5 \end{bmatrix}$ and $\begin{bmatrix} -1.9 & 4.8 \\ -2.2 & 3.0 \end{bmatrix}$ equals the product of the determinants of these matrices.

22. *(18)* **Fuel Economy** A dragster can consume 6 gallons of gasoline in $\frac{1}{4}$ mile. What is the fuel economy in miles per gallon? How far would a car with a 20-gallon tank get before needing a refill?

© Saxon. All rights reserved.

Connecting the Parabola with the Quadratic Function

23. (7) **Imports** The total imports of goods and services, in millions of dollars, for the U.S. in 2004, 2005, and 2006 was 5,971,007. The imports in 2005 were 228,100 more than in 2004 and 206,784 less than in 2006. What were the imports in millions of dollars in 2005?

24. (19) While buying a bird feeder, Karl discovers one in the shape of a rectangular prism. Karl is trying to determine the volume of bird food that the feeder will hold. He knows that the dimensions are as follows:

Length: x inches   Width: $(x - 3.75)$ inches   Height: $(x - 0.25)$ inches

Write an expression for the volume of the bird feeder that Karl can use in his calculations.

25. (11) **Error Analysis** A student says that the polynomial $ab^4 + a^2b^2 - 3$ is of higher degree than the polynomial $a^2b^3 + ab + 2$. Is this correct? Explain.

26. (20) **Statistics** The proceeds for three major fundraisers are represented by $f(x) = 35x - 100$, $g(x) = 52x - 60$, and $h(x) = 100x - 250$. Write a function $m(x)$ that would represent the mean of the proceeds in terms of x.

***27.** (25) The table shows the average salaries of various engineering jobs in 2006. Find the range and median of this data.

Job	Aerospace	Agricultural	Civil	Computer	Environmental	Mechanical	Petroleum
Average Salary	\$50,993	\$46,172	\$43,679	\$52,464	\$47,384	\$50,236	\$61,156

28. (17) **Verify** Show that $|1 - 3x| = 5x$ has two solutions, one of which is extraneous.

***29.** (26) **Medicine** The Centers for Disease Control has developed growth charts that pediatricians use to see if a child's height is within a certain average. The chart shows data for a girl's height in the 50th percentile. The three points are on a line. Use the data to write the equation of the line in slope-intercept form.

Age (years)	Height (inches)
3	37
4	40
5	43

***30.** (9) **Graphing Calculator** $A = \begin{bmatrix} -5 & 3 \\ 1 & 2 \end{bmatrix}$ $B = \begin{bmatrix} -6 & 0 \\ 0 & -6 \end{bmatrix}$ Use a graphing calculator to find AB and BA. Is $AB = BA$?

© Saxon. All rights reserved.

Name ________________________________ Date __________ Class ____________

Simplifying Rational Expressions

LESSON 28

*1. Convert $f(x) = (-x + 1)^2$ to standard form.
(27)

Identify any excluded values, then simplify each expression.

*2. $\dfrac{-2q^3}{16q}$
(28)

*3. $\dfrac{s + 1}{15(s + 1)^2}$
(28)

*4. $\dfrac{x^2}{x}$
(28)

*5. $\dfrac{4x^5}{12x}$
(28)

Use Cramer's Rule to solve the following systems of equations.

6. $x + y = 5$
(16) $x - y = 5$

7. $-5x + y = 7$
(16) $x - 3y = 7$

Simplify each of the following expressions.

8. $x^3y^{-3}x^{-5}y^8y^7$
(3)

9. $\dfrac{xx^{-2}y^5x^{-1}y^{-1}}{x^8y^{-3}y^2x^{-4}}$
(3)

10. $\dfrac{2x^6y^{-4}}{24xy^{-1}}$
(3)

Change each of the following to percents.

11. $\dfrac{3}{5}$
(6)

12. 0.8
(6)

13. 0.025
(6)

14. **Carnival** The entry cost at the local fair is \$9.00. Each ride costs \$1.50. If Matthew
(10) has \$45, how many rides could he go on? Write an inequality to help you answer the problem.

15. **Write** Write a situation explaining the problem: $\dfrac{20 \text{ hr}}{1} \times \dfrac{60 \text{ min}}{1 \text{ hr}} \times \dfrac{60 \text{ s}}{1 \text{ min}} = 72{,}000 \text{ s}$
(18)

*16. **Analyze** Compare and contrast the Quotient of Powers Property to the Product of
(28) Powers Property.

17. **Multiple Choice** Solve $-3|4x| - 2 \geq 22$.
(17)

A $-2 \leq x \leq 2$

B $x \leq -2$ or $x \geq 2$

C All real numbers

D No solution

*18. **Aviation** The Federal Aviation Administration tracks airline delays for airports
(26) around the country. During the first half of 2007, the flights delayed at Dallas-Fort Worth Airport averaged 4,500 per month. Use this information to write an equation in slope-intercept form that could be used to predict the total number of delays throughout the year. Let x equal the month of the year and y equal the cumulative delays.

© Saxon. All rights reserved.

*19. (25) **Data Analysis** A chemist weighs samples obtained from a production run. The weights of the samples are 13 g, 14 g, 65 g, 11 g, 15 g, 14 g, 14 g, 12 g, 13 g, 15 g, 14 g, and 12 g.

a. Find the mean of the data.

b. Find the standard deviation.

c. Identify any outliers.

d. Describe how any outlier affects the mean and the standard deviation of this data set.

20. (11) **Packaging Technology** An engineer has a box in the shape of a cube. He wants to know how the volume is affected if he adds 2 units to each base edge and subtracts 3 units from the height. Does the volume increase, decrease, or remain the same? Explain your answer.

21. (13) **Multi-Step** Use $-7x + 14y = -84$.

a. Find the x-intercept.

b. Find the y-intercept.

22. (24) **Geometry** Two angles are complementary and the difference between the larger angle and twice the smaller angle is 30°. Write a system to represent the scenario and solve the system to find the measures of the angles.

23. (16) **Error Analysis** Two students solved the system of equations $\begin{matrix} 7 - 5y - 4x = 0 \\ 16 - 2y - 5x = 0 \end{matrix}$.

Find the error or errors in these students' work and solve the system correctly.

Student A $\begin{matrix} 4x + 5y = 7 \\ 5x + 2y = 16 \end{matrix}$ $x = \dfrac{\begin{vmatrix} 7 & 5 \\ 16 & 2 \end{vmatrix}}{\begin{vmatrix} 4 & 5 \\ 5 & 2 \end{vmatrix}} = \dfrac{-66}{-17} \approx 3.88$ and $y = \dfrac{\begin{vmatrix} 5 & 7 \\ 2 & 16 \end{vmatrix}}{\begin{vmatrix} 4 & 5 \\ 5 & 2 \end{vmatrix}}$

$= \dfrac{66}{-17} \approx -3.88$

Student B $\begin{matrix} -5y - 4x = -7 \\ -2y - 5x = -16 \end{matrix}$ $y = \dfrac{\begin{vmatrix} -7 & -4 \\ -16 & -5 \end{vmatrix}}{\begin{vmatrix} -5 & -4 \\ -2 & -5 \end{vmatrix}} = \dfrac{-29}{17} \approx -1.71$ and $x = \dfrac{\begin{vmatrix} -5 & -7 \\ -2 & -16 \end{vmatrix}}{\begin{vmatrix} -5 & -4 \\ -2 & -5 \end{vmatrix}}$

$= \dfrac{66}{17} \approx 3.88$

*24. (20) **Graphing Calculator** Given $f(x) = 2x - 2$ and $g(x) = x^2$, find $(f + g)(x)$. Graph $(f + g)(x)$ using a graphing calculator. Explain what the graph shows.

© Saxon. All rights reserved.

25. (15) **Multi-Step** Set up and solve a system to find an equation of the line through points (2, 5) and (4, −3). Put the equation in the form $y = mx + b$.

a. Substitute the point (2, 5) for (x, y) in the form $y = mx + b$ to get a linear equation in unknowns m and b.

b. Substitute the point (4, −3) into the form $y = mx + b$ to get another linear equation in m and b.

c. Solve the system for m and b.

d. What is the equation of the line?

26. (21) **(Business School)** This table shows the change in rank of two undergraduate business schools from 2006 to 2007. If the rankings continue to change at these constant rates, in what year will University of Florida and University of Wisconsin have the same rank?

School	2006	2007	Change
University of Florida	47	43	−4
University of Wisconsin	27	28	+1

27. (22) **Error Analysis** Courtney determines that the relation shown at right fails the vertical line test. Write a response to correct her decision.

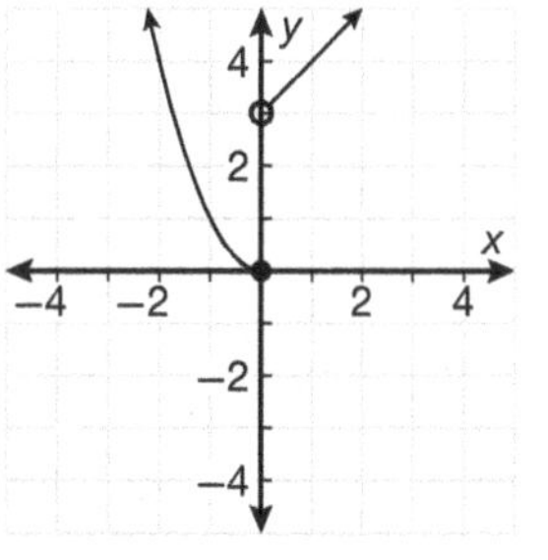

***28.** (27) **Verify** Verify that the roots of $f(x) = x^2 + 7x - 18$ are −9 and 2 by substituting −9 and 2 into the function.

***29.** (25) **Analyze** Cassie's job is to analyze a set of 100 scores that range from 0 to 10 from a recent survey. The set of values includes exactly 6 scores that are zero. She decides not to include the 6 zero scores in the analysis, based on the false assumption that zero is not really a number since it has no value.

a. Is it possible to determine whether the mean will be greater than, less than, or equal to the value using all 100 scores?

b. Is it possible to determine whether the standard deviation will be greater than, less than, or equal to the value using all 100 scores? Explain your answers.

30. (23) **(Artwork)** Jacob would like to buy a frame for some artwork he painted. His painting is 20 feet by 16 feet. He wants an equal-sized border around the outside of the painting, and he wants to increase the amount of area that the painting covers by 50%.

a. Write an expression to solve for the width of the border around the painting.

b. Calculate what size frame he should buy.

© Saxon. All rights reserved.

Name ______________________ Date __________ Class __________

Solving Systems of Equations in Three Variables

LESSON 29

Solve each system of equations.

*1. (29)
$$\begin{aligned} x - 5y + 2z &= 2 \\ 2x - y + z &= 1 \\ 7x - 3y + z &= 8 \end{aligned}$$

*2. (29)
$$\begin{aligned} -4x + 2y - z &= 2 \\ 4x + 8y - 6z &= 0 \\ 4x - 2y + z &= 2 \end{aligned}$$

Factor the polynomials.

3. (23) $144x^2 - 1$

4. (23) $9x^2 - 25$

Given the functions $f(x) = 2x + 1$ and $g(x) = x^2$,

5. (20) find $(f - g)(4)$.

6. (20) find $(f + g)(-3)$.

Given the functions $f(x) = -x - 7$ and $g(x) = -(x^2 + 3)$,

7. (20) find $(g + f)(0)$.

8. (20) find $(g - f)(-1)$.

Solve each equation.

9. (17) $|x + 3| = 4$

10. (17) $|2x + 6| + 2 = 1$

11. (17) $|1 - 3x| + 5 = 6$

12. (19) **Write** Explain FOIL for the multiplication of any two binomials in the form $(a + b)(a + b)$.

Convert the following to feet per minute.

13. (18) 18 in./hour

14. (18) 144 in./min

*15. (29) **Verify** Is the ordered triple $(-1, 2, -3)$ a solution of the system?

$$\begin{aligned} -x + y - z &= 6 \\ -x - 2y + 2z &= -9 \\ 3x - y + 2z &= -11 \end{aligned}$$

16. (13) Given the equation $6x + 3y = -9$, identify the slope and y-intercept.

17. (10) **Error Analysis** A student solved the inequality $-4x - 2 \geq 14$ and got the solution $x \geq -4$. Explain and correct the error.

*18. (14) **Graphing Calculator** Calculate the determinant of $\begin{bmatrix} 4 & -2 & 1 \\ 3 & 0 & 2 \\ 2 & -1 & 1 \end{bmatrix}$ using a graphing calculator.

*19. (26) **Multiple Choice** Using the data in the table, what is the equation in standard form of the line that passes through the three points?

A $y = -12.50x + 7.5$ **B** $y = 12.50x + 7.5$

C $125x + 10y = 75$ **D** $-125x + 10y = 75$

x	y
1	−5
2	−17.5
3	−30

© Saxon. All rights reserved.

*20. **Coordinate Geometry** A rectangle is drawn on a coordinate grid with one side along (23) the x-axis and one vertex at $(4 + v, 0)$. The area of the rectangle is $v^2 - 7v + 10$. Determine an expression for an adjacent vertex. Explain your answer.

21. If x varies directly with y and the constant of variation is 3, what is the value of (8) x when $y = 12$?

22. **Justify** A man records his height (22) every 5 years. Examine the table shown. Does this table represent a continuous, discontinuous, and/or discrete function? Justify your answer.

Age	5	10	15	20
Height	36 in.	48 in.	60 in.	72 in.

23. **Multi-Step** An online nut store sells nuts and raisins by the pound. Cora bought (21) 4 pounds of nuts and 2 pounds of raisins for \$37.20. Mark bought 2 pounds of nuts and 4 pounds of raisins for \$26.40.

   a. Write a system of equations that represents the price of the nuts, n, and the price of the raisins, r.

   b. How much should a pound of nuts and a pound of raisins cost together? Explain.

*24. **Write** Describe the steps used when solving a linear system by the elimination (24) method.

25. **Multiple Choice** Given $f(x) = -2x + 11$ and $g(x) = 6x - 1$, find $(f + g)(8)$. (20)

   A 42 **B** 52 **C** 74 **D** 76

26. The Olympic record time for swimming the 100-meter freestyle is held by P. van den (18) Hoogenband, who swam it in 47.84 seconds on September 19, 2000. What is his time in feet per second?

27. **Error Analysis** Explain the error in the statement and provide numerical support: The (17) transformation that occurs from $f(x) = |x|$ to $f(x) = |x - 3|$ results in a graph that shifts to the left 3 units.

*28. **Population** The table shows the population (29) in millions for the two most populated states. If the populations of the next three most populated states, New York, Florida, and Illinois, are added, the total population is 102.2 million. The difference between the populations of New York and Florida is 3 million. The difference between the populations of Florida and Illinois is 3.6 million. Find the populations of New York, Florida, and Illinois.

State	Population in Millions
California	33.9
Texas	20.9
New York	
Florida	
Illinois	

© Saxon. All rights reserved.

Solving Systems of Equations in Three Variables

29. (16) Use Cramer's Rule to solve the system $\begin{matrix} x + y = 2 \\ 2x - y = 7 \end{matrix}$.

***30.** (28) **Geometry** Suppose that the height of a square pyramid equals the length of one side of its base, s. Write the ratio of the area of the base to the volume of the pyramid as a simplified rational expression.

© Saxon. All rights reserved.

Name ______________________ Date __________ Class __________

Applying Transformations to the Parabola and Determining the Minimum or Maximum

LESSON 30

Determine the vertex and axis of symmetry of each function.

***1.** (30) $y = x^2 + 3$

***2.** (30) $y = 2(x - 1)^2 + 3$

***3.** (30) $y = -(x + 2)^2$

***4.** (30) $y = 3x^2 + 5$

***5.** (29) Solve the system of equations:

$$\begin{aligned} x + 3y - z &= 10 \\ 2x + 5y + z &= 9 \\ -3x + y - 3z &= 8 \end{aligned}$$

6. (27) Determine the domain and range of the function $f(x) = 2x^2$.

Find each product.

7. (19) $2x^2(2x - 4)$

8. (19) $\frac{4x^2}{3x^3}(x^3 + 9)$

Determine whether each of the following are functions.

9. (4) $y^2 = x + 5$

10. (4) $y + 3x^3 = 2x + 1$

11. (4) $y^2 - x^2 = 3$

***12.** (30) **Tall Structures** The height of an object, in meters, dropped from the roof of the Empire State Building after x seconds can be approximated by the function $y = -5x^2 + 381$, whereas the height of an object dropped from the Sears Tower can be approximated by $y = -5x^2 + 442$. Without graphing, tell how the graphs of each function compare to the parent quadratic function and to each other.

***13.** (29) **Estimate** Use

$$\begin{aligned} -5x - z &= -4 - 9y \\ 15x - 12 + 4z &= 6y \\ 20x - 36y &= -4z + 16 \end{aligned}$$

a. Rewrite the equations by lining up the variables.

b. Estimate the number of solutions. Explain your answer.

c. Solve the system of equations to verify your estimate.

***14.** (28) **Travel** The London Eye is a large Ferris wheel in England. Write the circumference to area ratio of the Eye as a simplified rational expression. Then find the ratio given that the diameter of the Eye is 135 meters.

***15.** (15) **Graphing Calculator** Solve the system of equations using a graphing calculator.

$$\begin{aligned} 5y &= 7 - 2x \\ 6x + 3y &= 9 \end{aligned}$$

© Saxon. All rights reserved.

16. (14) **Multi-Step** **a.** Calculate the determinant of $\begin{bmatrix} 0 & -2 & 3 \\ 1 & 4 & 2 \\ -3 & -1 & 1 \end{bmatrix}$.

b. Write the result of interchanging the first two rows of the matrix above.

c. Compare the determinants of the matrices in parts a and b. Explain what you see.

17. (25) **Model** Each week, Damien records his car's miles per gallon. Over a period of 10 weeks, he records:18, 17, 19, 18, 18, 25, 29, 30, 26, 19. Make a box-and-whisker plot of his data.

18. (24) **Justify** Which property of equality allows one equation to be added to another equation? Explain.

19. (23) **Error Analysis** Explain the error in the student's work below.

$$3x^2 - x - 4 = 0$$
$$2x = 4$$
$$x = 2$$

20. (21) **Analyze** Describe how a graph of 2 linear equations looks when the system has:

a. exactly one solution. **b.** an infinite number of solutions.

c. no solution.

21. (17) **Multiple Choice** Solve $|2x + 1| < 4$.

A $-\frac{5}{2} < x < \frac{3}{2}$ **B** $\frac{3}{2} < x < -\frac{5}{2}$

C $x < -\frac{5}{2}$ or $x > \frac{3}{2}$ **D** $x < \frac{3}{2}$

22. (22) **Mailing Weights** A customer visits the post office to weigh a package. The cost of mailing a package depends on its weight. Examine the table. Does this table represent a continuous, discontinuous, and/or discrete function? Justify your answer.

Weight	Cost
$0 \le x < 5$	\$2.00
$5 \le x < 10$	\$4.00
$10 \le x < 15$	\$6.00

23. (19) **Basketball** The length of a regulation high school basketball court is represented by the expression $(x + 24)$ feet. The width of a regulation high school basketball court is represented by the expression $(x - 10)$ feet.

a. Write an expression that represents the area of a regulation high school basketball court.

b. Evaluate the area of the court if $x = 60$.

© Saxon. All rights reserved.

24. (18) **Track and Field** Katie ran two miles to get ready for Thursday's meet. How many feet did Katie run?

25. (17) **Coordinate Geometry** A triangle on a coordinate grid has vertices at $(3, 0)$, $(-5, 0)$, and $(0, -6)$. Write the distance from each vertex to the origin as an absolute value expression. Then simplify the expression.

26. (11) **Multi-Step** Given the polynomial functions $f(x) = x^3 - x$, $g(x) = x^2 + 1$, and $h(x) = x^2 - 1$:

a. Write the polynomial function $g(x) + h(x)$.

b. Write the composite function $f(g(x) + h(x))$ in standard form.

27. (17) **Multiple Choice** Solve $-|2x + 9| \leq -3$.

A $-6 \leq x \leq -3$ **B** $x \leq -6$ or $x \geq -3$

C All real numbers **D** No solution

*28. (30) **Error Analysis** Two students are asked to find the axis of symmetry for the parabola of the function $f(x) = -(x + 4)^2 + 1$. Student A said the line was $x = 4$ and Student B said the line was $x = -4$. Which student is incorrect? Explain the error.

29. (27) **Justify** Identify the domain and range of $f(x) = 2x^2 - 7$. Explain how you know.

30. (26) **Geometry** The Mendez family is going to start a vegetable garden by their house and is going to enclose it within a fence on three sides. If the total amount of fencing they purchase is 300 feet, write an equation in standard form for finding all possible lengths and widths for the garden.

© Saxon. All rights reserved.

Name ______________________ Date __________ Class __________

Multiplying and Dividing Rational Expressions

LESSON 31

1. **Generalize** Given the dimensions of four matrices, A: 2 × 4, B: 2 × 2, C: 4 × 2, D: 4 × 4, determine all of the possible multiplication pairs and the dimensions of each product matrix.
(9)

*2. If $f(x) = \frac{x^2 - 100}{x^2 + 20x + 100}$ and $g(x) = \frac{10x + 100}{3x - 30}$, what is $f(x) \cdot g(x)$ in simplest form?
(31)

*3. **(Engineering)** The Channel Tunnel is a tunnel that runs under the English Channel. It is cylindrical in shape. Write the volume to lateral area ratio as a simplified rational expression. Then find the ratio given that the tunnel has an inner diameter of 7.6 meters. (Hint: The lateral area of a cylinder is the same as the surface area minus the area of the bases.)
(28)

4. When mixing concentrated fertilizer for a garden, the amount of fertilizer varies directly with the amount of water. If 2 cups of fertilizer are used in 16 gallons of water, how much fertilizer is used in 48 gallons of water?
(8)

5. **Geometry** Write a compound inequality using the fact that the sum of the lengths of any two sides of a triangle is greater than the length of the third side (Triangle Inequality) using the diagram. (Hint: Remember that length cannot be negative.)
(10)

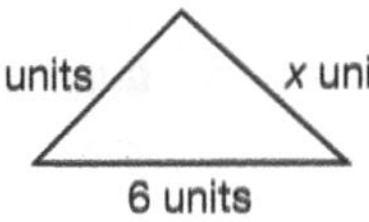

Use the description to write the vertex form of a quadratic equation.

*6. The parent function is shifted 4 units right and 6 units down.
(30)

*7. The parent function is reflected across the x-axis, and then shifted 3 units up.
(30)

8. **(Woodworking)** A lathe operator has a piece of wood in the shape of a square prism with dimensions $2x$, $2x$, and h. He wants to make the largest possible cylinder by turning the wood on the lathe and cutting it down. The cylinder will have radius x and length h. Write a polynomial that represents the volume of wood he will cut off to make the cylinder.
(11)

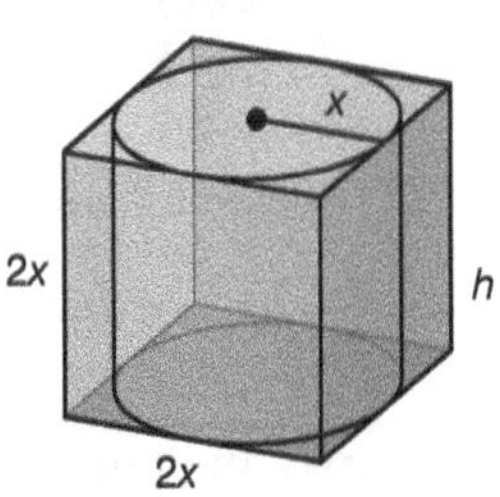

Multiply.

*9. $\frac{3a^3b^2}{5a^5} \cdot \frac{10a^3b}{7a^4b^2}$
(31)

*10. $\frac{2xy}{3y^{11}} \cdot \frac{6x^2y}{3xy}$
(31)

11. **Verify** Use FOIL to verify that $a = c + d$ and $b = cd$ in the formula:
(23)

$x^2 + ax + b = (x + c)(x + d)$.

12. **(Mountains)** Mt. Elbert in Colorado has an elevation of 14,433 ft and from the center, it runs horizontally approximately 22,105 ft. Find the approximate slope of Mt. Elbert, round your answer to the thousandths place.
(13)

13. **Multiple Choice** Which polynomial is in standard form?
(11)

A $\frac{1}{2}x^3 - x$ **B** $\frac{1}{3} - \frac{1}{3}x^3$ **C** $4x^2 + 3x^3 + 2x^4$ **D** $x^4 + x^5$

© Saxon. All rights reserved.

14. (18) Convert 87 ft^2 to square inches.

15. (10) **Analyze** Find the largest two consecutive even integers with a total sum less than or equal to 130.

16. (14) **Error Analysis** Explain the error in the student's work. Then find the correct determinant. $\begin{vmatrix} -2 & 6 \\ 3 & -1 \end{vmatrix} = (6)(3) - (-2)(-1) = 18 - 2 = 16$

***17.** (15) **Graphing Calculator** Solve the system of equations using a graphing calculator.

$$2x - 3y = 4$$
$$4x + y = 1$$

18. (17) **Multi-Step** $|ax + b| \leq c$, where $a > 0$ and $c > 0$.

a. Solve the inequality for x in terms of a, b, and c.

b. Apply this general solution to solve $|2x + 3| \leq 5$.

19. (13) **Coordinate Geometry** Graph the pentagon formed by these five equations on a coordinate plane.

$$x = 3 \qquad x = -3 \qquad y = -4 \qquad y = \frac{2}{3}x + 3 \qquad y = -\frac{2}{3}x + 3$$

a. Is the pentagon regular?

b. What are the coordinates of the vertices of the pentagon?

***20.** (30) **Error Analysis** A student said the graph of the function $y = (x - 6)^2$ is a shift of the parent function 6 units to the left because h is negative. Explain and correct the error in the student's thinking.

21. (19) **Multiple Choice** Multiply $(x + 11)(x - 8)$.

A $x^2 - 19x + 88$ **B** $x^2 + 3x - 88$ **C** $x^2 - 3x - 88$ **D** $x^2 + 19x - 88$

Identify the following equations as direct or inverse variations.

22. (12) $y = 3x$

23. (12) $y = \frac{20}{x}$

24. (21) **Analyze** Describe how a graph of 2 linear equations looks when the system has:

a. exactly one solution.

b. an infinite number of solutions.

c. no solution.

***25.** (31) **Write** Describe how to find the following product in simplest form: $\frac{a^2 - 49}{a - 7} \cdot \frac{a}{2a^2 + 14a}$.

***26.** (28) **Multi-Step** **a.** Simplify $\frac{4x^2 - 13x + 3}{9 - 6x + x^2}$.

b. Evaluate the simplified expression for $x = 9$.

© Saxon. All rights reserved.

Multiplying and Dividing Rational Expressions

27. (24) **Money** A parking meter contains 157 coins worth $26.95. If the meter only accepts quarters and dimes, how many of each type of coin are in the meter?

Given $f(x) = 5x - 9$ and $g(x) = 9x + 8$.

28. (20) Find $(f \cdot g)(3)$.

29. (20) Find $\left(\frac{f}{g}\right)(2)$.

30. (Inv 3) Find the intercepts of the equation $10x + 3y - 8z = 12$.

© Saxon. All rights reserved.

Name ______________________ Date __________ Class __________

Multiplying and Dividing Rational Expressions

LESSON 32

*1. **Verify** Is the ordered triple (5, −3, −1) a solution of the system:
(29)

$-2x - y - 2z = 5$
$x - 4y + 3z = 14$?
$-x + 4y - 3z = -6$

2. **Multi-Step** A data set consists of the following numbers: −4, −7, 12, −2, 8, 3, −1, 2, 4, −52
(25)

a. Find the mean of the data. **b.** Find the standard deviation.

c. Identify any outliers.

d. Describe how any outlier affects the mean and the standard deviation of this data set.

3. Solve the inequality: $3t + 4 < 2(t + 3) + t$. Show your work.
(10)

*4. **Multiple Choice** Which shows all the values of x that make the division expression $\frac{x^2 - 1}{x} \div \frac{3 - x}{2x + 2}$ undefined?
(31)

A 0, 3, −1 **B** 0, −3, 1 **C** 2, 3, −1 **D** 2, −3, 1

5. **Analyze** If the degree of every term of a polynomial is even and all the coefficients are positive (including the constant term), can the polynomial have a negative value? Explain.
(11)

*6. Write the matrix equation for the system and solve.
(32)

$$3x - y = 5 \text{ and } y = 2x - 4$$

7. **Multiple Choice** Choose the letter that best represents the equation of the graph:
(13)

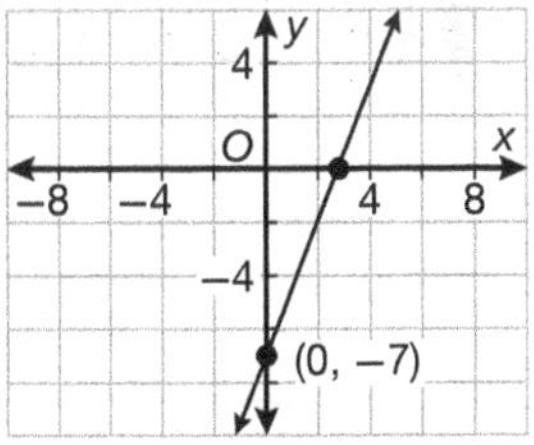

A $y = \frac{2}{5}x - 7$ **B** $y = -\frac{5}{2}x - 7$

C $y = \frac{5}{2}x - 7$ **D** $y = -\frac{2}{5}x - 7$

8. **Verify** Verify that (1.3, −2.7) is a solution of $\begin{matrix} 5.3x - 0.8y = 9.05 \\ -3.0x + 1.4y = -7.68 \end{matrix}$.
(15)

*9. Divide. $\frac{36x^5y^{10}}{7y^4} \div \frac{12y^4}{21x^2}$
(31)

10. **Recreational Planning** A playground that is to be rectangular in shape has an area modeled by the function $f(x) = -x^2 + 12x$ where x represent the length of one side of the playground in meters.
(27)

a. What value of x gives the playground the greatest possible area?

b. What is the greatest possible area?

© Saxon. All rights reserved.

*11. (30) **Graphing Calculator** An object dropped from a height 40 feet above the ground after x seconds is represented by $y = -16x^2 + 40$. When the object is dropped from 10 feet above the ground, the function becomes $y = -16x^2 + 10$.

a. Graph the functions on a graphing calculator and describe the transformation that changes the graph of the first function to the second.

b. For which quadrant or quadrants does the graph make sense? Why?

Write matrix equations for the systems of equations

*12. (32)
$$\begin{aligned} 2x + 4y + z &= 16 \\ x - 5y + z &= -5 \\ x + y + z &= 7 \end{aligned}$$

*13. (32)
$$\begin{aligned} 3x + 4z &= 13 \\ 15y - 2z &= 20 \\ 6z &= 6 \end{aligned}$$

14. (27) Written in vertex form, what are the values of a, h, and k in $f(x) = -2\left(x - \frac{1}{2}\right)^2 - 5$?

15. (11) **Write** Describe how to rewrite the polynomial $x + 4x + 12 - 5x^2 - x$ as an equivalent polynomial in standard form.

*16. (32) **Nutrition** A sandwich consists of Swiss cheese, ham, and rye bread. The sandwich contains 37.4 grams of carbohydrates, 46 grams of fat, and 36.6 grams of protein. How much of each ingredient is in the sandwich?

	Swiss Cheese	Ham	Rye Bread
Carbohydrates	6%	9%	77%
Fat	64%	48%	11%
Protein	30%	43%	12%

17. (28) **Error Analysis** Explain and correct the error a student made below.

$$\frac{10 - 2r}{r^2 - 10r + 25} = \frac{2(5 - r)}{(r - 5)(r - 5)} = \frac{2\cancel{(r - 5)}}{\cancel{(r - 5)}(r - 5)} = \frac{2}{r - 5}$$

18. (12) **Geometry** For each equation identify the kind of variation it represents.

a. Area of a circle $= \pi(\text{radius})^2$ **b.** Area of a rectangle = length × width

*19. (31) **Multi-Step** A container manufacturer is considering doubling the height of a cylindrical container.

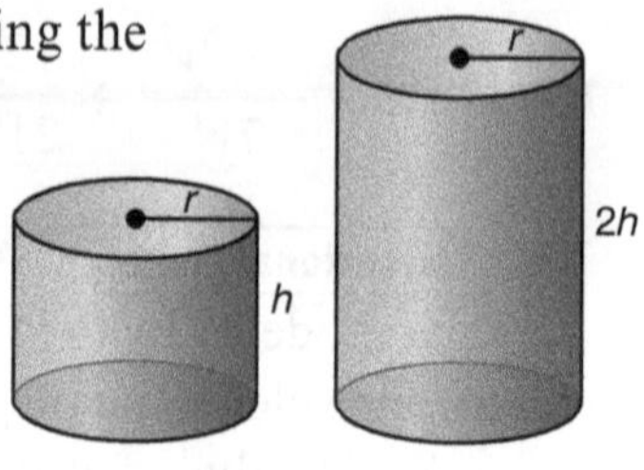

a. Find the ratio of surface area to volume for the small container.

b. Find the ratio of surface area to volume for the large container.

c. A smaller ratio of surface area to volume results in a more economical container. Which container is more economical? Explain.

© Saxon. All rights reserved.

20. (17) **Exercise** For a 20-year old to workout within his cardio range, his heart rate should be within 25 beats per minute of 155 bpm.

a. Write an absolute value inequality to determine the lowest and highest heart rate at which he will be in his cardio range.

b. Solve the inequality.

21. (3) Simplify $\frac{x^2x^0x^{-1}(x^{-2})^2yx^{-3}}{(x^2y)^{-3}xyx^{-2}x^2}$.

22. (19) **Basketball** The length of a regulation high school basketball court is represented by the expression $(x + 24)$ feet. The width of a regulation high school basketball court is represented by the expression $(x - 10)$ feet.

a. Write an expression that represents the area of a regulation high school basketball court.

b. Evaluate the area of the court if $x = 60$.

***23.** (32) **Analyze** Suppose matrix A has an inverse and the matrix equation $AX = B$ has a solution. Explain why $X = A^{-1}B$ is the solution, but $X = BA^{-1}$ is not the solution.

24. (20) Given $f(x) = -7x + 4$ and $g(x) = 9x + 2$, represent $(f + g)(x)$ geometrically.

25. (28) **Probability** A mathematician has a number of red, white, and blue marbles. The number of red marbles is the same as the number of blue marbles and the number of white marbles is the square of the number of red marbles. If the mathematician puts all the marbles in a bag and randomly chooses one marble, what simplified rational expression represents the probability of pulling out one red marble?

Solve.

26. (24)
$$\frac{3}{8}x - \frac{1}{3}y = -9$$
$$2x + 4y = 4$$

27. (7) $\frac{-3 - x}{2} - \frac{x}{2} = 7$

***28.** (29) Use
$$9x = y - 3z - 21$$
$$4y - 6z = 8x + 10$$
$$56x - 28y = 2 - 42z$$

a. Write the equations in standard form.

b. Estimate the number of solutions. Explain your answer.

c. Solve the system of equations to verify your estimate.

© Saxon. All rights reserved.

29. *(23)* Solve $x^2 - 5x - 36 = 0$

30. *(14)* **Error Analysis** Explain the error in the work below. Then find the correct determinant.

$$\begin{vmatrix} 1 & 2 & -2 \\ -1 & 4 & 3 \\ 0 & 1 & 2 \end{vmatrix} = 1\begin{vmatrix} 4 & 3 \\ 1 & 2 \end{vmatrix} - 1\begin{vmatrix} 2 & -2 \\ 1 & 2 \end{vmatrix} + 0\begin{vmatrix} 2 & -2 \\ 4 & 3 \end{vmatrix} = 5 - 6 + 0 = -1$$

© Saxon. All rights reserved.

Name ______________________ Date __________ Class __________

Applying Counting Principles

LESSON 33

*1. **Geometry** The function representing the area of a rectangle whose length is 12 units longer than its width is $f(x) = (x + 6)^2 - 36$ where x is the width of the rectangle. Graph this function. For which quadrant or quadrants does the graph make sense? Why?
(30)

2. Solve and graph the compound inequality $4 < 2(x - 2) \leq 16$.
(10)

Use the letters A-B-C-D-E-F-G.

*3. How many seven-letter passwords are possible if letters can be repeated?
(33)

*4. How many seven-letter passwords are possible if letters cannot be repeated?
(33)

5. Find the equation of the line through $(-3, -5)$ and $(4, -5)$.
(26)

6. **Airplanes** As an airplane ascends after takeoff, its altitude increases at a rate of 45 ft/s while its distance on the ground from the airport increases at 210 ft/s. Write parametric equations to model the location of the plane.
(Inv 2)

*7. Write the matrix equation that represents the system of equations.
(32)

$$p + q + r = 6$$
$$0.4p + 0.5q + 2r = 5.7$$
$$2.2p + 3.4q + r = 12$$

8. **Error Analysis** Two students evaluated $(f - g)(7)$, given $f(x) = 5x + 8$ and $g(x) = 9x + 2$. Who is correct? Explain the error.
(20)

Student A	Student B
$(f - g)(7)$	$(f - g)(7)$
$= 5(7) + 8 - (9(7) + 2)$	$= 5(7) + 8 - (9(7) + 2)$
$= 35 + 8 - 63 - 2$	$= 35 + 8 - 63 + 2$
$= -22$	$= -2$

9. Given the polynomial functions $f(x) = \frac{1}{2}x^2 - 3$, $g(x) = 2x^2$, and $h(x) = 4x$,
(11, 19)

a. write the sum $(f + g + h)(x)$ in standard form.

b. write the product $(f \cdot g \cdot h)(x)$ in standard form.

*10. **Justify** Is multiplication of rational expressions commutative? Is division of rational expressions commutative? Justify your answers.
(31)

11. **Multiply** Assume all expressions are defined. $\frac{2x^4y^5}{3x^2} \cdot \frac{15x^2}{8x^3y^2}$
(31)

*12. Using the numbers 2-4-6 and the letters P-A-R-K, how many one-digit, two-letter passwords can be made, if repeats are allowed and the password starts with a digit?
(33)

© Saxon. All rights reserved.

13. (14) **Multi-Step** $\begin{vmatrix} x & 2 \\ -6 & 4 \end{vmatrix} = 8$

a. Write the determinant as an equation.

b. Solve for x.

c. Check your answer by substituting for x and finding the determinant with a calculator.

***14.** (32) Find the inverse of $M = \begin{bmatrix} 4 & 8 \\ 2 & 6 \end{bmatrix}$, if it exists.

Write each equation in standard form.

15. (26) $y = 1.5x + 3$

16. (26) $y = -0.05x + 20$

17. (16) **Ticket Prices** A zoo charges $10.95 for each child's admission and $14.95 for each adult admission. If a busload of 45 people attend, and together they pay $516.75, how many adults and how many children are admitted?

a. Set up equations relating the number of children and adults to the total admissions. Let c represent the number of children and a the number of adults.

b. Use Cramer's Rule to solve the system of equations.

18. (21) **Write** Without solving the system, can you tell how many solutions this system of equations has? Explain. $\begin{aligned} y + x &= 2 \\ y + 1 &= -x \end{aligned}$

19. (19) Simplify: $\dfrac{(xm^{-2})^0 x^0 m^0}{xx^2 m^0 (2x)^{-2}}$

***20.** (33) **Write** Describe how to determine the number of different arrangements of the letters M, A, T, and H.

21. (23) **Multiple Choice** Factor the expression $-12x^4 + 6x^2 + 18x$.

A $-6x(2x^3 - x - 3)$

B $-6(2x^4 - x^2 - 3)$

C $-6x(2x^3 + x + 3)$

D $-6(2x^4 + x^2 + 3)$

***22.** (27) **Graphing Calculator** Use a graphing calculator to determine the y-intercept of the quadratic function $y = x^2 + x - 2$.

***23.** (33) **Sports** There were 12 players on the United States team that competed in the 2006 Women's Basketball (under 19) World Championship tournament. How many ways can 5 starters be chosen from 12 players?

© Saxon. All rights reserved.

24. *(16)* **Motion** A speed boat leaves a nearby shore of a lake and moves at 25 knots toward the opposite shore, 2 nautical miles away. At the same time, a pleasure boat leaves the opposite shore and moves at 10 knots toward the speed boat. When will the boats meet?

a. Set up a system of equations representing the position of each boat relative to the nearby shore.

b. Use Cramer's Rule to solve the system.

***25.** *(31)* **Measurement** Write a rational expression in simplest form for the ratio of area to perimeter for the right triangle.

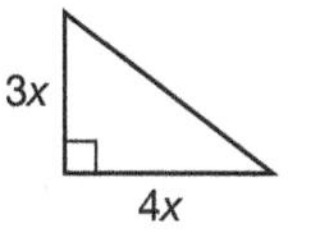

***26.** *(Inv 3)* Find the intercepts of the equation $40 + 8y - 2z = -5x$.

27. *(25)* **Analyze** The first quartile of some test scores is 55 and the third quartile is 74.

a. Is it possible for the median of the test scores to be 77? Explain why or why not.

b. The maximum score is 93 and the range of the test scores is 55. What is the minimum test score?

c. What is the range of test scores that will place a student in the middle 50% of the class?

28. *(24)* **Multi-Step** **a.** Write an equation in two variables to represent that the sum of two numbers is 73.

b. Write an equation with the same variables to represent that twice the second number minus the first number is 2.

c. Write and solve a linear system to find the two numbers.

29. *(18)* Convert 61 yd^2 to square inches

***30.** *(32)* What is the inverse of the matrix $\begin{bmatrix} 2 & 2 \\ 4 & 5 \end{bmatrix}$?

© Saxon. All rights reserved.

Name ______________________ Date __________ Class __________

Graphing Linear Equations II

LESSON 34

1. (Berries) Chuck and Nikita picked 173 quarts of berries. How many did each pick if Chuck picked 11 more quarts than Nikita?
(7)

2. Factor: $-2ab + abx + abx^2$.
(23)

Evaluate.

3. $x^2 - y^2(x - y)$ if $x = \frac{1}{2}$ and $y = \frac{1}{3}$.
(2)

4. $ax - a(a - x)$ if $a = -\frac{1}{2}$ and $x = \frac{1}{4}$.
(2)

5. Use substitution to solve: $\begin{aligned} x + 2y &= 5 \\ 3x - y &= 7 \end{aligned}$.
(21)

6. Expand: $\frac{4x^{-2}y^{-2}}{z^2}\left(\frac{3x^2y^2z^2}{4} + \frac{2x^0y^{-2}}{z^2y^2}\right)$.
(19)

Simplify.

7. $\frac{(0.0003 \times 10^8)(6000)}{(0.006 \times 10^{15})(2000 \times 10^5)}$
(3)

8. $\frac{3m}{x} - \frac{2x^{-1}}{m^0m^{-1}} + \frac{5x^2m^2}{x^3m}$
(3)

9. Write the equation $y = \frac{2}{3}x + \frac{4}{5}$ in standard form.
(26)

10. Solve for C: $[2 \quad -29 \quad 5] + C = [31 \quad -18 \quad 14]$.
(5)

*11. **Multiple Choice** Which statement is true about the graph of $y = 3x + 2$?
(34)
A The rate of change between any two points on the graph is 2.
B The rate of change between any two points on the graph is 3.
C The rate of change decreases along the graph from left to right.
D The rate of change increases along the graph from left to right.

*12. **Analyze** Given the functions $f(x) = \frac{3x - 2}{x + 2}$, $g(x) = \frac{10x^2 + 20x}{3x^2 - 2x}$, and $h(x) = 10$, compare the function product $f(x) \cdot g(x)$ and the constant function $h(x) = 10$. Describe how they are related.
(31)

13. (Population) The table lists the population estimates, in hundreds of thousands, for Vermont from 2000 to 2002.
(13)

Year	2000	2001	2002
Population	6.1	6.13	6.16

a. Write the data above as ordered pairs where x is the number of years after 2000 and y is the population in hundreds of thousands.

b. Estimate Use slope and y-intercept to find the equation of the line representing this data.

© Saxon. All rights reserved.

14. (24) **a.** Multiply the first equation in $\begin{matrix} 0.2x + 0.5y = -1 \\ x - y = 16 \end{matrix}$ by 10. How does this make solving the system easier?

b. Solve the system.

***15.** (30) **Graphing Calculator** Use a graphing calculator to graph $y = (x + 2)^2$ and $y = x^2$ on the same coordinate axes. How do the graphs compare?

16. (15) **River Current** A motor boat makes a 175-kilometer trip down the Mississippi River to New Orleans in 3.3 hours. But it takes an hour longer for the boat to return upstream to its starting point. How fast is the river's current?

***17.** (34) **Probability** A circle has a radius of 4 and center (0, 0). Suppose a point is chosen at random inside the circle. What is the probability that the chosen point is in quadrant I and below the line $y = x$?

18. (21) **Geometry** You are given the equation of a line on a coordinate grid. You are then given three other equations of lines that combine with the first to form a rectangle. How many of the three lines have an inconsistent solution with the original line? How many of the three lines have a consistent solution with the original line?

19. (32) **Multi-Step** Find the inverse of matrix A. Then prove your answer is correct.
Do not use a calculator. $A = \begin{bmatrix} 3 & 8 \\ 2 & 4 \end{bmatrix}$

20. (19) **Multiple Choice** Multiply $(x + 7)(x - 9)$

A $x^2 - 16x + 63$ **B** $x^2 - 2x + 63$ **C** $x^2 - 2x - 63$ **D** $x^2 + 2x - 63$

21. (7) **Verify** Is $x = 4$ the solution to the equation $6x - 4 = 20$?

22. (25) **Shipping Boxes** The table shows the measurements in inches of the side lengths of various shipping boxes available from the United States Postal Service.

Box	Measurement 1	Measurement 2	Measurement 3
1	11.875	3.375	13.625
2	11	8.5	5.5
3	7.5	5.125	14.375

Which measurement has the greatest range of side lengths? What is that range?

***23.** (34) **Roofing** The minimum slope (pitch) that is normally recommended for an asphalt shingle roof is $\frac{1}{3}$. Rectangle $ABCD$ represents the front wall of a building. Graph a line through point A to represent a roof with a slope of $\frac{1}{3}$. Write an equation of the line in slope-intercept form.

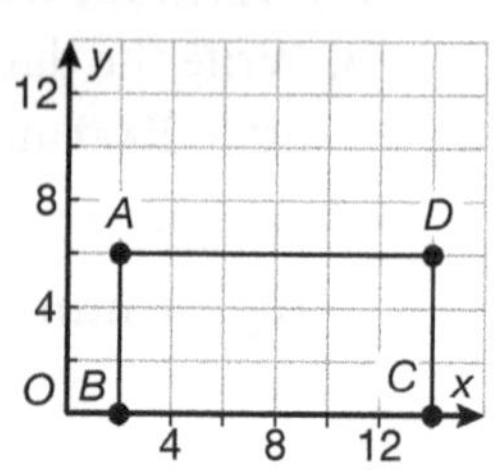

© Saxon. All rights reserved.

24. (33) **Passwords** A voicemail system password is 1 letter followed by a 3-digit number less than 600. How many different voicemail passwords are possible?

25. (15) **Analyze** Explain the difficulty you encounter when trying to use Cramer's Rule to solve the system $\begin{aligned} 4x - 12y &= -4 \\ -6x + 18y &= 6 \end{aligned}$

26. (33) **Error Analysis** A student is choosing a four-letter password. She wants to know how many passwords are possible if letters may not be repeated. To find out, she adds: $26 + 25 + 24 + 23 = 98$. What is the error? Find the correct answer.

27. (23) **Analyze** Is $x^2 + 7x + 12$ a basic quadratic polynomial, a perfect square trinomial, or a difference of two squares? Explain how you can tell by looking at the polynomial.

***28.** (34) **Write** Describe how to obtain the graph of $y = \frac{3}{4}x - 3$ by transforming the graph of $y = x$.

29. (15) **Error Analysis** A student solved the linear system $\begin{aligned} x + y &= 3 \\ x - y &= 1 \end{aligned}$ and got 2 as the answer. Explain and correct the student's error.

30. (23) Use $x^2 + 16x + 64$. Rewrite the expression in the form of a perfect square trinomial.

© Saxon. All rights reserved.

Name ______________________ Date __________ Class __________

Solving Quadratic Equations I

LESSON 35

Simplify.

1. (3) $\dfrac{(b^2c^{-2})^{-3}c^{-3}}{(b^2c^0b^{-2})^4}$

2. (3) $\dfrac{(2x^2ya)^{-3}ya^3}{x^2y(ay)^{-2}y}$

Solve.

3. (7) $3(-2x - 3) - 2^2 = -(-3x - 5) - 2$

4. (23) $x^2 + 26x - 56 = 0$

5. (26) Find the equation of the line that passes through $(-3, 4)$ and $(3, -2)$.

Use elimination to solve.

6. (24) $4x - 3y = -1$
$2x + 5y = 19$

7. (24) $5x + \frac{1}{2}y = -4$
$-x + y = 3$

8. (5) Solve for a and b: $\begin{bmatrix} a \\ 64 \end{bmatrix} = \begin{bmatrix} 102 \\ a - b \end{bmatrix}$.

9. (20) Find $(f \cdot g)(x)$, given $f(x) = 4x - 3$ and $g(x) = 8x + 9$.

10. (22) **Formulate** Describe a plan for determining if a function is continuous.

***11.** (35) **Multiple Choice** What are the zeros of the function $f(x) = x^2 - 5x + 6$?
A 0 and 6 **B** 0 and -6 **C** 2 and 3 **D** 2 and -3

12. (32) **Probability** Suppose you roll a pair of number cubes twice. What is the probability of rolling a sum greater than 10 on both rolls?

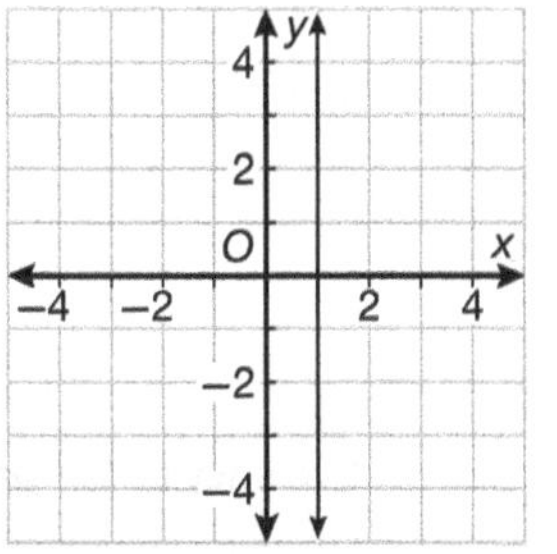

***13.** (34) **Error Analysis** A student described this line as having no slope, or zero slope. What is wrong with this description?

14. (11) If a polynomial of degree 3 is added to a polynomial of degree 4, what are all possible values for the degree of the result?

15. (31) **Analyze** The product $\frac{x^2-4}{x^2-3x-4} \cdot \frac{x-4}{x+2}$ in simplest form is $\frac{x-2}{x+1}$, as shown:

$\frac{x^2-4}{x^2-3x-4} \cdot \frac{x-4}{x+2} = \frac{\cancel{(x+2)}(x-2)}{(x+1)\cancel{(x-4)}} \cdot \frac{\cancel{(x-4)}}{\cancel{(x+2)}} = \frac{x-2}{x+1}$. When 4 is substituted for x in $\frac{x-2}{x+1}$, the value is $\frac{2}{5}$. Explain why the value of $\frac{x^2-4}{x^2-3x-4} \cdot \frac{x-4}{x+2}$ is not $\frac{2}{5}$ when $x = 4$.

16. (23) **Write** A square is drawn on a coordinate grid with one side along the x-axis and one vertex at $(a - 1, 0)$. The area of the square is $a^2 - 8a + 16$. Determine an expression for an adjacent vertex. Explain.

© Saxon. All rights reserved.

*17. **Justify** Explain why this paragraph describes a method of graphing the equation: (34)
$y + 1 = \frac{1}{4}(x - 2)$: Plot the ordered pair $(2, -1)$. Then from that point, count 1 unit up and 4 units to the right to plot another point. Then draw a line through the two plotted points.

18. Solve and graph the compound inequality: $4 < 2(x - 2) \leq 16$. (10)

19. **Average Velocity** If an object is thrown straight down with initial velocity 8 feet (31) per second, the number of feet it travels in t seconds is given by the expression $16t^2 + 8t$ (neglecting air resistance).

a. Write a rational expression for the average velocity of the object before it hits the ground over the time interval from 0 seconds to t seconds. Then simplify the expression. (Average velocity equals distance traveled divided by elapsed time.)

b. Evaluate the expression to find the average velocity of the object over the time interval from 0 seconds to 2.5 seconds.

20. **Chemistry** How many liters of a 15% acid solution should be mixed with a 35% acid (24) solution to make 7 liters of a 20% acid solution?

*21. **Write** State all possible numbers of real zeros a quadratic function can have. (35) Explain what information the number of real zeros provides about the point(s) of intersection of the graph and the x-axis.

22. Is the equation $y = \sqrt{2}x$ a direct or inverse variation? (12)

*23. **Geometry** The area of the right triangle is 24 square units. Find the (35) value of x.

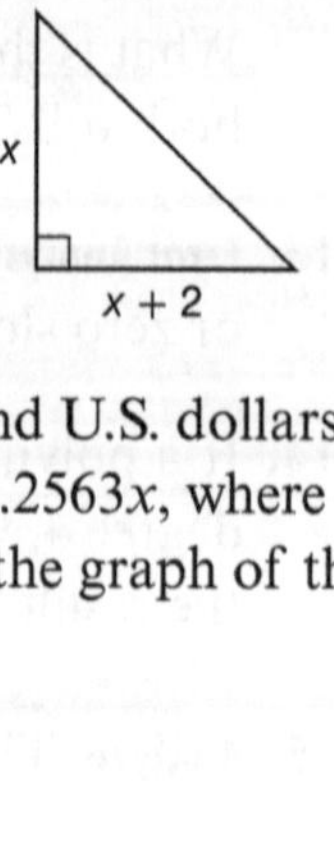

*24. **Currency Exchange** During 2006, the average exchange rate for euros and U.S. dollars (34) was \$1.2563 per euro. This relationship is given by the function $y = 1.2563x$, where y represents dollars and x represents euros. Describe how to transform the graph of the parent function $y = x$ to obtain the graph of $y = 1.2563x$.

25. **Multiple Choice** An example of a set of numbers that can be listed is: (22)

A real numbers **B** integers

C rational numbers **D** irrational numbers

© Saxon. All rights reserved.

***26.** (26) **Graphing Calculator** When you're traveling in a car that comes to an abrupt halt, the car continues forward even though the brakes have been pressed. The distance traveled is called the "stopping distance." The table below shows the stopping distance at three different speeds for a car traveling on wet pavement. Use your graphing calculator and the linear regression capabilities to write an equation in slope-intercept form for the stopping distance.

Initial Traveling Speed (mile/hour)	Stopping Distance (feet)
35	53.389
49	114.159
62	202.678

27. (21) **Coordinate Geometry** Which set of equations could be represented by this graph?

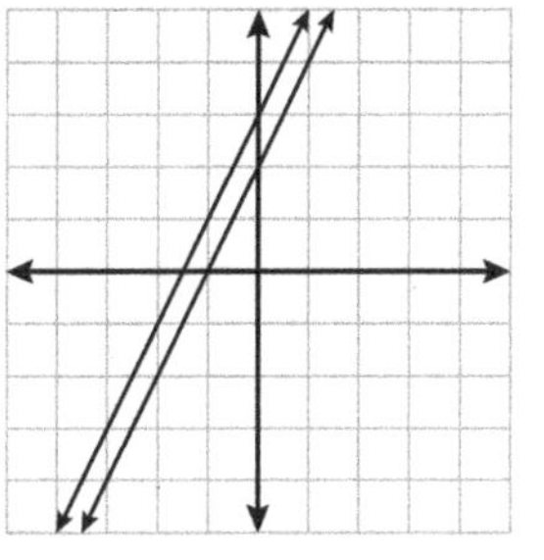

A $y = 2x + 4$, $2y - 2x = 8$

B $y = 2x + 4$, $12 - 3y = -6x$

C $2y = 4x - 12$, $y = 2x + 6$

D $-4x = 8 - 2y$, $y = 2x + 6$

28. (32) **Nutrition** A spaghetti entrée consists of spaghetti, ground beef, and tomato sauce. The entrée contains 118.68 grams of carbohydrates, 40.12 grams of fat, and 41.2 grams of protein. How much of each ingredient is in the entrée? To find the answer, write a system of equations and use an inverse matrix to solve it. Use the table below.

	Spaghetti	Ground Beef	Tomato Sauce
Carbohydrates	81%	0%	87%
Fat	5%	60%	3%
Protein	14%	40%	10%

***29.** (35) **Flags** There is no required size for a United States flag, but the ratio of width to length that is recommended in most cases is 1 : 1.9. Write and solve a quadratic equation to find the length and width of a United States flag that has an area of 17.1 square feet.

30. (18) What is the perimeter of this rectangle in feet?

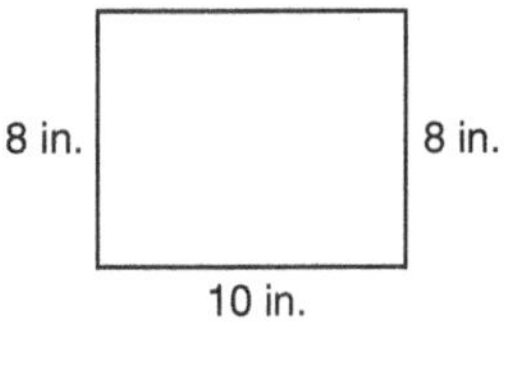

© Saxon. All rights reserved.

Name ______________________ Date __________ Class __________

Using Parallel and Perpendicular Lines

LESSON 36

Use the slope formula to find the slope of each line.

*1. (26) $(-3, 7)(1, 0)$

*2. (26) $(2, -5)(0, -6)$

Determine the kind of variation, if any, for each equation.

3. (12) $y = mx + b$, for $m, b \neq 0$

4. (12) $y = mx + b$, for $m \neq 0$ and any value of b

Simplify. Write answers with all exponential expressions in the numerator.

5. (3) $\dfrac{xx^2(x^0y^{-1})^2}{x^2x^{-5}(y^2)^5}$

6. (3) $\dfrac{m^2p^0(m^{-2}p)^2}{m^{-2}p^{-1}(m^{-3}p^2)^3}$

Solve.

7. (27) $x^2 + 2 = 4x + 7$

8. (24) $\begin{aligned} 12x - 5y &= 24 \\ 20y - 4x &= 3 \end{aligned}$

9. (26) Write the equation in standard form: $y = \frac{1}{11}x + \frac{1}{7}$.

10. (28) **Analyze** Explain how to create a rational expression with four excluded values. Then give an example.

11. (23) **Error Analysis** Carmen factored the polynomial $x^2 + 5x - 6$ into $(x - 5)(x - 1)$. Describe her error.

12. (22) **Verify** that the graph $y = 3x - 6$ is a continuous function.

*13. (14) **Graphing Calculator** Calculate the value of x in the matrix below. Substitute the value of x and use a graphing calculator to verify your answer. $\begin{vmatrix} -4 & 3 \\ 5 & x \end{vmatrix} = -x$

14. (31) **Multiply** Assume that all expressions are defined. $\frac{x}{15} \cdot \frac{x^7}{2x} \cdot \frac{20}{x^4}$

*15. (35) **Olympic Swimming Pool Size** An Olympic swimming pool has an area of 1250 square meters, and its length is 25 meters more than its width. Write and solve a quadratic equation to find the length and width of an Olympic swimming pool.

16. (32) **Geometry** In the triangle, x is 5 greater than y, and y is 21 less than 3 times z, and the perimeter is 180. What is the value of each variable? To find the answer, write a system of equations and use an inverse matrix to solve it.

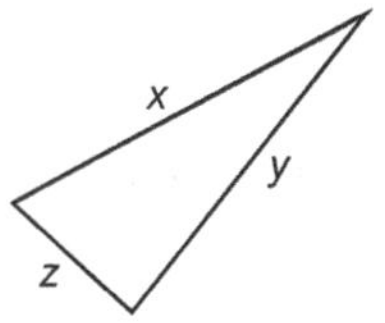

© Saxon. All rights reserved.

17. (29) **Data Analysis** The table represents the number of ice creams sold at an ice cream shop for the months of January (01), May (05), and October (10).

Month	Sales
01	124
05	4,476
10	3,796

Let x be the month and y be the sales. Use the data in the table to create a system of three equations to find a quadratic equation of the form $y = ax^2 + bx + c$ that models the data.

***18.** (34) **Cab Fares** The normal fares for taxicab rides in New York City in the year 2006 satisfied a linear function. The table shows the fares for rides of several different distances.

Number of Miles (x)	0.2	0.4	1	5
Fare in Dollars (y)	2.90	3.30	4.50	12.50

Graph the function, state the rate of change, and describe what it means.

19. (Inv 2) A helicopter takes off with a horizontal speed of 5 ft/s and a vertical speed of 20 ft/s. Write parametric equations to show the motion of the helicopter.

***20.** (36) **Error Analysis** Two students are finding the equation of the line parallel to $y = 5x - 3$ that crosses (1, 4) but get different results. Which student made the mistake? Explain.

Student A	Student B
$5 = \frac{y-4}{x-1}$	$5 = \frac{y-1}{x-4}$
$5x - 5 = y - 4$	$5x - 20 = y - 1$
$y = 5x - 1$	$y = 5x - 19$

21. (25) **Multiple Choice** Which data set gives a median of 8 and a mode of 4?
A {4, 5, 6, 8, 8, 9, 12} **B** {4, 4, 8, 9, 10}
C {2, 3, 4, 8, 8, 9} **D** {2, 3, 4, 4, 8, 8}

***22.** (36) **Write** Is the triangle defined by vertices (−4, 6), (4, 4), and (1, −8) a right triangle? How do you know?

23. (30) **Small Business** The profits, for x weeks, in one year for a small business can be modeled by the function $y = 0.45(x - 22)^2 - 840.50$. Does the graph of the function have a maximum or a minimum? What is that value? During what week did it occur?

© Saxon. All rights reserved.

***24.** (35) Find the roots of $x^2 + 7x + 6 = 0$.

25. (27) **Justify** In $f(x) = ax^2 + bx + c$, why is a the only constant that is not allowed to be zero?

***26.** (33) **Multiple Choice** There are 8 runners in a race. How many ways can runners finish in first, second, and third place?

A 21 **B** 24 **C** 336 **D** 512

27. (14) **Multi-Step** The matrix $\begin{bmatrix} a & c \\ b & d \end{bmatrix}$ represents a parallelogram, with vertices at (0, 0), (a, b), (c, d), and $(a + c, b + d)$.

a. Graph this parallelogram in the first quadrant, putting (a, b) clockwise from (c, d).

b. To find the area of this parallelogram, draw a rectangle around it and subtract off the areas of triangles and rectangles.

c. Show that the area of the parallelogram equals the determinant of the matrix.

***28.** (33) **Women's Basketball** There are 12 teams in the Atlantic Coast Conference of college women's basketball. How many ways can teams finish in first, second, and third place?

29. (30) **Write** Describe how symmetry can be used to graph $y = (x - 2)^2 + 2$.

30. (31) **Multiple Choice** What is the value of $\frac{x^2 + x}{x^2 - 9} \cdot \frac{3x - x^2}{3x + 3}$ if $x = 6$?

A $-\frac{4}{3}$ **B** $-\frac{4}{9}$ **C** $\frac{4}{9}$ **D** $\frac{4}{3}$

© Saxon. All rights reserved.

Name ______________________ Date ____________ Class ____________

Adding and Subtracting Rational Expressions

LESSON 37

1. Use elimination to solve the system $\begin{matrix} 5x + 2y = 70 \\ 3x - 2y = 10 \end{matrix}$.
(24)

2. Find the equation of the line that has a slope of $-\frac{3}{8}$ and passes through (4, 4).
(26)

*3. Add: $\frac{k^2}{2p} + c - \frac{4}{p^2c}$.
(37)

*4. Find the equation of the line that passes through the point (3, 5) and is parallel to the line $y = \frac{1}{6}x - 2$.
(36)

5. Expand: $\frac{x^2y^{-2}}{z^2}\left(\frac{z^2}{y^2\,(2x^{-2})^{-1}} - \frac{4x^2\,y^0}{z^{-2}}\right)$.
(20)

6. Multiply: $\begin{bmatrix} 4 & -1 \\ 3 & 7 \end{bmatrix} \cdot \begin{bmatrix} 2 & 4 & 3 \\ 1 & 0 & 8 \end{bmatrix}$.
(9)

Factor completely.

7. $x^2 + x - 6$
(23)

8. $x^3 - 9x$
(23)

*9. Find the difference. $\frac{1}{1 + \frac{1}{x+1}} - \frac{1}{1 + \frac{1}{x-1}}$
(37)

10. Given $f(x) = 2x - 7$ and $g(x) = -5x + 8$, graph $f(x)$ and $g(x)$ on the same grid.
(13)

11. **Write** Determine the four resulting inequalities that are used to solve $|x| > |2 + 7x|$.
(17)

12. **Multi-Step** **a.** Tell how to determine the values of a, b, and c for any quadratic function written in standard form.
(27)

b. Write a quadratic equation in standard form where $a = -1$, $b = -2$, and $c = 3$.

*13. **(Aviation)** Because of the jet stream, on a roundtrip flight from Washington, D.C. to California, the first part of the trip will take half an hour longer than the return trip. How much faster is the return trip?
(37)

14. **Error Analysis** A student multiplied rational expressions as follows:
(31)

$$\frac{\cancel{x^2} - 1}{\cancel{x^2} + 2x + 1} \cdot \frac{\cancel{x} + 1}{\cancel{x} - 3} = \frac{-1}{2x+1} \cdot \frac{1}{-3} = \frac{1}{3(2x+1)}.$$

What is the error? Find the correct product.

15. **Multiple Choice** Which is the solution to the linear system $\begin{matrix} y = x \\ y = 3x - 2 \end{matrix}$?
(15)

A (3, 3) **B** (2, 4) **C** (1, 1) **D** There is no solution.

© Saxon. All rights reserved.

16. (24) **Error Analysis** Find and correct the error a student made below.

$$\begin{array}{l} 2x + 2y = 6 \\ -2x + y = -12 \end{array} \longrightarrow \begin{array}{r} 2x + 2y = 6 \\ + -2x + y = -12 \\ \hline 2y = -6 \\ y = -3 \end{array} \longrightarrow \begin{array}{r} -2x + y = -12 \\ -2x - 3 = -12 \\ -2x = -9 \\ x = 4.5 \end{array}$$

The solution is (4.5, –3).

***17.** (36) **(Economics)** The exchange rate from dollars to different currencies is shown in the table. A company charges a fee of \$3 for amounts up to \$50 and \$5 for amounts above \$50. Write the equations for exchanging Euros to dollars. What do the graphs of the equations have in common?

Currency	US $
1 euro =	1.377
1 Canadian dollar =	0.9472
1 British pound =	2.0284

18. (35) **Probability** The right triangle is inscribed in the circle. The area of the triangle is 120 square units. Suppose a point is chosen at random inside the circle. What is the probability that the chosen point is inside the triangle?

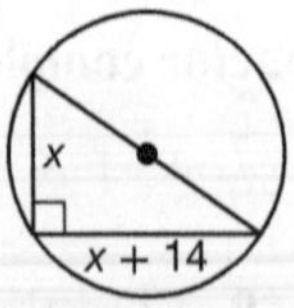

19. (34) **Multi-Step** **a.** Graph the equations $y = \frac{1}{2}x - 2$ and $y = \frac{1}{2}x + 3$.

b. What is the slope of each line?

c. State a property of lines and their slopes that is illustrated by the graphs.

***20.** (37) **Write** What must be true if the LCM of rational expressions $\frac{f(x)}{g(x)}$ and $\frac{h(x)}{i(x)}$ is $g(x)i(x)$?

***21.** (14) **Graphing Calculator** Use a graphing calculator to solve.

$$\det \begin{bmatrix} 2 & -3 & 5 \\ 2 & 0 & -1 \\ 2 & 3 & 1 \end{bmatrix}$$

22. (33) **Analyze** A card is chosen from a standard 52-card deck. Consider these four events: *Choose a red card. Choose a face card. Choose the jack of spades. Choose a black jack.* How many pairs of mutually exclusive events can be made from the events? List all the pairs.

23. (19) **(Basketball)** The length of a regulation high school basketball court is represented by the expression $(x + 24)$ feet. The width of a regulation high school basketball court is represented by the expression $(x - 10)$ feet.

a. Write an expression that represents the area of a regulation high school basketball court.

b. Evaluate the area of the court if $x = 60$.

***24.** (36) **Justify** Suppose that $y_1 = m_1x + b_1$ and $y_2 = m_2x + b_2$ are each perpendicular to $y_3 = m_3x + b_3$. Justify the statement $y_1 \parallel y_2$.

© Saxon. All rights reserved.

25. (21) **Verify** Solve the system of equations by solving the first equation for y then substituting. Verify your answer by solving the second equation for y, then substituting.

$2y - 3x = -10$

$4x = 7 - y$

26. (32) **Item Costs** An office worker ordered breakfast items for coworkers as shown below.
Monday: 6 muffins, 6 bagels, and 6 fruit cups; total bill \$24.00
Tuesday: 4 muffins, 12 bagels, and 4 fruit cups; total bill \$22.80
Wednesday: 8 muffins, 12 bagels, and 10 fruit cups; total bill \$39.30

What was the cost of each item? To find the answer, write a system of equations and use an inverse matrix to solve it.

27. (22) **Geometry** Examine the polygons given below. Each polygon has been divided up into triangles. Complete the table. Graph the function. State the domain and range. Determine if the graph is continuous, discontinuous, and/or discrete.

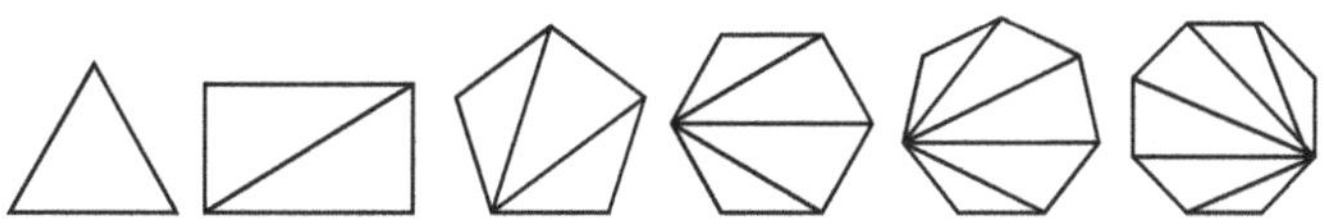

Number of sides of the polygon	Number of triangles
3	1
4	2
5	3
6	4
7	5
8	6

28. (31) **Multi-Step** Given the rational functions $f(x) = \frac{2x - 1}{x + 5}$ and $g(x) = \frac{14x - 7}{14x^2 + 70x}$:

a. Find the function quotient $f(x) \div g(x)$ in simplest form.

b. Find the value of $f(x) \div g(x)$ if $x = 10$.

***29.** (37) What is the sum of $\frac{1}{x^2 + x - 72}$ and $\frac{1}{x^2 - x - 56}$?

A $\frac{2}{x^2 + 16x + 63}$　　**B** $\frac{2}{x^2 + x - 72}$

C $\frac{2}{x^2 - x - 56}$　　**D** $\frac{2x + 16}{x^3 + 8x^2 - 65x - 504}$

30. (16) **Construction** A contractor is replacing the tile in two bathrooms. For one bathroom, she purchased 416 large tiles and 256 small tiles at a cost of \$233.60. For the other bathroom, she purchased 400 large tiles and 512 small tiles at a cost of \$251.20. How much does each size tile cost?

© Saxon. All rights reserved.

Name ______________________ Date __________ Class __________

Dividing Polynomials Using Long Division

LESSON 38

Use the descriptions below to write the vertex form of a quadratic equation.

1. (30) The parent function is shifted 10 units left.

2. (30) The parent function is shifted 1 unit right and 3 units down.

***3.** (38) Divide $x^3 - 10x^2 - 69x + 30$ by $(x + 5)$.

4. (32) Given $A = \begin{bmatrix} 4 & -2 \\ 8 & 4 \end{bmatrix}$ and $B = \begin{bmatrix} -2 & 0 \\ 0 & -2 \end{bmatrix}$, solve $AX = B$.

A number cube is rolled. Determine if the following events are mutually exclusive.

5. (33) *Roll an odd number* or *roll a 6*

6. (33) *Roll an even number* or *roll a number less than 3*

***7.** (37) Find the difference. $\frac{1}{x+3} - \frac{1}{x+2} - \frac{1}{x+1}$

8. (16) Use Cramer's Rule to solve $\begin{matrix} 3x - 12y = -15 \\ x + 2y = 7 \end{matrix}$.

Find the determinants of the following matrices.

9. (14) What is $|A|$ if $A = \begin{bmatrix} 2 & -12 \\ 7 & 13 \end{bmatrix}$?

10. (14) What is $|B|$ if $B = \begin{bmatrix} -1 & -24 \\ 0.25 & 0.5 \end{bmatrix}$?

***11.** (38) What are the slope and y-intercept of $3x + 10y = -1$?

12. (12) **Geometry** As the diameter (d) of circle increases in size, the circumference (C) increases. Likewise, as the diameter decreases in size, so does the circumference. The constant of variation between C and d is π. Describe the kind of variation between the circumference and diameter in a circle. Write the equation.

***13.** (35) **Write** State all the possible numbers of y-intercepts a quadratic function graph can have. Explain.

***14.** (38) **Justify** Consider the polynomial $x^2 + ax + bx + ab$. What is the remainder when this polynomial is divided by $x + a$? How do you know?

15. (29) **Hourly Pay** An employee makes three different rates of pay based on the type of work. The rates of pay are \$16 per hour, \$24 per hour, and \$32 per hour. The combined number of hours worked at the rate of \$16 per hour and \$24 per hour was 10 times the hours worked at the rate of \$32 per hour. If in one week the employee earned \$808 for working 44 hours, how many hours were worked at each rate of pay?

© Saxon. All rights reserved.

***16.** (38) **Error Analysis** Two students are dividing $-14x^3 + 46x^2 + 44x - 16$ by $x - 2$ but get different results. Which student made the mistake?

Student A	Student B
$-14x^2 + 18x + 80$	$-14x^2 + 18x - 8$
$(x - 2)\overline{)-14x^3 + 46x^2 + 44x - 16}$	$(x - 2)\overline{)-14x^3 + 46x^2 + 44x - 16}$
$\underline{-(-14x^3 + 28x^2)}$	$\underline{-(-14x^3 + 28x^2)}$
$0 + 18x^2 + 44x - 16$	$0 + 18x^2 + 44x - 16$
$\underline{-(18x^2 - 36x)}$	$\underline{-(18x^2 - 36x)}$
$0 + 80x - 16$	$0 + 8x - 16$
$\underline{-(80x - 160)}$	$\underline{-(8x - 16)}$
144	0

***17.** (27) **Graphing Calculator** Use a graphing calculator to determine the minimum of the quadratic equation $f(x) = x^2 - 4x - 2$.

***18.** (36) **Multiple Choice** Which is the equation of the line perpendicular to $y = 4x + 10$ that crosses the point (1, 1)?

A $y = 4x + \frac{5}{4}$ **B** $y = -\frac{1}{4}x + \frac{5}{4}$ **C** $y = -4x + \frac{5}{4}$ **D** $y = \frac{1}{4}x + \frac{5}{4}$

19. (34) **Multi-Step** Graph the equations $y = \frac{3}{2}x - 1$ and $y = -\frac{2}{3}x + 2$ on the same coordinate system.

a. What are the slopes of the lines?

b. What is the product of the slopes?

c. State a property of lines and their slopes that is illustrated by the graphs.

20. (28) **Geography** Crater Lake in southern Oregon lies inside a volcanic basin and is nearly circular in shape. Write the area to circumference ratio of the lake as a simplified rational expression. Then find the ratio given that the radius of the lake is about 3 miles.

21. (33) **Error Analysis** A card is drawn at random from a standard 52-card deck. How many outcomes are in the event *draw an ace or a spade*? A student solved this problem by reasoning as follows: There are 4 aces and 13 spades, so there are $4 + 13 = 17$ outcomes in the event. What is the error? Find the correct answer.

22. (24) **Multi-Step** **a.** Rewrite the system $\begin{matrix} y = 5 - 7x \\ 10 = 14x + 2y \end{matrix}$ so that both equations are in standard form.

b. By inspection, what do you think the solution is? Why?

c. Solve and classify the system.

© Saxon. All rights reserved.

23. (32) **Analyze** Students at a high school were asked if they visited a museum, public library, or historical site during the last month. The table shows data about the results of the survey. How many students in each grade were surveyed? To find the answer, write a system of equations and use an inverse matrix to solve it.

	Ninth Graders	Tenth Graders	Eleventh Graders	Total
Museum	20%	30%	25%	143
Public Library	40%	50%	45%	258
Historical Site	20%	20%	35%	142

24. (30) **Generalize** Describe shifts, stretches, and compressions of parabolas and discuss how those changes appear in the equations of parabolas.

25. (23) **Write** Explain in words how the Zero Product Property is useful in solving polynomial equations.

***26.** (37) **Aviation** Because of a strong head wind the return trip on an airplane takes 1.5 hours longer than the first part of the trip. How much slower is the return trip?

27. (27) **Justify** Graph $f(x) = -x^2 + 3$. Tell why the range of the function is the set of real numbers less than or equal to 3.

***28.** (38) **Multiple Choice** Which of the following is a factor of $3x^3 + 8x^2 - 31x + 20$?
A $(x + 2)$ **B** $(3x + 4)$ **C** $(x - 1)$ **D** $(x + 6)$

29. (26) **Medicine** The Centers for Disease Control has developed growth charts that pediatricians use to see if a child's height is within a certain average. The chart below shows data for a boy's height in the 75th percentile. The three points are on a line. Use the data to write the equation of the line in slope-intercept form.

Age (years)	Height (inches)
3	38.5
4	41.5
5	44.5

***30.** (37) **Probability** Two six-sided number cubes have labels $\frac{1}{x}$, $\frac{1}{2x}$, $\frac{1}{3x}$, $\frac{1}{4x}$, $\frac{1}{5x}$, and $\frac{1}{6x}$. If both number cubes are rolled, what is the probability that the sum of the expressions is $\frac{1}{x}$?

© Saxon. All rights reserved.

Name ______________________ Date __________ Class __________

Graphing Linear Inequalities in Two Variables

LESSON 39

Determine if the given points are solutions of the inequalities.

*1. (39) $y < 6x - 2$, (3, 18)

*2. (39) $y + 2x \geq -4$, (−1, −2)

3. (20) Add: $m + \frac{x}{c} + \frac{c}{x^2b}$

4. (29) Solve. $\begin{array}{c} -8x - 22 + 2y = 2z \\ -6x + 2y = 16 + z \\ 6 + 3y + z = -x \end{array}$

Solve by substitution:

5. (21) $\begin{array}{l} x = y + 1 \\ 3x + 2y = 8 \end{array}$

6. (21) $\begin{array}{l} 3x - y = 22 \\ 2x + 3y = -11 \end{array}$

7. (21) $\begin{array}{l} -7x + y = 8 \\ 5x - y = -6 \end{array}$

8. (38) Divide $6x^3 + 23x^2 - 20x - 9$ by $3x + 1$.

9. (28) Find the excluded values of $\frac{x^2 - 25}{3x^2 + 15x}$.

10. (23) Factor the polynomial $2x^4 + 4x^3 - 4x$.

11. (28) **Verify** Show why the x's cannot be divided out in $\frac{x + 2}{x + 5}$.

*12. (39) **Multiple Choice** The graph of which inequality is shown?

A $-3y - 4x \geq 24$

B $-3y - 4x \leq 24$

C $-3y - 4x > 24$

D $-3y - 4x < 24$

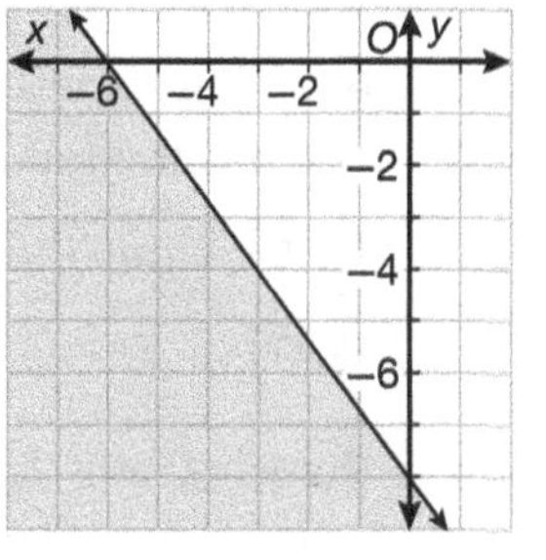

*13. (37) **Statistics** The fraction of students that are interested in a new brand of sneakers is twice the fraction of those that are not. The fraction of students who are not interested is $\frac{1}{x}$. Those who expressed no opinion in the sneakers were 10% of the students who were interested. What percent of students were interested?

14. (16) **Baseball Equipment** Last month, a baseball coach bought 4 bats and 9 balls for \$355. This month, the coach bought 2 bats and a dozen balls for \$290. The prices did not change from last month to this month. How much did each bat and ball cost?

a. Set up equations relating the monetary values of the bats and balls last month and this month. Let T represent the cost (in dollars) per bat, and B represent the cost per ball.

b. Use Cramer's Rule to solve the system of equations.

© Saxon. All rights reserved.

Graphing Linear Inequalities in Two Variables

LESSON 39

***15.** *(39)* **Verify** Using the graph, choose a point in the shaded region and test it. Choose a point in the unshaded region and test it. Is the graph correct? Explain.

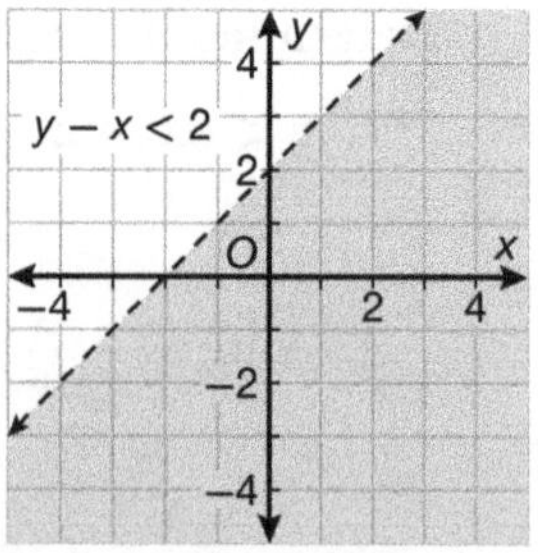

***16.** *(22)* **Graphing Calculator** Graph $y = 4$ on your graphing calculator. Determine if this relation is a function. Determine if the graph is continuous, discontinuous, and/or discrete.

***17.** *(35)* **U.S. Postal Service** The United States Postal Service uses size, shape, and weight to determine pricing for first class mail. One category of first class mail is large envelope. The maximum length of a large envelope is 3 inches greater than its maximum width, and its maximum area is 180 square inches. Write and solve a quadratic equation to find the maximum length and maximum width of a large envelope.

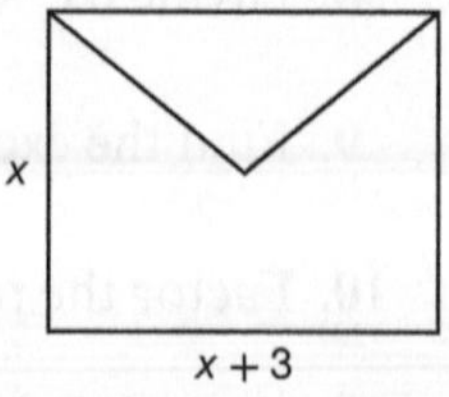

18. *(23)* **Multi-Step** Use $x^2 + 8x - 48$.

a. Find the factors of -48.

b. Which of the factors have a sum of 8?

c. What is the factored form of the polynomial?

19. *(34)* **Multiple Choice** If the graph of $y = x$ is reflected over the x-axis, and then the resulting graph is translated 4 units up, which equation is represented by the final graph?

A $y = -\frac{1}{4}x$ **B** $y = -4x$ **C** $y = x - 4$ **D** $y = -x + 4$

20. *(21)* **Multi-Step** A store sells granola and dried fruit by the pound. Dillon bought 4 pounds of granola and 2 pounds of dried fruit for $22. Carmen bought 2 pounds of granola and 4 pounds of dried fruit for $26.

a. Write a system of equations that represents the price of the granola, g, and the price of the dried fruit, f.

b. How much should one pound of granola and one pound of dried fruit cost individually and together?

***21.** *(33)* **Model** The figure at the right is a Venn diagram. It shows that jacks and clubs are not mutually exclusive events when choosing a card from a standard 52-card deck. Draw a Venn diagram to show that kings and hearts are not mutually exclusive events when choosing a card from a standard 52-card deck.

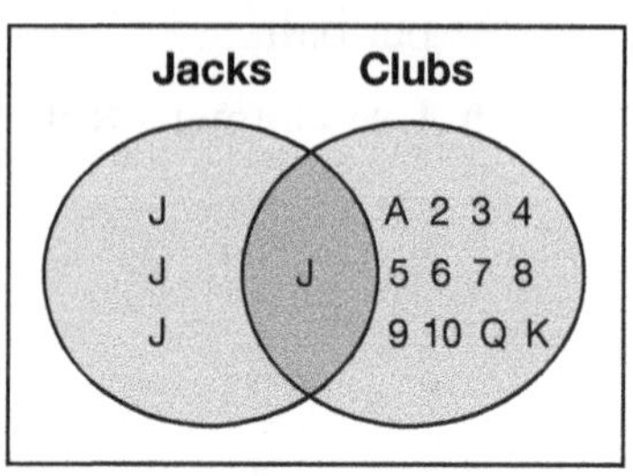

© Saxon. All rights reserved.

22. *(32)* **Analyze** What system of equations is represented by the matrix equation shown below? Solve the system mentally.

$$\begin{bmatrix} 2 & 0 & 0 \\ 0 & 3 & 0 \\ 0 & 0 & 5 \end{bmatrix} \begin{bmatrix} x \\ y \\ z \end{bmatrix} = \begin{bmatrix} 10 \\ 12 \\ 50 \end{bmatrix}$$

23. *(28)* **Error Analysis** A student divided rational expressions as follows: $\frac{20x^2}{y} \div \frac{y}{x^3} = \frac{20\cancel{x^2}}{\cancel{y}} \div \frac{\cancel{y}}{x \cdot \cancel{x^2}} = \frac{20}{x}$. What error did the student make? Find the correct quotient.

***24.** *(38)* **Model** Show that the ratio of an odd number to an even number, when each is expressed as a polynomial, has a nonzero remainder.

25. *(30)* **Verify** Suppose a rocket is fired straight into the air such that the graph of the function representing the height of the rocket after x seconds has its vertex at (3.75, 225) and passes through the point (5, 200). Verify that the value of a in the equation written in vertex form is -16.

***26.** *(38)* **Geometry** What is the ratio of the volume to the surface area for the rectangular prism shown? Does the ratio have a remainder?

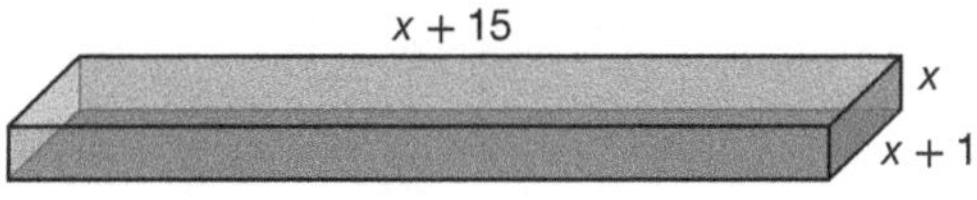

27. *(29)* **Investing** A person invests \$50,000 for one year; some is invested at 7%, some at 8%, and the remainder at 12%. The combined interest earned at the end of the year from these investments was \$4,770. The amount invested at 8% is \$4,000 more then the amount invested at 7% and 12% combined. Find the amount of money invested at each rate.

***28.** *(39)* **Money** Nelson is building a tower of coins with half-dollars and dimes. He wants the tower to be less than 15 centimeters high. Each half dollar is 2.15 mm thick and each dime is 1.35 mm thick. Write an inequality that represents how many of each coin are needed. Then show how to use the inequality to see if using 30 half-dollars and 70 dimes is a possibility.

29. *(27)* **Business** Mr. Jing makes and sells carved animals. His monthly profit function can be modeled by $f(x) = -0.15x^2 + 7x$ where x represents the number of carved animals he sells each month.

a. For how many animals does he make the maximum profit? How much profit is it?

b. At what point would Mr. Jing begin to lose money?

***30.** *(36)* Write the equation of the line in slope intercept form that is parallel to $y = 5x - 3$ and goes through (1, 4).

© Saxon. All rights reserved.

Name ______________________ Date __________ Class __________

Simplifying Radical Expressions

LESSON 40

*1. (39) Make a table of values to satisfy the inequality $2x - 4y \geq 12$.

Write the equation in standard form for the line that crosses the two points.

2. (26) (4, 5.5), (−1, 2.5)

3. (26) (3, 5), (6, 4)

Multiply then simplify.

*4. (40) $\sqrt{30} \cdot \sqrt{6}$

*5. (40) $\sqrt{180} \cdot \sqrt{10}$

Factor:

6. (23) $5x^2y^2 - 2xy + 10xy^2$

7. (23) $x^2y^3m^5 + 12x^3ym^4 - 3x^2y^2m^2$

8. (20) Given the rational functions $f(x) = \frac{1}{x}$ and $g(x) = \frac{x^2}{x+4}$, find the value of $f(x) \cdot g(x)$ if $x = -2$.

Solve:

9. (35) $-x + x^2 = 12$

10. (35) $-48x = -2x^2 - x^3$

*11. (40) **Multi-Step** **a.** Expand the expression as much as possible. Do not simplify: $\sqrt{x^8}$

b. Explain how can you rewrite your answer from part a so the expression can be easily simplified.

c. Simplify the expression as much as possible. The variable represents non-negative real numbers.

12. (28) **Error Analysis** Explain and correct the error a student made below.

$$\frac{x^2}{x^5} = x^{5-2} = x^3$$

13. (32) **Multiple Choice** If $A = \begin{bmatrix} 2 & 3 \\ 3 & 4 \end{bmatrix}$ and $B = \begin{bmatrix} -1 & 2 \\ 5 & 0 \end{bmatrix}$, what is the solution to the matrix equation $AX = B$?

A $X = \begin{bmatrix} 19 & -8 \\ -13 & 6 \end{bmatrix}$

B $X = \begin{bmatrix} 11 & -8 \\ -13 & 6 \end{bmatrix}$

C $X = \begin{bmatrix} 19 & 8 \\ -13 & 6 \end{bmatrix}$

D $X = \begin{bmatrix} 19 & -8 \\ 13 & 6 \end{bmatrix}$

*14. (38) **(Chemistry)** Water has a unique property that causes it to increase in volume as it changes from liquid to ice. In the illustration, water just fills a cube-shaped container. The water is frozen, and increased volume of ice changes in one direction. What is the ratio of the new volume to the original volume?

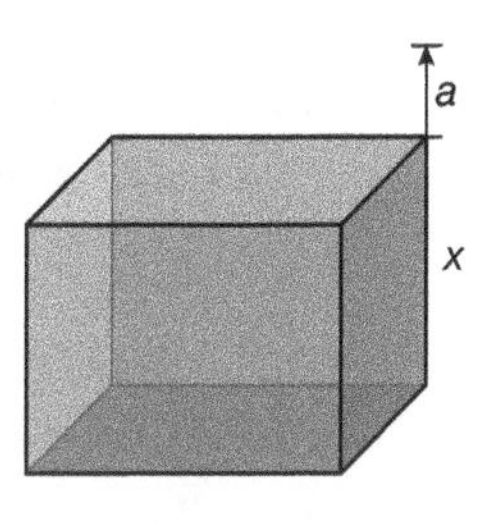

© Saxon. All rights reserved.

15. **Multiple Choice** Subtract. $\frac{2}{x^2 - 4x - 45} - \frac{1}{x^2 + 9x + 20}$
(37)

A $\frac{x + 17}{x^2 - 61x - 180}$ B $\frac{x + 17}{x^3 - 61x - 180}$ C $\frac{1}{x^3 - 61x - 180}$ D $\frac{1}{x^2 - 61x - 180}$

16. **Error Analysis** A chemist weighs samples obtained from a production run. The weights of the samples are 12 g, 14 g, 65 g, 11 g, 15 g, 12 g, 13 g, 15 g, 14 g, and 11 g. She eliminated the outlier and calculated the mean of the data. What is her error?
(25)

$$\overline{x} = \frac{12 + 14 + 11 + 15 + 12 + 13 + 15 + 14 + 11}{10} = \frac{117}{10} = 11.7$$

17. **Geometry** For the circle shown, the line $y_1 = \frac{4}{3}x + \frac{1}{3}$ passes through the center of the circle at (2, 3). How do you know that the equation of the tangent at (−2, 6) is parallel to y_1?
(36)

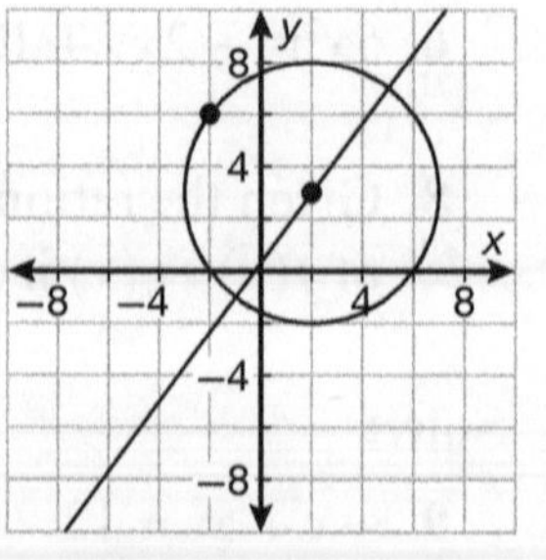

18. **Predict** Use your knowledge of the factoring formulas to find the product of $(5x^6 + 3)$ and $(5x^6 - 3)$ without multiplying the polynomials. Explain your prediction.
(23)

19. **Analyze** Does the table of values represent a linear function? Explain your answer without graphing.
(34)

x	−4	0	2	8
y	11	5	2	−7

20. **Sports** There are 4 teams in the National Football Conference East division. How many ways can the teams finish in first, second, third, and fourth place?
(33)

21. **Write** Describe how to graph $y - 1 \leq 5x$ on a graphing calculator.
(39)

22. **Multi-Step** Consider this question: Which is the larger area that a piece of rope of length x will enclose, a circle or a square?
(31)

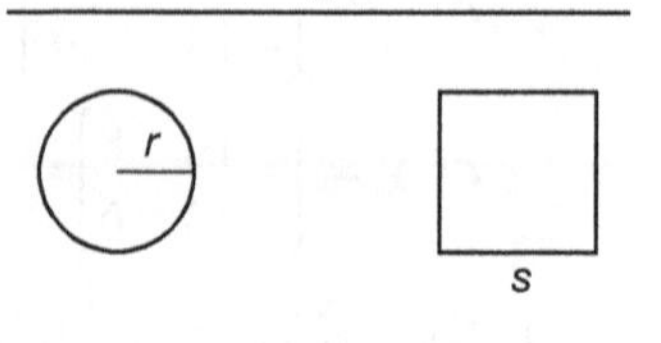

a. Write a simplified expression for the area of the circle in terms of x.

b. Write a simplified expression for the area of the square in terms of x.

c. Which area is larger? Find the ratio of the areas.

d. Express the larger area as a percent of the smaller area. Round to the nearest percent.

© Saxon. All rights reserved.

23. (35) **Write** For the function $f(x) = x^2 + 12x + 36$, describe the relationship among the zero(s) of $f(x)$, the x-intercept(s) of $f(x)$, and the root(s) of $f(x) = 0$.

***24.** (27) **Graphing Calculator** Determine the vertex of the function $f(x) = x^2 - 6x + 1$ using a graphing calculator.

***25.** (40) **Biology** The metabolism rate of an 18 pound animal is approximately $73\sqrt[4]{625}$ Calories per day. Simplify the metabolism rate.

26. (24) **Work** In one month, Angela worked a total of 20 hours, some of it spent babysitting and the rest spent washing cars. She earned a total of \$96.25. If she gets paid \$5.50 per hour for babysitting and \$2.75 per hour for washing cars, how many hours of each type of work did she do?

27. (39) **Sports** In American football, a touchdown with a conversion is worth 7 points and a field goal is worth 3 points. Suppose the only scoring in a game was due to touchdowns with conversions and field goals. Write the inequality that represents how many of each could have occurred if the total number of points earned in the game was less than or equal to 105. Give a solution that would be on the boundary line if the inequality were graphed.

28. (21) **Coordinate Geometry** You are given equations of three lines on a coordinate grid that intersect to form a triangle. Explain in words how you could find the vertices of the triangle.

***29.** (40) **Verify** Supply two examples to show that b and the value of $\sqrt[n]{b}$ can be negative when n is odd.

***30.** (26) **Aviation** The Federal Aviation Administration tracks airline delays for airports around the country. From the beginning of the year to the end of March, there were 6,000 delays at Atlanta-Hartsfield Airport. By the end of May, there were 10,000 cumulative delays. Use this information to write an equation in slope-intercept form that could be used to predict the total delays throughout the year. Let x equal the month of the year as a number and y equal the cumulative delays.

© Saxon. All rights reserved.

Name ________________________ Date __________ Class __________

Using the Pythagorean Theorem and the Distance Formula

LESSON 41

Find the distance between the points.

***1.** (41) $(-3, 8)$ and $(3, 0)$

***2.** (41) $(-1, -1)$ and $(13, 6)$

3. (26) Write the equation of the line that is perpendicular to $y = \frac{1}{3}x - 1$ and passes through the point $(2, -3)$.

Simplify.

***4.** (40) $3\sqrt{3} \cdot 4\sqrt{12} - 5\sqrt{300}$

***5.** (40) $4\sqrt{3}(2\sqrt{3} - \sqrt{6})$

Add.

6. (37) $2 + \frac{1}{x}$

7. (37) $\frac{5x^2}{y} + p^2 - \frac{3x}{py}$

8. (36) Find the equation of the line that passes through the point $(2, 2)$ and is parallel to $y = -\frac{3}{7}x + 4$.

Expand.

9. (20) $xy^{-2}\left(\frac{x^0y^2}{x} - \frac{3x^0y^2}{x^2}\right)$

10. (20) $\frac{xy^{-2}}{p^2}\left(\frac{p^2y^2}{x} + \frac{5x^2y^3}{p^{-2}}\right)$

11. (28) **Geography** The state of Wyoming is roughly square in shape. Write the area to perimeter ratio of the state as a simplified rational expression. Then find the ratio given that the length of each side of the state is roughly 300 miles long.

***12.** (41) **Multi-Step** If the origin represents a pier, and one boat travels 4 units due east and 6 units due north, while a second boat travels 4 units due west and 6 units due south, how far apart are the boats in units? Write the answer as both a simplified radical expression and as a decimal rounded to the nearest tenth. Then approximate the distance given that each unit represents 2.5 miles.

13. (30) **Multi-Step** **a.** Identify the vertex and axis of symmetry of $y = (x + 3)^2 - 5$.

b. Find the values of y when $x = -6, -5,$ and -4.

c. Use symmetry to find the values of y when $x = -2, -1,$ and 0.

***14.** (40) **Geometry** The radius of a right circular cylinder can be represented by $\frac{\sqrt{V}}{\sqrt{\pi h}}$, where V is the volume of the cylinder and h is the height. Simplify the expression.

15. (33) **Multiple Choice** How many three-digit passwords are possible if digits may be repeated?

A 27 **B** 30 **C** 720 **D** 1000

16. (38) **Write** Suppose that $f(x)$ is a polynomial of degree m, and $g(x)$ is a polynomial of degree $n < m$. What can you conclude about $\frac{f(x)}{g(x)}$ if it has a zero remainder?

© Saxon. All rights reserved.

17. (34) **Error Analysis** A student solved the equation $x^2 - 16 = 0$ as shown below. $x^2 - 16 = 0 \rightarrow (x - 4)^2 = 0 \rightarrow x = 4$. What is the error? Solve the equation correctly.

***18.** (41) **Multiple Choice** The legs of a right triangle are 18 mm and 80 mm. What is the length of the hypotenuse?

A 80 mm **B** 82 mm **C** 89 mm **D** 98 mm

19. (34) **Model** Graph the line represented by the table of values.

x	−2	0	2	4
y	−5	−2	1	4

***20.** (39) **Justify** Why does (0, 0) usually make for a good test point for determining which half-plane to shade? When can it not be used?

21. (35) **Graphing Calculator** Use a graphing calculator to estimate the root(s) of the equation $x^2 - 78 = 0$ to the nearest integer(s).

22. (32) **Nutrition and Cost** A one-kilogram container of mixed nuts costs $17.70 and contains 86 grams of protein. The mix contains almonds ($15 per kilogram, 13% protein), cashews ($18 per kilogram, 9% protein), and pecans ($19 per kilogram, 5% protein). How much of each type of nut is in the mix? To find the answer, write a system of equations and use an inverse matrix to solve it.

23. (29) **Ticket Sales** At a college basketball game 350 tickets were sold. Tickets cost $5 for children and senior citizens, $7 for students, and $10 for all others. The total income from ticket sales was $2,665. The combined number of $7 and $10 tickets sold was 6 times more than the number of $5 tickets sold. How many tickets of each type were sold?

***24.** (40) **Justify** Explain why the expression $\frac{3}{\sqrt{5}}$ is allowed to be written as $\frac{3}{\sqrt{5}} \cdot \frac{\sqrt{5}}{\sqrt{5}}$.

25. (37) **Physics** A satellite has an orbital acceleration of $\frac{v^2}{r}$, where v is the speed of the satellite and r is the distance from the satellite to the Earth's center. Find the difference in acceleration between satellite 1 and satellite 2.

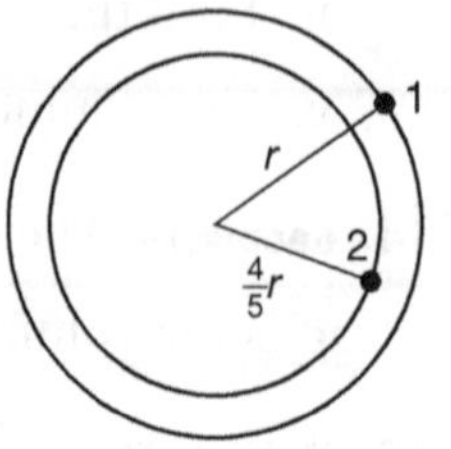

26. (25) **Rainfall** Annual rainfall amounts in inches for Austin, Texas for 2006 are listed in the table below. What was the mean amount of rainfall in Austin during that year and what was the standard deviation?

Month	J	F	M	A	M	J	J	A	S	O	N	D
Amount (in.)	1.80	0.89	7.54	2.89	5.28	3.18	0.48	0.22	3.00	3.93	1.29	4.20

Using the Pythagorean Theorem and the Distance Formula

LESSON 41

*27. **Error Analysis** Find and correct the error a student made in finding the distance between the point (7, 2) and the point (8, −5).
(41)

$$d = \sqrt{(8-7)^2 - (-5-2)^2}$$
$$= \sqrt{1^2 - (-7)^2}$$
$$= \sqrt{1-49}$$
$$= \sqrt{-48}$$

28. **Justify** Is the equation $2\pi x + 3y = 20$ in standard form? Explain your reasoning.
(26)

29. Create a truth table for $s \wedge \neg t$.
(Inv 1)

30. **Coordinate Geometry** Use the set of ordered pairs {(2, 3), (2, 1), (2, 0), (2, 4)}. Is the graph of this relation continuous, discontinuous, and/or discrete?
(22)

Name ______________________ Date __________ Class __________

Finding Permutations and Combinations

LESSON 42

Use multipliers to convert.

1. (18) 32 mi^3 to cubic inches

2. (18) 10 square miles to square feet

Use the point-slope formula to write the equation of the line with slope *m* that passes through the given point.

3. (26) $m = -1$, $(4, 5.5)$

4. (26) $m = 1.8$, $(-10, 0)$

Find the distance between the following points.

*5. (41) $(-2, 2)$ and $(4, 6)$.

*6. (41) $(-3, 2)$ and $(5, 2)$

Evaluate.

*7. (42) $P(5, 3)$

*8. (42) $C(8, 4)$

*9. (42) $11!$

Find the sum.

10. (37) $\frac{1}{x+1} + \frac{1}{x+2} + \frac{1}{x+3}$

11. (37) $\frac{1}{1+\frac{1}{x+1}} + \frac{1}{1+\frac{1}{x-1}}$

12. (24) **Verify** Show that $\begin{matrix} 2x + 3y = 13 \\ 4x - 9y = -79 \end{matrix}$ can be solved by eliminating either the x-terms or the y-terms.

*13. (42) **Dog Show** In a dog show, how many ways can 3 beagles, 2 poodles, and 5 grey hounds line up if the dogs of the same breed are considered identical?

14. (32) **Error Analysis** Given the matrix $A = \begin{bmatrix} 1 & 2 \\ 1 & -3 \end{bmatrix}$, a student found the inverse matrix as follows:

$$A^{-1} = \frac{1}{-5}\begin{bmatrix} -1 & 1 \\ 2 & 3 \end{bmatrix} = \begin{bmatrix} 0.2 & -0.2 \\ -0.4 & -0.6 \end{bmatrix}.$$

What is the error? Find the correct inverse matrix.

15. (11) **Multi-Step** The graph of a polynomial function is continuous. That is, there are no breaks in the graph. The x-intercepts of a function are the x-coordinates of the points at which the graph of the function crosses the x-axis.

a. Complete the table of values for the polynomial function $f(x) = x^3 - 4x - 2$.

x	-2	-1	0	1	2	3
$f(x)$						

b. The function $f(x) = x^3 - 4x - 2$ has three x-intercepts. Between what pair of consecutive integer values of x does each x-intercept lie?

© Saxon. All rights reserved.

*16. (42) **Write** Describe the difference between a permutation and a combination if you select two-letter sets from the three-letter set {A, B, C}.

*17. (30) **Graphing Calculator** Use a graphing calculator to graph $f(x) = -x^2 - 8x - 11$. Explain how the graph differs from the parent function $y = x^2$.

18. (35) **Multiple Choice** What are the x-intercept(s) of the function $f(x) = x^2 + 2x + 1$?
A -1 only **B** 1 only **C** -1 and 1 **D** -1 and -2

*19. (41) **Probability** A teacher writes the numbers shown below on 6 sheets of paper and a student randomly chooses two papers from the hat, without replacement. What is the probability that the two papers chosen show measures that could be the sides of a right triangle?

30, 72, 78	24, 45, 51	12, 18, 20	25, 60, 65	9, 40, 41	14, 50, 54

20. (39) **Analyze** Suppose you test a point that is on the boundary line of the graph of an inequality. What information does the result give about making the graph? What information does it not give about making the graph?

21. (28) **Multiple Choice** Which of the following shows $\frac{3x^2 + 6x + 3}{x^2 - 3x - 4}$ completely simplified?
A $-\frac{1}{4}$ **B** $\frac{1}{x - 4}$ **C** $\frac{3(x + 1)}{x - 4}$ **D** $\frac{(x + 1)^2}{x - 4}$

*22. (41) **Cartography** A cartographer constructs a map of Montana over a grid system such that Hamilton is at (132, 4) and Missoula is at (146, 72). Find the distance between the cities to the nearest kilometer if each unit represents one kilometer.

23. (31) **Multi-Step** If an object is thrown straight down with an initial velocity of 32 feet per second, the number of feet it travels in t seconds is given by the expression $16t^2 + 32t$ (neglecting air resistance).

a. Write a rational expression for the average velocity of the object before it hits the ground over the time interval from 0 seconds to t seconds. Then simplify the expression. (Average velocity equals distance traveled divided by elapsed time.)

b. Evaluate the expression to find the average velocity of the object over the time interval from 0 seconds to 2 seconds.

© Saxon. All rights reserved.

24. (38) **Error Analysis** Two students are dividing $2x^5 - 7x^4 - 4x^3 + 27x^2 - 18x$ by $x + 1$ but get different results. Which student made the mistake?

Student A	Student B
$2x^4 - 9x^3 + 5x^2 + 32x$	$2x^4 - 9x^3 + 5x^2 + 22x$
$(x+1)\overline{)2x^5 - 7x^4 - 4x^3 + 27x^2 - 18x}$	$(x+1)\overline{)2x^5 - 7x^4 - 4x^3 + 27x^2 - 18x}$
$-(2x^5 + 2x^4)$	$-(2x^5 + 2x^4)$
$0 - 9x^4 - 4x^3$	$0 - 9x^4 - 4x^3$
$-(-9x^4 - 9x^3)$	$-(-9x^4 - 9x^3)$
$0 + 5x^3 + 27x^2$	$0 + 5x^3 + 27x^2$
$-(5x^3 + 5x^2)$	$-(5x^3 + 5x^2)$
$0 + 32x^2 - 18x$	$0 + 22x^2 - 18x$
$-(32x^2 + 32x)$	$-(22x^2 + 22x)$
$0 - 50x$	$0 - 40x$

25. (33) **Model** A lunch special includes soup (tomato or chicken noodle), a sandwich (tuna, roast beef, or ham), and a beverage (juice or milk). Draw a tree diagram to show all the different possible lunches. How many different lunches are possible?

26. (29) **Multi-Step** Use

$$y = -5x + 2z - 18$$
$$-6x = 2y - 3z + 23$$
$$z = -10 - 4x + y$$

a. Write the equations with the variables aligned.

b. Estimate the number of solutions. Explain your answer.

c. Solve the system of equations to verify your estimate.

27. (36) **(Physics)** To convert from Fahrenheit to Celsius, use the formula $F = \frac{9}{5}C + 32$. Find the formula to convert Celsius to Fahrenheit and determine if the graphs of the equations are parallel, perpendicular, or neither.

*28. (40) **Multi-Step** **a.** Identify the like radicals in the expression $4\sqrt[3]{5k} - 4\sqrt{5} + \sqrt[3]{4k} + \sqrt{5}$

b. Simplify the expression by combining the like radicals.

29. (34) **Geometry** Give all the names that apply to the polygon that is formed by the graphs of $y = \frac{3}{4}x + 2$, $y = 6$, $y = \frac{3}{4}x - 1$, and $y = 2$.

30. (27) **Model** Make sketches of parabolas to show that there can be zero, one, or two x-intercepts in the graph of a quadratic function.

© Saxon. All rights reserved.

Name ______________________ Date __________ Class __________

Solving Systems of Linear Inequalities

LESSON 43

Factor.

1. (23) $63x^3 + 108x^2 + 81x$

2. (23) $x^{10} - 400$

Determine if there are any excluded values. If so, list them.

3. (28) $\dfrac{10}{5x^2 - 20x - 60}$

4. (28) $\dfrac{4 - x}{3}$

***5.** (43) **Justify** Explain why all solutions of the system below lie in quadrant III.

$$y > \frac{1}{2}x$$
$$y < -2$$

6. (30) **Small Business** The profits, in dollars, for x weeks in one year for a small business can be modeled by the function $y = -0.55(x - 12)^2 + 630$. Does the graph of the function have a maximum or a minimum? What is that value and during what week did it occur?

7. (16) **Analyze** Explain the difficulty you encounter when trying to use Cramer's Rule to solve the system $\begin{array}{l} 4x - 12y = -4 \\ -6x + 18y = -6 \end{array}$

***8.** (43) **Ticket Prices** Two of the ticket prices for a baseball game are $45 for a right field box seat and $90 for a pavilion box seat. Suppose it is the year 2007 and you are a business owner. You decide to buy tickets to give away as prizes to customers. You decide to buy up to 15 tickets and to spend up to $900. Let x represent a number of right field box seats and y represent a number of pavilion box seats.

a. Write and graph a system of linear inequalities that represents the situation.

b. Describe the points in the graph of the system that represent all the possible combinations of right field box seats and pavilion box seats you can buy.

c. Determine the point of intersection of the boundary lines in the graph and explain its meaning.

9. (20) **Tennis** The length of a regulation tennis court is given by the function $f(x) = x + 42$ feet. The width of a regulation tennis court is given by the function $g(x) = x$ feet. Write a function $h(x)$ that represents how many feet longer the court is than it is wide.

***10.** (29) **Graphing Calculator** Use a graphing calculator to solve. $\begin{array}{l} 9z - 7 = 10x + 7y \\ -x - 3 = -8y + 11z \\ z = -2 - x + y \end{array}$

11. (36) **Generalize** Suppose that $y_1 = m_1x + b_1$ is perpendicular to $y_2 = m_2x + b_2$. What must be true for b_1 to equal b_2?

© Saxon. All rights reserved.

*12. **Multiple Choice** Which system has no solution?
(43)

A $y \leq 2x + 2$, $y \geq 2x + 3$ **B** $y \leq 2x + 2$, $y \leq 2x + 3$ **C** $y \geq 2x + 2$, $y \leq 2x + 3$ **D** $y \geq 2x + 2$, $y \geq 2x + 3$

13. **Write** In the difference of 2 squares, explain why the product of the two binomials $(a + b)$ and $(a - b)$ is $a^2 - b^2$.
(23)

Determine whether the given points are solutions of the systems of linear inequalities.

*14. $y + x \leq 6$, $2x - 3y > 12$ (6, 0)
(43)

*15. $10x + 5y \geq 16$, $4x - 6y < 22$ (1, 3)
(43)

16. **Multiple Choice** What are the excluded value(s) for $\frac{x+4}{2x^2 - x - 21}$?
(28)

A -4 **B** -3 **C** -3 and 3.5 **D** $-4, -3$, and 3.5

17. **a.** Show the steps to multiply $\sqrt{12} \cdot \sqrt{24}$ by simplifying each radical first.
(40)

b. Show the steps to multiply $\sqrt{12} \cdot \sqrt{24}$ by multiplying the radicands first.

18. **Justify** Suppose that the graph of $y = ax^2 + bx + c$, for real numbers a, b, and c, does not cross the x-axis. Is there a linear polynomial $x + d$, for real number d, such that $\frac{ax^2 + bx + c}{x + d}$ has a zero remainder? Explain.
(38)

19. **Data Analysis** Students at a high school were asked how they traveled to and from school. The table shows data about the results of the survey. How many students in each grade were surveyed? To find the answer, write a system of equations and use an inverse matrix to solve it.
(32)

	Tenth Graders	Eleventh Graders	Twelfth Graders	Total
Walk	30%	20%	16%	114
School Bus	50%	50%	40%	245
Other	20%	30%	44%	171

*20. **Error Analysis** Find and correct the error a student made in finding the distance between the point at $(-1, 3)$ and the point at $(0, 2)$.
(41)

$$d = \sqrt{(0 - (-1))^2 + (2 - 3)^2}$$
$$= \sqrt{1^2 + (-1)^2}$$
$$= \sqrt{4}$$
$$= 2$$

© Saxon. All rights reserved.

21. (21) **Business School** This table shows the change in rank according to Business Week of two undergraduate business schools from 2006 to 2007. If the rankings continue to change at these constant rates, at what rank will University of Florida and University of Wisconsin be equal?

School	2006	2007	Change
University of Florida	47	43	–4
University of Wisconsin	27	28	+1

State the expanded form.

***22.** (42) 8!

***23.** (42) $\frac{10!}{3!}$

24. (39) **Geometry** Suppose 5 inch by 5 inch squares and 5 inch by 10 inch rectangles are placed end to end to make a long strip that is 5 inches high. Write and graph the inequality that shows how many of each shape can be used if the area of the strip must remain less than 1500 square inches.

25. (31) **Multi-Step** A container manufacturer is comparing a cubic container and a cylindrical container with the dimensions shown.

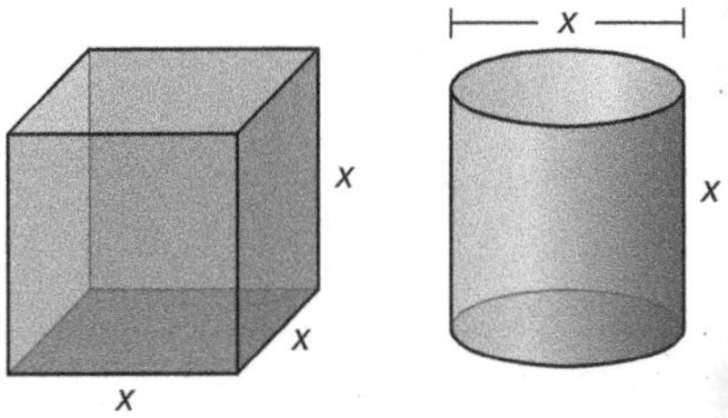

a. Write a rational expression in simplest form for the ratio of surface area to volume for the cubic container.

b. Write a rational expression in simplest form the ratio of surface area to volume for the cylindrical container.

c. Explain the meaning of the results in parts *a* and *b*.

26. (27) **Error Analysis** A student was asked to convert a function written in vertex form to its standard form. The student's work is shown below. Find and correct the error the student made.

$$\begin{aligned} f(x) &= -2(x-4)^2 - 1 \\ &= -2(x^2 - 8x + 16) - 1 \\ &= -2x^2 - 8x + 16 - 1 \\ &= -2x^2 - 8x + 15 \end{aligned}$$

Divide and identify the roots.

27. (38) $15x^3 - 17x^2 - 66x + 56$ by $x + 2$

28. (38) $-8x^3 + 50x^2 - 93x + 45$ by $x - 3$

***29.** (42) **Student Government** There are nine seniors and six juniors running for the class officer positions (President, Secretary, and Treasurer). Each class must elect 3 officers. How many possible outcomes are there for this election? Explain.

© Saxon. All rights reserved.

30. (19) **Multi-Step** The diagram at the right shows the garden in Lucy's backyard.

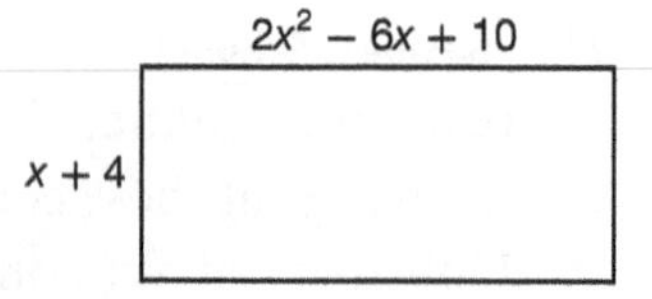

a. Write an expression for the area of the garden.

b. Simplify the expression using multiplication.

c. Find the area of the garden if $x = 4$ feet.

© Saxon. All rights reserved.

Name ______________________ Date ____________ Class ____________

Rationalizing Denominators

LESSON 44

Simplify:

***1.** (44) $\dfrac{5}{3\sqrt{3}}$

***2.** (44) $\dfrac{4}{2+\sqrt{7}}$

***3.** (44) $\sqrt{\dfrac{9}{10}}$

***4.** (41) **Hiking** If the origin represents a campsite, and one hiker hikes 3 units due east and 4 units due south, while a second hiker hikes 5 units due west and 7 units due south, how much further from the campsite is the second hiker hike than the first? Write the answer as a decimal to the nearest tenth of a mile, given that each unit represents 1.5 miles.

5. (24) Solve $\begin{array}{l} 4x = 12 - 5y \\ 24 = 8x + 10y \end{array}$.

***6.** (43) **Error Analysis** The graph at the right is a student's incorrect graph of the system below. What is the error? Graph the system correctly.

$y \geq \dfrac{1}{2}x + 2$

$2x - y \leq 2$

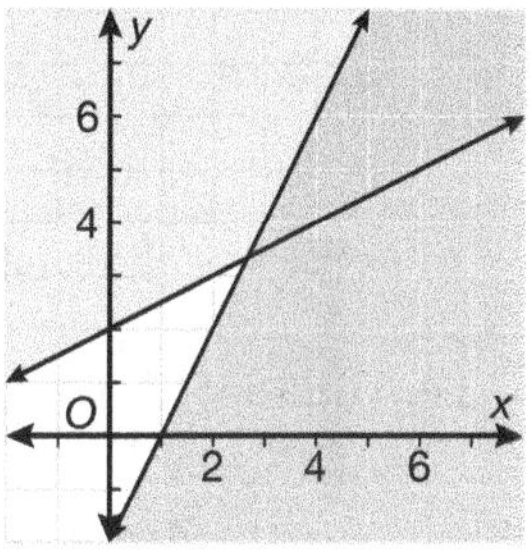

***7.** (Inv 4) Describe a substitution cipher.

***8.** (43) **Justify** Are there more arrangements of 10 items taken 4 at a time with order not important, or 10 items taken 6 at a time with order not important?

***9.** (40) **Physics** The time in seconds it takes for an object to fall from a certain height can be given by $\dfrac{\sqrt{h}}{\sqrt{16}}$ where h is the initial height of the object in feet.

Find how long it takes for a rock to fall from the top of the Hoover Dam which has a height of 726 feet.

***10.** (39) **Multiple Choice** The graph of which inequality is shown?

A $x \leq -2$ **B** $x < -2$

C $y \leq -2$ **D** $y < -2$

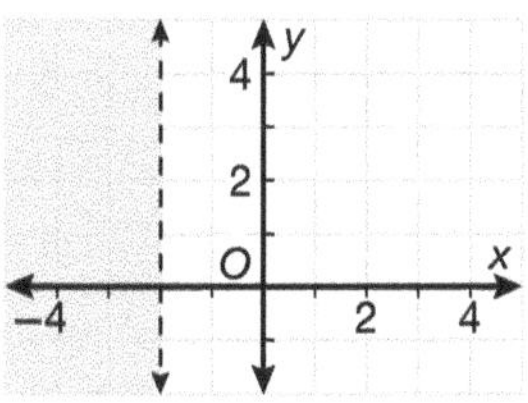

***11.** (38) **Generalize** Suppose the polynomial $ax^2 + bx + c$ has no real roots. Is there a linear factor $x + d$ such that the remainder is zero? Explain.

12. (33) **Geometry** Are the events mutually exclusive? Explain your answer.

a. Draw an obtuse triangle or draw an isosceles triangle.

b. Draw an acute triangle or draw a right triangle.

© Saxon. All rights reserved.

13. **Analyze** Suppose that $y_1 \parallel y_2$, $y_2 \perp y_3$, and $y_3 \perp y_4$. What must be true for y_1 and y_4 to share the same y-intercept?
(36)

14. Factor $x^3y^2z^3 + x^2yz^2 - 3x^3yz$.
(23)

15. Given $f(x) = \frac{x}{x+1}$ and $g(x) = \frac{3}{2x}$, find $g(f(x))$ in simplest form.
(34)

16. **Graphing Calculator** Use a graphing calculator to find the inverse of $A = \begin{bmatrix} 6 & -2 \\ 4 & 12 \end{bmatrix}$.

17. How does the graph of $y = 5x^2$ differ from the graph of $y = x^2$?
(30)

18. **Multi-Step** Use $\begin{aligned} 2x + 3y &= 2z \\ 4x &= -5y + 4z. \\ 3x + 5z &= 2y \end{aligned}$
(29)

a. Write the equations with the variables aligned.

b. Estimate the number of solutions. Explain your answer.

c. Solve the system of equations to verify your estimate.

19. **(Utilities)** A utility cable is hung between two poles that are 150 feet apart. The height of the cable between the two poles can be modeled by $f(x) = 0.0005x^2 + 35$ where x is the distance from the halfway point to either pole. How far up each pole is the cable attached? Round to the nearest tenth of a foot.
(27)

20. Written in standard form, what are the values of a, b, and c in $f(x) = 3x^2$?
(27)

21. **Write** Consider a quadratic function $f(x) = ax^2 + bx + c$ with $a < 0$ and whose vertex is in Quadrant III. How many real zeros does the function have? Explain.
(35)

22. **Error Analysis** Two students used the point-slope form to write the equation of a line with slope 3 that passes through the point (5, 2). One student wrote the equation as $y = 3x - 13$, while the other wrote the equation as $y = 3x - 1$. Which student is correct? What error did the other student make?
(26)

Student A	Student B
$y - 5 = 3(x - 2)$ $y = 3x - 6 + 5$ $y = 3x - 1$	$y - 2 = 3(x - 5)$ $y = 3x - 15 + 2$ $y = 3x - 13$

23. **Measurement** Convert $36x^2 + 72x + 96$ inches to feet.
(23)

24. Factor $16m^2p^3y - 8y^4mp^3 + 4m^2p^2y^2$
(23)

25. The United States Postal Service will mail a letter that is no greater than $2x + 1.5$ inches long and no more than $x + 1$ inches high. The total area of an envelope with the maximum dimensions is approximately 69 in^2. Calculate the approximate maximum dimensions of an envelope that can be mailed through the USPS.
(23)

© Saxon. All rights reserved.

26. Divide $x^4 - 2$ by $x + 1$ and check.
(38)

27. **Write** Assume you have graphed the boundary line for $x + 2y > 6$. Describe two ways to determine which half-plane to shade.
(43)

28. **Multi-Step** If the origin represents a parking lot, and one mountain biker is located at $(6, k)$ and another is located at $(-2, -7)$:
(41)

a. Find two possible values of k if the bikers are 10 units apart.

b. Determine the first biker's coordinates given that his distance from the parking lot is about 6.1 units.

29. **Error Analysis** At an ice cream store, there are five different flavors of frozen yogurt. A customer orders three scoops. One customer says that there could be 60 different variations, and another customer says there could be only 10. Who is correct? Explain your reasoning.
(42)

30. Divide $3x^3 - 3$ by $-x - 2$ and check.
(38)

© Saxon. All rights reserved.

Name ____________________ Date __________ Class __________

Finding the Line of Best Fit

LESSON 45

***1.** (45) **Multi-Step**

x	1	5	2	7	4	8	4	7
y	−75	−20	−32	−31	−44	−16	−64	−39

a. Make a scatter plot of the data set. **b.** Sketch a line of best fit.

c. Give the equation of the line.

***2.** (45) **Graphing Calculator** Use a graphing calculator to find the value of r for the data set below. Tell what this value means.

Weight of Bicycle (lb)	21.1	20.4	38.4	41.3	29.9	29.5	14.2	15.6	26.9
Price of Bicycle ($)	650	710	490	330	650	535	4500	5610	2200

***3.** (43) **Measurement** Find the area of the graph of the system of linear inequalities.

$$y \leq 10 \text{ and } y \geq \frac{3}{4}x + 2 \text{ and } y \geq -\frac{5}{2}x + 15$$

4. (42) **Window Display** A video store wants to display 4 identical DVD movies, 3 identical CDs, and 2 identical hand-held devices. How many distinguishable displays are possible?

5. (41) **Verify** Show that 16 cm, 40 cm, and 43 cm *cannot* be the lengths of the sides of a right triangle.

Simplify.

6. (40) $2\sqrt{27} - 3\sqrt{75}$

7. (40) $3\sqrt{2}\left(2\sqrt{2} - \sqrt{6}\right) \cdot 4\sqrt{3} + 2$

8. (44) $\frac{3}{5\sqrt{12}}$

9. (44) $\frac{14}{3\sqrt{75}}$

10. (44) $\frac{2}{3\sqrt{6}}$

11. (40) **Multiple Choice** Simplify $\sqrt[3]{250}$.

A 10 **B** $\sqrt[3]{10}$ **C** $2\sqrt[3]{5}$ **D** $5\sqrt[3]{2}$

12. (39) **Sightseeing** In 2007, tickets to the Space Needle's Observation Deck in Seattle Washington cost $16 per adult and $8 per child. A group of tourists has up to $200 to spend on tickets. Write and graph an inequality that shows how many of each ticket they could buy. Use the graph to explain whether they could buy 6 adult tickets and 15 children's tickets.

13. (45) **Error Analysis** A student claimed that the correlation coefficient for a set of data was 1.25. Why is the student incorrect?

© Saxon. All rights reserved.

14. (38) **Physics** One of the properties of metals is that they expand in size when heated. The coefficient of thermal expansion is an indication of how a particular metal increases in size. A metal cube is heated. The cube has side lengths, x. After heating, the linear dimensions of the cube increase by a value of a. What is the ratio of the new volume to the original volume?

15. (40) **Generalize** When do roots of negative numbers exist and when are they undefined?

16. (28) **Geography** On a map, a square is drawn around Washington DC. Write the perimeter to area ratio of the square as a simplified rational expression. Then find the ratio given that the length of each side of the square is 10 miles long.

17. (37) **Write** Can a rational number be a rational expression? Can a rational expression be a rational number? Explain.

Expand.

18. (19) $(x - 1)^3$

19. (19) $(x + 5)^3$

20. (36) Which is the equation of the line parallel to $y = -5x + 7$ that crosses the origin?

A $y = -5x$ B $y = -\frac{1}{5}x + 7$ C $y = 5x$ D $y = \frac{1}{5}x + 7$

21. (35) **Error Analysis** A student solved the equation $4x^2 - 20x + 25 = 0$ as shown below.

$$4x^2 - 20x + 25 = 0$$
$$(2x + 5)(2x - 5) = 0$$
$$2x + 5 = 0 \quad \text{or} \quad 2x - 5 = 0$$
$$2x = -5 \quad \text{or} \quad 2x = 5$$
$$x = -\frac{5}{2} \quad \text{or} \quad x = \frac{5}{2}$$

What is the error? Solve the equation correctly.

22. (34) **Temperature** The function $C = \frac{5}{9}(F - 32)$ describes the relationship between Celsius temperature and Fahrenheit temperature. Write the function in point-slope form. Graph the function, state the rate of change, and describe what it means.

23. (33) **Analyze** These characters are written on 10 index cards, a different character on each card: A, B, C, D, E, 1, 2, 3, 4, and 5. A letter card is chosen and then a number card is chosen. How many outcomes are in the event *choose a vowel and then choose an odd number*? List all those outcomes.

24. (31) **Geometry** An isosceles right triangle is inscribed in a circle as shown. Its hypotenuse is the diameter of the circle. Write the ratio of the area of the circle to the area of the right triangle in simplest form.

© Saxon. All rights reserved.

25. *(32)* **Write** Describe how to determine whether two matrices are inverses.

Solve.

26. *(35)* $-x + x^2 = 12$

27. *(35)* $-48x = -2x^2 - x^3$

28. *(27)* Write a quadratic function in vertex form where $a = -1$, $h = -2$, and $k = 3$.

Add.

29. *(37)* $\frac{4x}{x + 4} + \frac{6}{x + 2}$

30. *(37)* $\frac{3m}{m^2 + 3m + 2} - \frac{5m}{m + 1}$

© Saxon. All rights reserved.

Name ______________________ Date __________ Class __________

Finding Trigonometric Functions and their Reciprocals

LESSON 46

For each equation and point, find the equation of the lines that are parallel and perpendicular to the line, and that pass through the point.

1. (36) $y = 3x - 6$; $(3, 4)$

2. (36) $y = -2x + 8$; $(-7, 0)$

Convert:

3. (20) 1800 seconds to hours.

4. (20) 16 yd^2 to in^2.

5. (30) Write the vertex form of a quadratic equation if the parent function is shifted 5 units right.

Use the right triangle to find the value of the following trigonometric functions:

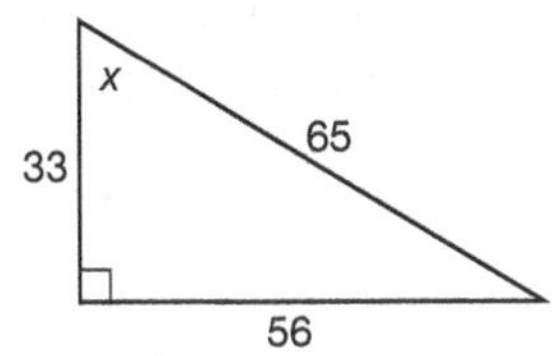

***6.** (46) $\tan(x)$

***7.** (46) $\csc(x)$

Factor the expressions:

8. (23) $-12x^4 - 18x^2 - 6$

9. (23) $x^2 - 28x + 196$

Write the equation of the line with slope *m* that passes through the point, in slope-intercept form.

10. (26) $m = -8, (-2, 9)$

11. (26) $m = \frac{4}{9}, (6, 3)$

***12.** (46) **Multiple Choice** What is the value of the cosecant of $\angle M$?

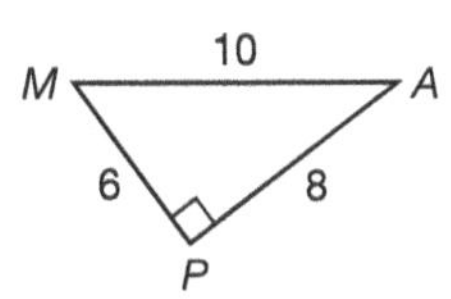

A 0.6
B 0.8
C 1.25
D $1.\overline{7}$

***13.** (16) **Coordinate Geometry** Use Cramer's Rule to find the intersection of the lines with equations $9x + 3y = 21$ and $2x - 2y = 2$.

14. (35) **Gravity** The height of a free-falling object (neglecting air resistance) is given by the function $h(t) = -16t^2 + v_0t + h_0$, where h_0 is the initial height in feet, v_0 is the initial velocity in feet per second, and $h(t)$ is the height in feet at t seconds. An object is dropped from a height of 56 feet. How long does it take for the object to reach a height of 20 feet? (Hint: The initial velocity of a dropped object is zero.)

15. (43) **Analyze** What ordered pair of integers in the solution set of the system below has the least sum? Explain your answer.

$$y < \frac{3}{4}x - 3$$

$$y > \frac{1}{3}x + 4$$

© Saxon. All rights reserved.

*16. **Multi-Step** The graph compares students' quiz and test grades.
(45)

a. Write an equation for the line of best fit.

b. Describe the slope in terms of the data.

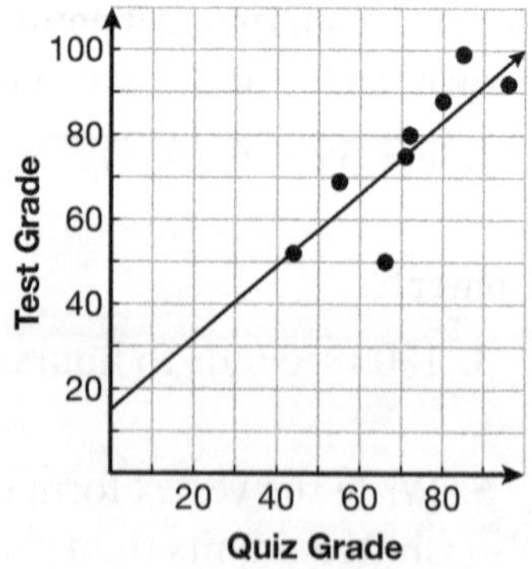

17. **Error Analysis** Find and correct the error made below where a student was determining if (4, −8) was a solution to $2y + 3 \leq -4x$.
(39)

$2(4) + 3 \overset{?}{\leq} -4(-8)$

$8 + 3 \overset{?}{\leq} 32$

$11 \leq 32$ True, (4, −8) is a solution.

18. **Multiple Choice** Circle the letter that represents the complete factorization of $x^2 - 9x - 36$.
(23)

A $(x + 6)(x - 6)$ **B** $(x + 4)(x - 9)$

C $(x + 3)(x - 12)$ **D** $(x + 2)(x - 18)$

19. **(Density)** The side length of a metal cube, in centimeters, is given by $\frac{\sqrt[3]{m}}{\sqrt[3]{p}}$, where m is its mass in grams and p is its density.
(40)

a. Write the expression in simplified form.

b. Approximate the side length of a 1000 gram cube of nickel given that the density of nickel is 88 g/cm^3.

*20. **Justify** Why does a table showing number of feet and the corresponding number of inches have a correlation of 1?
(45)

21. **(Baseball)** There are 5 teams in the American League East division of professional baseball. How many ways can teams finish in first and second place?
(33)

22. **(Physics)** Through the process of annealing, metals are made more flexible, allowing a piece of metal to be flattened without breaking. Suppose a rectangular piece of metal with square ends goes through the annealing process and is flattened into a thin sheet. What is the ratio of the new surface area to the original? Does the quotient have a zero remainder? Explain.
(38)

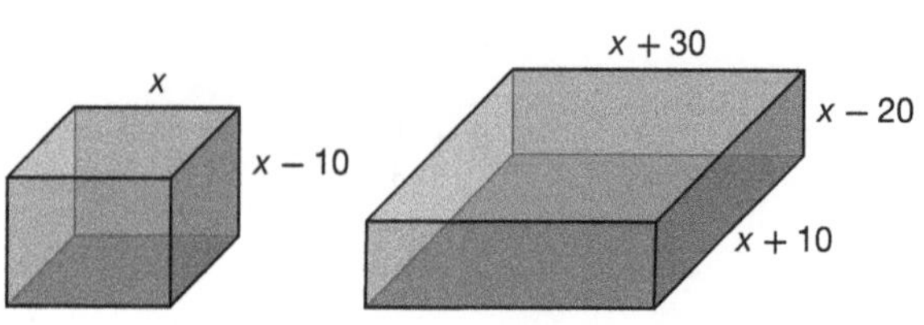

23. (41) **Cartography** A cartographer constructs a map of North Dakota over a grid system such that Bismarck is at (225, 87) and Minot is at (192, 232). Find the distance between the cities to the nearest kilometer if each unit represents one kilometer.

***24.** (32) **Graphing Calculator** If $A = \begin{bmatrix} 2 & 4 \\ 6 & 8 \end{bmatrix}$ and $B = \begin{bmatrix} 10 & 12 \\ 14 & 16 \end{bmatrix}$, use a graphing calculator to find $AX = B$.

***25.** (46) **Write** How are the sine and cosine functions alike? How are they different?

26. (27) **Error Analysis** A student was asked to convert a function written in vertex form to its standard form. The student's work is shown below. Find and correct the error the student made.

$$\begin{aligned} f(x) &= -(x+3)^2 + 14 \\ &= -(x^2 + 9) + 14 \\ &= -x^2 - 9 + 14 \\ &= -x^2 + 5 \end{aligned}$$

27. (42) **Chess Tournament** Ten people enter a chess tournament. How many ways can matches be determined for the first round?

28. (36) **Formulate** A staircase needs to be built that crosses a horizontal distance of 10 feet and a vertical distance of 15 feet. Write an equation of a line that could model the handrail that is 3 feet above the stairs.

***29.** (46) **Sports** A baseball diamond is shaped like a square that is 90 feet on each side. A line drawn from second base to home plate forms a right triangle with acute angles measuring 45°.

a. Show how to use a trigonometric function to find the distance from second base to home base to the nearest tenth of a foot.

b. Check your answer to part a by using the Pythagorean Theorem.

30. (37) **Geometry** What is the ratio of the area of the shaded region to that of the unshaded region in the square to the right?

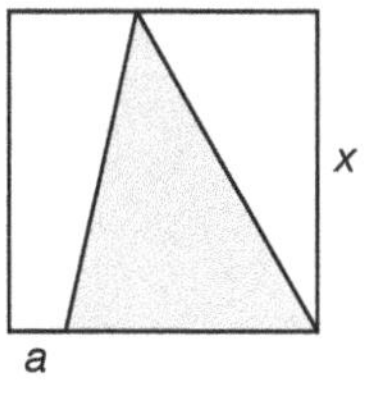

© Saxon. All rights reserved.

Name ______________________ Date __________ Class __________

Graphing Exponential Functions

LESSON 47

1. (19) **Probability** The local amusement park has a dart game where you win a prize if you can throw a dart into the shaded area of a rectangle. The probability of getting a dart to land in the shaded area is $\frac{\text{area of the shaded area}}{\text{total area of the rectangle}}$. Write an expression that represents the probability of winning a prize for the dart game.

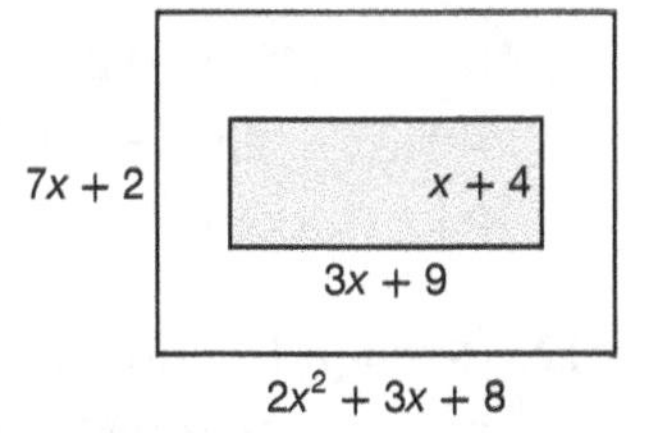

2. (38) **Multiple Choice** Which of the following is the remainder when dividing $3x^3 - 16x^2 + 12x + 16$ by $(x + 1)$?

A -16 **B** -15 **C** 0 **D** 15

3. (27) **Generalize** If the x-intercepts of a quadratic function are x_1 and x_2, give a general equation for the x-coordinate of the vertex.

***4.** (47) **Graphing Calculator** Graph the functions $y_1 = 2.3^x$, $y_2 = \frac{1}{6}(2.3)^x$ and $y_3 = -\frac{1}{6}(2.3)^x$ on a calculator.

Add:

5. (37) $\frac{5x^2}{pm} - 4 + \frac{c}{p^2m}$

6. (37) $3xy^2m + \frac{4}{x}$

7. (23) **Running** The expression representing a runner's speed is $120x^2 - 60x - 240$ feet per minute. Find the expression for the runner's speed in feet per second.

***8.** (43) **Multi-Step** A college student earns \$10 per hour working in the library and \$15 per hour on a landscaping crew. He decides to work not more than 20 hours in a week, and his goal is to earn at least \$240 in a week. Let x represent a number of hours working in the library and y represent a number of hours working on the landscaping crew.

a. Write and graph a system of linear inequalities that represents the situation.

b. Describe the portion of the solution set that contains meaningful solutions for this situation.

c. Determine the vertices of the polygon you described in part b. Describe what each vertex represents.

***9.** (39) **Formulate** Write a list of rules describing which half-plane to shade and what type of line to use (dashed or solid) based on the inequality symbol in an inequality.

10. (35) **Gravity** The height of a free-falling object (neglecting air resistance) is given by the function $h(t) = -16t^2 + v_0t + h_0$, where h_0 is the initial height in feet, v_0 is the initial velocity in feet per second, and $h(t)$ is the height in feet at time t seconds. How long does it take for an object to hit the ground after it is thrown straight up at a speed of 36 feet per second from a height of 52 feet?

© Saxon. All rights reserved.

11. Graph the system below. Describe the shape that the lines form.
(15)

$0.9x - 1.5y = 0.21$

$-1.2x + 2.0y = -0.28$

$0.6x - y = 0.14$

***12.** **Savings** London deposited $3000 into a savings account when she got her first job after graduating from college. How much will be in her account when she finishes graduate school in 2 years if the account earns 8.3% compounded daily?
(47)

Determine whether the ordered triples are solutions of the systems.

13. Is (2, −5, 3) a solution of the system $\begin{array}{l} 4x + 3y + 5z = 8 \\ -6x + 3y + 7z = -6 \\ 8x + y - 2z = 5 \end{array}$?
(29)

14. Is (0, 1, 2) a solution of the system $\begin{array}{l} 10x + 9y + 6z = 21 \\ -x + 4y - 7z = -10 \\ -9x + 5y + 2z = 9 \end{array}$?
(29)

***15.** **Write** Explain why multiplying a radical denominator by its radical conjugate eliminates the radical from the denominator.
(44)

16. **Analyze** Explain the difficulty you encounter when trying to use Cramer's Rule to solve the system $\begin{array}{l} 4x - 12y = -4 \\ -6x + 18y = -6 \end{array}$
(16)

17. **Verify** Show that 30 cm, 72 cm, and 78 cm can be the lengths of the sides of a right triangle.
(41)

***18.** **Depreciation** The table shows the trade-in value for seven cars in good condition with typical mileage and standard equipment. Make a scatter plot of the data, using the number of years before and after 2000 on the x-axis. Sketch a line of best fit.
(45)

	A	B	C	D	E	F	G
Year	1987	1992	1996	1999	2002	2005	2007
Value ($)	450	650	1950	2050	3435	4265	8610

19. **Error Analysis** A student submitted the work below and reported that $\sqrt{8} \cdot \sqrt{6}$ simplifies to $2\sqrt{12}$. Explain her error.
(40)

$\sqrt{8} \cdot \sqrt{6} = \sqrt{4} \cdot \sqrt{2} \cdot \sqrt{6} = 2\sqrt{2}\sqrt{6} = 2\sqrt{12}$

20. **Geometry** Write a rational expression in simplest form for the ratio of the triangle's perimeter to its area.
(31)

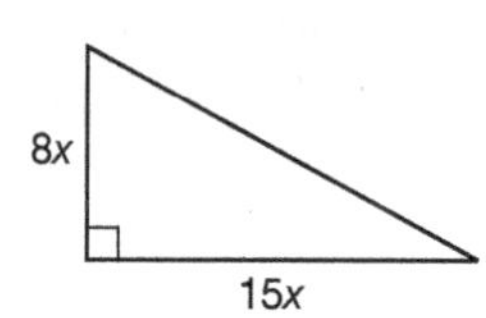

© Saxon. All rights reserved.

21. (36) **Economics** The exchange rate from dollars to different currencies is shown. A company charges a fee of \$2.50 for amounts up to \$50 and \$7.50 for amounts above \$50. Write the equations for exchanging British pounds to dollars. What do the graphs of the equations have in common?

Currency	US $
1 Euro =	1.377
1 Canadian dollar =	0.9472
1 British pound =	2.0284

22. (13) **Error Analysis** A student incorrectly graphed the equation $x = -2$ as shown. What equation does the graph represent? Explain how you know.

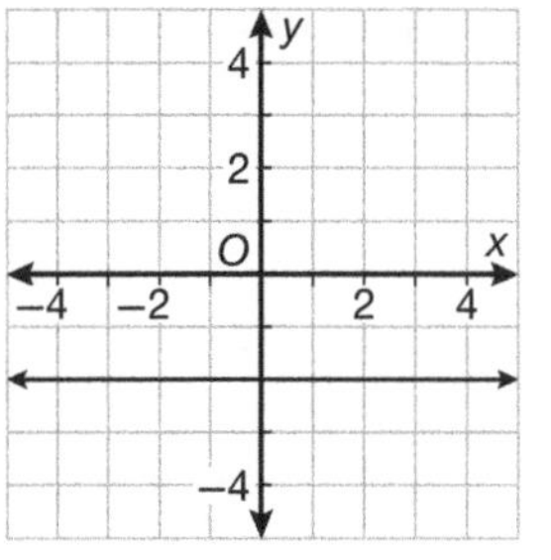

23. (28) **Multi-Step** Consider the expression $\frac{3x-6}{2}$.

a. Is the expression simplified? Tell why or why not.

b. Are there any excluded values? Explain.

***24.** (46) **Tourism** The angle of elevation from a tourist on the beach in Cape May, New Jersey to the top of the lighthouse is 38°. The lighthouse has a height of 158 feet. To the nearest foot, how far away is the tourist from the base of the lighthouse?

25. (15) Graph the system below. Describe the shape that the lines form.

$$4x - 2y = 2$$
$$-6x - 3y = 3$$
$$x - 2y = 6$$

26. (42) **Multiple Choice** How many different committees of three people can be formed from a group of 15?

A 455 **B** 910 **C** 1365 **D** 2370

Write the distance from each point to the origin as an absolute value expression. Then simplify the expression.

27. (17) (5, 0) **28.** (17) (−7, 0) **29.** (17) (0, 9)

***30.** (44) Which of the following shows the simplified radical expression for $\frac{4\sqrt{7}-2}{5\sqrt{7}+3}$?

A $\frac{73 - 11\sqrt{7}}{83}$ **B** $\frac{54}{83}$ **C** $\frac{134 + 22\sqrt{7}}{184}$ **D** $\frac{108}{146 + 19\sqrt{7}}$

© Saxon. All rights reserved.

Name ______________________ Date __________ Class __________

Understanding Complex Fractions

LESSON 48

Simplify:

***1.** (48) $\dfrac{\dfrac{x}{m+p}}{\dfrac{y}{m+p}}$

***2.** (48) $\dfrac{x+\dfrac{4xy}{x}}{\dfrac{1}{x}-y}$

***3.** (48) $\dfrac{\dfrac{m}{p}+\dfrac{3}{xp}}{\dfrac{y}{p}}$

4. (20) **Basketball** The length of a regulation NCAA basketball court is given by the function $f(x) = x + 24$ feet. The width of a regulation NCAA basketball court is given by the function $g(x) = 2x - 90$ feet. Write a function $h(x)$ that represents how many feet longer the court is than it is wide.

5. (Inv 2) **Airplane Altitude** A plane's altitude increases at a rate of 40 ft/s as it ascends after takeoff. Its ground distance from the airport is increasing at a rate of 240 ft/s. What is the location of the plane 20 seconds after takeoff?

6. (36) **Justify** Is the triangle defined by vertices $(-3, 6)$, $(4, 4)$, and $(1, -8)$ a right triangle? Explain your answer.

7. (44) **Geometry** The area of a rectangular garden is 30 ft^2. The width of the garden is $(\sqrt{3} + 1)$ ft. Find a simplified expression for the length of the garden.

Use the description to write the vertex form of a quadratic equation.

8. (30) The parent function is shifted 5 units right.

9. (30) The parent function is shifted 2 units to the left and 7 units up.

10. (40) **Write** Explain why absolute value symbols are used in the following sentence. For any real number x, $\sqrt{x^2} = |x|$.

11. (22) **Data Analysis** A store records the number of video games sold each month. Examine the table. Does this table represent a continuous, discontinuous, and/or discrete function? Justify your answer.

Month	Games Sold
1	10
2	8
3	9
4	20

***12.** (42) **Verify** If you have 5 digits that can be arranged in any order, then specify that one digit must be in the second position; verify that the number of arrangements of the other four digits must be 4!

13. (25) **Error Analysis** A chemist weighs samples obtained from a production run. The weights of the samples are 12 g, 14 g, 65 g, 11 g, 15 g, 14 g, 14 g, 12 g, 13 g, 15 g, 14 g, and 11 g. He eliminated the outlier and drew a box-and-whisker plot to represent the data. What is his error?

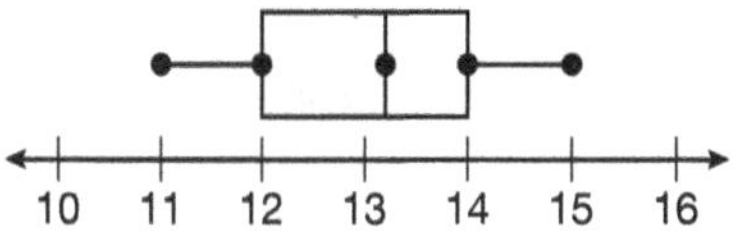

© Saxon. All rights reserved.

*14. (48) Simplify $\dfrac{\frac{5}{2x} - \frac{2}{x+5}}{\frac{1}{2(x+5)} + \frac{1}{x}}$.

15. (27) **Formulate** a. Use a table to graph $f(x) = (x - 2)^2 + 6$.

b. Compare the graph to its function. Formulate a conjecture about how you can find the vertex of a parabola based on its related function given in vertex form.

Simplify:

16. (40) $5\sqrt{18} - 10\sqrt{50} + 3\sqrt{72}$

17. (40) $3\sqrt{18}\left(4\sqrt{2} - 2\sqrt{3}\right)$

18. (40) $2\sqrt{\frac{2}{9}} - 3\sqrt{\frac{9}{2}}$

19. (40) $-3\sqrt{\frac{2}{3}} + 2\sqrt{\frac{3}{2}}$

20. (40) $3\sqrt{24}\left(2\sqrt{6} - 3\sqrt{12}\right)$

21. (30) **Multi-Step** a. Graph the function $y = (x - 5)^2 + 1$.

b. On the same graph, sketch the reflection of the parabola across the x-axis.

c. Give the equation of the function represented by the reflected parabola.

22. (24) **Multiple Choice** To solve by elimination, which linear system will require that both equations first be multiplied by a constant before the equations are added?

A $\begin{matrix} 4x - 4y = 0 \\ -4x + 6y = 2 \end{matrix}$ **B** $\begin{matrix} 4x - 4y = 0 \\ 4x + 5y = 9 \end{matrix}$ **C** $\begin{matrix} 4x - 4y = 0 \\ -\frac{1}{4}x + \frac{5}{4}y = 1 \end{matrix}$ **D** $\begin{matrix} 4x - 4y = 0 \\ 3x + 5y = 8 \end{matrix}$

23. (37) **Error Analysis** Two students are adding the rational expressions $\frac{1}{x+3}$ and $\frac{1}{x-3}$ but get different results. Which student made the mistake?

Student A	Student B
$\frac{1}{x+3} + \frac{1}{x-3} = \frac{x-3}{(x+3)(x-3)} + \frac{x-3}{(x-3)(x+3)} = \frac{2x-6}{x^2-9}$	$\frac{1}{x+3} + \frac{1}{x-3} = \frac{x-3}{(x+3)(x-3)} + \frac{x+3}{(x-3)(x+3)} = \frac{2x}{x^2-9}$

*24. (47) **Write** Describe the transformations you need to make to the graph of $y = \left(\frac{1}{5}\right)^x + 3$ to get the graph of $y = 5^x + 1$.

*25. (15) **Graphing Calculator** Solve the system of equations using a graphing calculator.

$$5x + y = 15$$
$$2y = 5 + 10x$$

© Saxon. All rights reserved.

***26.** (48) **Verify** Simplify the expression on the left side of the equation; verify that it is equal to the right side.

$$\frac{\frac{4}{x+2} - \frac{2}{x+3}}{\frac{2}{x+3}} = \frac{x+4}{x+2}$$

27. (39) **Money** Dejah is collecting pennies and nickels for a charity event. She's going to continue until her collection of coins weighs at least 2 kilograms. Every penny weighs 2.5 grams and every nickel weighs 5 grams. Write and graph an inequality that represents how many of each coin are needed.

28. (18) **Swimming** In order to qualify for the 2008 Olympic Swim Team, a male swimmer must swim the 100-meter freestyle in under 51.59 seconds.

a. What is this time in feet per second? (Hint:1 meter = 3.2808399 feet)

b. If a male swimmer swims the 100-meter freestyle in 48.62 seconds, what is his time in feet per second?

***29.** (47) **Compound Interest** Ann deposits \$2,800 in a savings account. How much will be in her account in 3 years if the account earns 4% compounded annually? If it is compounded semi-annually?

30. (41) **Write** When using the Pythagorean Theorem to find a missing side of a right triangle, how is finding the length of a leg different from finding the length of the hypotenuse?

© Saxon. All rights reserved.

Name ______________________ Date __________ Class __________

Using the Binomial Theorem

LESSON 49

Simplify.

1. (23) $\dfrac{4xy + 4x^2y^2}{4xy}$

2. (23) $p^5x^3 + p^4x^2 - p^3x$

***3.** (48) $\dfrac{ax^2 - \dfrac{4}{a}}{\dfrac{x^2}{a} + 6}$

***4.** (48) $\dfrac{\dfrac{m^2p}{x} - 6}{m^2p - \dfrac{4}{x}}$

5. (40) $6\sqrt{18} + 5\sqrt{8} - 3\sqrt{50}$

6. (40) $2\sqrt{5}(3\sqrt{15} - 2\sqrt{5})$

7. (24) Solve by using either substitution or elimination. $3x - 2y = 10$, $y = -\dfrac{1}{2}$

Expand.

***8.** (49) $(b - 2)^4$

***9.** (49) $(2x + y)^6$

10. (36) Find the equation of the line that passes through (2, 4) and is perpendicular to the line that passes through the points (2, 4) and (−3, −2).

11. (31) **Analyze** Given the functions $f(x) = \frac{2x - 2}{x}$ and $g(x) = \frac{x^2 + 3x}{x - 1}$, describe the graph of the product function $f(x) \cdot g(x)$. Include points of discontinuity in the description. (Note: If a function is undefined at some value of x, then there is a point of discontinuity in the function graph at that value of x.)

***12.** (49) **Baseball** A baseball player has a batting average of 0.32 (32 hits in 100 times at bat). Find each probability for the next 4 times at bat.

a. P(exactly 2 hits) **b.** P(at least 1 hit)

13. (45) **Multi-Step**

x	0	1	3	3	4	5	5	6	7	7	7
y	8	11	5	8	6	3	7	5	7	3	1

a. Make a scatter plot of the data

b. Sketch the line of best fit and write its equation.

c. Estimate the value of r.

14. (22) **Data Analysis** A customer visits the post office to weigh a package. The cost of mailing a package depends on its weight. Examine the table below. Does this table represent a continuous, discontinuous, or discrete function? Justify your answer.

Weight	Cost
$0 \le x < 5$	\$2.00
$5 \le x < 10$	\$4.00
$10 \le x < 15$	\$6.00
$15 \le x < 20$	\$8.00
$20 \le x < 25$	\$10.00

© Saxon. All rights reserved.

15. (43) **Ticket Prices** Two of the ticket prices for a 2007 baseball game were: $27 for an outfield grandstand seat and $45 for a right field box seat. Suppose you are an automobile dealer. You decide to buy tickets to give away during a sale. You decide to buy up to 24 tickets and to spend up to $720. Let x represent a number of outfield grandstand seats and y represent a number of right field box seats.

a. Write and graph a system of linear inequalities that represents the situation.

b. Describe the points in the graph of the system that represent all the possible combinations of outfield grandstand seats and right field box seats you can buy.

c. Determine the point of intersection of the boundary lines in the graph and explain its meaning.

16. (41) **Multiple Choice** Which could be the sides of a right triangle?
A 21, 72, and 75 **B** 30, 35, and 45 **C** 35, 58, and 48 **D** 41, 82, and 90

17. (17) **Health** An adult is considered to be in a healthy weight range if his or her BMI (Body Mass Index) is within 3.2 of 21.7. Write an absolute value equation to determine the minimum and maximum BMI that is considered healthy. And then solve the equation.

*18. (49) **Write** Describe how to expand the binomial $(y + z)^5$ using Pascal's Triangle.

19. (25) **Geometry** The table below shows the measurements in inches of various shipping boxes available from the United States Postal Service.

Box	Measurement 1	Measurement 2	Measurement 3
1	11.875	3.375	13.625
2	11	8.5	5.5
3	7.5	5.125	14.375

a. What is the range of volumes?

b. If you had to choose from these boxes to ship something, how could the range of volumes be useful?

20. (42) **Lottery** A lottery game contains 24 numbers. In order to win, four numbers must be chosen that match the winning numbers. If the winning numbers are selected one at a time and not replaced, how many possible ways are there for the winning numbers to be determined?

21. (30) **Estimate** The graphs of the parent quadratic function and a second function are shown. Use the graph to estimate the value of a for the equation of the second function.

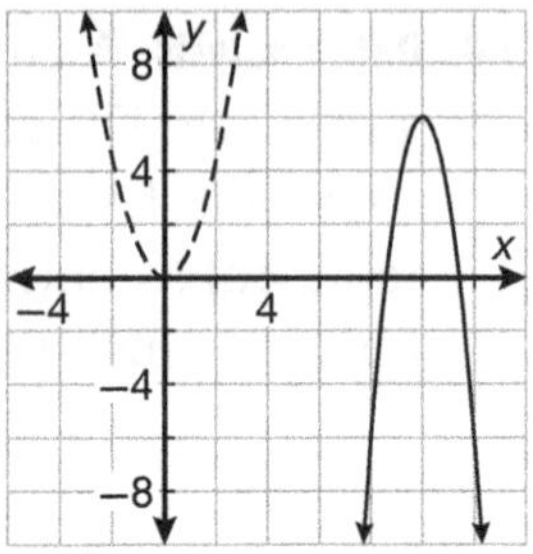

© Saxon. All rights reserved.

22. **Error Analysis** A student worked out the problem below using radical conjugates. Is the procedure correct? If not, identify and correct the error. Simplify: $\frac{2\sqrt{2}+6}{3\sqrt{2}+\sqrt{5}}$.
(44)

Student work: $\frac{2\sqrt{2}+6}{3\sqrt{2}+\sqrt{5}} \cdot \frac{2\sqrt{2}-6}{3\sqrt{2}-\sqrt{5}} = \frac{8-36}{18-5} = -\frac{28}{13}$

23. **Multi-Step** The speed of an object at time t is based on its initial speed (v_o) and its acceleration (a): $v = v_o + at$.
(36)

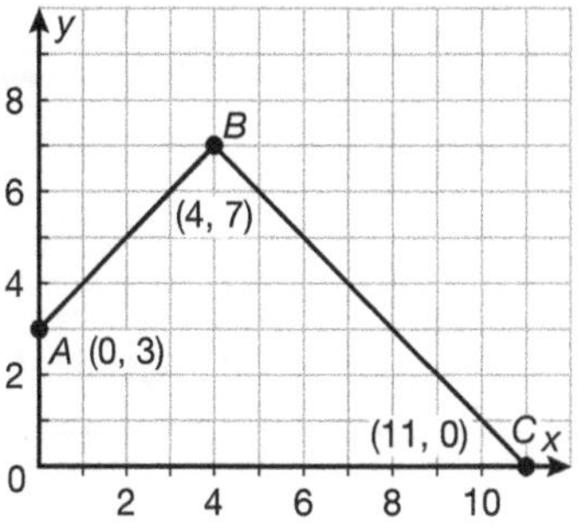

a. Find the equations of the lines from A to B and B to C and describe the motion of the object.

b. What is the relationship between the equations of motion?

24. **Architecture** The Petronas Towers in Malaysia are two twin towers joined by a sky bridge that is 192 feet long and 558 feet above the ground. The angle of elevation from either end of the sky bridge to the top of the opposite tower is about 78.27°. Find the height of the towers to the nearest foot.
(46)

25. **Verify** Prove that $2x - 7 = -(7 - 2x)$. Supply a reason for every step.
(28)

*26. **Graphing Calculator** Graph $y = \sqrt[3]{x}$ and $y = \sqrt[4]{x}$ on a graphing calculator. (Use the equivalent equations of $y = x^{\frac{1}{3}}$ and $y = x^{\frac{1}{4}}$.) How do the graphs confirm the differences in rules for $\sqrt[n]{b}$ as far as n being odd or even?
(40)

*27. **Multiple Choice** What is the fifth term of the expansion of $(y - 3)^8$?
(49)

A $-13{,}608y^3$ **B** $5670y^4$ **C** $1890y^5$ **D** $1458y^6$

*28. **Multi-Step** Use the formula $r = \frac{d}{t}$ relating rate, distance, and time. A car traveled a distance of $3x + 60$ miles in 2 hours. A second car traveled $2x + 40$ miles in 3 hours.
(48)

a. Write a rational expression to represent the ratio of the rate of the first car to the rate of the second car.

b. Simplify the rational expression. What does this expression tell you about the rates of the two cars?

29. **Error Analysis** Explain the error(s) the student made when graphing $-4 > y$.
(39)

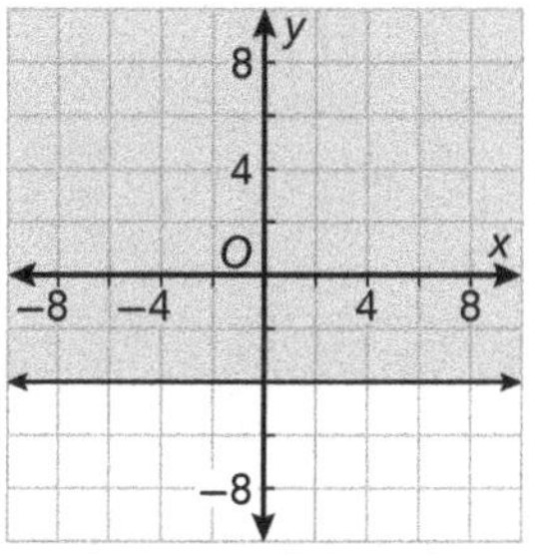

*30. **Multiple Choice** Which of the following equations does **not** represent an exponential function?
(47)

A $y = -3^x$ **B** $y = x^3$ **C** $y = \left(\frac{1}{3}\right)^x$ **D** $y = 3^{-x}$

© Saxon. All rights reserved.

Name ______________________ Date __________ Class __________

Finding Inverses of Relations and Functions

LESSON 50

Multiply:

1. (19) $(3x^3 - 2x)(2x^2 - x - 4)$

2. (19) $(4x + 2)(x^3 - 2x + 4)$

Write the equation in standard form for the line that crosses the two points.

3. (26) $(-3, 0), (-5, 1)$

4. (26) $(-7, 9), (-10, 11)$

Expand:

***5.** (49) $(2 - m)^7$

***6.** (49) $(3g + 2h)^3$

Find the inverse of each linear function.

***7.** (50) $y = 3x^2 - 1$

***8.** (50) $y = \sqrt{x}$

***9.** (50) $y = \frac{1}{2}x + 6$

***10.** (45) **Graphing Calculator** The table shows the category and amount of damage to the United States from seven hurricanes that hit the US after the year 2000. Use a graphing calculator to find the value of r for the data set. Tell what this value means.

	Wilma	Charley	Ivan	Rita	Isabel	Lili	Francis
Category	3	4	3	3	2	1	2
Damage to US ($, billions)	20.6	15	14.2	11.3	3.37	0.86	8.9

11. (31) **Velocity** The velocity of a certain automobile during the first 40 seconds starting from rest is approximated by the rational function $f(t) = \frac{90t}{t+6}$, where t is the number of elapsed seconds and $f(t)$ is velocity in feet per second.

Write a division expression for the average acceleration of the automobile over the time interval from 0 seconds to t seconds. Then simplify the expression. (Average acceleration equals change in velocity divided by elapsed time.)

***12.** (49) **Probability** You have a fifty-fifty chance of correctly guessing each answer on a test. Suppose you guess at 10 true/false questions. Find the probability that you will get exactly 4 questions correct.

13. (17) **Multiple Choice** Solve $|2x + 1| < 4$.

A $-\frac{5}{2} < x < \frac{3}{2}$

B $\frac{3}{2} < x < -\frac{5}{2}$

C $x < -\frac{5}{2}$ or $x > \frac{3}{2}$

D $x < \frac{3}{2}$

14. (42) **Error Analysis** In selecting five items out of ten, a student says there would be ten times more permutations than combinations. Is the student correct? If not provide the correct answer.

© Saxon. All rights reserved.

15. (25) **Model** The table below shows the measurements in inches of various shipping boxes available from the United States Postal Service. Draw a box-and-whisker plot to represent the approximate areas of all sides of the boxes. Consider that a box has 6 faces.

Box	Measurement 1	Measurement 2	Measurement 3
1	11.875	3.375	13.625
2	11	8.5	5.5
3	7.5	5.125	14.375

16. (30) **Multi-Step** The graph of a quadratic function has a vertex $(2, -3)$ and passes through the point $(5, -12)$. Give the equation of the function. Tell if the function has a maximum or minimum.

17. (17) **Grizzly Bears** The table shows amounts of three foods that a 200-lb grizzly bear can eat in a day.

Type	Amount (lbs)
Deer	24
Salmon	30
Vegetation	67

a. Write an inequality to show the amounts of these foods that a 200-lb grizzly bear can eat in a day.

b. Verify that your answer is equivalent to the absolute value inequality $|f - 45.5| \le 21.5$.

18. (40) **Multiple Choice** Which number has two fourth roots?

A -27 **B** 4 **C** 16 **D** 125

19. (27) **Geometry** **a.** Write a quadratic equation in standard form to represent the area of the shaded region.

b. Identify the values of a, b, and c in the equation in part a.

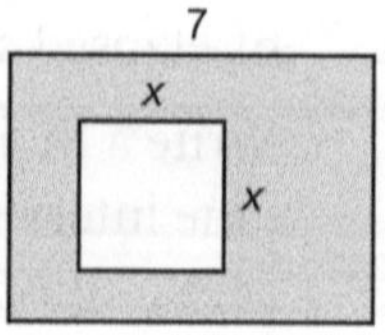

20. (19) **Error Analysis** Two students completed the problem $(x - 8)(x + 8)$. Who is correct? Explain your answer.

Student A	Student B
$= x^2 + 8x + 8x - 64$	$= x^2 + 8x - 8x - 64$
$= x^2 + 16x - 64$	$= x^2 - 64$

21. (43) **Justify** Explain why the system $\begin{matrix} y > 3x + 1 \\ y < 3x - 1 \end{matrix}$ has no solution.

22. (20) **Births** From 1990 to 1999, the number of births $b(x)$ in the U.S. can be modeled by the function $b(x) = -27x + 4103$, and the number of deaths $d(x)$ can be modeled by the function $d(x) = 23x + 2164$. Write a function for the net increase in population, $p(x) = b(x) - d(x)$ from 1990 to 1999.

© Saxon. All rights reserved.

23. **Justify** Explain why $4x^2 + 3x$ is a rational expression.
(28)

24. **Cartography** A student constructs a map of the eastern United States over a grid system such that Indianapolis, IN is the origin and Raleigh, NC is at $(6, -3)$. Find the distance between the cities to the nearest kilometer if each unit represents 120 kilometers.
(41)

25. If $g(x) = \frac{1}{x+2}$, what is $g(x)^2$ in simplest form?
(31)

26. **Analyze** Why are the sine and cosine values of an acute angle in a right triangle always less than 1?
(46)

27. **Engine Size** In past years, engine size for American automobiles was usually measured in cubic inches. Today, most engine sizes are measured in liters. The table shows three typical engine sizes for modern automobiles in both liters and cubic inches.
(34)

Liters (x)	2.3	2.5	3.0
Cubic Inches (y)	140.3	152.5	183

Graph the linear function that relates liters and cubic inches, state the rate of change, and describe what it means.

28. Use $\begin{array}{l} 9x = y - 3z - 21 \\ 4y - 6z = 8x + 10 \\ 56x - 28y = 2 - 42z \end{array}$.
(29)

a. Rewrite the equations lining up the variables.

b. Estimate the number of solutions. Explain your answer.

c. Solve the system of equations to verify your estimate.

29. **Analyze** In the Pythagorean Theorem, why are a, b, and c all greater than 0?
(41)

30. **Write** Explain in words what you are doing when you "factor out the GCF" to factor a polynomial.
(11)

© Saxon. All rights reserved.

Name ______________________ Date __________ Class __________

Using Synthetic Division

LESSON 51

Use synthetic division to divide.

*1. (51) $2x^4 - x$ by $(x - 2)$

*2. (51) $2 + 4x - 2x^2 + 4x^3$ by $(-3 + x)$

Find the distance between the given points.

3. (41) $(-3, 5)$ and $(-1, 2)$

4. (41) $(2, 4)$ and $(6, -2)$

5. (41) $(-3, 5)$ and $(4, -2)$

*6. (14) **Computer Graphics** A computer programmer wants a shape to rotate and expand on the screen. The programmer multiplies the coordinates of each vertex by the matrix $\begin{bmatrix} 1.5 & 0.71 \\ -0.71 & 1.5 \end{bmatrix}$. The area of the shape expands by an amount that equals the determinant of this matrix. By what amount does that area expand?

Add.

7. (37) $\frac{m^2}{x^2a} + \frac{5}{ax} - \frac{m}{a}$

8. (37) $\frac{a}{x^2} - a - \frac{3x}{2a^4}$

9. (25) **Multiple Choice** Which data set is represented by the box-and-whisker plot shown?

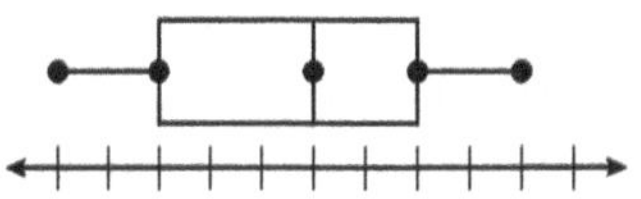

A {15, 8, 10, 13, 11, 12, 6, 13, 7, 15}

B {6, 9, 10, 12, 7, 8, 12, 15, 12, 14}

C {8, 10, 12, 6, 15, 12, 6, 13, 14, 8}

D {6, 11, 12, 7, 12, 8, 14, 15, 9, 12}

Simplify.

10. (44) $\frac{3}{4\sqrt{15}}$

11. (44) $\frac{5\sqrt{3} - \sqrt{2}}{4\sqrt{3} + 3\sqrt{2}}$

12. (44) $\frac{5}{2\sqrt{7} - \sqrt{5}}$

Use synthetic substitution to evaluate the polynomials.

*13. (51) Find $f(3)$ for $f(x) = 3x^3 - 7x + 15$

*14. (51) Find $f(6)$ for $f(x) = -3x^5 - 12x^4 + 30x^3 - 16x^2 - x$

*15. (48) **Electronics** If two resistors in an electrical circuit have resistances R_1 and R_2 (both in ohms), then the total resistance R_t (in ohms) is given by $R_t = \frac{1}{\frac{1}{R_1} + \frac{1}{R_2}}$.

a. Simplify the complex fraction.

b. If there are two resistors in an electrical circuit with resistances 3 ohms and 6 ohms, what is the total resistance of the circuit?

© Saxon. All rights reserved.

16. **Verify** Determine if the graph is correct by choosing points in the shaded and unshaded regions and testing them.
(39)

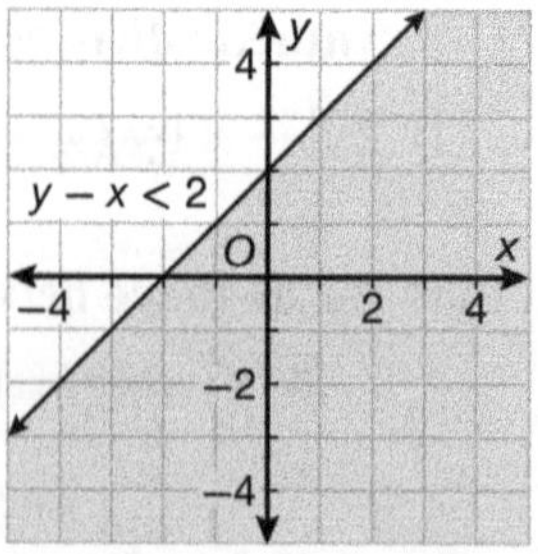

17. **Generalize** Suppose that $f(x)$ is a polynomial of degree m and $g(x)$ is a polynomial of degree n. What must be true for rational expression $\frac{f(x)}{g(x)}$ to be of degree $m - 2$ in the numerator and $n - 2$ in the denominator?
(37)

18. **Error Analysis** Explain the error in the student's work.
(11)

$(3x^4 - 2x^3 + 1) - (x^4 - x^3 + 5)$
$= 3x^4 - 2x^3 + 1 - x^4 - x^3 + 5$
$= 2x^4 - 3x^3 + 6$

*19. **Graphing Calculator** The table shows the elevation of where each record cold temperature reading took place. Use a graphing calculator to find the value of r and the equation for the line of best fit. Use it to predict the record cold temperature for an elevation of 5000 feet.
(45)

	Arizona	Idaho	Wyoming	Rhode Island	Alabama	Tennessee	Virginia	Mississippi
Elev. (ft)	8180	6285	6650	425	760	2471	3870	420
Temp. (°F)	−40	−60	−66	−25	−27	−32	−30	−19

20. **Mountain Bikers** If the origin represents a parking lot, and one mountain biker bikes 2 units due north and 9 units due west, while a second mountain biker bikes 8 units due north and 5 units due east, how much farther from the parking lot is the second mountain biker than the first? Write the answer as a decimal to the nearest tenth of a mile, given that each unit represents 3 miles.
(41)

21. **Estimate** Estimate the values of the x- and y-intercepts.
(27)

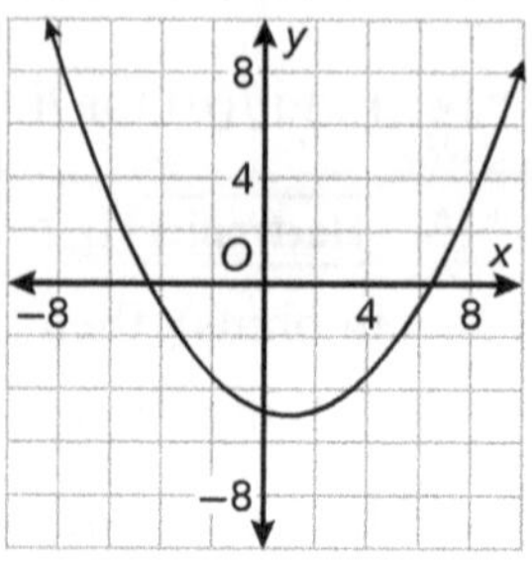

22. **Multiple Choice** What is the value of the cotangent of $\angle A$ if the tangent of $\angle A$ is 0.75?
(46)

A 0.6 **B** 0.75
C 1.25 **D** $1.\overline{3}$

© Saxon. All rights reserved.

23. (11) **Multi-Step** Al's grandfather deposited the amounts shown in Bank A as gifts on Al's birthday during the years 2002 through 2005. His aunt deposited the amounts shown in Bank B. The value of the accounts on 7/2/06 is represented by these polynomials, where $x = 1 + r$, and r is the interest rate for both accounts:

	Bank A	Bank B
7/2/02	\$500	\$1000
7/2/03	\$1000	\$200
7/2/04	\$600	\$200
7/2/05	\$500	\$200

Bank A $500x^4 + 1000x^3 + 600x^2 + 500x$

Bank B $1000x^4 + 200x^3 + 200x^2 + 200x$

a. Write the polynomial that represents the total value of both accounts on 7/2/06.

b. What is the total value of both accounts on 7/2/06 if the interest rate is 5%?

24. (36) **Verify** Show that the equation of the line parallel to $y = mx + b$ through (x_1, y_1) is $y = mx + (y_1 - mx_1)$.

25. (13) **Write** Explain how to graph $y = \frac{3}{4}x + 9$ using a table. Be sure to show each step.

26. (42) **Probability** Two cards are drawn at random from a deck of 52 cards, without replacement. What is the probability that both cards drawn are aces?

27. (23) **Error Analysis** The factored form of $x^2 + 5x + 6$ is given as $(x - 1)(x + 6)$. Find and explain the error and give the correct factorization.

***28.** (49) **Geometry** The sides of a cube have length s. If each dimension of the cube is increased by 0.5, write a binomial expression for the volume of the cube. Expand the binomial.

29. (43) **Employment** A student earns \$8 per hour working for the recreation department and \$12 per hour at a candy store. She is not allowed to work more than 16 hours in a week, and her goal is to earn at least \$150 in a week. Let x represent a number of hours working for the recreation department and y represent a number of hours working at the candy store.

a. Write and graph a system of linear inequalities that represents the situation.

b. Describe the portion of the solution set that contains meaningful solutions for this situation.

c. Determine the vertices of the polygon you described in part **b.** Describe what each vertex represents.

***30.** (49) **Generalize** Write the expansion of $(a + b)^5$. Make a generalization about terms that have the same coefficient in a binomial expansion of the form $(a + b)^n$.

© Saxon. All rights reserved.

Name ____________________ Date __________ Class __________

Using Two Special Right Triangles

LESSON 52

1. (36) Find the equation of the line parallel to the line $3y - x = 3$, and passing through the point $(2, -1)$.

Use elimination to solve.

2. (24) $8y - 3x = 22$; $2y + 4x = 34$

3. (24) $3x + y = 11$; $3x - 2y = 2$

4. (24) $3x + 4y = 20$; $-4x + 3y = 15$

Add.

5. (37) $2 + \frac{a}{2x^2}$

6. (37) $\frac{4}{cx} + c - \frac{3}{4c^2x}$

Use the properties of special right triangles to find *x* and *y*.

***7.** (52)

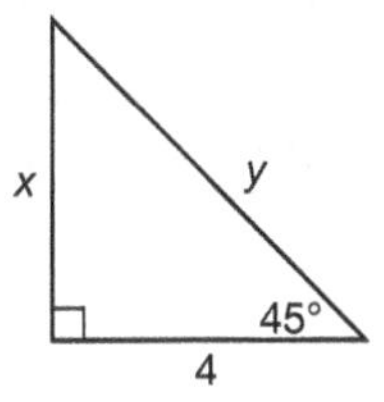

***8.** (52)

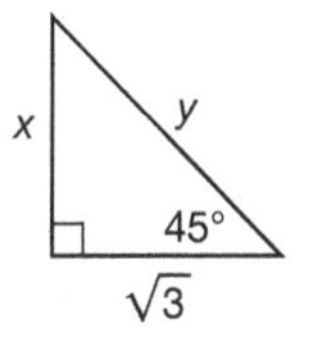

***9.** (51) Divide $(4x^4 + 21x^3 + 10x^2 + 25x) \div (x^2 + 5x)$ using polynomial long division.

10. (40) **Aviation** The radical expression $3.56\sqrt{A}$ can be used to approximate the distance in kilometers to the horizon from an altitude of A meters. What is the approximate distance to the horizon observed by a pilot flying a Boeing 747 at an altitude of 13,225 meters?

11. (31) What are all the values of x for which the multiplication expression $\frac{x+5}{x+2} \cdot \frac{x}{x^3 + 2x^2 + x}$ is undefined?

***12.** (52) **Write** Explain why all 45°-45°-90° triangles are similar.

13. (38) **Physics** Through the process of annealing, metals are made more flexible, allowing a piece of metal to be flattened without breaking. Suppose a rectangular piece of metal with square ends goes through the annealing process and is flattened into a thin sheet. What is the ratio of the new surface area to the original?

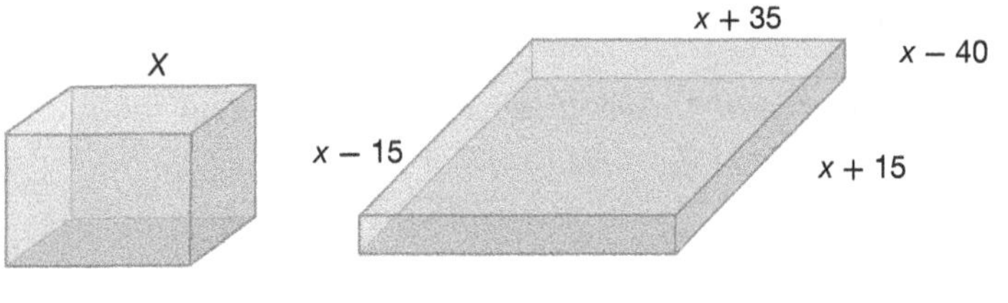

© Saxon. All rights reserved.

14. **Multiple Choice** A _________ function is a function with a connected graph.
(22)
A discrete B continuous C discontinuous D relation

*15. **Multi-Step**
(51)
a. Divide the polynomial $x^5 + 4x^4 - 13x^3 - 52x^2 + 36x + 144$ by $x^2 - x - 6$ using long division.

b. Divide the quotient of part **a** by $(x + 5)$ to find its quotient and remainder using synthetic division.

16. **(Monuments)** A painter at the top of one of the two towers at the Tower Bridge in London throws a length of rope down from his position 63 meters above the ground to another painter who secures the rope to the ground so that it makes a 68° angle with the ground. To the nearest meter, what is the length of the rope from the ground to the top of the tower?
(46)

17. **Error Analysis** Find and explain the error in solving the system. Correct the error and solve:
(29)

$$\begin{aligned} -9x + 4y + 5z &= -16 \\ x - 4y - 6z &= 25 \\ -x + y - z &= -3 \end{aligned}$$

Step 1:

$$\begin{array}{r} -9x + 4y + 5z = -16 \\ + \; x - 4y - 6z = 25 \\ \hline -8x \qquad\quad -z = 9 \end{array}$$

Step 2:

$$\begin{array}{r} x - 4y - 6z = 25 \\ + \; -x + y - z = -3 \\ \hline -3y - 7z = 22 \end{array}$$

*18. **Estimate** The hypotenuse of a 30°-60°-90° triangle is 20 inches. Estimate the length of the side opposite the 60° angle. Give your answer to the nearest whole inch.
(52)

19. **Multiple Choice** What is the value of h in the vertex form of $f(x) = x^2 - 3$?
(27)
A −3 B 0 C 1 D 3

20. **Model** Model FOIL for the multiplication of any two binomials in the form $(a + b)(a - b)$.
(19)

21. **Predict** Describe how the graph $y = 0.25(x + 6)^2$ differs from the graph of the parent function.
(30)

22. **Geometry** Find the area of the shape formed by the linear inequalities $x \geq 1, y \geq 1, y \leq 5, y \leq -2x + 9$.
(43)

© Saxon. All rights reserved.

23. *(15)* **Data Analysis** One day Irma hikes up a mountain. The table shows times of day and her distances from the base of the mountain. She camps overnight, and then hikes down the same path the next day.

Time of Day	8 am	10 am	12 pm	2 pm	4 pm
Distances 1st day (mi)	0	2	4	6	8
Distances 2nd day (mi)	8	5.75	3.5	1.25	0

a. Write equations that relate her distances from the bottom to the times of day. Represent the distance by d and the number of hours after 8 a.m. by t.

b. Graph those equations.

c. Is there a point on the path at which Irma arrives at the same time of day on both days? Explain.

24. *(49)* **Error Analysis** A student expanded the binomial $(m - 2)^3$ as shown. Explain the error.

$$(m-2)^3 = {}_3C_0 m^3 2^0 + {}_3C_1 m^2 2^1 + {}_3C_2 m^1 2^2 + {}_3C_3 m^0 2^3$$
$$= m^3 + 3m^2(2) + 3m(2)^2 + (2)^3$$
$$= m^3 + 6m^2 + 12m + 8$$

25. *(23)* **Architecture** The volume of a building is $5x^2 + 50x - 280$ yd^3. If the height of the building is 5 yd, find the length and width of the building.

***26.** *(50)* **Multi-Step** Consider the function $y = 3x + 2$.

a. Find an equation for its inverse.

b. Graph the function and its inverse on the same grid.

c. How are the slopes of the function and its inverse related?

27. *(42)* **Playing Cards** A deck of cards has 4 suits of 13 cards each for a total of 52 cards.

a. How many ways can one 5-card hand be dealt?

b. How many ways can one 5-card hand be dealt that includes 2 hearts and 3 cards from the other suits?

28. *(25)* **Model** The table shows the measurements in inches of various shipping boxes. Draw a box-and-whisker plot to represent the lengths of all edges of the boxes. Consider that a box has 12 edges.

Box	Length	Width	Height
1	11.875	3.375	13.625
2	11	8.5	5.5
3	7.5	5.125	14.375

© Saxon. All rights reserved.

29. (37) **Physics** A satellite has an orbital acceleration of $\frac{v^2}{r}$, where v is the speed of the satellite and r is the distance from the satellite to the Earth's center. Find the difference in acceleration between satellite 1 and satellite 2. Assume that each is traveling at the same speed, v.

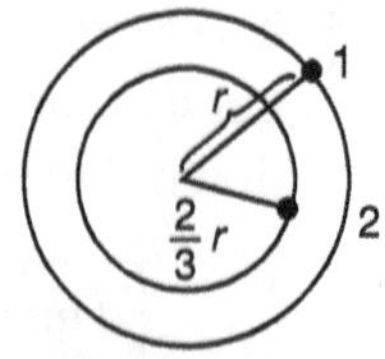

***30.** (45) **Graphing Calculator** The table shows the average number of tropical storms per year compared to the average number of hurricanes per year. Use a graphing calculator to find the value of r and the equation for the line of best fit. Use it to predict the average number of hurricanes per year when there was an average of 9.5tropical storms.

Tropical Storms	8.7	10.6	10.7	11.1	11.4	12.6	14.5
Hurricanes	5.3	6.1	6	6.2	6.3	6.8	7.8

© Saxon. All rights reserved.

Name ______________________ Date __________ Class __________

Performing Compositions of Functions

LESSON 53

Solve.

1. (7) $2\frac{1}{4}x - 3\frac{1}{2} = -\frac{1}{16}$

2. (7) $0.002x - 0.02 = 6.6$

3. (7) $\frac{3 - 2x}{4} + \frac{x}{3} = 5$

Use the properties of special right triangles to find x and y.

***4.** (52)

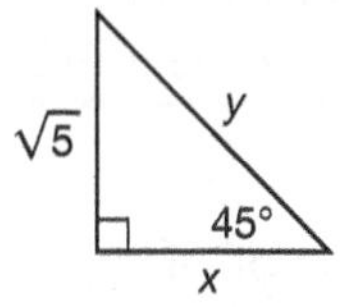

***5.** (39)

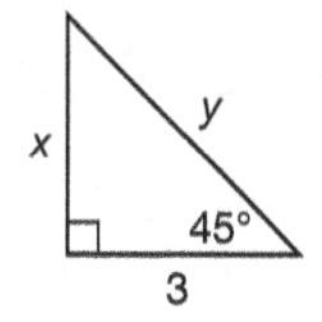

Use $3x + 10 > 4y$.

6. (39) Find a point that is a solution.

7. (39) Find a point that is not a solution.

8. (49) How many terms does the binomial expansion of $(3r + s)^{17}$ contain?

***9.** (53) Let $x(t) = 3$ and $y(t) = -7t + 6$. Find $x(y(t))$ and $y(x(t))$.

***10.** (53) Let $p(x) = 3$ and $q(x) = -x^2 + 3x$. Find $p(q(x))$ and $q(p(x))$.

11. (33) **Analyze** Suppose there are three tiles in a bag, labeled A, B, and C. A tile is chosen at random, then a second tile is chosen at random, and then the third tile is chosen. Each tile that is chosen is not replaced in the bag. List all the outcomes in the sample space of this experiment. How many outcomes are in the sample space?

***12.** (53) **Multi-Step** A bookstore gives you a 10% student discount, but you still must pay the 6% sales tax. Use composite functions to:

a. Determine how much you save if the discount is calculated first.

b. Determine how much you save if the tax is calculated first.

c. Determine which method will save you the most.

13. (44) **Multi-Step** A rectangle has an area of 60 square centimeters and a length of $\frac{3\sqrt{3}}{2}$ centimeters.

a. Find the width of the rectangle.

b. Find the perimeter of the rectangle.

14. (39) Find a point that is a solution of $-7x + 18 < 3y$ and a point that is not a solution.

15. (51) **Write** Determine the polynomial divisor, dividend, and quotient represented by the synthetic division shown.

$$\begin{array}{r|rrrrr} -1 & 10 & 5 & 4 & 0 & -9 \\ & 0 & -10 & 5 & -9 & 9 \\ \hline & 10 & -5 & 9 & -9 & \boxed{0} \end{array}$$

© Saxon. All rights reserved.

16. **Error Analysis** Find and correct the error(s) the student made.
(40)
$$\frac{3}{\sqrt[3]{3}} \cdot \frac{\sqrt[3]{3}}{\sqrt[3]{3}} = \frac{3\sqrt[3]{3}}{\sqrt[3]{9}} = \frac{3\sqrt[3]{3}}{3} = \sqrt[3]{3}$$

*17. **Graphing Calculator** At the start of the year, there are 23 rabbits living in a field.
(47) The growth of the rabbit population is modeled by the equation $P(x) = 1.2^x + 22$, where $P(x)$ is the number of rabbits in the field x weeks into the year. Use a graphing calculator to predict how many weeks it will take for there to be more than 100 rabbits.

*18. **Multiple Choice** Let $h(x) = x^{-3} + x^3$ and $k(x) = x^{-1}$. What is the value of $h(k(2))$?
(53)

A 8 B $\frac{1}{8}$ C $8\frac{1}{8}$ D $\frac{8}{65}$

19. **Geometry** The altitude of an isosceles triangle bisects its base. Find the length
(46) of the base of an isosceles triangle whose legs measure 20 inches and whose base angles measure 70°. Round to the nearest hundredth.

20. **Gravity** The height of a free-falling object (neglecting air resistance) is given by
(35) the function $h(t) = -4.9t^2 + v_0t + h_0$, where h_0 is the initial height in meters, v_0 is the initial velocity in meters per second, and $h(t)$ is the height in meters at time t seconds. How long does it take for an object to hit the ground after it is thrown straight up at a speed of 4.9 meters per second from a height of 29.4 meters? (Hint: Factor −4.9 from the trinomial.)

*21. **Analyze** Suppose $p(u) = 2u + 5$ with domain $\{1, 3, 5, 7\}$ and $r(u) = u - 3$ with
(53) domain $\{6, 8\}$. Then the domain of $p(u)$ limits the domain and range of the composite function. Can you change the domains of functions p and r so that the domain of $r(u)$ limits the domain and range of the composite function?

22. **Cartography** A cartographer constructs a map of Montana over a grid system
(41) such that Great Falls is at (125, 150) and Conrad is at (86, 220). Find the distance between the cities to the nearest kilometer if each unit represents one kilometer.

23. **Probability** Suppose the probability of you scoring a goal in a soccer game is $\frac{1}{3}$ for
(49) every shot taken. If you take 8 shots in a game, what is the probability that you will score 2 goals?

24. **Analyze** What must be true of a and b if the following equation is true? Explain.
(37)
$$\frac{1}{x^2 + ax + bx + ab} = \frac{1}{x^2 - 1}$$

25. **Irrigation** An irrigation pipeline starts from the top of a hill and has an angle of
(52) elevation of 45°. If the length of the pipe line is 720 meters, what is the vertical rise of the pipe? Round your answer to the nearest meter.

© Saxon. All rights reserved.

26. (48) **Generalize** Consider the following sequence of complex fractions.

$$1, \frac{1}{1+1}, \frac{1}{1+\frac{1}{1+1}}, \frac{1}{1+\frac{1}{1+\frac{1}{1+1}}}, \frac{1}{1+\frac{1}{1+\frac{1}{1+\frac{1}{1+1}}}}, \frac{1}{1+\frac{1}{1+\frac{1}{1+\frac{1}{1+\frac{1}{1+1}}}}}, \ldots$$

Simplify the first 6 terms. Describe any patterns you see. Can you predict the next term without writing and simplifying the complex fraction?

27. (42) **Multiple Choice** Evaluate $\frac{8!}{5!}$.

A 1.6 B 336 C 1680 D 6720

28. (36) **Speed** The speed of an object at time t is based on its initial speed v_o and its acceleration a: $v = v_o + at$.

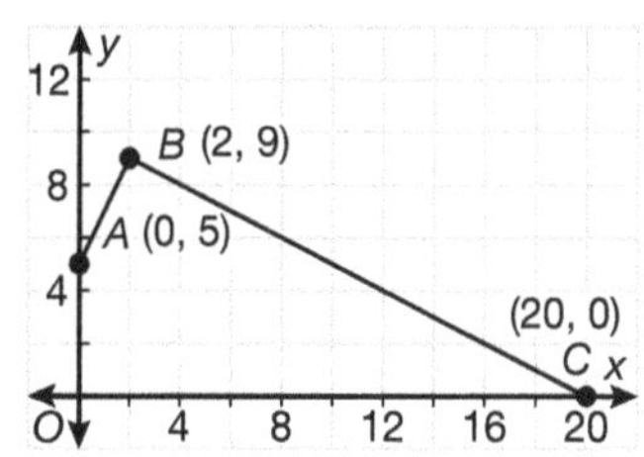

a. Find the equations of the lines from A to B and B to C and describe the motion of the object.

b. What is the relationship between the equations of motion?

29. (50) **Population** The population p of a city for the years from 1998 is modeled by $p = 326{,}000 + 8526t$, where $t = 0$ represents the year 1998. Solve the equation for t and use it to predict the year in which the population of the city exceeds 450,000.

30. (43) **Ticket Prices** Two of the ticket prices for a football game were \$92 for a field seat and \$54 for an upper view seat. You decide to buy up to 15 tickets and to spend up to \$1000. Let x represent a number of field seats and y represent a number of upper view seats.

a. Write a system of linear inequalities that represents the situation.

b. Describe the points in the graph of the system that represent all the possible combinations of field seats and upper view seats you can buy.

© Saxon. All rights reserved.

Name ______________________ Date __________ Class __________

Using Linear Programming

LESSON 54

Given the objective function *P* and the constraints, find the minimum and maximum values for the objective function.

*1. (54) $P = 2x + 3y$ given $x \geq 0$, $y \geq 0$, $0.4x + 0.9y \leq 25$

*2. (54) $P = 5x + 9y$ given $x \geq 0$, $y \geq 0$, $25x + 35y \leq 25$

Simplify.

3. (48) $\dfrac{a^2x - \dfrac{a}{x}}{ax - \dfrac{4}{x}}$

4. (48) $\dfrac{\dfrac{m}{m+x}}{\dfrac{x}{m+x}}$

5. (48) $\dfrac{\dfrac{s}{a+b} + \dfrac{x}{b}}{\dfrac{a}{s+x}}$

6. (22) **Multiple Choice** A point of discontinuity is a point at which the graph

A increases. **B** is disconnected. **C** ends. **D** decreases.

Identify which equations are direct variations and which are inverse variations.

7. (12) $y = \frac{1}{2}x$

8 (12) $xy = 15$

9 (12) $y = -\frac{1}{2}x + 5$

10. (18) **Saving Money** Jason has 300 nickels in his money jar. How many dollars does Jason have in nickels?

*11. (54) **Coordinate Geometry** Find the coordinates of the vertices for the feasible region.

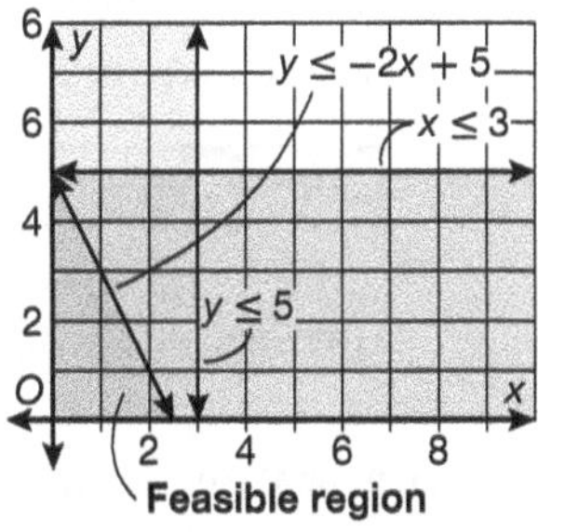

12. (54) Give an example of a problem situation where the feasible region might include negative values.

13. (21) **Error Analysis** Two students were asked which of these lines were intersecting. Their answers are below. Which student is correct? What is the relationship between the lines that the incorrect student answered?

Equation 1: $3y + 4x = 5$; Equation 2: $8x = 10 - 6y$;

Equation 3: $6y - 10 = 8x$

Dietrich: Equations 1 and 2 intersect.

Shelby: Equations 1 and 3 intersect, so equations 2 and 3 intersect as well.

© Saxon. All rights reserved.

14. (11) **Aquarium Design** Two aquariums each require the same amount of space on a shelf. The shapes of the aquariums are given in the picture. Write a polynomial that represents how much less water the cylindrical aquarium holds than the aquarium in the shape of a cube. (*Hint:* The formula for the volume of a cylinder is $V = \pi r^2 h$.)

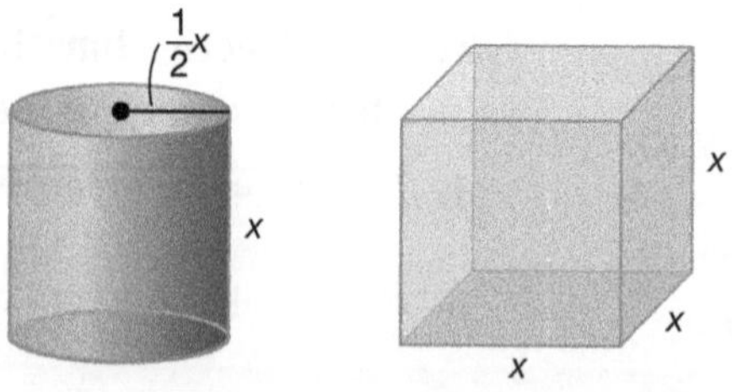

***15.** (53) **Write** Describe how to find a composite function $f(g(x))$ if the functions $f(x)$ and $g(x)$ are known.

16. (52) **Analyze** A chord in a circle makes an angle of 45° with the radius. If the chord is 4 cm long, what is the radius of the circle?

17. (22) **Verify** Explain how to show that the graph is an example of a function. Is the function continuous, discontinuous, and/or discrete?

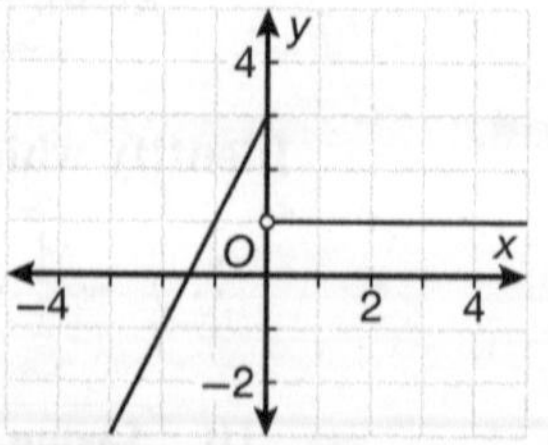

18. (25) **Rainfall** Annual rainfall amounts in inches for Austin, Texas, for 2005 are listed in the table below. If the mean amount of rainfall in Austin during that year was 1.861 inches, find x.

2005	J	F	M	A	M	J	J	A	S	O	N	D
Amount (inches)	2.25	2.21	x	0.72	3.13	0.89	2.75	2.44	1.44	1.78	0.33	0.09

19. (51) **Error Analysis** Jenny and Haley each tried to divide the polynomial $2x^4 - 6x^3 + x^2 - 3x - 3$ by $x - 3$. Who is correct? Explain your reasoning.

Jenny

3	2	−6	1	−3	−3
	0	6	0	3	0
	2	0	1	0	−3

Haley

−3	2	−6	1	−3	−3
	0	−6	36	−111	342
	2	−12	37	−114	339

20. (30) **Justify** Max said that it is possible to write the standard form of a quadratic equation given its vertex and y-intercept. Show that Max is correct by writing the equation of a quadratic function in standard form whose vertex is (1, 9) and y-intercept is 13.

21. (46) **Generalize** Tell how to find the cotangent of an angle when given the tangent of the angle. Give an example.

© Saxon. All rights reserved.

22. **Multiple Choice** Circle the letter that represents the number and type of solutions (29) of the system

$$-2x - 10y - 6z = -2$$
$$x + 5y + 3z = -16$$
$$5x + 25y + 15z = 5$$

A No solution, Inconsistent
B One solution, Inconsistent
C One solution, Consistent
D Infinitely many solutions, Consistent

*23. **Graphing Calculator** Use a graphing calculator to solve the following. (14)

$$\det\begin{bmatrix} 9 & 3 & 0 \\ 6 & 12 & 1 \\ -3 & -9 & 15 \end{bmatrix}$$

24. **Geometry** Write a rational expression in simplest form for the ratio of the rectangular prism's surface area to its volume. (31)

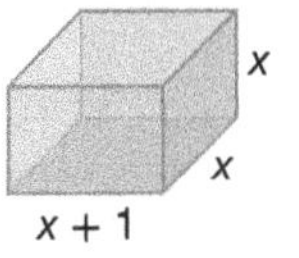

*25. Let $a(t) = t$ and $b(t) = 3.1t^2 - 2.0t + 4.3$. What is $a(b(t))$? (53)

*26. **(Cost of Lobster)** At a restaurant on the Maine coast, the supply of fresh new shell lobsters during the season (July through October) is given by the function $L(t) = -0.006t^2 + 0.733t$, where t is the number of days after July 1. If the restaurant has x lobsters for a day, it charges $C(x) = 37 - x$ dollars for each one. What function gives the restaurant's price per lobster in terms of the number of days after July 1? (53)

27. **(Pendulums)** The time t in seconds a pendulum takes to complete one full swing is given by the equation $t = 2\pi\sqrt{\frac{l}{9.8}}$, where l is the length of the pendulum in meters. Suppose a pendulum has a length of 5 meters. How much time will the pendulum take to complete one full swing? (44)

28. **Multi-Step** (45)

a. Make a scatter plot of the data set.

b. Sketch a line of best fit.

x	20	30	42	58	64	75	83	90
y	1	4	2.5	3	6	4.5	7	6.5

29. Factor $5x^2 + 4x^3 - x^4$ completely. Always factor the GCF as the first step. (23)

30. Give an example of how to use a number cube to make a binomial experiment. (Inv 5)

© Saxon. All rights reserved.

Name ____________________ Date __________ Class __________

Finding Probability

LESSON 55

Simplify.

1. (44) $\frac{1}{-2\sqrt{24}}$ **2.** (44) $\frac{\sqrt{5}+3}{\sqrt{2}+\sqrt{45}}$ **3.** (44) $\frac{-1}{\sqrt{12}+3}$

4. (40) $5\sqrt{5}(2\sqrt{5}-3\sqrt{10})$ **5.** (40) $3\sqrt{200}-5\sqrt{18}+7\sqrt{50}$ **6.** (40) $2\sqrt{3}\cdot 2\sqrt{2}(6\sqrt{6}-3\sqrt{2})$

7. (43) **Write** Explain why all solutions of the system $\begin{matrix} x \geq 1 \\ y > x \end{matrix}$ lie in quadrant I.

***8.** (54) Given the objective function P and the constraints, find the minimum and maximum values for the objective function. $P = 7x + 8y$ given $x \geq 0$, $y \geq 0$, $2x + 3y \leq 100$, $4x + 5y \geq 75$

9. (37) **Error Analysis** Two students are subtracting the rational expressions $\frac{2x}{2x^2+7x-15}$ and $\frac{1}{x+5}$ but get different results. Which student made the mistake? Explain.

Student A	Student B
$\frac{2x}{2x^2+7x-15}-\frac{1}{x+5}$ $=\frac{2x}{(2x-3)(x+5)}-\frac{(2x-3)}{(x+5)(2x-3)}$ $=\frac{3}{2x^2+7x-15}$	$\frac{2x}{2x^2+7x-15}-\frac{1}{x+5}$ $=\frac{2x}{(2x-3)(x+5)}-\frac{(2x-3)}{(x+5)(2x-3)}$ $=\frac{4x-3}{2x^2+7x-15}$

10. (49) **Multi-Step** Suppose one term in the expansion of $(a+b)^n$ is $1716a^7b^6$.
a. To what power was $(a+b)$ raised? **b.** Which term is $1716a^7b^6$?

11. (41) **Geometry** Write the length of the diagonal of a 3 ft by 3 ft square as a simplified radical expression.

***12.** (55) **Pet Shelter** In a pet shelter, there are two pairs of related kittens among 14 other kittens. What is the probability that someone randomly selecting two kittens will choose either pair of the related kittens?

13. (45) **Multiple Choice** Which value of r describes the set of points which are *farthest* from forming a line?
A $r = -0.99$ **B** $r = -0.4$ **C** $r = 0.22$ **D** $r = 0.81$

14. (50) **Doppler Effect** When something making a sound moves in relation to a stationary listener, the frequency heard by the listener is not the same as the actual frequency of the sound at its source. In normal atmospheric conditions, if f_l is the frequency (in hertz, or cycles per second) heard by the listener, f_s is the frequency at the source, and

© Saxon. All rights reserved.

v is the velocity of the sound source (in miles per hour), then
$f_l = \frac{740f_s}{740 - v}$.

Suppose you are standing still and a police car is moving away from you with its siren blaring at 1800 hertz. You estimate its speed at about 6000 feet per minute. What frequency do you hear?

*15. (54) **Analyze** Mobile-1 has two cell phone plans, the Star Plan and the Silver Plan. The cost for each plan is shown in the table. A small company is comparing the two plans. The company needs at least 10 cell phones, one for each sales rep, and each rep will use at least 800 minutes per month. What options does this company have?

Monthly Phone Rates

	Star Plan	Silver Plan
Start-up fee	\$75	\$125
Free minutes	2200	1500
Per minute rate above free minutes	7 cents	5 cents
Monthly service charge	\$25 × the number of cell phones	\$30 × the number of cell phones

*16. (47) **Graphing Calculator** Plot the graphs of $y = 3^x$ and $y = 3^x + 5$ on the same axes on a graphing calculator. Compare the domain and the range.

17. (42) **Multi-Step** How many 6-letter words (including nonsense words) can be formed from the letters **A B C D E F**?

a. If the order of the six letters doesn't matter?

b. If the letter **B** must be in the first place?

c. Is the answer in part **a** different from the answer for part **b**? Explain.

18. (33) **Analyze** Suppose there are three tiles in a bag, labeled A, B, and C. A tile is chosen at random, then a second tile is chosen at random, and then a third tile is chosen at random. Each tile that is chosen is replaced in the bag. List all the outcomes in the sample space of this experiment. How many outcomes are in the sample space?

19. (46) **Coordinate Geometry** The vertices of a triangle are $A(-3, 6)$, $B(2, -4)$, and $C(-3, -4)$. Find the value of the cotangent of $\angle B$.

*20. (55) **Error Analysis** The odds in favor of an event are 3 to 5. Which student made an error in finding the probability of the event? What is the error?

Student A	Student B
$P(\text{event}) = \frac{3}{3+5} = \frac{3}{8} = 37.5\%$	$P(\text{event}) = \frac{3}{5} = 60\%$

© Saxon. All rights reserved.

*21. (53) **Compound Interest** You deposit p dollars into a savings account. If the account earns interest at a rate of 1% per quarter, then after one quarter your account is worth $f(p) = (1.01)p$ dollars.

a. What does the function $f(f(p))$ represent?

b. What's the value of $f(f(p))$?

c. How much is your account worth after a year?

22. (23) **Architecture** Many famous works of architecture have sides whose proportions follow the Golden Ratio. To derive the Golden Ratio, look at the diagram to the right.

a. The line segment is divided into two segments, one of length a and one of longer length b. Write the ratio of the shorter segment to the longer segment.

b. Now write the ratio of the longer segment to the sum of the lengths of both segments.

c. The Golden Ratio is for values of a and b such that both ratios are equal to each other. Write this as an equation.

d. Multiply both sides by the expression $b(a + b)$.

e. If $a = 1$ and $b = x$, find the roots of this quadratic equation using the quadratic formula.

f. Which root can you ignore? Why?

g. To the nearest thousandth, what is the value of the Golden Ratio?

*23. (55) **Multiple Choice** The probability of an event is $\frac{x}{y}$. Which shows the odds in favor of the event?

A x to y **B** y to x **C** x to $(x - y)$ **D** x to $(y - x)$

24. (50) **Temperature** The formula to convert degrees Fahrenheit to degrees Celsius is $C = \frac{5}{9}(F - 32)$.

Find the formula to convert degrees Celsius to degrees Fahrenheit by finding the inverse for this function.

25. (52) **Explain** Explain why all 30°-60°-90° triangles are similar.

26. (40) Find the area of this isosceles triangle. Dimensions are in inches.

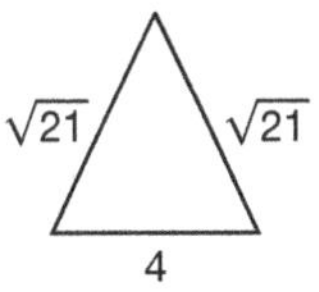

© Saxon. All rights reserved.

Finding Probability

LESSON 55

Divide using synthetic division.

27. $x^3 - 2$ by $x - 5$ *(51)*

28. $2x^3 - 1$ by $x - 2$ *(51)*

29. Find the equation of the line that passes through $(6, 0)$ and $(-3, -3)$. *(26)*

30. **Predict** The result of dividing one polynomial by another is $x^2 - 6x + 8 - \frac{2}{x-4}$. *(51)*
What two polynomials might have been divided?

© Saxon. All rights reserved.

Name ______________________ Date __________ Class __________

Finding Angles of Rotation

LESSON 56

Determine the kind of variation, if any, for each equation.

1. (12) $y = ax^2 + bx + c$, for $a, b, c \neq 0$

2. (12) $y = ax^2 + bx + c$, for any values of a, b, and c

Point P is located on the terminal side of angle θ. Find the exact values of the 6 trigonometric functions for θ with the given coordinates for P.

***3.** (56) $P(7, -24)$

***4.** (56) $P(-\sqrt{5}, 2)$

5. (11) Identify the leading coefficient and the constant term in the polynomial $-x^3 + 5x - 2$.

6. (49) Find the sixth term of the expansion of $(a + b)^9$.

7. (20) Given $f(x) = 2x - 7$ and $g(x) = -5x + 8$. Graph the sum $(f + g)(x)$.

8. (54) The odds in favor of an event are 4:12. What is the probability of the event happening?

9. (23) **Justify** A square room has an area of 196 square feet. What are the measurements of the room? Use a polynomial to explain.

10. (47) **Error Analysis** Consider the graph shown. Donnie says the equation of this graph is $y = -5^x$. Chris disagrees; he says it is $y = (-5)^x$. Who is correct? Explain the error.

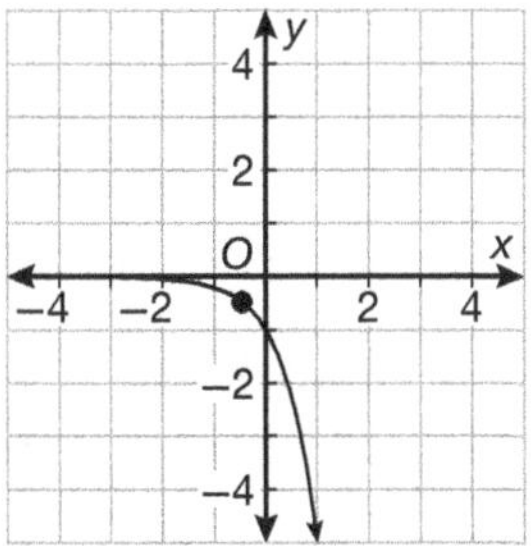

11. (18) **Exercise** Kellie's last three walks were 2.25 mi, 3.29 mi, and 2.318 mi. Use significant digit to find the sum of Kellie's walking distances.

***12.** (55) **Multi-Step** A brown bag contains 12 peaches and 8 nectarines.

a. Which has the greater probability: randomly selecting 2 peaches or 2 nectarines?

b. How much greater is the probability?

13. (27) **Multiple Choice** What is the range of the function?

A all real numbers between −4 and 4

B all real numbers less than −5

C all real numbers greater than −5

D all real numbers

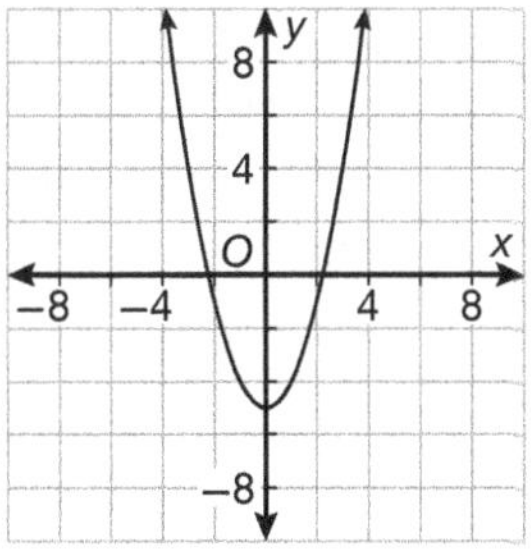

14. (49) Find the seventh term of the expansion of $(g + 2)^{12}$.

© Saxon. All rights reserved.

15. (Sea Level) From an observation point 435 feet above sea level, a tourist spots a buoy at an angle of depression of 57° and another in the same line of sight at an angle of depression of 13°. To the nearest foot, how far apart are the buoys?
(46)

16. (Investments) A couple has saved \$20,000. An advisor suggests that they invest this amount in treasury bonds and in certificates of deposit (CDs). The couple can get a one-year CD that pays 5.42% (annual) interest, and a 2-year treasury bond that will yield 4.18% annually. If the couple wants to earn \$1000 per year from the investment, how much should they invest in treasury bonds?
(15)

17. (Food Preparation) Antonio is making a dip for a school function. Each tablespoon of olive oil has 15 grams of fat and each tablespoon of mayonnaise has 5 grams of fat. He wants the snack to have less than 75 grams of fat. Graph the inequality that represents the possible amounts of each ingredient in the dip. Choose a point in the shaded area. Tell what it means.
(39)

18. **Error Analysis** A student said that the correlation coefficient for the data graphed is 1 because it follows a perfect pattern. Why is the student incorrect?
(45)

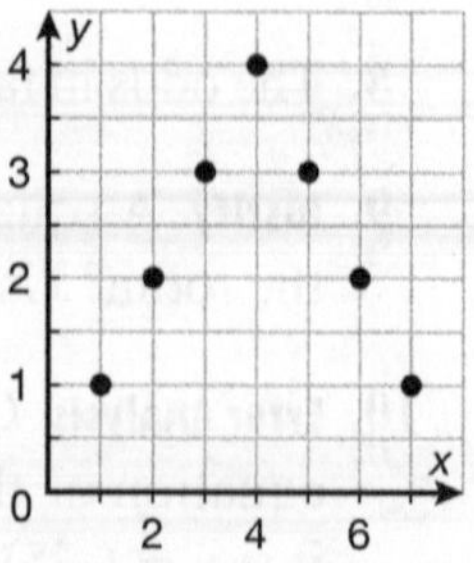

Draw each of the indicated angles in standard position.

*19. 70° (56)

*20. −200° (56)

*21. −90° (56)

22. **Verify** Verify that the value of the complex fraction $3 + \frac{1}{7 + \frac{1}{15 + 1}}$ is a good approximation of π.
(48)

23. **Analyze** Create two 2 × 2 matrices that are inverses of each other. Calculate and compare their determinants. Explain your findings.
(14)

*24. **Graphing Calculator** Describe the feasible region for the set of inequalities $x \leq 4, y \geq 2, y \leq -0.25x + 5$
(54)

25. (Acceleration) A car increases its speed from 0 to 50 miles per hour. It then drives 50 miles per hour for the rest of the trip. Examine the graph shown. Does this graph represent a continuous, discontinuous, and/or discrete function? Justify your answer.
(22)

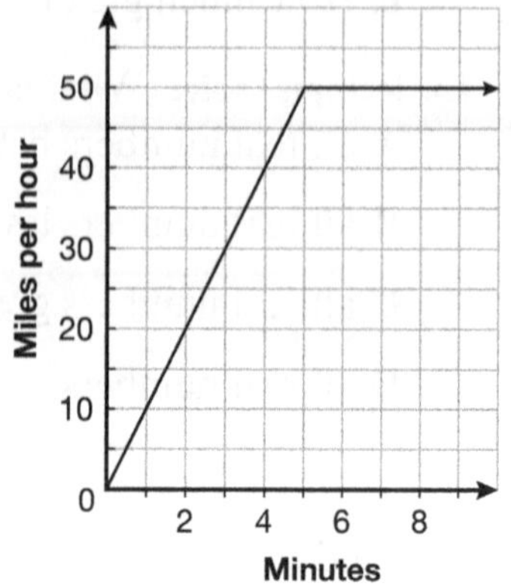

© Saxon. All rights reserved.

*26. (55) **Probability** In 2006, the U.S. Census Bureau estimated there were 18,089,888 people living in Florida and 299,398,484 living in the United States.

a. Estimate the probability that a person randomly selected in the United States lives in Florida.

b. Estimate the odds in favor that a person randomly selected in the United States lives in Florida.

27. (42) **Multi-Step** A bag of marbles contains 6 red marbles, 5 blue marbles, and 1 green marble. Two marbles are selected at random. Which is more likely: selecting 2 red marbles or 1 red and 1 blue marble?

28. (30) **Write** Describe how the graph of $y = -2.5(x - 5)^2 + 2$ differs from the graph of the parent function.

*29. (54) A community center wants to build a rectangular playground and fence around it. The cost of fencing is $25 per foot. The cost for painting the fence is $14 per foot. The center cannot spend more than $2500 on fencing. The playground cannot be any longer than 40 ft and needs to be at least 20 ft wide. What is the maximum area, in square feet, the center can get for the size of the playground?

30. (53) **Geometry** Suppose that function $f(x)$ rotates every point on the plane clockwise 180 degrees about the origin, and $g(x)$ translates every point to the right 2 units.

a. What is the effect of $(g \circ f)(x)$ on the point with coordinates (0, 1)?

b. What is the effect of $(f \circ g)(x)$ on that same point?

© Saxon. All rights reserved.

Name ______________________ Date __________ Class __________

Finding Exponential Growth and Decay

LESSON 57

1. (29) Is the ordered triple (4, 0, −1) a solution of the system $\begin{aligned} 2x - y + z &= 7 \\ -3x + 5y - 3z &= -9 \\ 4x - 2y + 2z &= -14 \end{aligned}$?

Simplify.

2. (40) $4\sqrt{3} \cdot 3\sqrt{12} \cdot 2\sqrt{3}$

3. (40) $3\sqrt{75} - 4\sqrt{48}$

4. (40) $2\sqrt{5}(5\sqrt{5} - 3\sqrt{15})$

5. (31) What are all the values of x for which the division expression $\frac{x}{x-2} \div \frac{6x-2}{3x+6}$ is undefined?

Given the objective function *P* and the constraints, find the minimum and maximum values.

***6.** (54) $P = 15x + 7y$ given $x \geq 0$, $y \geq 0$, $1.5x + y \leq 35$, $0.25x + 5y \leq 15$

***7.** (54) $P = 50x + 75y$ given $x \geq 0$, $y \geq 0$, $2x + y \geq 30$, $0.75x + y \leq 20$, $0.5x + y \leq 18$

8. (11) If a trinomial in standard form is added to a binomial in standard form and the result is written in standard form, how many terms can be in the result?

9. (53) **Error Analysis** A student says: If $f(x) = \frac{5}{x}$ and $g(x) = \frac{-3}{x}$, then $f(g(x)) = \frac{5}{\frac{-3}{x}} = -\frac{5}{3}x$. Explain the reasoning.

10. (11) **Multi-Step** **a.** Complete the table of values for the polynomial function $f(x) = x^3 - 5x + 8$.

x	−3	−2	−1	0	1	2
$f(x)$	4	10	12	8	4	6

b. Using only integer values of x, what is the smallest x-interval whose associated portion of the graph contains a relative maximum? What is the smallest x-interval whose associated portion of the graph contains a relative minimum? Justify your answers.

***11.** (56) **Skateboarding** In the 1999 X Games, skateboarder Tony Hawk became the first to land a 900—a rotation of 900° in the air from a half-pipe. Find an angle with measure between 0° and 360° that is coterminal with 900°. Describe the skateboarding move.

12. (41) **Cartography** A student constructs a map of Montana over a grid system such that Lewiston is at (1, 4) and Havre is at (0.5, 10). Find the distance between the cities to the nearest kilometer if each unit represents 25 kilometers.

© Saxon. All rights reserved.

13. $f = \{(3, 4), (6, 8), (2, 1), (3, 6)\}$ represents a ________.
(22)
A continuous function **B** discrete function
C continuous relation **D** discrete relation

14. **Geometry** The height of a right triangle is 6 ft and the base is 8 ft. Find the slope of the hypotenuse of the right triangle.
(13)

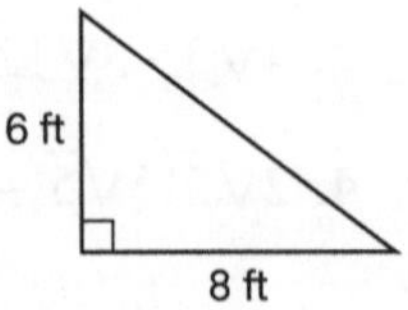

15. **Write** Describe two ways to graph $2y - x < 6$.
(39)

16. **Error Analysis** The factored form of $9x^2 - 6x - 15$ is given as $3x(3x - 7)$. Find and explain the error and give the correct factorization.
(23)

Determine whether the function shows exponential growth or decay.

*17. 1.4^x
(57)

*18. $10(0.4)^x$
(57)

19. **Analyze** Find all the angle measures between 0° and 360° for which $\tan\theta$ is undefined.
(56)

20. **Coordinate Geometry** A point is randomly chosen in one of the four quadrants of the coordinate plane. Construct a theoretical probability model to show the probabilities of the point being in each quadrant.
(55)

21. **Error Analysis** Given matrices $A = \begin{bmatrix} 2 & -3 \\ 5 & -8 \end{bmatrix}$ and $B = \begin{bmatrix} 0 & 2 \\ 1 & 4 \end{bmatrix}$, a student solved $AX = B$ as follows:
(32)

$X = BA^{-1} = \begin{bmatrix} 0 & 2 \\ 1 & 4 \end{bmatrix}\begin{bmatrix} 8 & -3 \\ 5 & -2 \end{bmatrix} = \begin{bmatrix} 10 & -4 \\ 28 & -11 \end{bmatrix}$. What is the error? Find the correct solution.

22. **Multiple Choice** To solve $\begin{matrix} 6x - 7y = -1 \\ 3x + 2y = 5 \end{matrix}$ by elimination, what should the second equation be multiplied by in order to eliminate the x-terms?
(24)

A -6 **B** -3 **C** -2 **D** 2

23. **Write** Identify some mathematical patterns found in Pascal's Triangle. For example, the third diagonal has the **Triangular Numbers.**
(42)

24. **Model** Graph the equation $2x + 3y = 3$.
(34)

25. **Electricity** Ohm's Law states that the current I, in amps, equals $\frac{\sqrt{P}}{\sqrt{R}}$ where P is power, measured in watts, and R is resistance measured in ohms. Simplify the expression.
(40)

26. **Analyze** If you apply expansion by minors to the 2×2 matrix $\begin{bmatrix} 3 & -2 \\ 4 & 1 \end{bmatrix}$, you
(14)

© Saxon. All rights reserved.

get $3|1| - 4|-2|$. How must you define the determinant of a single number so that the result agrees with the formula for the determinant of a matrix this size?

***27.** (57) **Formulate** Write the equation of an exponential function whose graph passes through the points (0, 2) and (2, 18). Determine whether the function is increasing or decreasing.

28. (43) **Catering** A caterer is ordering salmon and shrimp for an event. The salmon costs \$7.50 per pound and the shrimp costs \$15 per pound. She needs at least as much shrimp as salmon, and the most she can spend is \$300. Let x represent the number of pounds of salmon and y represent the number of pounds of shrimp.

a. Write and graph a system of linear inequalities that represents the situation.

b. Determine the point of intersection of the boundary lines in the graph. Round to the nearest hundredth.

c. Assume that the salmon and shrimp can be ordered in quarter-pound increments. Determine the point closest to the point of intersection of the boundary lines that represents a possible purchase. Describe what it means.

***29.** (57) **Life Insurance** From 1950 through 1980, the total amount, l (in billions), of life insurance in the United States is shown in the table below.

Year	1950	1955	1960	1965	1970	1975	1980
Amount	234	373	586	901	1402	2314	3541

Write an exponential model that approximates this data. How much money does this model predict will be invested in life insurance by the year 2010?

***30.** (27) **Graphing Calculator** Use a graphing calculator to determine the y-intercept of the quadratic function $y - 1 = -3x^2 - 6x$.

© Saxon. All rights reserved.

Name ______________________ Date ____________ Class ____________

Completing the Square

LESSON 58

Solve by using either substitution or elimination.

1. (24) $2y - 2x = 8$, $y + x = -2$

2. (24) $y - 2x = 1$, $y = -2$

3. (24) $3x + 2y = 12$, $5x - 4y = 8$

4. (10) Solve the inequality $-3 < d + 2$ and $d + 2 < 12$.

5. (10) Solve and graph the inequality $-4 \leq 4x - 8 < 12$.

Determine the kind of variation, if any, for each equation.

6. (12) $y = \frac{1}{x}$, for $x \neq 0$

7. (12) $z = \frac{1}{xy + a}$, for $x, y \neq 0$ and any value of a

Solve.

***8.** (58) $x^2 - 8x + 16 = 3$

***9.** (58) $x^2 + 26x + 169 = 81$

10. (30) **(Physics)** An object dropped from a height 4 meters above the ground after x seconds is modeled by the function $y = -4.9x^2 + 4$. If measured in feet, the height is modeled by $y = -16x^2 + 1.2$. Without graphing, tell how the graphs of each function compare to each other.

11. (22) **Error Analysis** Sam listed the following points $\{(2, 3),(1, 6), (5, -3),(1, 2)\}$ when giving an example of a discrete function. Correct his example.

12. (51) **Multiple Choice** What is the result of dividing $x^3 - 7x + 3$ by $x - 2$?

A $x^2 + 2x + 3 - \frac{3}{x - 2}$

B $x^2 + 2x - 3$

C $x^2 + 2x - 3 - \frac{3}{x - 2}$

D $x^2 + 2x$

***13.** (58) **Multi-Step** Use $x^2 + 104x - 97 = 4$.

a. What is the first step before you can complete the square?

b. What constant can be added to the binomial to create a perfect square trinomial?

c. What is the factored form of the perfect square trinomial?

d. Solve the equation for x.

14. (46) **Justify** Show that it is possible to solve for x by using either the sine or cosine function.

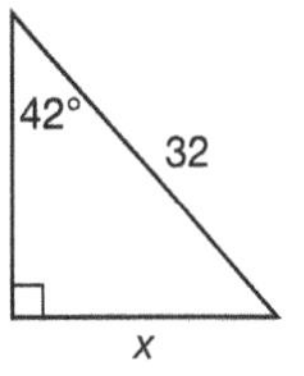

© Saxon. All rights reserved.

***15.** (57) **Formulate** Formulate an expression for the amount Stu will have in his bank account at the end of a year if he invests a principal of $1,850 at an annual interest rate of 2.4%, compounded monthly.

***16.** (58) **Multiple Choice** Chose the letter that best represents the value of x in the equation $x^2 - 42x + 441 = 2$.

A $x = -21 \pm \sqrt{2}$ **B** $x = 20, 22$

C $x = 21 \pm \sqrt{2}$ **D** $x = -20, -22$

17. (26) **Geometry** Miriam is going to create a rectangular vegetable garden along the side of her house and is going to enclose it within a fence on three sides. If the total amount of fencing she purchases is 80 feet, write an equation in standard form for finding all possible lengths and widths for the garden.

18. (19) **Write** Explain how to multiply $(2x + 8)(3x - 6)$ using the FOIL method.

19. (45) **Formulate** Describe the correlation coefficient r using a compound inequality and absolute value symbols.

***20.** (55) **(Pass Codes)** A computer generates temporary pass codes to users. Each pass code is exactly 3 letters long and it can have repeating letters. What is the probability of getting a pass code with 3 vowels (A, E, I, O, or U)?

21. (23) **(Deck Building)** The area of a triangular section of a deck is $72x^2 - 98$ ft^2. If the base of the section of deck is $12x + 14$ ft, find the height of the section.

22. (52) **(Agriculture)** Lee and his brother own a piece of land that has the shape of an equilateral triangle with side length 200 m. They divide the land between them into two equal parts along the altitude of the triangle by putting a fence. What is the length of the fence? What area of land does each of them own? Use a graphing calculator and round your answers to the nearest hundredth.

***23.** (54) **Graphing Calculator** Describe the feasible region for the set of inequalities

$$x \geq 0, y \geq 0, y \leq -0.75x + 8.$$

24. (24) **Error Analysis** Find and explain the error in solving the system $\begin{matrix} x - 10y = 10 \\ 2x - 20y = 23 \end{matrix}$ in the step below.

$$\begin{array}{r} -2(x - 10y = 10) \\ +2x - 20y = 23 \\ \hline \end{array} \qquad \begin{array}{r} -2x + 20y = -20 \\ +2x - 20y = 23 \\ \hline 40y = 3 \end{array}$$

© Saxon. All rights reserved.

25. (50) **Pendulums** The period T (in seconds) of a simple pendulum as a function of its length l (in meters)is given by the equation $T = 2\pi\sqrt{\frac{l}{9.8}}$. Express the length l as a function of the time t.

***26.** (57) **Multi-Step** The half-life of Uranium-234 is 245,000 years.

a. Formulate an exponential function representing the amount of a grams Uranium-234 remaining after t years.

b. Use the function to find how much of a 150-gram sample of Uranium-234 will be left after 182,000 years.

27. (53) Let $f(x) = 3x$ and $g(x) = 3x + 2$. Find the composite function $g(f(x))$.

28. (40) **Justify** A student saw his friend write that $-\sqrt{81} = -9$, and he told his friend that it is wrong because a square root cannot yield a negative number. Why is the student wrong and his friend correct?

29. (44) **Generalize** How might you rationalize the denominator for the expression $\frac{1}{\sqrt[3]{5}}$, when there is a *cube* root in the denominator?

***30.** (58) **Projectile Motion** The world record for the World Championship Punkin Chunkin, held each year in the state of Delaware, is held by an air cannon named "2nd Amendment." The height of a pumpkin t seconds after being shot from this machine can be described by the equation $h = -16t^2 + 880t + 70.7$. After how many seconds will a pumpkin shot from this machine land on the ground? Round your answer to the tenths place.

© Saxon. All rights reserved.

Name ______________________ Date __________ Class __________

Using Fractional Exponents

LESSON 59

1. Find the probability of getting exactly 0 heads if a coin is tossed 3 times.
(49)

Simplify.

2. $3\sqrt{\frac{7}{5}} + 2\sqrt{\frac{5}{7}}$ (40)

3. $\frac{2}{5\sqrt{18}}$ (40)

4. $\sqrt{\frac{2}{3}} + \sqrt{\frac{3}{2}}$ (40)

Complete the square and factor the resulting perfect square trinomial.

*5. $x^2 + 3x$ (58)

*6. $x^2 - 14x$ (58)

7. Find the equation of the line that is perpendicular to $2x + y = 4$ and passes through the point $(-2, -1)$.
(36)

Write the rational exponent as a radical expression.

*8. $27^{\frac{1}{3}}$ (59)

*9. $16^{\frac{3}{4}}$ (59)

*10. $64^{\frac{1}{6}}$ (59)

11. **Verify** Use FOIL to verify the perfect square trinomial formulas.
(23)
a. $a^2 + 2ab + b^2 = (a + b)^2$ **b.** $a^2 - 2ab + b^2 = (a - b)^2$

*12. **Music** Frets are small metal bars placed across the neck of a guitar so that the guitar can produce notes of a specific scale. To find the distance a fret should be placed from the bridge, multiply the length of the string by $2^{-\frac{n}{12}}$, where n is the number of notes higher than the string's root note. Where should a fret be placed to produce a G note on the A string (2 notes higher), if the length of the string is 66 cm, rounded to the nearest tenth place?
(59)

13. **Multiple Choice** Which ordered pair is a solution of the system below?
(39)

$$y \le x$$
$$x > -4$$
$$2x - 5y > 5$$

A $(-3, -3)$ **B** $(-3, 3)$ **C** $(-5, -5)$ **D** $(-5, 5)$

*14. **Coordinate Geometry** Graph the function $f(x) = \frac{1}{2}x^2 - 1$ by making a table.
(27)

*15. **Graphing Calculator** Graph $y \le 2x + 3$ on your graphing calculator. Find a point that is a solution and is not on the boundary line and then find a point that is a solution and is on the boundary line.
(39)

*16. **Verify** Explain why radical expressions with even indices and negative radicands have no real roots. Use $\sqrt[4]{-256}$ to demonstrate your explanation.
(59)

17. **Analyze** Suppose that the expression $\frac{(x^2 - a^2)}{(x - d)}$, for integers a and d, has no remainder. What must be true of a and d?
(38)

© Saxon. All rights reserved.

18. (42) **Decorative Tiles** A 4 in. by 8 in. picture is formed using square tiles that are 2 in. on each side. If there are 8 tiles of different colors, how many different patterns can be created?

*19. (58) **Multi-Step** Use $x^2 - 90x - 15 = -2037$.

a. What is the first step before you can complete the square?

b. What constant can be added to the binomial to create a perfect square trinomial?

c. What are the factors of the perfect square binomial?

d. Solve the equation for x.

20. (51) **Carpentry** A carpenter plans to use wooden plywood to make a wardrobe. He needs a total area of $A = 20x^2 - 23x - 21$ and a minimum width of $5x + 3$. Find the length of the rectangular plywood the carpenter would use to make the wardrobe.

21. (50) **Geometry** The formula for the circumference of a circle is $C = 2\pi r$. Find the inverse of the function. Use the inverse to find the radius of the circle whose circumference is 44 square inches.

22. (45) **Geometry** Find the area and perimeter of each rectangle. Then sketch a scatter plot comparing the area and perimeter. Describe the correlation.

Dimensions	1 by 6	4 by 4	2 by 9	3 by 10	1 by 1	2 by 3	5 by 5
Area (unit^2)							
Perimeter (unit)							

*23. (57) **Marine Biology** The estimated worldwide population $P(t)$ of humpback whales, in thousands, is shown in the table below for various years.

Year	1900	1910	1920	1930	1940
Number (in thousands)	150	100	66	44	29

Model the data with an exponential function, and use the model to estimate the humpback population in 1950.

24. (46) **Error Analysis** Explain and correct the error made: $\tan x = \frac{4}{3} = 1.\overline{3}$.

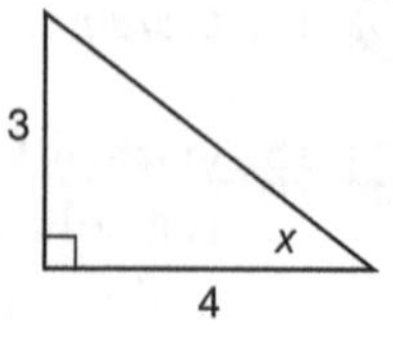

25. (55) **Multiple Choice** What is the probability that 3 out of 5 books randomly chosen from a box where all the titles are different are chosen in alphabetical order?

A about 0.02% **B** about 1% **C** about 1.7% **D** about 10%

© Saxon. All rights reserved.

26. **Justify** Explain the following statement: The triangles formed by the origin, the point (x, x), and the point $(x, 0)$, for any real x, are similar.
(52)

27. **Write** What is a conditional probability? Give an example.
(55)

28. Order the numbers $\frac{3}{\sqrt{5}}, \frac{3\sqrt{5}}{2\sqrt{2}}$, and $\frac{6}{\sqrt{10}}$ from least to greatest, without using a calculator.
(44)

29. **Error Analysis** A student is working with function $m(t) = t^{-3}$ and $n(t) = t^{-2}$. The student claims that the domain of $m(n(t))$ consists of all real numbers. Explain the error.
(53)

30. Name two different angles that have a reference angle of 15°.
(56)

© Saxon. All rights reserved.

Name ____________________ Date __________ Class __________

Distinguishing Between Mutually Exclusive and Independent Events

LESSON 60

1. (36) Find the equation of the line that passes through the point (2, 2) and is perpendicular to the line $y = 3x - 5$.

2. (54) Given the objective function $P = 111x + 95y$ and the constraints $x \leq 4$, $y \geq 0$, $x + 2y \leq 50$, $3x + y \geq 15$, find the minimum and maximum values for the objective function.

3. (41) Find the distance between $(4, -2)$ and $(-3, -5)$.

Divide using synthetic division.

4. (51) $x^3 - 7$ by $x - 5$

5. (51) $x^3 + 3x^2 + 7x + 5$ by $x + 1$

Divide using long division.

6. (38) $x^3 + 2$ by $x + 1$

7. (38) $x^4 - 2$ by $x + 1$

***8.** (60) **Multiple Choice** A jar contains 19 black blocks and 25 gray blocks. The black blocks are numbered 1–19 and the gray blocks are numbered 20–44. Choose the answer that best represents the probability of selecting a black block or a number greater than 21.

A 0.8864 **B** 0.9545 **C** 0.9773 **D** 0.9318

9. (43) **Error Analysis** A student stated that (1, 3) is a solution of the system below. What is the error?

$$y \leq x + 2$$
$$y > -x + 4$$

10. (38) **Generalize** Suppose that $ax^2 + bx + c$ is divisible by $x + d$ with no remainder, for real numbers a, b, c, and d. What can you conclude about the graph of the parabola?

11. (14) **Coordinate Geometry** Matrix multiplication can represent transforming a geometric figure. For example, suppose the three vertices of a triangle are given by the three rows of the matrix A. Then multiplying on the right by the matrix T gives a result that represents a new triangle.

$$A = \begin{bmatrix} 2 & 0 \\ 0 & 2 \\ 0 & 0 \end{bmatrix} \quad T = \begin{bmatrix} 3 & 3 \\ -3 & 3 \end{bmatrix}$$

a. Calculate the product of these matrices.

b. Graph this new triangle.

c. Calculate the areas of the original and the transformed triangles.

d. How do these areas relate to the determinant of matrix T?

12. (52) **Estimate** The hypotenuse of a 30°-60°-90° triangle is 16 inches. Estimate the length of the side adjacent to the 30°. Give your answer to the nearest whole inch.

© Saxon. All rights reserved.

***13.** (60) **Multi-Step** A number cube is rolled once and a fair coin is flipped.
   a. Are the events, a number less than 5 and heads, dependent or independent? Explain why.
   b. Find the probability of the number cube showing less than 5. Round to the hundredths place.
   c. Find the probability of the coin showing heads. Round to the hundredths place.
   d. Use the probabilities found in parts **b** and **c** to find the probability that a roll and flip will show a number less than 5 and heads. Round to the hundredths place.

14. (53) **Chemistry** Seventy percent of a compound is sodium chloride. If 660 grams of other chemicals are in the compound, what is the total weight of the compound?

15. (44) **Physics** The formula $t = \sqrt{\frac{2s}{g}}$ can be used to determine the time t, in seconds, it takes an object initially at rest to fall s meters. In this formula, g stands for the acceleration due to gravity, which on Earth is about 9.8 m/s^2. Use the formula to find out how long it takes a rock initially at rest to fall 110 meters. Write your answer in radical form.

***16.** (15) **Graphing Calculator** Use a graph to estimate the solution of $\begin{matrix} 3.1a + 2.8b = -12.2 \\ -0.9a - 1.1b = 3.85 \end{matrix}$.

17. (51) **Explain** Can synthetic division be used to simplify $\frac{x^3 - 5x + 3}{x^2 + 2}$?

***18.** (60) **Write** Two number cubes are tossed once. Explain why the events, one cube shows 2 and the sum of the two cubes is greater than 5, are dependent.

19. (24) **Geometry** Write a rational expression in simplest form for the ratio of the rectangular prism's surface area to its volume.

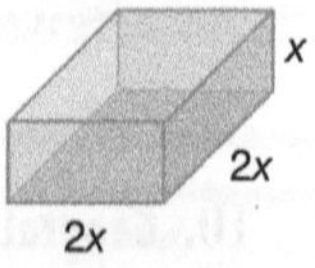

***20.** (58) **Projectile Motion** Gravity on the planet Jupiter is almost three times stronger than on Earth. If an object is thrown into the air, with an initial velocity of 90 feet per second, from the surface of Jupiter, the height, h, of the object in feet after t seconds can be approximated by the equation $h = -42t^2 + 90t$. Find the time at which the object will return to the surface. Round your answer to the tenths place.

21. (41) **Justify** Given the lengths of three sides of a right triangle, how do you know which side is the hypotenuse?

22. (29) **Multiple Choice** Circle the letter that represents the number and type of solutions of the system of three equations: $\begin{matrix} -4x + 12y - 16z = -28 \\ 3x - 9y + 12z = 21 \\ -x + 3y - 4z = -7 \end{matrix}$.

A No solution, inconsistent **B** One solution, inconsistent
C One solution, consistent **D** Infinitely many solutions, consistent

© Saxon. All rights reserved.

Distinguishing Between Mutually Exclusive and Independent Events

23. (58) **Error Analysis** Find and explain the error in the work below. Then find the correct solution.

$$x^2 - 34x - 15 = 15 \qquad (x - 17)^2 = 30$$
$$x^2 - 34x = 30 \qquad x - 17 = \pm\sqrt{30}$$
$$x^2 - 34x + 289 = 30 \qquad x = 17 \pm \sqrt{30}$$

***24.** (59) **Statistics** Given that the variance of a data set is $425^{\frac{5}{3}}$ find the standard deviation for the data set. (Hint: standard deviation $= \sqrt{\text{variance}}$)

25. (46) **History** The Red Pyramid is an Egyptian pyramid with a square base length of 220 meters. The slope is approximately 43°. Approximate the length of an edge of the pyramid to the nearest tenth.

26. (57) **Medicine** If a patient ingests medicine containing a grams of a drug, the amount left in the patient's bloodstream after t hours is given by the equation $y = ab^t$. If one-fourth of the medicine is left after 3 hours what portion is left after 4 hour?

27. (45) **Verify** Use the following data to verify that exchanging the x and y values does not change the value of r for the data set.

x	1	2	3	4
y	67	56	84	70

28. (53) **Investment** You invest in a business. The first month your investment gains 5%. The second month your investment loses 5%. Write a composition function to show whether the investment equals the original investment after two months.

***29.** (59) **Verify** Show the steps needed to write $\sqrt{3} \cdot \sqrt[5]{3}$ as $\sqrt[10]{2{,}187}$.

30. (55) **Geography** The table shows the number of states in the continental U.S. that fall into each time zone. The total exceeds 48 because some states are in two time zones. What is the probability that a randomly chosen state is not in the Pacific time zone?

Time Zone	Eastern	Central	Mountain	Pacific
Number of States	22	20	13	5

© Saxon. All rights reserved.

Name ______________________ Date __________ Class __________

Understanding Advanced Factoring

LESSON 61

Graph.

1. (13) $x = -5$

2. (13) $2x - y = 4$

3. (13) $7y + 7x = 21$

4. (Inv 3) Find the intercepts of the equation $5x - 4y + 7z = 21$.

Simplify.

5. (59) $-16^{-\frac{1}{2}}$

6. (59) $27^{-\frac{1}{3}}$

7. (59) $9^{\frac{3}{2}}$

Find an inverse for the equations.

8. (50) $y = \frac{2}{3}x - 3$

9. (50) $y = 5x + 15$

10. (53) Let $K(u) = 17$ and $L(u) = -13$. Find $K(L(u))$ and $L(K(u))$.

***11.** (54) Minimize $P = 4x + 3y$ for the constraints $\begin{array}{l} x \le 4 \\ y \le 6 \\ x + y \ge 7 \end{array}$

***12.** (57) Mary deposited $980 at 7.0% compounded continuously. How much money will she have after 9 years?

13. (55) **Meteorology** The number of tornadoes in the United States in 2006 is shown in the table.

Season	Jan-Feb	Mar-Apr	May-Jun	Jul-Aug	Sep-Oct	Nov-Dec
Number of Tornadoes	59	395	258	151	160	82

What is the experimental probability that a tornado occurs in the first six months of the year?

***14.** (61) **Write** Tell how factoring a sum of cubes is similar to factoring a difference of cubes.

15. (45) **Probability** A student graphed a set of data points and found that the correlation coefficient was -0.73. What is the probability that the slope of the line of best fit is greater than $\frac{1}{2}$? Explain.

***16.** (60) **Geometry** The probability that a randomly selected point lies within a region can be found using the ratio of the area the point would lie in to the total area. Find the probability that a random point within the region lies within one of the smaller circles.

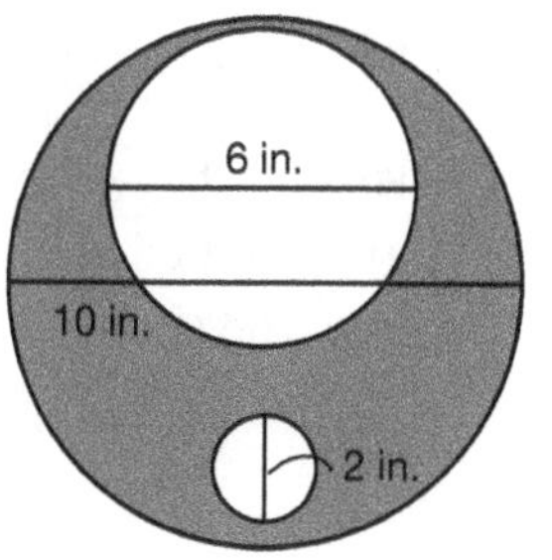

© Saxon. All rights reserved.

17. (46) **Buildings** One building is 310 feet tall and a nearby building is 374 feet tall. From the top of the taller building, you can spot the top of the shorter building at an angle of depression of 30°. How far apart are the two buildings? Round to the nearest foot.

18. (53) **Walking Shadows** While walking the dog one night, you notice how the length of your shadow changes as you approach each lamppost. The length of the shadow seems to be $\frac{1}{5}$ of your distance to the lamppost. Your dog is dragging you along at about 3 feet per second, aiming for a lamppost. Show how to write a composite function that gives the length of your shadow in terms of time as you approach the lamppost.

*19. (59) **Error Analysis** Is the work below correct? If not, find and explain the error, and give the correct solution.

$$x^{\frac{3}{8}} = 3 \longrightarrow \left(x^{\frac{3}{8}}\right)^{\frac{3}{8}} = (3)^{\frac{3}{8}} \longrightarrow x^1 = 3^{\frac{3}{8}} \longrightarrow x = \sqrt[8]{27}$$

20. (49) **Analyze** Suppose you spin the spinner shown 8 times. What is the probability that you will spin black 5 times?

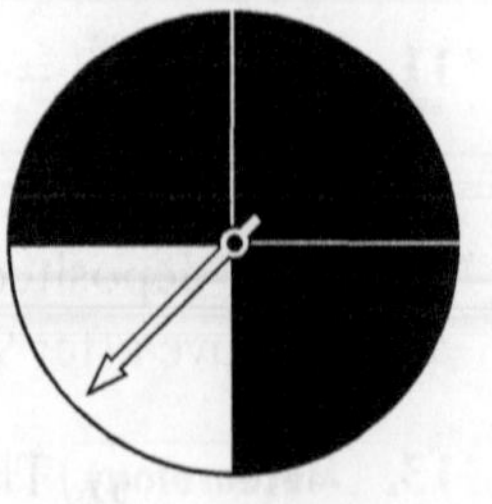

21. (58) **Verify** Use the form $x^2 + 2cx + c^2$ for a quadratic perfect square trinomial to verify the method of completing the square.

*22. (54) **Graphing Calculator** Describe the feasible region for the inequalities:

$$x \geq 0, y \geq 0, y \leq -0.75x + 8$$

23. (45) **Multiple Choice** Which value of r, the correlation coefficient, describes the set of points that are *closest* to forming a line?
A $r = -0.75$ **B** $r = 0$ **C** $r = 0.6$ **D** $r = 0.65$

*24. (60) **Commuting to Work** According to data collected in the 2005 American Community Survey, approximately 10.67% of workers carpool to work, 4.66% use public transportation, and 2.47% walk. Find the probability that a randomly selected worker carpools or uses public transportation.

25. (47) **Write** A few different equations of the form $y = b^x$ are graphed to the right. Describe in your own words how the shape of the graph depends on the value of b.

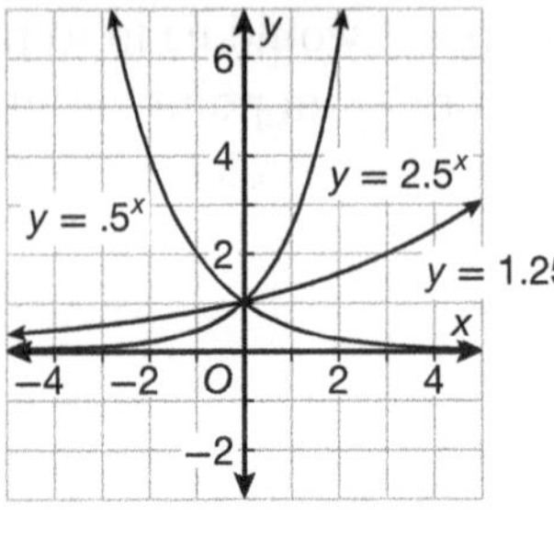

© Saxon. All rights reserved.

***26.** (59) **Multi-Step** Use $\frac{5^{\frac{3}{5}} \cdot 5^{\frac{3}{5}}}{5^{\frac{4}{5}}}$.

a. Which property of rational exponents should be applied first to simplify the expression? Explain.

b. Apply the property from part a.

c. Which property of rational exponents should be applied next?

d. Apply the property from part c.

e. If possible, finish simplifying the expression from part d.

27. (52) **Multiple Choice** In the diagram to the right, find the l ength of the hypotenuse of triangle LMN.

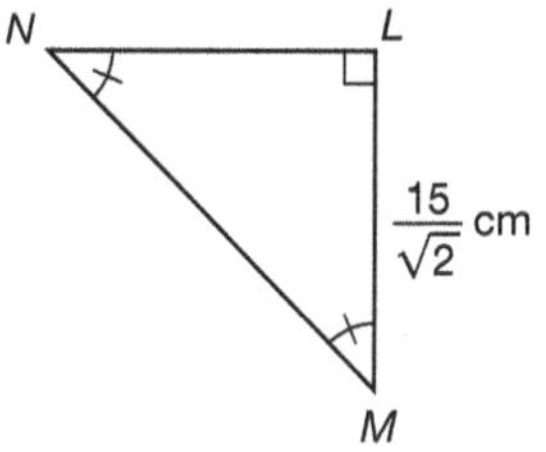

A 7.5 **B** $\sqrt{2}$

C 15 **D** $15\sqrt{3}$

***28.** (61) **Multi-Step** The area of a twin size mattress is $x^2 - 275 - 11x + 25x$ square inches.

a. Factor the polynomial by grouping.

b. Find the area given that $x = 50$.

29. (56) **(Amusement Parks)** The Giant Swing at Silver Dollar City in Branson, Missouri, rotates through an angle measuring 230°. Find the reference angle for this angle.

***30.** (61) **Verify** Show that there are two different ways to group the terms in $3d + 6f + d^2 + 2df$ and that both lead to the same factorization.

© Saxon. All rights reserved.

Name ______________________ Date __________ Class __________

Using Complex Numbers

LESSON 62

Factor.

***1.** (61) $125x^4 + 375x^3 - x - 3$

***2.** (61) $64x^{12} - 125y^9$

Add or subtract.

3. (37) $a + \frac{a}{b}$

4. (37) $\frac{ax^2}{m^2p} - c + \frac{2}{m}$

5. (37) $-\frac{gh^2}{x^3} + xh + \frac{g^2h^2}{gx^3}$

Factor the greatest common factor.

6. (23) $35x^7y^5m - 7x^5m^2y^2 + 14y^7x^4m^2$

7. (23) $6x^2ym^5 - 2x^2ym + 4xym$

Simplify.

8. (59) $\frac{1}{81^{\frac{-3}{4}}}$

9. (59) $(-27)^{\frac{-2}{3}}$

10. (59) $\frac{1}{-3^{-2}}$

11. (49) **School** It is estimated that 15% of students walk to school. What is the probability that exactly 2 out of 5 randomly selected students will walk to school?

12. (50) Find an equation for the inverse of $y = \frac{1}{5}x^3 + 6$.

13. (55) What are the odds in favor of rolling a 3 on a number cube?

***14.** (62) **Multiple Choice** Which is a real number?
A $15i$ **B** $0 + 15i$ **C** $5 + 0i$ **D** $15 + 15i$

***15.** (37) **Verify** Show that the expression $\frac{1}{1 + \frac{1}{x+1}}$ is equivalent to $\frac{x+1}{x+2}$.

***16.** (62) **Electrical Engineering** A circuit has a current of $(4 - 2i)$ amps, and a second circuit has a current of $(6 - 6i)$ amps. Find the sum of the currents.

17. (55) **Analyze** Explain why the odds in favor of an event with a probability of 50% are 1 to 1.

18. (58) **Projectile Motion** The Leaning Tower of Pisa measures 180.4 feet. If an object is thrown into the air, with an initial velocity of 80 feet per second, from the top of the lower side, the height, h, of the object in feet after t seconds can be described by the equation $h = -16t^2 + 80t + 180.4$. Find the time at which the object will reach a height of 200 feet. Round your answer to the tenths place.

***19.** (60) A number cube is rolled once. Are the events a number greater than 3 or a multiple of 2 mutually exclusive or inclusive? Explain why.

***20.** (61) **Transportation** The approximate volume of a moving truck, in cubic feet, can be given by $x^3 - 6x^2 + 8x + 5x^2 - 30x + 40$. Factor this expression by grouping. Then find the volume when $x = 10$.

21. (56) **Multiple Choice** Which of the following angles is *not* coterminal with 225°?
A 585° **B** −135° **C** 935° **D** −495°

© Saxon. All rights reserved.

22. (57) **Multi-Step** The population of an insect colony is growing at a rate of 1.5% per week.

a. Write an expression for the function $N(P)$ that gives the population one week after the population is P.

b. What composite function gives the population three weeks after the population is P?

***23.** (61) **Graphing Calculator** Factor $2x^5 - x^4 - 2x + 1$. Then enter the original expression for Y1 and the factored expression for Y2 on a graphing calculator. Access the Table function and study the table of values for the expressions. What is true? What does it mean?

24. (59) **Write** Explain why radical expressions with even indices and positive radicands have two real roots. Use $\sqrt[6]{64}$ to demonstrate your explanation.

***25.** (51) **Geometry** An expression for the volume of the rectangular prism is $V = 2x^3 + 7x^2 - 14x - 40$. Find an expression for the missing dimension.

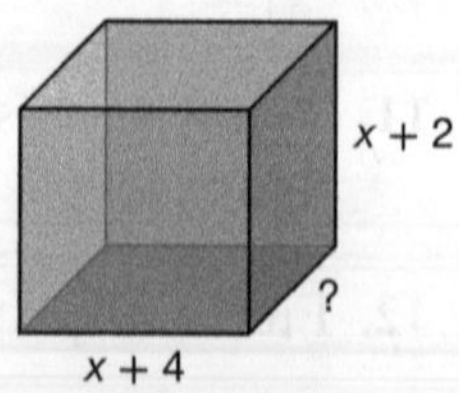

26. (57) **Analyze** Suppose the graph of $y = b^x + k$ passes through the points $(3, -3)$ and $(5, 0)$. Determine whether the equation models exponential growth or decay.

27. (52) **Error Analysis** A student made an error while studying the relation between the two triangles shown. Explain the error.

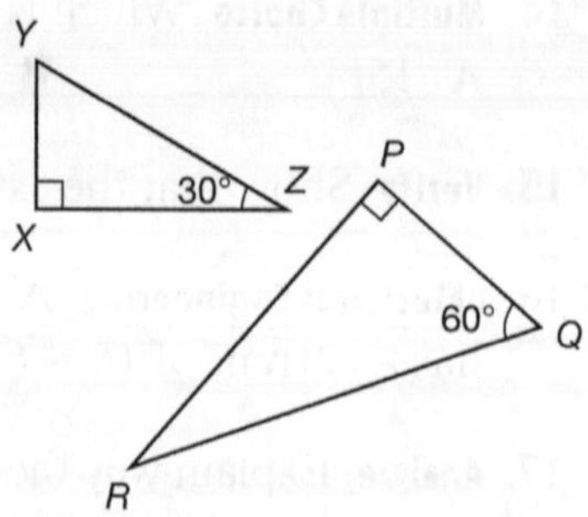

Find the missing angles.

$m\angle Y = 90° - 30° = 60°$ $m\angle R = 90° - 60° = 30°$

$m\angle X = 90°$ $m\angle Y = 60°$ $m\angle Z = 30°$

$m\angle P = 90°$ $m\angle Q = 60°$ $m\angle R = 30°$

The corresponding angles are congruent. So, the triangles are congruent.

28. (58) **Probability** A sales clerk has a weekly quota of 15 sales. The probability, p, that the sales clerk will meet this quota after working d days, in a 5-day work week, can be approximated by $p = -0.04d^2 + 0.4d$. How many days a week should the sales clerk work for the probability of making 15 sales to be 0.8?

***29.** (62) **Verify** Show that $11i$ and $-11i$ are solutions of $x^2 = -121$.

© Saxon. All rights reserved.

30. (54) **Cell Phones** Mobile-U has two cell phone plans, the Metropolitan Plan and the Continental Plan. The cost for each plan is shown in the table. A company is comparing the two plans. The company needs at least 12 cell phones, one for each sales representative. Each representative will use at least 500 minutes per month. What options does this company have?

	Continental Plan	**Metropolitan Plan**
Start-up Fee	\$50	\$100
Free minutes	2000	1200
Per minute rate above free minutes	10 cents	7 cents
Monthly charge	\$20 × # of cell phones	\$25 × # of cell phones

© Saxon. All rights reserved.

Name ______________________ Date __________ Class __________

Understanding the Unit Circle and Radian Measures

LESSON 63

Simplify.

1. (48) $\dfrac{\frac{1}{x} + \frac{4}{y}}{3 + \frac{1}{xy}}$

2. (48) $\dfrac{\frac{4}{x} - 3}{\frac{7}{x} + 2}$

3. (48) $\dfrac{x + \frac{1}{x^2}}{x^2 - \frac{2}{x^2}}$

Determine if the following probability experiments are binomial experiments. If not, explain why.

4. (Inv 5) Rolling a number cube 18 times and recording the results

5. (Inv 5) Flipping 2 coins 20 times to test if they match half of the time

Simplify.

6. (40) $5\sqrt{45} - 2\sqrt{75} + 2\sqrt{108}$

7. (40) $3\sqrt{12}\left(4\sqrt{3} - 3\sqrt{3}\right)$

Expand.

8. (19) $(x + 5)^3$

9. (19) $(x + 4)^3$

Solve.

10. (35) $36x^2 - 36 = 0$

11. (35) $24x = -11x^2 - x^3$

12. (50) **Error Analysis** Julian is finding the inverse of the function $y = 2x^3$. Which step is incorrect?

Step One: $y = 2x^3 \longrightarrow$ Step Two: $x = 2y^3 \longrightarrow$ Step Three: $\frac{x}{2} = y^3 \longrightarrow$
Step Four: $\pm\sqrt{\frac{x}{2}} = y$

*13. (62) Write the expression in terms of i and then add: $\left(15 - \sqrt{-4}\right) + \left(10 + \sqrt{-1}\right)$.

14. (44) **Geometry** In the triangle to the right, find x.

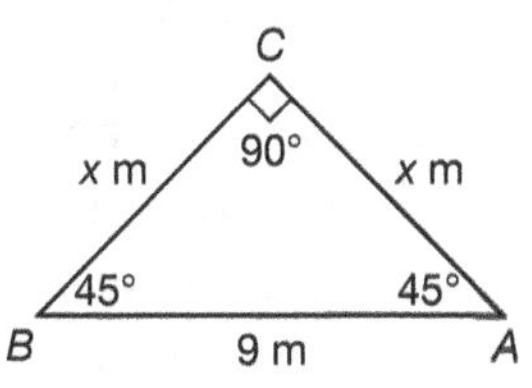

*15. (63) **Planet Rotation** Jupiter is the largest planet. Its radius is approximately 44,365 miles. Jupiter rotates faster than Earth. It takes approximately 9.8 hours for Jupiter to make one complete rotation. If an object is fixed on Jupiter's equator, how far does it travel in 1 hour due to Jupiter's rotation?

16. (57) **Multiple Choice** Which of the following functions could be used to model exponential growth?

A $y = \dfrac{1}{e^x}$ **B** $y = 2e^{-x}$ **C** $y = \dfrac{2}{e^{2x}}$ **D** $y = \dfrac{2.4}{e^{-2x}}$

© Saxon. All rights reserved.

17. (46) **Surveying** A surveyor stands on the roof of a building that is 180 feet above the ground and spots the top of a taller building at an angle of elevation of 34°. The two buildings are 480 feet apart. Find the height of the taller building. Round to the nearest foot.

*18. (54) **Graphing Calculator** Describe the feasible region for the set of inequalities $x \geq 0$, $y \geq 0, y \leq -1.5x + 9.5$.

*19. (60) **Formulate** A fair coin is flipped. Write the equation that can be used to solve for the probability that three flips result in heads, then four flips, and seven flips. Write a formula using exponents that can be used to find the probability that the same independent event will occur n times.

20. (48) **Multiple Choice** Which of the following expressions is equivalent to $\frac{\frac{1}{x}+\frac{1}{y}}{1-\frac{1}{x}}$?

A $\frac{1-x}{x+y}$ **B** $\frac{x^2-xy-x-y}{x^2y}$ **C** $\frac{x+y}{xy-y}$ **D** $\frac{2(1-x)}{x+y}$

*21. (62) **Write** How is adding and subtracting complex numbers similar to adding and subtracting polynomials?

*22. (45) **Model** Sketch a graph of five points whose correlation coefficient is about 0.1.

23. (56) **Multi-Step** The formula $\theta = \frac{180°(n-2)}{n}$ gives the measure of each interior angle of an n-sided regular polygon.
a. Use the formula to find the measure of an interior angle of a regular decagon.
b. Find the reference angle for this angle.

24. (63) **Estimate** Use what you know about the unit circle and special angles to estimate $\cos(0.3\pi)$. Do not use a calculator. Explain your method.

25. (58) **Jupiter** Gravity on the planet Jupiter is almost three times stronger than on Earth. If an object is thrown into the air, with an initial velocity of 100 feet per second, from the surface of Jupiter, the height, h, of the object in feet after t seconds can be approximated by the equation $h = -42t^2 + 100t$. Find the time at which the object will first reach 50 feet. Round your answer to the tenths place.

26. (53) **Analyze** Let $f(x) = ax + b$ and $g(x) = cx + d$. Under which conditions will the composite functions $f(g(x))$ and $g(f(x))$ be equal?

27. (61) **Construction** The volume of a typical American-made brick in cubic millimeters can be represented by the polynomial $x^3 - 20x^2 - 4500x + 126{,}000$ where the length is given by $x + 70$. Fully factor the expression for the volume of a brick.

© Saxon. All rights reserved.

28. (59) **Coordinate Geometry** Sketch a graph of the equation $y = \sqrt[3]{x}$, where y is the side length of a cube and x is the volume of the cube. Use the graph to estimate the volume of a cube with side lengths of 2.4 in. Use the graph to estimate the side length of a cube with a volume of 6.9 in^3.

***29.** (63) **Error Analysis** A student incorrectly found s, the length of the indicated arc, as shown below.

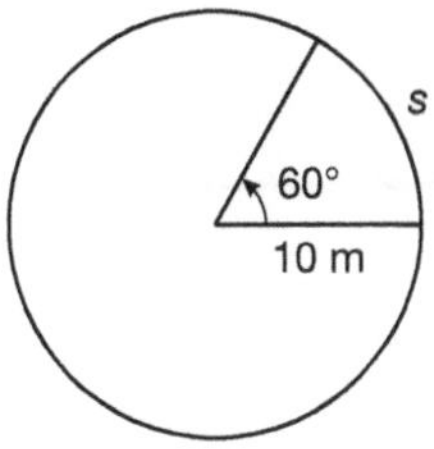

$s = r\theta$

$= 10 \cdot 60$

$= 600$ m

What is the error? Find the correct arc length.

***30.** (55) **Pass codes** A computer generates temporary pass codes for users. Each pass code is exactly 3 letters long with no repeating letters. What is the probability of getting a pass code with 3 vowels (A, E, I, O, or U)?

© Saxon. All rights reserved.

Name ______________________________ Date __________ Class __________

Using Logarithms

LESSON 64

Use synthetic substitution.

1. (51) Find $f(6)$ for $f(x) = x^4 - 4x^3 + 2x^2 + 4x - 18$.

2. (51) Find $f(-7)$ for $f(x) = x^4 + 5x^3 - 12x^2 - 4x + 8$.

3. (26) Find the equation of the line that passes through $(-2, 5)$ and $(-6, -3)$.

4. (41) The sides of a triangle measure 7 in., 6 in., and 8 in. Is the triangle a right triangle?

Find the zeros of each quadratic function.

5. (35) $f(x) = 2x^2 + x - 15$ **6.** (35) $f(x) = -32x^2 - 28x$ **7.** (35) $f(x) = x^2 - 9$

Determine if (0, −3) is a solution of the inequalities.

8. (39) $5x + 2y < -4$ **9.** (39) $y - 2x > 6$ **10.** (39) $16y - 2 \geq x$

11. (52) **Formulate** A parasail is attached to a boat with a rope 300 feet long. The angle of elevation from the boat to the parasail is 48 degrees. Write a formula that would help you to estimate the parasail's height above the boat.

***12.** (63) **Coordinate Geometry** Find the area of triangle OQR. Give the answer in exact form and to the nearest tenth of a square unit.

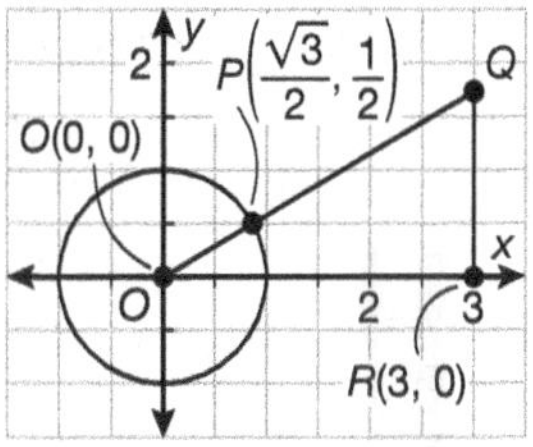

13. (50) Find an equation for the inverse of $y = 5x - 8$. Identify the domain and range of the inverse function.

***14.** (64) **Write** Explain why $\log_0 9$ and $\log_1 9$ do not exist.

15. (53) **Population** Currently the U.S. population is growing at a rate of approximately 0.6 percent per year. According to the 2000 census, the population was about 281 million. Use composite functions to predict the U.S. population in the year 2015, and justify your prediction.

***16.** (59) **Multi-Step** Use $\left(\frac{9}{7}\right)^{\frac{1}{4}}\left(\frac{9}{7}\right)^{\frac{1}{4}}$.

a. Which property of rational exponents should be applied first to simplify the expression? Explain.

b. Apply the property from part a.

c. Which property of rational exponents should be applied next?

d. Apply the property from part c.

e. If possible, finish simplifying the expression from part d.

© Saxon. All rights reserved.

*17. **Transportation** The approximate volume of a moving truck, in cubic feet, that can (61) move four to five household rooms can be given by $x^3 - 15x^2 + 56x + 6x^2 - 90x + 336$. Factor this expression by grouping. Then find the dimensions when $x = 15$.

18. **Geometry** The figures below show how to create Sierpinski's Triangle. Start with a (57) solid black equilateral triangle (Iteration 0); at every iteration, join the midpoints of the sides of each black triangle to get a smaller triangle, and color the interior of that triangle white.

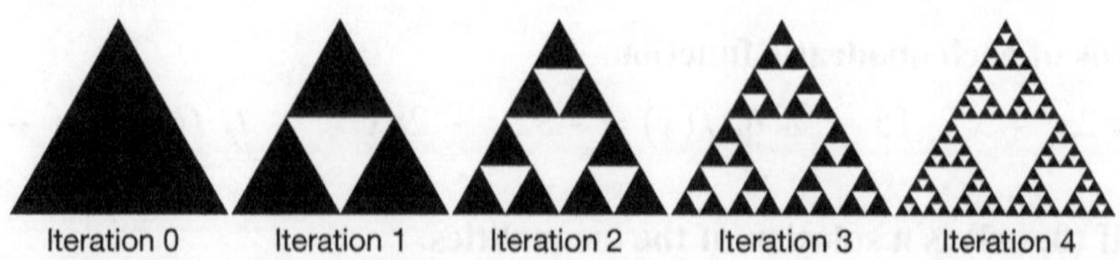

Formulate an exponential function for the number of black triangles $N(x)$ in the xth iteration.

19. Find the slope of the line that passes through the points $A\left(\frac{3}{x}, \frac{1}{3}\right)$ and (31) $B\left(\frac{1}{5}, \frac{5}{x}\right)$, where x is any non-zero real number.

*20. **Windshield Wipers** A rear windshield wiper moves (63) through an angle of 135° on each swipe. To the nearest inch, how much greater is the length of the arc traced by the top end of the wiper blade than the length of the arc traced by the bottom end of the wiper blade?

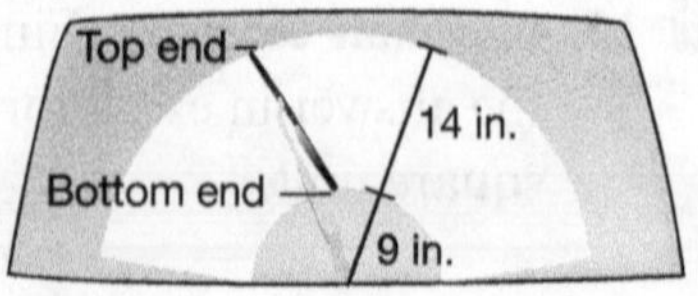

21. **Multiple Choice** Which of the following expressions is equivalent to $\frac{3}{5 - \sqrt{2}}$? (44)

A $\frac{3 - 15\sqrt{2}}{21}$ **B** $\frac{15 + 3\sqrt{2}}{23}$ **C** $\frac{15 - 2\sqrt{3}}{21}$ **D** $\frac{21 - 3\sqrt{2}}{15}$

22. **Multi-Step** What number needs to be added to both sides of the equation to make (Inv 6) $x^2 + 12x + 42 = 0$ a perfect square? Solve the equation.

*23. **Rainwater** The acidity of a liquid is measured in pH, given by the function (64) $\text{pH} = -\log[\text{H}^+]$, where $[\text{H}^+]$ represents the concentration of hydrogen ions in moles per liter. In 1999, the hydrogen ion concentration of rainwater in the Chesapeake Bay region of Maryland was found to be approximately 0.0000316 moles per liter. What was the pH of the rainwater, to the nearest tenth? Show how to check your answer by writing a logarithmic equation and its equivalent exponential equation. (*Hint*: You will need to use the ≈ symbol instead of the = symbol.)

*24. **Write** Two number cubes are tossed once. Explain why the events, one cube shows a (60) number less than 5 and the sum of the two cubes is a multiple of 2, are dependent.

© Saxon. All rights reserved.

25. (55) **Justify** Give an example of an event that has a probability of 0. Explain why the probability is 0.

***26.** (62) **Graphing Calculator** Set the mode on your graphing calculator to $a + bi$ by pressing the Mode key and using the arrow keys. Then find $\sqrt{-1296} \div \sqrt{-324}$.

27. (56) **Error Analysis** Rizwan tried to find the value of $\cos\theta$, where θ is an angle in standard position with the point $Q(-6, 8)$ on its terminal side. His work is shown below. What was Rizwan's error?

$$r = \sqrt{x^2 + y^2}$$

$$r = \sqrt{(-6)^2 + 8^2}$$

$$r = \sqrt{100}$$

$$r = 10$$

$$\cos\theta = \frac{x}{r}$$

$$\cos\theta = \frac{6}{10} = 0.6$$

***28.** (64) **Multiple Choice** Which equation is equivalent to $\log_2 16 = x$?

A $2^x = 16$ **B** $x^2 = 16$ **C** $16^2 = x$ **D** $2^{16} = x$

29. (45) **Analyze** Compare and contrast correlation coefficient values of -0.45 and 0.45.

***30.** (58) **Falling Objects** The height, in feet, of an object that is falling or is projected into the air can be described by $h = -16t^2 + v_0t + h_0$, where h is the height in feet after t seconds, v_0 is the initial velocity of the object in feet per second, and h_0 is the initial height of the object in feet per second. A coin is tossed from the top of a 100 foot tall building, with an initial velocity of 92 feet per second. Write the equation that models the height of the coin. Find the time when the coin will reach the ground. Round your answer to the tenths place.

© Saxon. All rights reserved.

Name ______________________ Date ____________ Class ____________

Using the Quadratic Formula

LESSON 65

1. Secret ingredient X has a half-life of 23 hours. What portion of 360 kg will remain after 7 hours?
(57)

Use long division.

2. Divide $(3x^3 + 12x^2 - 15x + 15)$ by $(3x - 9)$
(38)

3. Divide $(2x^3 + 14x^2 - 4x - 48)$ by $(2x + 4)$
(38)

Solve.

*4. $x^2 = 7 + 3x$
(58)

*5. $x^2 = -x + 1$
(58)

Simplify.

6. $2\sqrt{3}(5\sqrt{3} - 2\sqrt{6})$
(40)

7. $4\sqrt{63} - 3\sqrt{28}$
(40)

8. $3\sqrt{2} \cdot 2\sqrt{6} \cdot 3\sqrt{6}$
(40)

9. Jordon spins a spinner with six equal-sized sections numbered 1–6. In one spin, what is the likelihood that the spinner will stop on a 1 or a 5?
(55)

*10. **Error Analysis** Find and correct the error a student made in solving $4x^2 - 37x + 9 = 0$.
(65)

$$x = \frac{-b \pm \sqrt{b^2 - 4ac}}{2a}$$

$$= \frac{-37 \pm \sqrt{(-37)^2 - 4(4)(9)}}{8}$$

$$= \frac{-37 \pm \sqrt{1369 - 144}}{8}$$

$$= \frac{-37 \pm \sqrt{1225}}{8} = \frac{-37 \pm 35}{8} = -\frac{1}{4} \text{ and } -9$$

11. List the coefficients in the 6th row of Pascal's Triangle.
(49)

12. **Probability** A history test has 20 questions, 7 of which are about the Civil War. Students are asked to answer 5 of the 20 questions. What is the probability that a student randomly selecting questions will select 5 Civil War questions?
(55)

*13. **Write** Describe how to determine $\sin \frac{3\pi}{2}$ by using the unit circle.
(63)

14. Find an equation of a line perpendicular to $y = \frac{1}{3}x - 4$.
(36)

15. **Analyze** In what type of right triangles will the sine and cosine values of the acute angles be equal?
(46)

© Saxon. All rights reserved.

Find x and y.

16. (52)

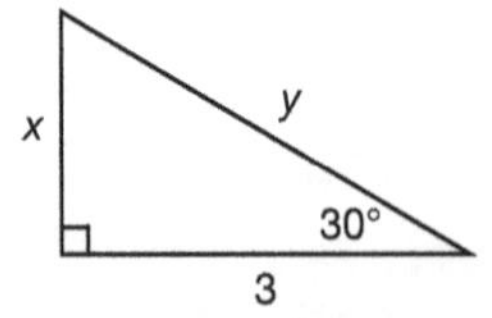

17. (52)

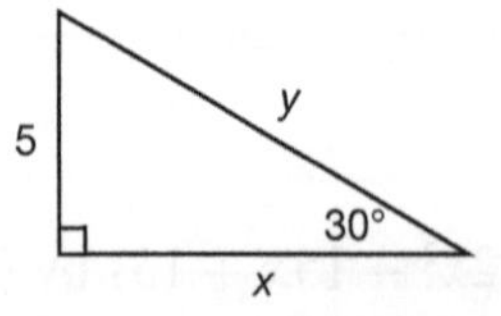

***18.** (64) **Multi-Step** Complete parts a–d to graph a logarithmic function and use the graph to estimate a logarithm.

a. Write the equation $y = \log_2 \frac{1}{4}$ in exponential form. What value of y makes both equations true?

b. Writing exponential equations if needed, complete the table of values for the function $y = \log_2 x$.

x	$\frac{1}{4}$	$\frac{1}{2}$	1	2	4	8
$y = \log_2 x$						

c. Plot the points and sketch the graph of the function.

d. Use your graph to estimate the value of $\log_2 6$. Check your estimate by evaluating the appropriate power of 2 on a calculator.

19. (58) **Multiple Choice** Choose the letter that best represents the value of x in the equation $x^2 + 2x + 7 = 8$.

A $x = -1 \pm \sqrt{2}$ **B** $x = -2, 0$ **C** $x = 2, 0$ **D** $x = 1 \pm \sqrt{2}$

20. (39) **Measurement** Given that 1 strip of red ribbon = 3 inches and 1 strip of blue ribbon = 4 inches, write and graph the inequality that represents that the total number of inches must be no less than 60.

21. (Inv 1) **Multi-Step** A car is sitting outside in a driveway. Consider the following statement, "If it starts raining, the car will get wet."

a. Is the converse of the statement true? Explain.

b. Is the contrapositive true? Explain.

22. (44) **Geometry** The base of a triangle is $5\sqrt{2}$ feet, and its height is $\frac{1}{\sqrt{3}}$ feet. Find the area of the triangle.

***23.** (62) **Physics** A fireworks technician wants a firework to explode 70 feet below the top of the Gateway Arch in St. Louis. The Gateway Arch has a height of 630 feet. The technician has figured the height of the firework to be modeled by $-16t^2 + 160t$, where t is the time in seconds after it is launched. The solutions of $-16t^2 + 160t = 560$ give the number of seconds it will take for the firework to reach the desired height. Solve the equation. Will the firework reach the desired height? If so, when?

© Saxon. All rights reserved.

24. (53) **Justify** Let $f(x) = 3x - 7$ and $g(x) = \frac{1}{3}x + \frac{7}{3}$.

a. Justify the claim that $f(g(x)) = x$.

b. Does $g(f(x)) = x$ also? Explain.

25. (61) **Error Analysis** Find and correct the error a student made in factoring the expression below.

$$9x^4 - 63x^3 - 8x + 56$$
$$9x^3(x - 7) - 8(x - 7)$$
$$(x - 7)(9x^3 - 8)$$
$$(x - 7)(3x - 2)(6x^2 + 6x + 4)$$

***26.** (65) **Physical Science** The North Falls waterfalls in Silver Falls State Park in Oregon are 136 feet high. The equation $-16t^2 + 136 = 0$ gives the number of seconds it takes for a drop of water at the top of the falls to reach the pool of water below. Solve the equation by using the quadratic formula. Round to the nearest hundredth of a second.

27. (56) **Formulate** Let θ be an angle in standard position and let n be any integer. You can use the expression $\theta + n(360°)$ to indicate all the angles coterminal with θ. Write an expression for all the angles coterminal with 15°, and find 3 different ones.

***28.** (65) **Graphing Calculator** Solve $5x^2 - 2x - 16 = 0$ by using a graphing calculator.

29. (59) **Velocity of an Electron** The velocity at which an electron orbits the nucleus of an atom is known as the Fermi-Thomas velocity and can be found using the equation $\frac{Z^{\frac{2}{3}}}{137}c$, where Z is the number of protons in the nucleus and c is the speed of light. What is the Fermi-Thomas velocity for platinum, which has 78 protons, in terms of c? Round to the nearest thousandths place.

***30.** (64) **Analyze** Write the following equations in exponential form. What property of exponents is illustrated?

$$\log_2 1 = 0, \log_3 1 = 0, \log_{15} 1 = 0$$

© Saxon. All rights reserved.

Name ______________________ Date __________ Class __________

Solving Polynomial Equations

LESSON 66

Simplify each expression.

1. (59) $\dfrac{81^{\frac{2}{4}}}{81^{\frac{3}{4}}}$

2. (37) $\dfrac{p - 4px}{p}$

3. (37) $\dfrac{4a}{a + 4} + \dfrac{a + 2}{2a}$

4. (37) $\dfrac{x}{x + 2} + \dfrac{3 + x}{x^2 + 4x + 4}$

5. (59) $(4^6)^{\frac{1}{3}}$

6. (59) $343^{\frac{1}{3}} \cdot 343^{\frac{1}{3}}$

***7.** (60) There are 7 cherries and 3 grapes in a bag. What is the probability of selecting 2 grapes at random without replacement?

8. (36) Find the equation of the line that passes through (2, −3) and is parallel to $y = -\frac{3}{8}x + 2$.

***9.** (66) **Packaging** A new food product is to be sold in cylindrical cans. The designer wants the height of the can to be 6 inches greater than the radius. The manager wants the can to have a volume of about 125 in^3.

a. Write a polynomial equation in standard form that can be used to find the radius. Leave in terms of π. Hint: The formula for the volume of a cylinder is $V = \pi r^2 h$.

b. Find the approximate radius that should be used for the can by using a graphing calculator. Round the radius to the nearest tenth.

10. (50) Find an equation for the inverse of $y = 7x^2 + 21$ for $x \geq 0$. Identify the domain and range of the inverse function.

11. (22) **Multiple Choice** $f(x) = x - 5$ is an example of a:

A continuous function
B discrete function
C discontinuous function
D both B and C

12. (58) **Write** Explain why it is necessary to add the constant term $\left(\frac{b}{2}\right)^2$ to both sides of the equation when using the method of completing the square to solve a quadratic equation.

***13.** (Inv 5) **Graphing Calculator** Calculate the binomial probability, to the nearest hundredth of a percent, of 8 successes out of 50 trials, if the probability of success for each trial is 0.17.

14. (56) **Geometry** Consider the circle with radius 5 units, centered at the origin. A 270° angle in standard position cuts the circle into a larger and a smaller sector. Find the area of the larger sector.

***15.** (64) **Error Analysis** A student converted the logarithmic equation $\log_2 64 = x$ to exponential form by writing $x^2 = 64$. What is the error? Write the correct exponential equation.

© Saxon. All rights reserved.

*16. (65) **Multi-Step** A 24 in. by 36 in. photo is framed and the total area of the photo and the frame is 1200 in^2.

a. Write a quadratic expression in standard form to represent the situation.

b. Find the width of the frame to the nearest hundredth of an inch.

17. (57) **Formulate** Write the equation of an exponential function whose graph passes through the points (0, 5) and (−2, 125). Determine whether the function is increasing or decreasing.

*18. (65) **Analyze** If using the quadratic formula to solve $16 = -3x^2$, what would be the values of a, b, and c?

*19. (63) **Tires** The diameter of a certain tire is 24 inches. Through how many degrees does the tire rotate when the automobile travels 5 feet? Give your answer to the nearest degree.

20. (55) **Population** In 2006, the U.S. Census Bureau estimated there were 36,457,549 people living in California and 299,398,484 living in the United States.

a. Estimate the probability that a person randomly selected in the United States lives in California.

b. Estimate the odds in favor that a person randomly selected in the United States lives in California.

21. (62) **Probability** A student taking a test has enough time to solve 2 out of the 5 equations shown.

$$x^2 + 1 = 0, \quad x^2 + 4 = 0, \quad x^2 - 25 = 0, \quad x^2 - 16 = 0, \quad x^2 + 9 = 0$$

If she chooses equations randomly, what is the probability that both equations have imaginary solutions?

Use trigonometric ratios to solve for each of the variables.

22. (52) $\cos 30° = \frac{\sqrt{3}}{2}$ and $\cos 30° = \frac{y}{12}$

23. (52) $\sin 30° = \frac{1}{2}$ and $\sin 30° = \frac{x}{12}$

24. (60) **Multi-Step** A student creates a chart classifying his books by subject and cover.

a. Are the events math textbook or paperback textbook mutually exclusive or inclusive? Explain why.

b. Find the probability that four books, selected randomly with replacement, are math or paperback. Round to the thousandths place.

	Cover	
Subject	**Hardcover**	**Paperback**
Math	7	3
Sciences	23	14
Social Sciences	6	16
History	1	4

© Saxon. All rights reserved.

25. (59) **Music** Frets are small metal bars placed across the neck of a guitar so that the guitar can produce notes of a specific scale. To find the distance a fret should be placed from the bridge, multiply the length of the string by $2^{-\frac{n}{12}}$, where n is the number of notes higher than the string's root note. Where should a fret be placed on the low E string to produce a note that is 5 notes higher, if the length of the string is 64 cm, rounded to the nearest hundredths place?

***26.** (61) **Generalize** Tell how to factor by grouping.

27. (49) **Probability** Find the probability of getting at least 1 tail if a coin is tossed 4 times.

***28.** (66) **Multiple Choice** Which is not a possible rational root of $2x^3 + 2x^2 - 21x - 27 = 0$?

A -3 **B** -1 **C** $\frac{2}{3}$ **D** $\frac{9}{2}$

29. (53) Let $f(x) = 8x - 6$ and $g(x) = 4x^2 + 1$. Evaluate the composition $(f \circ g)(-2)$ using two different methods.

***30.** (64) **Write** Explain why $\log_0 5$ and $\log_1 5$ do not exist.

© Saxon. All rights reserved.

Name ______________________ Date __________ Class __________

Finding Inverse Trigonometric Functions

LESSON 67

1. Given $\theta = -1787°$, find the measure of the reference angle.
(56)

Convert each measure from degrees to radians.

2. $60°$ (63)
3. $125°$ (63)
4. $-240°$ (63)

5. Use synthetic substitution to find $f(-3)$ for $f(x) = 7x^4 - 3x^3 + x^2 + 11$.
(51)

6. Complete the square and factor the resulting perfect square trinomial: $x^2 + 6x$.
(58)

Simplify.

7. (48) $\dfrac{\frac{a}{b}}{\frac{a+b}{b}}$

8. (48) $\dfrac{\frac{s}{a+b} + \frac{x}{b}}{\frac{a}{s+x}}$

*9. **Error Analysis** A student incorrectly solved the equation $\sin\theta = -0.55$, for $90° \le \theta \le 270°$, as shown below. What error did the student make? Find the correct solution.
(67)

$$\sin\theta = -0.55$$
$$\sin^{-1}(-0.55) \approx -33.4°$$
$$\theta \approx 180° - 33.4°$$
$$\theta \approx 146.6°$$

*10. **(Tennis)** A tennis player 6 feet from the net hits an overhead shot, hitting the ball at a height of 8.5 feet. Assume that the path of the ball is a straight line. To the nearest degree, what is the maximum angle θ at which the ball can be hit and land within the court?
(67)

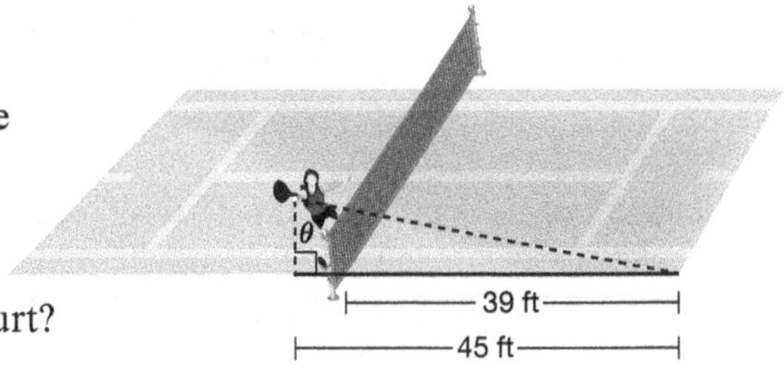

*11. **Graphing Calculator** **a.** Graph $y = x^4 + 2x^3 - 12x^2 + 14x - 5$ on a graphing calculator. What are the x-intercepts?
(66)

b. Find the multiplicity of each root of $x^4 + 2x^3 - 12x^2 + 14x - 5 = 0$ by factoring.

12. Minimize $P = 4x + 6y$ for the constraints $0 \le x \le 4$, $y \ge 1$, $y \ge -x + 4$
(54)

*13. **Multiple Choice** Which is a solution of $5 + 2x^2 = -3x$?
(65)

A 1 **B** $\frac{5}{2}$ **C** $\frac{3}{4} + \frac{\sqrt{31}}{4}$ **D** $-\frac{3}{4} - \frac{\sqrt{31}}{4}i$

© Saxon. All rights reserved.

***14.** (Inv 5) **Contact Lenses** The contact lens prescription for Asia's left eye is stronger than the prescription for her right eye. If Asia accidentally mixed up her contact lenses, what is the probability that she will put the correct lens in either eye on the first try? Explain.

***15.** (63) **Multi-Step** Complete parts a–d to determine the measure of the angle formed by the hands of a clock when the time is 3:24. Find all measures in radians.

a. Find x, the angle formed at 3:00.

b. Find $(x + y + z)$, the angle through which the minute hand moves in 24 minutes.

c. Find y, the angle through which the hour hand moves in 24 minutes.

d. Find z, the angle formed by the minute hand and hour hand when the time is 3:24.

16. (62) **Model** Make a Venn Diagram to illustrate how the complex numbers, real numbers, and imaginary numbers are related.

17. (61) **Finance** The value of a stock over the past five years where x is the number of years is modeled by $x^3 - 2x^2 + 5x - 10$. Factor this expression.

18. (54) **Geometry** The Community Center wants to build a playground area and enclose it within a wooden, split rail fence. The cost of fencing is \$20 per finished foot. The cost for painting the fence is \$12 per finished foot. The Center cannot spend more than \$2000 on fencing. The playground cannot be any longer than 30 ft and needs to be at least 15 ft wide. What is the maximum area the Center can get for the size of the playground? How much will this cost?

19. (60) **Error Analysis** A cup contains 15 pink beads, 24 purple beads, and 18 gold beads. Three beads are individually selected with replacement. The work below is used to find the probability that one of each color bead is selected in the order pink, purple, gold. Is the work correct? If not, explain the error and find the correct solution. If so, explain each step of the work.

K = event of pink bead drawn

U = event of purple bead drawn

G = event of gold bead drawn

$$P(K,U,G) = P(K) \cdot P(U) \cdot P(G) = \frac{5}{19} \cdot \frac{8}{19} \cdot \frac{6}{19} \approx 0.035$$

$$P(K) = \frac{15}{57} = \frac{5}{19} \quad P(U) = \frac{24}{57} = \frac{8}{19} \quad P(G) = \frac{18}{57} = \frac{6}{19}$$

20. (59) **Multiple Choice** Choose the letter that best represents $\sqrt[3]{\frac{216x^{12}}{4}}$ simplified.

A $\frac{3x^4\sqrt[3]{4}}{2}$ **B** $3x^4\sqrt[3]{2}$ **C** $6x^4\sqrt[3]{4}$ **D** $\frac{3x^4\sqrt[3]{2}}{2}$

© Saxon. All rights reserved.

*21. **Analyze** When solving $x^3 + 7x^2 + 7x - 6 = 0$, why is it not necessary to use synthetic substitution after one of the roots is found?
(66)

22. **Write** A ball is tossed with an initial velocity of 74 feet per second from the top of a building that is 50 feet tall. The height, h, of the ball in feet after t seconds can be approximated by the equation $h = -16t^2 + 74t + 50$. The ball will be 20 feet from the ground when $t = -0.375$ second and $t = 5$ seconds. Explain why you would not use the solution $t = -0.375$ second.
(58)

*23. **Coordinate Geometry** Find $m\angle AOB$ to the nearest tenth of a degree, using these points: $A(8, 3)$, $O(0, 0)$, and $B(8, 0)$.
(67)

24. **Verify** Explain why the probability of choosing first, second, and third place winners for a photo when randomly choosing from the top 10 athletes is $\frac{1}{_{10}C_3}$.
(55)

*25. **Storage** The volume of a can of dog food is 450 cubic inches. The height of the can is 5 inches greater than its radius. Write a polynomial in standard form, using 3.14 for π, that can be used to find the radius. (Round the constant to the nearest integer.) Then find the approximate radius by using a graphing calculator.
(66)

26. **Generalize** Suppose θ is an angle in standard position and $Q(x, y)$ is a point on the terminal side of the angle. Explain how the signs (positive or negative) of $\sin\theta$, $\cos\theta$, and $\tan\theta$ depend on which quadrant Q lies in.
(56)

27. **School** A teacher has 3 red crayons, 7 yellow crayons, 5 green crayons, and 2 blue crayons. A yellow crayon and then a blue crayon are chosen at random without replacement. Are these events dependent or mutually exclusive?
(60)

28. The number of rabbits increases exponentially. At first there were 400. Three years later there were 1600. How many rabbits would there be after 10 years?
(57)

29. Maximize $P = 5x + 2y$ for the constraints
(54)

$$\begin{aligned} y &\geq 0 \\ x &\geq 0 \\ y &\leq -x + 10 \\ y &\leq 2x + 1 \end{aligned}$$

*30. **Physical Science** The South Falls waterfalls in Silver Falls State Park in Oregon are 177 feet high. The equation $-16t^2 + 177 = 0$ gives the number of seconds it takes for a drop of water at the top of the falls to reach the pool of water below. Solve the equation by using the quadratic formula. Round to the nearest hundredth of a second.
(65)

© Saxon. All rights reserved.

Name ______________________ Date ___________ Class ___________

Finding Conditional Probability

LESSON 68

1. Solve $s^2 - 22 = -112$. Write the solutions in terms of i.
(62)

Factor completely.

2. $-3pax + pax^2 + 2pa$
(23)

3. $30 + 3x^2 - 21x$
(23)

4. Multi-Step Use $x^2 - 62x + 961 = 26$.
(58)

a. Explain why the left side of the equation is a perfect square trinomial.

b. Factor $x^2 - 62x + 961$.

c. Solve the equation for x.

***5. Error Analysis** Find and correct the error a student made in determining the roots and their multiplicity in $x^3 - 4x^2 + 4x = 0$.
(66)

$$x^3 - 4x^2 + 4x = 0$$
$$x(x^2 - 4x + 4) = 0$$
$$x(x - 2)(x - 2) = 0$$
The only root is 2 and its multiplicity is 2.

6. Analyze What does it mean for an event to have the first number in the odds in favor ratio greater than the second number?
(55)

7. Geometry Write an expanded expression for the volume of the cube shown.
(49)

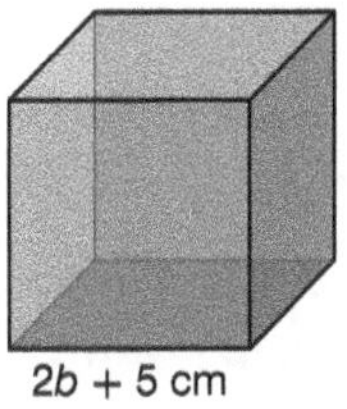

***8. Housing** The table shows estimated housing occupancy for three states for the year 2006.
(68)

Find the probability that a randomly selected house from one of these states is in Nevada. Then find the probability that a randomly selected house from one of these states is in Nevada given that it is vacant. Round each percent to the nearest tenth.

	Occupied Houses	Vacant Houses
Mississippi	1,075,521	165,918
Nevada	936,828	128,439
New York	7,088,376	819,138

Simplify.

9. $-64^{-\frac{2}{3}}$
(59)

10. $\dfrac{-3}{-9^{-\frac{3}{2}}}$
(59)

11. $(-8)^{\frac{1}{3}}$
(59)

12. Find the arc length of a sector with a radius of 4 in. and central angle $\theta = \frac{\pi}{6}$.
(63)

© Saxon. All rights reserved.

*13. **Probability** A bag contains 30 red marbles and 10 white marbles. If three marbles are randomly chosen without replacement, what is the probability of selecting all red or all white marbles?
(68)

14. **Surveying** A surveyor is standing on top of a hill that is 600 meters from a bridge. Her angle of elevation to the top of the bridge is 14° and her angle of depression to the bottom of the bridge is 26°. To the nearest tenth of a meter, what is the height of the bridge?
(46)

*15. **Generalize** Insert = or ≠ to make each statement true.
(68)

If A and B are independent events, then $P(B|A)$ ☐ $P(B)$.

If A and B are dependent events, then $P(B|A)$ ☐ $P(B)$.

16. **Statistics** How do probability and statistics compare and contrast?
(60)

17. **Multiple Choice** Which angle does *not* have a reference angle of 30°?
(56)

A $-30°$ **B** $120°$ **C** $570°$ **D** $-150°$

*18. **Estimate** Use what you know about the unit circle and special angles to estimate $\mathrm{Cos}^{-1}(0.48)$ in degrees. Do not use a calculator. Explain your method.
(67)

19. **Write** Describe how to determine cos 150° by using its reference angle.
(63)

Simplify.

20. $3\sqrt{\frac{5}{2}} - 2\sqrt{\frac{2}{5}}$
(44)

21. $3\sqrt{18} + 2\sqrt{50} - \sqrt{98}$
(44)

22. Calculate the binomial probability $P(12, 200, 0.09)$ to the nearest hundredth of a percent using the formula $P(n, N, p) = \frac{N!}{n!(N-n)!}p^n(1-p)^{N-n}$.
(Inv 5)

*23. **Graphing Calculator** Describe the feasible region for the set of inequalities $x \geq 0$, $x \leq 4$, $y \geq 0$, $2y + x \leq 25$.
(54)

24. **Error Analysis** Find and correct the error a student made in subtracting complex numbers.
(62)

$$(7 - 4i) - (2 + 3i)$$
$$5 - i$$

*25. **Multiple Choice** Which describes all the values of $\sin^{-1}\frac{1}{2}$?
(67)

A $\frac{5\pi}{6}$ **B** $\frac{\pi}{6}$

C $\frac{2\pi}{3}$ **D** $\frac{\pi}{3}$

© Saxon. All rights reserved.

26. (59) **Estimate** Sketch a graph of the equation $y = \frac{\sqrt[3]{6\pi^2 x}}{2\pi}$, where y is the radius of a sphere and x is the volume of the sphere. Use the graph to estimate the volume of a sphere with a radius of 2 cm. Use the graph to estimate the radius of a sphere with a volume of 14 cm^3.

27. (61) **Volume** The volume of a California king size mattress is $12x^3 - 36x^2 - 432x - 384$ cubic inches. Factor the polynomial given that $x - 8$ is a factor. Then find the volume given that $x = 20$.

***28.** (64) **Plant Nutrition** The pH of a soil is given by the function pH $= -\log [H^+]$, where $[H^+]$ represents the concentration of hydrogen ions in moles per liter. Most plants require soil with a hydrogen ion concentration between 0.0001 and 0.00000001 moles per liter. What pH values correspond to these hydrogen ion concentration values?

***29.** (65) **Travel** A driver leaves a parking lot and heads due south at a rate of 40 miles per hour. An hour later, another driver leaves the same parking lot and heads due west at a rate of 60 miles per hour. Approximately how long will it take for the cars to be 300 miles apart?

***30.** (68) **Multi-Step** Two bags each contain papers labeled with numbers 1 through 5. One paper is selected from each.

a. Explain why selecting a 5 from the first bag and the sum of the numbers is greater than 5 are dependent events.

b. Find the probability of both events.

© Saxon. All rights reserved.

Name ______________________ Date __________ Class __________

Simplifying Complex Expressions

LESSON 69

Solve using the quadratic formula.

1. (65) $f(x) = x^2 + 8x - 3$

2. (65) $f(x) = 3x^2 - 10x + 4$

3. (55) **Probability** A bag holds 53 yellow marbles, 17 red marbles, and 30 green marbles. What is the probability of not choosing a red marble?

4. (57) A savings account earns interest at an annual rate of 3.8%, compounded quarterly. If the account begins with a principal amount of $2,700, what will its value be after 14 years?

Solve for *x*.

5. (59) $x^{\frac{1}{7}} = 5$

6. (59) $x^{\frac{2}{3}} = 36$

***7.** (69) **Multiple Choice** In which quadrant of the complex plane is $5 - i$ located?
A Quadrant I **B** Quadrant II **C** Quadrant III **D** Quadrant IV

8. (61) **Write** Explain how to use synthetic division to determine if $x + 6$ is a factor of $x^3 + 3x^2 - 28x - 60$ and then perform the division.

Simplify.

9. (62) $\frac{1}{4}\sqrt{-256}$.

10. (62) $\frac{1}{2}\sqrt{-2500}$.

11. (56) Given $\theta = -920°$, find the measure of the reference angle.

***12.** (69) **Generalize** Show that the product of any two complex conjugates, $a + bi$ and $a - bi$, is a real number.

***13.** (67) Evaluate the inverse trigonometric function $\text{Sin}^{-1}\left(-\frac{\sqrt{2}}{2}\right)$. Give your answer in both radians and degrees.

14. (Inv 4) Why can't the matrix below be used as an encoding matrix for a cipher?

$$\begin{bmatrix} 5 & -2 & 3 \\ 0 & 0 & 7 \\ 0 & 0 & 13 \end{bmatrix}$$

15. (56) **Amusement Parks** You get on a ferris wheel ride, and the ferris wheel turns through 1370°. How much further must the wheel turn before you are at the bottom again?

***16.** (68) **Error Analysis** Find and correct the error a student made in finding $P(\text{AM}|\text{Male})$.

$$P(\text{AM}|\text{Male}) = \frac{16}{24} = \frac{2}{3} = 66.7\%$$

	Male	Female
AM	16	4
PM	8	12

© Saxon. All rights reserved.

*17. **Graphing Calculator** (66) **a.** Graph $y = x^3 + 6x^2 - 32$ on a graphing calculator. What are the x-intercepts?

b. Find the multiplicity of each root of $x^3 + 6x^2 - 32 = 0$ by factoring.

*18. **Formulate** (68) Give a rule for finding $P(B|A)$. *Hint:* Consider the rule for $P(A \text{ and } B)$ for dependent events.

19. **Multiple Choice** (64) Which equation is equivalent to $10^x = 0.1$?

A $\log_{0.1}10 = x$ **B** $\log_{0.1}x = 10$

C $\log_{10}0.1 = x$ **D** $\log_{10}x = 0.1$

20. **Formulate** (60) Write a formula for $P(A \text{ or } B \text{ or } C)$. Use the diagram to the right to help you.

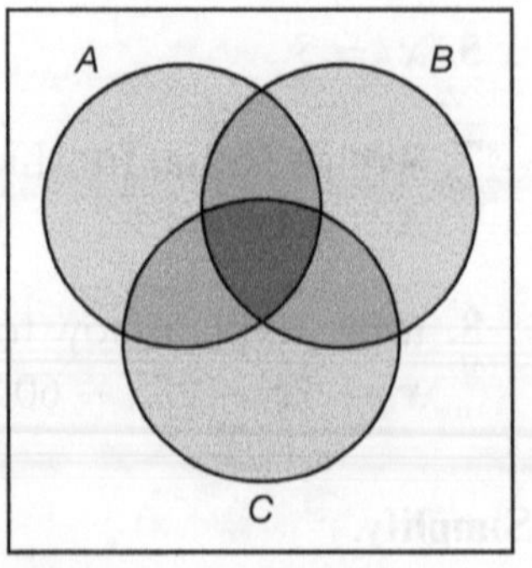

21. **Multi-Step** (67) Let $f(\theta) = \text{Sin}\,\theta$ and $g(\theta) = \text{Sin}^{-1}\theta$, where θ is in radians.

a. Evaluate $f\left(g\left(\frac{1}{2}\right)\right)$. Show your steps.

b. Evaluate $g\left(f\left(\frac{\pi}{6}\right)\right)$. Show your steps.

c. Based on part a, what is the value of $f(g(x))$? Based on part b, what is the value of $g(f(x))$?

22. **Error Analysis** (58) Examine the work below. Find and explain the error. Then find the correct solution.

$$x^2 - 44x + 484 = 121$$
$$(x - 22)^2 = 121$$
$$x - 22 = 11$$
$$x = 33$$

*23. **Probability** (65) A student graphs $y = 9x^2 - 29x + 22$ and uses a graphing calculator to find the value of the zeros one at a time. What is the probability that the first zero the student finds is negative? Why?

*24. **Multi-Step** (69) Simplify $i^{22} + i^{15}$. Then graph the number on the complex plane.

25. **Planet Rotation** (63) Venus is only slightly smaller than Earth; its radius is approximately 3757 miles. But it rotates much more slowly; it takes 243 Earth days for Venus to make one complete rotation. If an object is fixed on Venus's equator, how far does it travel in 1 hour due to Venus's rotation?

© Saxon. All rights reserved.

26. **Analyze** Describe the value(s) of b^x when $b = 1$ and when $b \neq 1$.
(64)

*27. Find the absolute value of $|3 - 4i|$.
(69)

*28. Find the absolute value of $|6 + 2i|$.
(69)

29. **Sports** A football player playing in a domed stadium kicks a football straight up into the air. The height of the football after t seconds can be modeled by $-16t^2 + 80t$. The dome has a height of about 288 feet. The solutions of $-16t^2 + 80t = 288$ give the number of seconds it will take for the football to reach the top of the dome. Solve the equation. Will the football reach the top of the dome? If so, when?
(62)

30. **Geometry** Find the area of the triangle to the right.
(59)

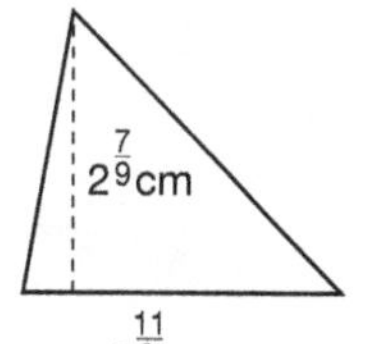

© Saxon. All rights reserved.

Name ______________________ Date __________ Class __________

Solving Radical Equations

LESSON 70

Solve the equations. Write the solutions in the form $a + bi$.

1. (62) $3p^2 + 7 = -9p^2 + 4$

2. (62) $2x^2 + 31 = 9$

***3.** (66) Find the roots and give the multiplicity of each root: $x^3 - 7x^2 + 11x - 5 = 0$

4. (53) Let $f(x) = 3x + 1$ and $g(x) = x - 2$. Find the composite function $f(g(x))$.

5. (60) Of the 220 people who came into the Italian deli on Friday, 104 bought pizza and 82 used a credit card. Half of the people who bought pizza used a credit card. What is the probability that a customer bought pizza or used a credit card?

Solve for x by completing the square.

6. (58) $x^2 = 9x - 7$

7. (58) $-5x - 6 = -x^2$

***8.** (70) **Lighthouses** The number of miles m a person can see on a clear day is approximated by $m = 1.2116\sqrt{h}$, where h is the person's height in feet above sea level. If a person standing at the top of the Barnegat Lighthouse in New Jersey on a clear day can see a distance of 16 miles, what is the person's height above sea level?

9. (55) **Error Analysis** The odds in favor of an event are 9 to 2. To the nearest percent, what is the probability of the event?

10. (61) **Multiple Choice** What is $P(-3)$ if $x + 3$ is a factor of $2x^3 + 2x^2 - 10x + 6$?

A -3 **B** 0 **C** 3 **D** 6

11. (59) **Velocity of an Electron** The velocity at which an electron orbits the nucleus of an atom is known as the Fermi-Thomas velocity and can be found using the expression $\frac{Z^{\frac{2}{3}}}{137}c$, where Z is the number of protons in the nucleus and c is the speed of light. What is the Fermi-Thomas velocity for cobalt, which has 27 protons, in terms of c? Round to the nearest thousandths place.

***12.** (70) **Write** What is an extraneous solution? When can it occur?

13. (63) **Estimate** Use what you know about the unit circle and special angles to estimate tan 43°. Do not use a calculator. Explain your method.

***14.** (69) **Graphing Calculator** With your calculator in a + bi mode, find the following.

a. $(64 - 82i)(26 + 31i)$ **b.** $-3.7i(2.25 + 4.5i)$

15. (62) **Electrical Engineering** A circuit has a current of 5 amps, and a second circuit has a current of $(14 - 9i)$ amps. Find the sum of the currents.

© Saxon. All rights reserved.

16. (54) **Temporary Employees** A department store is planning to hire up to 24 temporary employees for a tent sale. Experienced workers will be paid \$20 per hour and inexperienced workers will be paid \$15 per hour. The company can pay up to \$400 per hour for the temporary employees. Experienced workers produce 1.5 times more profit than inexperienced workers. How many of each type of worker should be hired to maximize the company's profits?

*17. (69) **Multi-Step** The product of a number and its multiplicative inverse is 1.
   a. State the multiplicative inverse of $2 + 3i$.
   b. Simplify the multiplicative inverse.
   c. **Verify** Show that your answer in part b is the multiplicative inverse by multiplying it by $2 + 3i$.

Factor each expression completely.

18. (61) $8c^3 + 343$

19. (61) $-5z^3 + 320$

20. (66) **Generalize** How does the Rational Root Theorem make factoring polynomials easier? What must be true about a polynomial before it used?

*21. (67) **Wheelchair Accessibility** A contractor designed the wheelchair ramp shown in the diagram. The ramp must satisfy a building code that specifies 4.7° as the maximum angle of elevation, labeled θ in the diagram. Does the design satisfy the building code? Justify your answer.

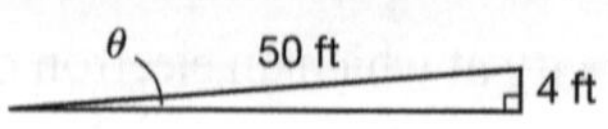

22. (50) Find an equation for the inverse of $y = 5x^3 - 20$. Determine whether each relation is a function.

23. (65) **Verify** A student used factoring to find that the solutions of $4x^2 - 11x - 20 = 0$ are -1.25 and 4. Show how to verify these solutions with the Quadratic Formula.

24. (54) Maximize $P = 4.5x + 2.4y$ for the constraints
$$\begin{aligned} y &\geq 0 \\ x &\geq 0 \\ y &\geq x \\ y &\leq -2x + 9 \end{aligned}$$

25. (64) **Error Analysis** A student converted the exponential equation $4^{-2} = \frac{1}{16}$ to logarithmic form by writing $\log_4(-2) = \frac{1}{16}$. What is the error? Write the correct logarithmic equation.

26. (52) **Geometry** Each side of the regular hexagon shown is 7 cm. Find the length of the diagonal $\overline{AE}$. Round your answer to the nearest tenth. (The measure of one interior angle of an n-gon is $\frac{(n-2)180°}{n}$.)

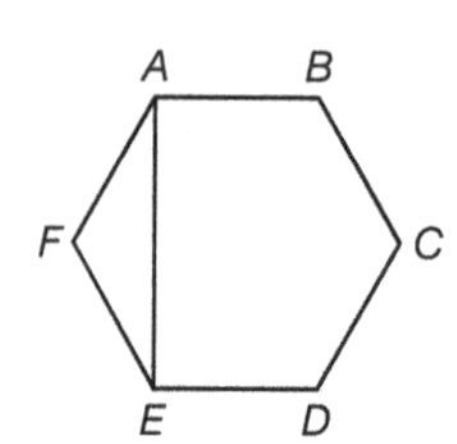

© Saxon. All rights reserved.

27. (60) **Write** Examine the formula for the probability of two inclusive events. Explain why $P(A \text{ and } B)$ is subtracted from the formula.

$$P(A \textbf{ or } B) = P(A) + P(B) - P(A \textbf{ and } B)$$

28. (53) **Multi-Step** A clothing store has a sale in which all the shirts are 20% off. On the last day of the sale, all shirts have an additional 25% off. Find a function describing how much a shirt with price p will cost on the last day. Solve the function.

***29.** (70) **Probability** A number cube is rolled twice. What is the probability that the number facing up on each roll shows a solution of $\sqrt{2x - 8} = x - 4$?

***30.** (68) **Multiple Choice** A bag of grapes contains 9 green grapes and 15 red grapes. If 4 grapes are chosen at random, without replacement, what is the approximate probability that the first two grapes are green and the last two grapes are red?

A 4.6% **B** 5.9% **C** 7.1% **D** 13%

© Saxon. All rights reserved.

Name ______________________ Date __________ Class __________

Using the Law of Sines

LESSON 71

Solve.

1. (66) $3x(x^2 + 7x - 25) = 0$

2. (66) $4x(2x^2 + 9x - 45) = 0$

Use synthetic division to divide.

3. (51) $5x^3 - 10x^2 + 20x - 15$ by $x - 1$

4. (51) $4x^5 - 129$ by $4x - 8$

5. (58) **Write** The square root property states: If $x^2 = a$, then $x = \pm\sqrt{a}$. Explain why x must be positive or negative.

6. (50) Find an equation for the inverse of $y = -3x$. Identify the domain and range of the inverse function.

7. (61) **Coordinate Geometry** Because $x - a$ is a factor of $P(x)$ when $P(a) = 0$, a is an x-intercept of the graph of $P(x)$. Which of the following ordered pairs must be on the graph of $P(x) = x^3 - 7x^2 + 36$?

(−6, 0) (−4, 0) (−2, 0) (1, 0) (3, 0) (6, 0)

8. (54) **Flowers** Jay is planting a maximum of 40 bulbs of lilies and tulips in her garden. She wants more tulips, x, than lilies, y. Write a system of inequalities and find the maximum number of lily bulbs Jay can plant.

9. (59) **Multiple Choice** Choose the letter that best represents $\sqrt[4]{625x^{28}}$ simplified.

A $5x^7$ B $25x^{14}$ C $25x^7$ D $5x^{14}$

***10.** (71) **Geography** On a map, line segments connecting three southeast Texas cities form a triangle as shown to the right. To the nearest mile, what is the distance from Mathis to Cuero?

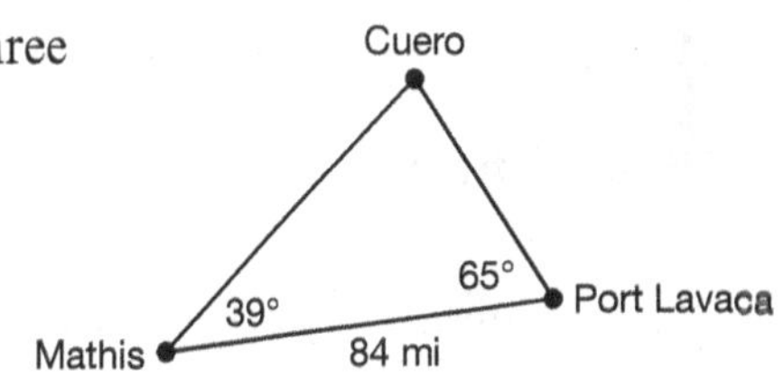

11. (65) **Write** Why must you write a quadratic equation in standard form before using the Quadratic Formula?

12. (52) Angle θ is an acute angle of a right triangle and $\cos\theta = \frac{7}{11}$. Find the sine of angle θ.

13. (66) **Analyze** $3 - 6\sqrt{2}$ is a root of a polynomial equation. What must be another root of the equation? Why?

© Saxon. All rights reserved.

***14.** (71) **Error Analysis** Explain and correct the error a student made in finding the value of x.

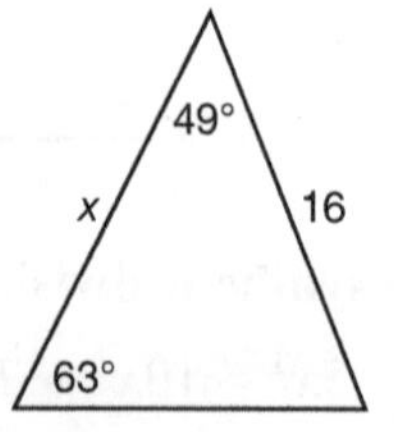

$$\frac{\sin 63°}{16} = \frac{\sin 49°}{x}$$

$$x = \frac{16 \sin 49°}{\sin 63°} \approx 13.55$$

***15.** (68) **Quality Control** In a factory, a sample of items is checked during all three work shifts. During the first shift, 2 out of 11 items were found defective. During the second shift, 0 out of 13 items were found defective. During the third shift, 4 out of 20 items were found defective. What is the probability that an item was checked during the first shift, given that it was not defective?

***16.** (70) **Graphing Calculator** Estimate the solution of $\sqrt{3x+1} - 4 + \sqrt[3]{x} = 0$ to the nearest hundredth.

17. (57) **Formulate** The half-life of Thorium-229 is 7340 years. Formulate an exponential function representing the amount of a grams of Thorium-229 remaining after t years. Use the function to find how much of a 200 gram sample of Thorium-229 will be left after 10,000 years.

***18.** (63) **Error Analysis** To find the tangent of 300°, a student used its reference angle as follows: $\tan 60° = \sqrt{3}$, therefore $\tan 300° = \sqrt{3}$. What is the error? Find the correct value of $\tan 300°$.

19. (53) Let $f(x) = 5x^2$ and $g(x) = -4x$. Find the composite function $f(g(x))$.

20. (52) **Geometry** Find the area of the shaded region of the regular hexagon.

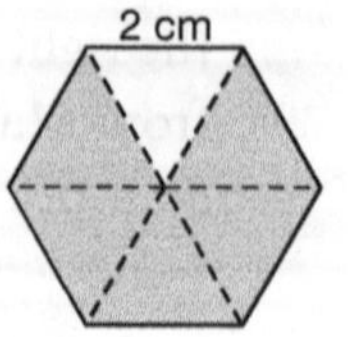

21. (54) Maximize $P = 2x + y$ for the constraints $x \geq 0$, $y \geq 0$, $x + y \leq 6$

***22.** (70) **Analyze** Explain why $x - \sqrt{5} = 2x$ is not a radical equation.

23. (38) Use long division to divide $-x^4 - 7x^3 + 6x^2 - 1$ by $x - 3$.

***24.** (69) **Multi-Step** Simplify $\frac{4 - 8i + 2 + i}{7 + 3i + 2i}$. Write the answer in the form $a + bi$.

25. (Inv 7) **Multi-Step** A dietician asked 26 high school students how often they eat breakfast. The students eat breakfast a mean of 2.5 days per week and there is a standard deviation of 1.36.

a. If Stephanie eats breakfast 5 days per week, how many standard deviations above the mean is she?

b. If Darryl eats breakfast 1 day per week, how many standard deviations below the mean is he?

c. Who is closest to the sample mean?

© Saxon. All rights reserved.

26. (62) **Bay Bridge** A sailor in a boat beneath the San Francisco Bay Bridge shoots a flare straight up. The height of the flare after t seconds is modeled by $-16t^2 + 96t$. The bridge is 220 feet above the water and the sailor is 12 feet above the water. The solutions of $-16t^2 + 96t = 208$ give the number of seconds it will take for the flare to reach the bridge. Will the flare reach the bridge? If so, when?

*27. (71) **Multiple Choice** What is the area of $\triangle ABC$ if $a = 7$ in., $b = 9$ in., and $m\angle C = 23°$?
A about 12.3 in^2 **B** about 24.6 in^2 **C** about 29 in^2 **D** about 49.2 in^2

Simplify.

*28. (69) $\frac{2 + 5i}{i}$

*29. (69) i^7

30. (59) $49^{\frac{5}{12}} \cdot 49^{\frac{1}{12}}$

© Saxon. All rights reserved.

Name ______________________ Date __________ Class __________

Using the Properties of Logarithms

LESSON 72

1. Find the distance between (6, 0) and (−3, −3).
(41)

2. Find the equation of the line that has a slope of $\frac{2}{5}$ and passes through (3, −5) in slope-intercept form.
(26)

Simplify.

3. $4\sqrt{3} \cdot 5\sqrt{2} \cdot 6\sqrt{12}$
(40)

4. $4\sqrt{63} - 3\sqrt{28}$
(40)

*5. **Write** Explain why $\log_2 2^x = x$.
(72)

6. **Tennis** A tennis player 8 feet from the net hits an overhead shot, hitting the ball at a height of 8 feet. Assume that the path of the ball is a straight line. To the nearest degree, what is the maximum angle θ at which the ball can be hit and land within the court?
(67)

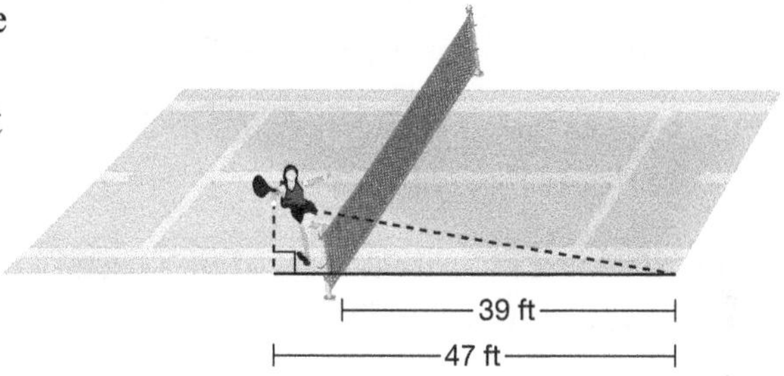

7. **Formulate** Formulate an expression for the amount Imani will have in her bank account at the end of ten years if she invests a principal of $2500 at an annual interest rate of 6.4%, compounded quarterly.
(57)

8. Find the absolute value of $|3 + i|$.
(69)

9. Describe the feasible region for the set of inequalities $0 \leq x \leq 15$, $y \geq 0$, $3y + 4x \leq 75$.
(54)

*10. Solve $\triangle DEF$ given that $m\angle D = 65°$, $m\angle E = 47°$, and $d = 102$.
(71)

11. **Multiple Choice** If an angle in standard position has a measure of $\frac{3\pi}{4}$ radians, in what point does its terminal side intersect the unit circle centered at the origin?
(63)

A $\left(-\frac{\sqrt{2}}{2}, \frac{\sqrt{2}}{2}\right)$ **B** $\left(-\frac{\sqrt{2}}{2}, -\frac{\sqrt{2}}{2}\right)$ **C** $\left(-\frac{1}{2}, \frac{\sqrt{3}}{2}\right)$ **D** $\left(-\frac{1}{2}, -\frac{\sqrt{3}}{2}\right)$

12. **Travel** A driver leaves a gas station and heads due north at a rate of 50 miles per hour. Two hours later, a truck driver leaves the same gas station and heads due east at a rate of 40 miles per hour. Approximately how long will it take for the vehicles to be 450 miles apart?
(65)

© Saxon. All rights reserved.

***13.** **Multi-Step** Suppose that the population of a certain town increases at the rate of 6% per year and that the current population is 2210.
(72)

a. Write an exponential function that gives the population as a function of x, the number of elapsed years.

b. Write a logarithmic function that gives the number of elapsed years as a function of x, the population.

c. To the nearest tenth, how many years will it take for the population to exceed 3000?

***14.** **Analyze** Explain why the probability of events that involve selection of items without replacement involve conditional probabilities.
(68)

***15.** **Multiple Choice** Which is equal to $5^{\log_5 x}$?
(72)

A 1 **B** x **C** $5x$ **D** 5^x

16. **Clock Face** The minute hand of a certain clock is 20 inches long. How far does the tip of the minute hand travel in 45 minutes, to the nearest inch?
(63)

***17.** **Graphing Calculator** Find the solution to the following system of equations using the Matrix functionality of the calculator.
(Inv 3)

$-2x + y + 4z = -24$

$-5x + 7y - z = -36$

$8x - 3y + z = 43$

18. **Error Analysis** Kyle carefully measures two sides of a triangle and finds that the longest side has a length of 2 inches, and the second longest side has a length of $\sqrt{3}$ inches. He comes to the conclusion that the shorter leg must have length 1. What is wrong with his reasoning?
(52)

***19.** **Verify** Show that the value of x can be found by either using the sine ratio or the Law of Sines.
(71)

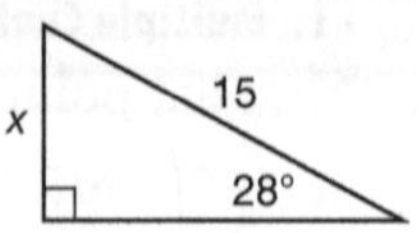

Add or subtract. Write the answer in the form $a + bi$.

20. $(6 - 3i) + (5 + 4i)$
(62)

21. $(8 + 20i) - (-8 + 12i)$
(62)

***22.** **Coordinate Geometry** Explain how to use the Law of Sines to find the area of a triangle whose vertices are at $(-4, 0)$, $(6, 0)$, and $(0, 6)$. Then find the area.
(71)

23. Find the inverse of $\begin{bmatrix} 16 & 8 \\ 2 & 0 \end{bmatrix}$.
(32)

24. **Analyze** Explain how to add a real number to a complex number. Provide an example.
(62)

© Saxon. All rights reserved.

***25.** (70) **Lighthouses** The number of miles m a person can see on a clear day is approximated by $m = 1.2\sqrt{h}$, where h is the person's height above sea level. Suppose a person standing at the top of the Little Sable Point Lighthouse in Michigan on a clear day can see a distance of 12.4 miles. To the nearest foot, what is their height above sea level?

***26.** (69) **Geometry** The sum of two complex numbers can be found by graphing each number on the complex plane, drawing segments from the origin to each point, completing the parallelogram that has these two segments as sides, and finding the point opposite the origin. Use this method to find $(-2 + 3i) + (5 + i)$.

27. (Inv 6) **Error Analysis** Isaiah added 196 to both sides of the equation $x^2 + 16x + 60 = 0$ so he could make the perfect square. What error did he make?

28. (Inv 7) Write the polar equation of a circle with a radius of 7.

Solve by substitution.

29. (21) $2y - x = 6$; $y - 2x = -3$

30. (21) $3x + 2y = 12$; $8x - 2y = 10$

© Saxon. All rights reserved.

Name ______________________ Date __________ Class __________

Using Sampling

LESSON 73

Write the logarithmic equation in exponential form.

1. (64) $\log_{10} 10{,}000{,}000 = 7$

2. (64) $\log_6 216 = 3$

3. (52) **Explain** Explain why all 45° –45° –90° triangles are similar.

*4. (71) State the case applicable to the given measurements (AAS, ASA, or SSA). Then decide whether the measurements determine one triangle, two triangles, or no triangle. A = 40°; C = 75°; c = 20

Solve for the roots of the polynomial:

5. (66) $6x(x^2 + x - 20) = 0$

6. (66) $2x(x^2 + 9x - 52) = 0$

7. (66) **Probability** For $x^3 + 8x^2 + 3x - 4 = 0$, what would be the probability of randomly selecting a root on the first try from the list of possible roots given by the Rational Root Theorem?

Solve for x by completing the square:

8. (58) $-x^2 + 6x = -12$

9. (58) $-4 = -x^2 - 3x$

*10. (73) **Business** The owner of a frozen food company wants to know how many people would agree to pay slightly more for products sold in recycled packages than non-recycled packages. She hires a surveyor to stand in the aisles of randomly selected grocery stores which sell the company's product to survey buyers of frozen food products. Define the population and sample in this situation. What groups of people would not be represented in the sample and why?

11. (53) **Multi-Step** Let $f(x) = x - 6$ and $g(x) = 3x$.
   a. Find the composition functions $(f \circ g)(x)$ and $(g \circ f)(x)$.
   b. Evaluate the composite functions $(f \circ g)(x)$ and $(g \circ f)(x)$ for $x = -1$.

*12. (64) **Write** Explain why there is no value of x that makes the equation $\log_1 10 = x$ true.

Convert each measure from radians to degrees.

13. (63) $\dfrac{6\pi}{4} =$

14. (63) $\dfrac{2\pi}{3} =$

*15. (67) **Navigation** A camper plans to canoe to an island. The island is 1500 meters south and 950 meters west of her starting point. To the nearest degree, in what direction should she head?

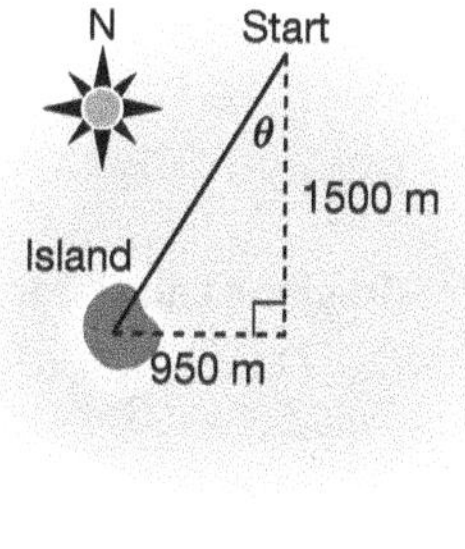

*16. (73) **Multi-Step** Explain why the question below is biased. Then rewrite the question without bias. "Do you not agree that junk food should not be sold in school vending machines?"

© Saxon. All rights reserved.

17. Multiple Choice Which is a solution of $3x^2 - 7x - 2 = 0$?
(65)

A $\frac{1}{3}$ B 2 C $\frac{7 + \sqrt{73}}{6}$ D $\frac{7}{6} - \frac{\sqrt{73}}{6}i$

18. Write What is a conditional probability? Give an example.
(68)

***19. Estimate** A researcher using the stratified sampling method has chosen a sample of 12 female athletes and 17 non-female athletes from a population of 305 female students. About how many students in the population are athletes?
(73)

20. Error Analysis Is the work below correct? If not, find and explain the error, and give the correct solution.
(59)

$$x^{\frac{1}{7}} = 2$$
$$\left(x^{\frac{1}{7}}\right)^{\frac{7}{1}} = 2$$
$$x^1 = 2$$
$$x = 2$$

21. Solve to the nearest tenth using the given restrictions. Tan $\theta = 2.42$, for $180° \leq \theta \leq 360°$
(67)

***22. (Geology)** The Richter magnitude M of an earthquake is expressed by $M = \frac{2}{3}\log\left(\frac{E}{10^{11.8}}\right)$, where E is the energy released in ergs. An earthquake near Peru in 2007 had a magnitude of 8.0. Find the energy released by that earthquake.
(72)

23. Multi-Step Use $x^2 + 30x + 225 = 13$.
(58)

a. Explain why the equation is a perfect square.

b. Factor $x^2 + 30x + 225$.

c. Solve the equation for x.

***24. Error Analysis** To rewrite $\ln 4e^3$ without an exponent, a student wrote $\ln 4e^3 = \ln 4 \cdot \ln e^3 = (\ln 4)(3) = 3 \ln 4$.
(72)

What is the error? Rewrite $\ln 4e^3$ without an exponent correctly.

25. (Population) The population of the state of Florida in various years is shown below.
(57)

Year	1900	1950	1990	2005
Population (thousands)	529	2771	12,937	17,789

Write an exponential model that approximates this data. What population is predicted by this model for the year 2010?

***26. Graphing Calculator** Find the area of $\triangle BCD$ given $c = 3.62$, $b = 1.45$, and $m\angle D = 33.25°$. Round to the nearest hundredth.
(71)

© Saxon. All rights reserved.

27. **Geometry** Find the probability that a point chosen randomly inside the figure is in the shaded region.
(55)

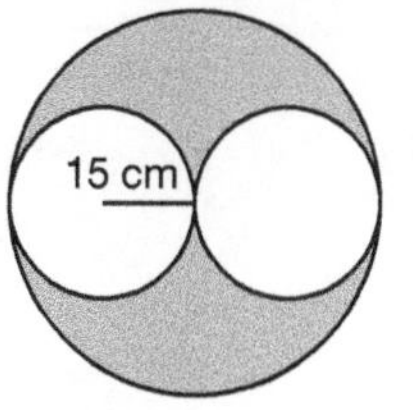

*28. **Multiple Choice** Solve $x = \sqrt{-14x - 45}$.
(70)
A no solutions B -9 C -5 D -9 and -5

29. **Analyze** How is graphing in the complex plane similar to, and different from, graphing in the *xy*- coordinate plane?
(69)

30. Write the equation of a line in slope intercept form that is parallel to $y = -\frac{3}{2}x + 4$ and passes through (1, 5).
(36)

© Saxon. All rights reserved.

Name ______________________ Date __________ Class __________

Finding the Discriminant

LESSON 74

Use synthetic division to divide.

1. $x^4 - 2$ by $x + 1$ *(61)*

2. $x^3 - 2$ by $x - 5$ *(61)*

***3.** *(57)* **Graphing Calculator** Use a graphing calculator to investigate the behavior of the following 4 functions for the domain $x \geq 0$: $y = e^x$, $y = x$, $y = x^2$, and $y = x^3$. Write a short paragraph comparing the growth rate of these four functions as the value of x increases.

***4.** *(74)* **Rock Climbing** A rock climber at the bottom of the King and Queen Seat outcropping in Rocks State Park in Maryland shoots a flare from a flare gun. The height of the flare, in meters, can be modeled by $y = -5x^2 + 32x + 1$, where x is number of seconds after the flare is set off. Use the discriminant to explain if the flare will reach the height of the outcropping, given that the outcropping has a height of 58 meters.

5. *(66)* **Storage** The volume of a cylindrical bucket is 1696 cubic inches. The height of the bucket is 9 inches greater than its radius. Write a polynomial in standard form, without π, that can be used to find the radius (Round the constant to the nearest integer.)

6. *(56)* Given $\theta = 400°$, find a positive and negative coterminal angle.

7. *(61)* **Multiple Choice** Which is *not* a factor of $x^3 + 9x^2 + 2x - 48$?

A $x - 4$ **B** $x - 2$ **C** $x + 3$ **D** $x + 8$

8. *(68)* A prize box contains 5 stickers, 13 smiley erasers, 20 pencils, and 2 binders. Find the probability that the student randomly chooses 2 prizes, a sticker first and then a pencil.

9. *(57)* The number of mice increased exponentially. At first there were 85 mice. Twelve years later there were 1700 mice. How many mice would there be at the end of 130 years?

***10.** *(74)* **Analyze** How does the discriminant of a quadratic equation indicate if the real solutions are rational or irrational?

11. *(69)* Multiply $2(3i)$. Write the result in the form $a + bi$.

12. *(63)* **Automobiles Tires** The diameter of a certain automobile tire, mounted on the wheel, is 25 inches. How far does the automobile go when the tire rotates 10 times? Give your answer to the nearest foot.

Solve.

13. *(70)* $\sqrt{9x} + 11 = 14$

14. *(70)* $-4\sqrt{x} - 6 = -20$

© Saxon. All rights reserved.

15. (65) **Analyze** When using a graphing calculator to solve a quadratic equation, for what type of solutions can exact answers be found?

16. (69) **Electrical Engineering** The flow of a current, I, the resistance to the flow, Z, and the voltage, E, are related by $E = I(Z)$. Find the resistance of a circuit (in ohms) if the voltage is $265 - 135i$ volts and the current is $26 - 30i$ amps.

***17.** (71) **Geometry** Find the perimeter of $\triangle XYZ$ given $m\angle X = 40°$, $m\angle Z = 70°$, and $y = 33$ cm.

18. (62) **Error Analysis** Which student incorrectly added the complex numbers? Explain the error.

Student A
$(6 + 2i) + (-3 - 9i)$ $8i - 12i$ $-4i$

Student B
$(6 + 2i) + (-3 - 9i)$ $3 - 7i$

***19.** (73) **Government** Suppose a politician must visit 5 counties in Maine. His human resource personnel form a simple random sample by listing each county and numbering it as shown below. If they use the line of random digits shown below, which 5 counties will the politician visit?

50: Androscoggin	51: Aroostook	52: Cumberland	53: Franklin
54: Hancock	55: Kennebec	56: Knox	57: Lincoln
58: Oxford	59: Penobscot	60: Piscataquis	61: Sagadahoc
62: Somerset	63: Waldo	64: Washington	65: York

62010	60482	89824	08705	57913	46815	76221	25650	89337	53603	73597

***20.** (73) **Multiple Choice** Which sampling method would introduce the greatest possible amount of bias?

A systematic sampling **B** stratified sampling

C convenience sampling **D** simple random sampling

21. (60) Katie rolls a 1–6 number cube twice. What is the probability she will roll an odd number and then an even number?

***22.** (72) **Justify** Explain why $3^{\log_3 2x} = 2x$.

Factor each expression completely.

23. (61) $3y^5 - 48y^3$

24. (61) $x^3 + x^2 + x + 1$

© Saxon. All rights reserved.

*25. **Multi-Step** (74) **a.** Write $16x^2 = 25$ in standard form.

b. Find the discriminant of the equation in part a.

c. Use the discriminant to describe the solutions of the equation in part a.

d. Verify Solve the equation in part a.

26. **Estimate** (52) The hypotenuse of a $45° - 45° - 90°$ triangle is between 120 and 130 cm long. Estimate the length of each leg.

*27. **Generalize** (70) Raise both sides of the equation $x = 4$ to the second, third, fourth, and fifth powers. Solve each equation. In which cases are there extraneous solutions? In general, when could raising both sides by the same power generate extraneous solutions?

28. **Multi-Step** (67) Let $f(\theta) = \text{Tan}\ \theta$ and $g(\theta) = \text{Tan}^{-1}\ \theta$, where θ is in radians.

a. Evaluate $f(g(1))$ and $g\left(f\left(\frac{\pi}{4}\right)\right)$. Show your steps.

b. Based on part a, what is the value of $f(g(x))$?

c. Rename $g(\theta)$ as $f^{-1}(\theta)$. What property of inverse functions is illustrated in part a?

29. **Data Analysis** (68) Use the double-bar chart to estimate the conditional probabilities.

a. $P(\text{boy} \mid \text{10th grade})$

b. $P(\text{10th grade} \mid \text{boy})$

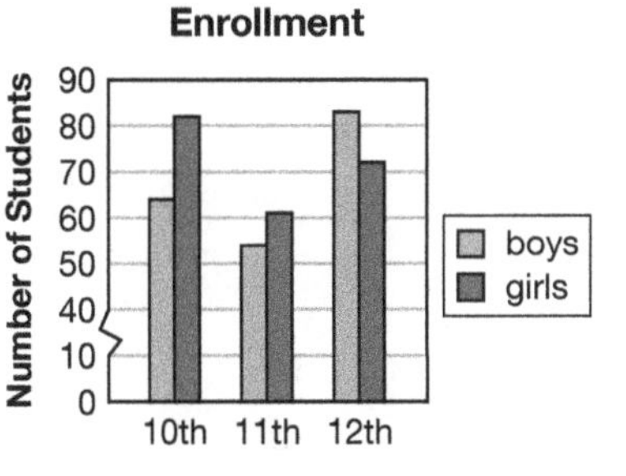

30. **Error Analysis** (61) What error did the student make in factoring the difference of cubes?

$$c^6 - 216$$
$$(c^2 - 6)(c^4 - 6c^2 + 36)$$

© Saxon. All rights reserved.

Name ______________________ Date __________ Class __________

Graphing Radical Functions

LESSON 75

*1. Find the area of $\triangle ABC$ with the given side lengths and included angle. $b = 11$, $c = 7$, $m\angle A = 120°$
(71)

2. Find the roots and give the multiplicity of each root: $2x^3 - 4x^2 + 2x = 0$
(66)

3. **Medicine** If a patient ingests medicine containing a grams of a drug, the amount left in the patient's bloodstream after t hours is given by the equation $y = ae^{-0.119t}$. After how much time will exactly one-third of the drug still be circulating in the bloodstream?
(57)

*4. **Multi-Step** **a.** Find the radical function that is the inverse of $y = (x - 3)(x^2 + 3x + 9)$.
(75)
b. Identify its domain and range.

5. **Error Analysis** Which student made an error in finding $|4 + 11i|$? Describe the error.
(69)

Student A	Student B
$\sqrt{4^2 + 11^2}$ $\sqrt{16 + 121}$ $\sqrt{137}$	$\sqrt{4^2 - 11^2}$ $\sqrt{16 - 121}$ $\sqrt{-105} = i\sqrt{105}$

*6. **Celebrating** On the Fourth of July, a technician on Bedloe's Island is planning to shoot confetti straight up behind the Statue of Liberty. The function $y = -4.9x^2 + 45x + 1$ gives the height of a piece of confetti, in meters, after x seconds. The statue has a height of 93 meters. Use the discriminant to explain if a piece of confetti will reach the top of the statue.
(74)

7. **Sports** In basketball, the basket through which the ball is thrown consists of a metal hoop that has a 9-inch radius. Use the formula $r = \sqrt{\frac{A}{\pi}}$ to find the area of the hoop.
(70)

8. **Multiple Choice** What is the solution set of the equation $2 \cos \theta + \sqrt{2} = 0$, for $0° \leq \theta \leq 360°$?
(67)

A {30°, 330°} **B** {45°, 135°} **C** {30°, 150°} **D** {135°, 225°}

*9. **Predict** Consider the radical function $f(x) = (g(x))^{\frac{1}{\pi}}$. Suppose that the graph of $f(x)$ is a straight line for increasing values of x. What can you conclude about $g(x)$?
(75)

10. **Write** Describe how to determine tan 240° by using its reference angle.
(63)

*11. **Probability** In a factory, a sample of items produced is checked during all three work shifts. The table shows the results of these checks for one day. What is the probability that an item was checked during the third shift given that it was found to be defective?
(68)

	1st Shift	2nd Shift	3rd Shift
Defective	3	5	18
Not Defective	119	109	132

© Saxon. All rights reserved.

12. **Multi-Step** **a.** Given the triangle, find the lengths of side x and y.
(52)
b. Draw a perpendicular line to the hypotenuse from vertex A, calling the new point of intersection D. Find the length of AD and DC.

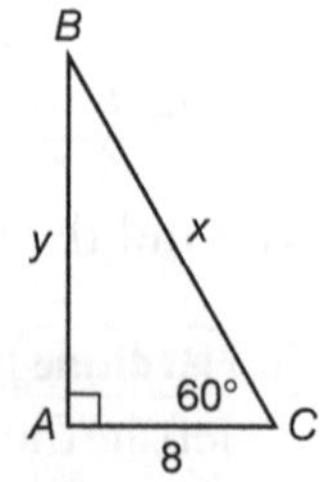

***13.** **Write** What is meant by *triangulation*?
(71)

14. **Geometry** The volume of a right prism is the product of the area of its base and its height. The height of a right prism with a volume of $6x^3 + 69x^2 + 3x - 330$ cubic units is $x + 11$ units. Find a polynomial expression for the area of the base.
(61)

15. Write each expression in terms of i, and then subtract:
(62)
$(-1 + \sqrt{-9}) - (-1 - \sqrt{-64})$.

16. **Physics** The number of seconds it takes for a rocket fired from a deck 10 feet off the ground at a velocity of 50 feet per second to return to the ground is given by $-16t^2 + 50t + 10 = 0$. Solve the equation. Round to the nearest hundredth.
(65)

Determine whether the linear binomial is a factor of the polynomial.

17. $P(x) = x^3 - 10x^2 + 19x + 30$; $x - 6$
(61)

18. $P(x) = 3x^3 - 2x^2 - 61x - 20$; $x - 4$
(61)

19. **Write** Tell what is meant by the *multiplicity* of a root.
(66)

Write the logarithmic equations in exponential form.

20. $\log_{10} 100{,}000 = 5$
(64)

21. $\log_4 1024 = 5$
(64)

***22.** **Error Analysis** Two students are finding the inverse of $y = \sqrt[4]{x^2 + 4}$ but get different results. Which student made the mistake?
(75)

Student A	Student B
$x = \sqrt[4]{y^2 + 4}$ $x^4 = y^2 + 4$ $y = \sqrt{x^4 - 4}$	$x = \sqrt[4]{y^2 + 4}$ $x^{\frac{1}{4}} = y^2 + 4$ $y = \sqrt{x^{\frac{1}{4}} - 4}$

23. Find all the possible values of $\text{Sin}^{-1}\left(\frac{1}{2}\right)$.
(67)

24. A calculator is programmed to generate random integers from 1 to 100 inclusive when the enter button is pressed. If the enter button is pressed twice, what is the probability of getting a multiple of 10 then a number greater than 60?
(55)

© Saxon. All rights reserved.

*25. (74) **Multiple Choice** The discriminant of a quadratic equation is −2. Which describes the solutions of the equation?
A 1 real solution **B** 1 complex solution **C** 2 real solutions **D** 2 complex solutions

Solve.

26. (72) $\log_6 \frac{5}{8}$

27. (72) $\log_6 40$

28. (62) **Multiple Choice** What are the solutions of $x^2 + 8x = -25$?
A $\pm 3i$ **B** $\pm 5i$ **C** $-4 \pm 3i$ **D** $4 \pm 5i$

*29. (73) **Graphing Calculator** To generate single digit random numbers on a calculator, press MATH and select [**randInt(**] from the PRB menu and type 0, 9 in parentheses. Then press enter.

a. Form a simple random sample of 3 individuals from the 10 listed below.

0: Greg	1: Pam	2: Tyler	3: Lakisha	4: Jon
5: Larry	6: Mark	7: Tammy	8: Li	9: Diane

b. Under what circumstances would you have to press enter more than 3 times?

*30. (72) **Justify** Explain why $\ln e^{2x-1} = 2x - 1$.

© Saxon. All rights reserved.

Name ______________________ Date __________ Class __________

Finding Polynomial Roots I

LESSON 76

***1.** (76) Let $f(x) = x^2 - 4$ and $g(x) = x + 1$. Find the roots of $f(g(x))$.

2. (50) Find an equation for the inverse of $y = -2x^5 - 10$.

***3.** (75) The volume of an ice cube has decreased from x^3 to $\frac{x^3}{3} - 9$, while still maintaining its cubic shape. What is the new length of each side of the cube?

4. (63) Find the sine, cosine, and tangent of 270°.

5. (50) Find an equation for the inverse of $y = 4x^2 + 12$.

***6.** (76) **Multiple Choice** Which of the following is not a factor of $x^3 - 6x^2 + 11x - 6$?
A $(x - 4)$ **B** $(x - 3)$ **C** $(x - 2)$ **D** $(x - 1)$

***7.** (75) **Geometry** Derive the function that can be used to find the hypotenuse of the right triangle. For what value of x is the hypotenuse part of a Pythagorean triple?

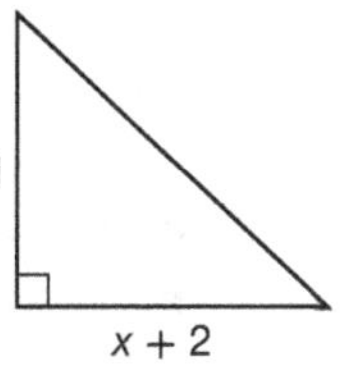

***8.** (75) **Physics** The equation for finding the period of a pendulum is the radical function $T = 2\pi\sqrt{\frac{L}{9.8}}$. The period is the amount of time it takes for the pendulum to complete one back-and-forth sweep. How much longer does a pendulum need to be to double the period?

9. (57) **Biology** In the absence of predators and diseases, and with enough food, a population of brown rats can increase by 6300% per year. Suppose you start with an initial population of three breeding pairs of rats. Write an exponential function to model the population size after t years.

10. (73) **Sports** A reporter went to a baseball game and asked fans that passed through the front gate at the end of the game if they thought the town could use a larger, more improved stadium. 98% of those surveyed answered *yes.* The reporter wrote in the paper that "98% of the city's population wants a new stadium." Discuss the problems with this situation.

11. (66) **Multiple Choice** Which is a possible rational root of $2x^3 + x^2 - 72x = 36$?
A 7 **B** 9 **C** 10 **D** 72

© Saxon. All rights reserved.

12. (72) **Multi-Step** Two measures of sound are loudness and intensity. They are related by the function $L(I) = 10\log\frac{I}{I_0}$, where $L(I)$ is loudness in decibels, I is intensity in watts per square meter, and $I_0 \approx 10^{-12}$ watt per square meter, the intensity of a barely audible sound.

a. The loudness of conversational speech is about 60 decibels. Find the intensity of a sound with a loudness of 60 decibels. Write your answer without an exponent.

b. The threshold of discomfort to the human ear is about 120 decibels. Find the intensity of a sound with a loudness of 120 decibels.

c. When the loudness doubles from 60 dB to 120 dB, by what factor is the intensity multiplied?

13. (68) **(Horses)** A paddock contains 5 thoroughbreds, 6 quarter horses, 8 mustangs, and 2 ponies. Find the probability that one thoroughbred and one quarter horse will be chosen at random without replacement for the upcoming horse show.

***14.** (76) **Multi-Step** Suppose that $f(x) = (x - 5)(x^2 - 12) + (x - 5)(-3x - x)$.

a. Find the zeros of the function.

b. Based on the solution in part **a**, how many x-intercepts does the graph of $f(x)$ have?

c. Simplify $f(x)$ and determine its degree.

15. (71) **Analyze** In $\triangle PQR$, $m\angle P = 35°$, $r = 18$, and $p = 21$. Are there one or two possible triangles that can have these measures? Explain.

16. (61) The volume of a rectangular solid with a length of $x - 8$ feet has a volume of $x^3 - 2x^2 - 40x - 64$ cubic feet. Factor the expression for the volume completely.

***17.** (74) **Graphing Calculator** Graph $y = -3.25x^2 - 0.3x + 7.5$ to determine if $-3.25x^2 - 0.3x + 7.5 = 0$ has one, two, or zero real solutions.

18. (70) **Error Analysis** Explain the error the student made below.

$$x - 2 = \sqrt{3x}$$
$$(x - 2)^2 = (\sqrt{3x})^2$$
$$x^2 - 4 = 3x$$
$$x^2 - 3x - 4 = 0$$
$$(x - 4)(x + 1) = 0$$
$$x = 4 \quad \text{or} \quad x = -1$$

19. (58) **(Projectile Motion)** The Leaning Tower of Pisa in Italy measures 180.4 feet from the ground on the lower side of the tower. If an object is thrown into the air, with an initial velocity of 96 feet per second, from the top of the lower side, the height, h, of the object in feet after t seconds can be described by the equation: $h = -16t^2 + 96t + 180.4$. Find the time at which the object will reach the ground. Round your answer to the tenths place.

© Saxon. All rights reserved.

20. **Estimate** Use properties of the unit circle and special angles to estimate (67) $\cos^{-1}(0.48)$ in degrees. Do not use a calculator. Explain your method.

21. **Error Analysis** Find and correct the error a student made in solving $6x^2 + 5 - x = 0$. (65)

$$x = \frac{-b \pm \sqrt{b^2 - 4ac}}{2a}$$
$$= \frac{-5 \pm \sqrt{25 - 4(6)(-1)}}{12}$$
$$= \frac{-5 \pm \sqrt{49}}{12}$$
$$= \frac{-5 \pm 7}{12} = \frac{1}{6} \text{ and } -1$$

22. A tree casts a shadow as shown in the picture. What is (52) the height of the tree?

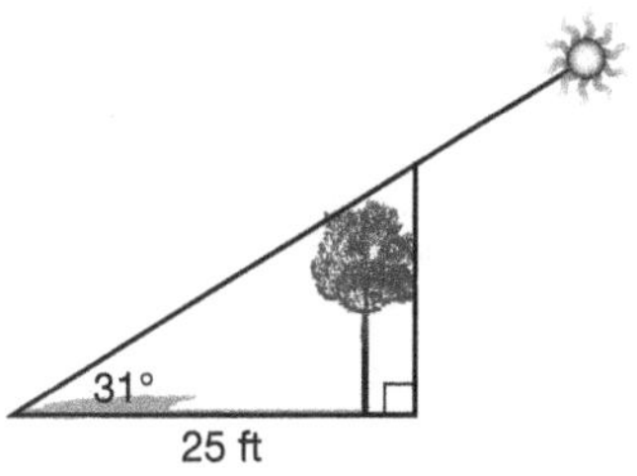

23. **Verify** Show why $2i\sqrt{2}$ is a square root of -8. (69)

24. A patient is injected with medication. $C(t) = Ae^{-0.42t}$ gives the amount of the (57) medication in the bloodstream after t hours. If the initial dose is 300 mg, after how many hours will it be 70 mg?

*25. **Analyze** Suppose that polynomial function $f(x)$ has n zeros and polynomial function (76) $g(x)$ has m zeros. What must be true for $f(x) \cdot g(x)$ to have $n + m$ zeros?

26. Mark rolled a 1–6 number cube four times. What is the probability of Mark rolling (60) an odd number each time?

*27. Find the roots of the polynomial function $3x(2x - 9)(x + 5)$. (76)

28. **Probability** A photo documentary includes 36 slides in a portfolio. If the teacher (55) randomly chooses 5 slides from the portfolio, what is the probability that the teacher picks either the first five slides or the last five slides?

Find the discriminant of the quadratic equation and give the number and type of solutions of the equation.

29. $x^2 - 8x + 16 = 0$ (74)

30. $s^2 + 7s + 11 = 0$ (74)

© Saxon. All rights reserved.

Name ______________________ Date __________ Class __________

Using the Law of Cosines

LESSON 77

*1. (17) **Safety Regulations** A company's safety regulations require the wire rope used to suspend a 100-ton load to have a thickness that is within $\frac{3}{8}$ inch of $1\frac{3}{4}$ inches. Write and solve an absolute value equation to find the minimum safe thickness of rope.

Write the exponential equations in logarithmic form.

2. (64) $3^7 = 2187$

3. (64) $12^2 = 144$

*4. (74) Find the discriminant of the quadratic equation $7r^2 - 5 = 2r + 9r^2$. Give the number and type of solutions of the equation.

Combine into one logarithm.

5. (72) $6 \ln x + 4 \ln y$

6. (72) $\ln 40 + 2\ln \frac{1}{2} + \ln x$

*7. (77) **Generalize** A student said that every time the Law of Cosines is used to find an angle measure, both sides of the equation will be divided by a negative number. Is the student correct or incorrect? Explain.

8. (52) Find the exact values of x and y.

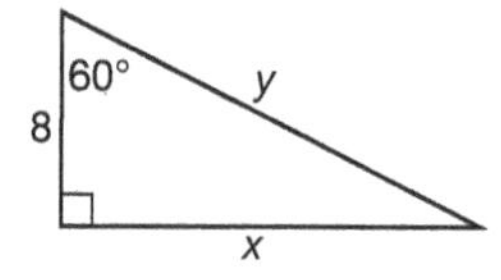

*9. (75) **Multiple Choice** Which of the following is equivalent to $y = \sqrt[4]{\sqrt[3]{x^3 + 2x^2 + 4}}$?

A $y = (x^3 + 2x^2 + 4)^{\frac{1}{12}}$

B $y = (x^3 + 2x^2 + 4)^{\frac{3}{4}}$

C $y = (x^3 + 2x^2 + 4)^{\frac{4}{3}}$

D $y = (x^3 + 2x^2 + 4)^{12}$

*10. (68) **Graphing Calculator** A school is made up of 334 freshmen and 229 sophomores. Four students are chosen at random for a newspaper interview. Use a calculator to find the probability that all four students are freshmen.

*11. (77) **Coordinate Geometry** Explain how to use Heron's formula to find the area of a triangle whose vertices are at $(-7, -5)$, $(1, 7)$, and $(2, -1)$. Then find the area.

12. (73) **Formulate** Write a formula that estimates an animal population N, when M are marked on the first visit, and m of the n captured on the second visit are marked.

13. (62) **Error Analysis** Describe and correct the error in simplifying the expression.

$$(1 + 2i)(4 - i) = 4 - i + 8i - 2i^2 = 2i^2 + 7i + 4$$

*14. (Inv 4) A message is put into matrix A and encoded using cipher matrix C. Will the same encoded message result from AC as CA? Why?

15. (26) Find the equation of the line in slope-intercept form that passes through $(5, -3)$ and has a slope of $\frac{2}{9}$.

© Saxon. All rights reserved.

16. **Multiple Choice** Which expression is *not* equivalent to 1?
(69)
A i^{18} B i^{24} C i^{32} D i^{56}

***17.** A triangle has side lengths of 14 feet, 15 feet, and 21 feet. Use Heron's formula to find the area of the triangle.
(77)

18. P is a point on the terminal side of θ in standard position. Find the exact value of the six trigonometric functions for θ where $P(-5, 5)$.
(56)

19. **Multi-Step** A rectangular prism with a square base has a height that is 8 inches longer than the length of one side of the base. Its volume is 325 cubic inches.
(66)

a. Write a polynomial equation in standard form that can be used to find the length of one side of the base.

b. List the possible rational roots.

c. Find the length of one side of the base.

***20.** **Error Analysis** A student is solving for the roots of $y = (x^2 - 3)(x^2 + 2) - (x^2 - 3)(6x + 5)$, what mistake did he make?
(76)

$$(x^2 - 3)(x^2 + 2) - (x^2 - 3)(6x + 5) = (x^2 - 3)(x^2 + 6x + 7)$$

Use the quadratic formula,

$$x = \frac{-6 \pm \sqrt{6^2 - 4(1)(7)}}{2(1)} = \frac{6 \pm \sqrt{36 - 28}}{2} = 3 \pm \sqrt{2}$$

There are a total of four roots of $f(x)$: $x = \pm\sqrt{3}$ and $3 \pm \sqrt{2}$

21. Solve using the quadratic formula. Write the solution as complex numbers in standard form. $f(x) = x^2 + 4$
(65)

***22.** **Generalize** Suppose that the polynomial functions $f(x)$ and $g(x)$ are each a sum of square terms. Give an example where $f(x) \cdot g(x) = 0$ has exactly two complex solutions.
(76)

23. **Verify** Explain how to check that $x = 7$ is a solution of $\sqrt{6 + x} - \sqrt{2x - 1} = 0$ by using a graphing calculator.
(70)

***24.** **Geology** The Richter magnitude M of an earthquake is expressed by $M = \frac{2}{3}\log\left(\frac{E}{10^{11.8}}\right)$, where E is the energy released in ergs. The 1906 San Francisco earthquake, with a magnitude between 7.7 and 8.3, was the worst earthquake disaster in U.S. history. Describe the amount of energy released by that earthquake.
(72)

25. **Geometry** What is the measure of the base angle θ of the isosceles trapezoid, to the nearest tenth of a degree?
(67)

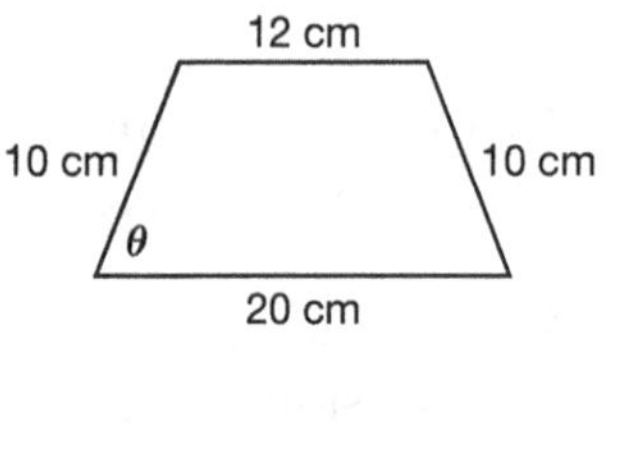

© Saxon. All rights reserved.

26. (61) **Sports** The area of a tennis court being used for the Special Olympics has an area that can be represented by $x^2 - 24x - 432 + 18x$ square feet. Factor this polynomial by grouping.

27. (60) There are 20 orange marbles and 13 green marbles in a sack. An orange marble is randomly selected and replaced. Then a green marble is randomly selected. Are these events dependent or mutually exclusive?

28. (74) **Generalize** What will be the value of the discriminant of an equation if the vertex of the related function is located in Quadrant II and the parabola opens upward? Why?

29. (59) **Probability** A farmer has four sheepdogs and three beagles. If he randomly chooses a dog to accompany him on a walk, what is the probability of him taking a walk with a sheepdog?

30. (58) Solve: $2x + 5 = x^2$

© Saxon. All rights reserved.

Name ______________________ Date __________ Class __________

Solving Quadratic Equations II

LESSON 78

***1.** (77) In $\triangle LMN$, $MN = 13$, $LN = 3$, and the $m\angle N = 36°$. Find LM.

2. (56) Given $\theta = -164°$, find a positive and negative coterminal angle.

Solve.

3. (66) $4x(2x^2 + 9x - 45) = 0$

4. (66) $2x(x^2 - 4x + 6) = 0$

***5.** (78) $2x^2 + 9x + 4 = 0$

***6.** (78) $3x^3 - 12x = 0$

7. (52) **Multiple Choice** In the diagram, triangle ABC is dilated to get triangle LMN. What is the scale factor?

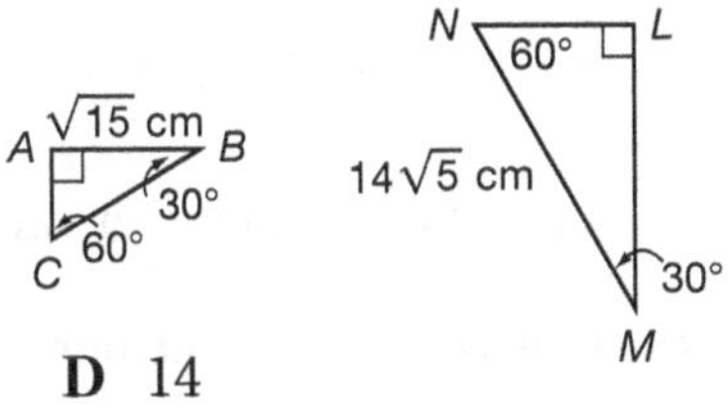

A $\sqrt{5}$ **B** $2\sqrt{5}$ **C** 7 **D** 14

8. (65) **Multi-Step a.** Write the equation $\frac{3}{4}x^2 + \frac{3}{8}x + 1 = 0$ without fractions.

b. Find the roots of the equation.

***9.** (78) **Analyze** Describe how to solve the equation $2.5x^2 - 0.4 = 0$ by factoring the difference of two squares.

***10.** (77) **Multiple Choice** What is the area of $\triangle ABC$ if $a = 34$ m, $b = 25$ m, and $c = 48$ m?

A about 54 m² **B** about 404 m² **C** about 6147 m² **D** about 163,529 m²

***11.** (54) **Graphing Calculator** Describe the feasible region for the inequalities. $0 \leq x \leq 20$, $y \geq 10$, $6y + 8x \geq 105$.

12. (57) **Error Analysis** To graph the function $y = 3^x + 2$, Eric started out by graphing $y = 3^x$ (the dashed curve). He then translated it 2 units to the right. Explain Eric's error, and write an equation for the function he graphed.

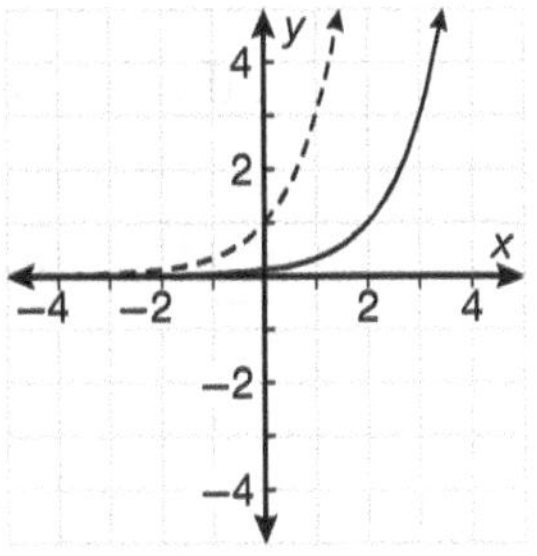

13. (59) **Multi-Step** Use $\left(5^{\frac{1}{2}} \cdot 5^{\frac{2}{7}}\right)^{\frac{2}{11}}$

a. Which property of rational exponents should be applied first to simplify the expression? Explain.

b. Which property of rational exponents should be applied next?

c. Simplify the expression.

© Saxon. All rights reserved.

14. **Data Analysis** The following table summarizes data obtained by the U.S. Census Bureau on computers in households. If one of the surveyed members of the household is randomly selected, find the probability that the member of the household is male or has a computer. Round to the ten thousandths place.
(60)

Gender of Household Member

Computer	Male	Female
Yes	39,475	30,461
No	20,583	22,607

Use synthetic division to divide.

15. $4x^2 + 7x + 10$ by $x + 2$
(51)

16. $2x^2 - 6x - 12$ by $x - 5$
(51)

17. Identify any excluded values for $\frac{2x - 10}{10 - 2x}$. Then simplify the expression.
(28)

18. **Analyze** Classify the number $a + bi$ when both a and b are equal to 0. Explain.
(62)

19. **Write** Describe how to use the sine function to define the inverse sine function.
(67)

20. **Physical Science** The number of miles m a person can see on a clear day is approximated by $m = 1.2116\sqrt{h}$, where h is the person's height above sea level. Suppose a person standing on a pier can see for 6 miles. To the nearest tenth of a foot, what is their height above sea level?
(70)

21. **Predict** If every complex number with an absolute value of $\sqrt{58}$ is graphed, what geometric figure is formed and why?
(69)

22. **Geometry** The angle measures of five different triangles are given below.
(68)

30°, 60°, 90° 45°, 45°, 90° 60°, 60°, 60° 20°, 20°, 140° 50°, 60°, 70°

a. If three triangles are chosen at random, without replacement, what is the probability that the first two triangles are right triangles and the last triangle is obtuse?

b. If three triangles are chosen at random, without replacement, what is the probability that all three are right triangles?

c. If three triangles are chosen at random, without replacement, what is the probability that all three are isosceles triangles?

23. **Error Analysis** Alex and Robert each tried to simplify the expression $\frac{4 + \sqrt{3}}{5 - \sqrt{3}}$. Who is correct? Explain your reasoning.
(44)

Robert

$$\frac{4 + \sqrt{3}}{5 - \sqrt{3}} = \frac{4 + \sqrt{3}}{5 - \sqrt{3}} \cdot \frac{4 - \sqrt{3}}{4 - \sqrt{3}}$$
$$= \frac{4^2 - (\sqrt{3})^2}{20 - 5\sqrt{3} - 4\sqrt{3} + 3}$$
$$= \frac{13}{23 - 9\sqrt{3}}$$

Alex

$$\frac{4 + \sqrt{3}}{5 - \sqrt{3}} = \frac{4 + \sqrt{3}}{5 - \sqrt{3}} \cdot \frac{5 + \sqrt{3}}{5 + \sqrt{3}}$$
$$= \frac{4(5) + 4\sqrt{3} + 5\sqrt{3} + (\sqrt{3})(\sqrt{3})}{5^2 - (\sqrt{3})^2}$$
$$= \frac{23 + 9\sqrt{3}}{22}$$

© Saxon. All rights reserved.

***24.** (78) **Gravity on the Moon** The height of a free-falling object on the moon (neglecting air resistance) is given by the function $h(t) = -0.8t^2 + v_0t + h_0$, where h_0 is the initial height in meters, v_0 is the initial velocity in meters per second, and $h(t)$ is the height in meters at time t seconds. How long does it take for an object to hit the surface of the moon after it is dropped from a height of 20 meters? (Hint: Multiply both sides of the quadratic equation by the number that makes the coefficient of the quadratic term a perfect square.)

***25.** (77) A triangle has side lengths of 12 feet, 16 feet, and 18 feet. Use Heron's formula to find the area of the triangle.

26. (54) Maximize $P = 2x + 5y$ for the constraints
$$\begin{aligned} x &\geq 0 \\ y &\geq 0 \\ y &\leq 1.5x + 1. \\ y &\leq -x + 6 \end{aligned}$$

***27.** (76) **Generalize** Suppose that polynomial functions $f(x)$ and $g(x)$ are each a difference of square terms. What can you say about the roots of $f(x) \cdot g(x)$?

***28.** (74) **Fencing** A homeowner has 90 feet of fencing material to enclose a rectangular dog pen. He wants the dog to have 600 square feet of space inside the pen. The equation $w(20 - w) = 600$ gives the width of a pen that meets these requirements. Use the discriminant to explain whether or not these requirements can be met.

Use the change of base formula to evaluate the logarithm.

29. (72) $\log_7 19$

30. (72) $\log_6 \frac{24}{5}$

© Saxon. All rights reserved.

Name ______________________ Date __________ Class __________

Understanding Piecewise Functions

LESSON 79

1. (55) **Probability** A bag contains 3 white marbles and 7 purple marbles. What is the probability of picking a white marble, keeping it out of the bag, and then picking a purple marble?

Solve.

2. (70) $\sqrt[3]{x} - 10 = -3$

3. (70) $\sqrt[3]{x-3} + 2 = 4$

***4.** (77) **Generalize** What information must be known to be able to use the Law of Cosines to find a missing measure in a triangle?

Solve.

***5.** (78) $x^4 - 81 = 0$

***6.** (78) $12x = 9x^2 + 4$

***7.** (78) $8x^3 - 392x = 0$

8. (46) **Multi-Step** **a.** A box in the shape of a rectangular prism has a 4 ft × 4 ft square base, and a volume of $64\sqrt{6}$ cubic feet. Find the height of the box.

b. Find the length of the longest stick that can fit inside the box.

c. When this stick is placed inside the box, what is the measure of the angle it forms with the vertical face of the box?

9. (Inv 5) **Verify** Suppose you are conducting an experiment consisting of rolling a number cube 40 times to find the probability of rolling a 2 seven times. Is this a binomial experiment? State why or why not.

10. (53) **Multi-Step** Let $f(x) = 2x$ and $g(x) = x^2$.

a. Find the composition functions $(f \circ g)(x)$ and $(g \circ f)(x)$.

b. Evaluate the composite functions $(f \circ g)(x)$ and $(g \circ f)(x)$ for $x = 2$.

11. (57) **Multiple Choice** Which of the following equations represents the graph shown?

A $y = -3^x + 2$

B $y = -3^{x+1} + 2$

C $y = \left(\frac{1}{3}\right)^{x+1} - 2$

D $y = -\left(\frac{1}{3}\right)^{x-1} + 2$

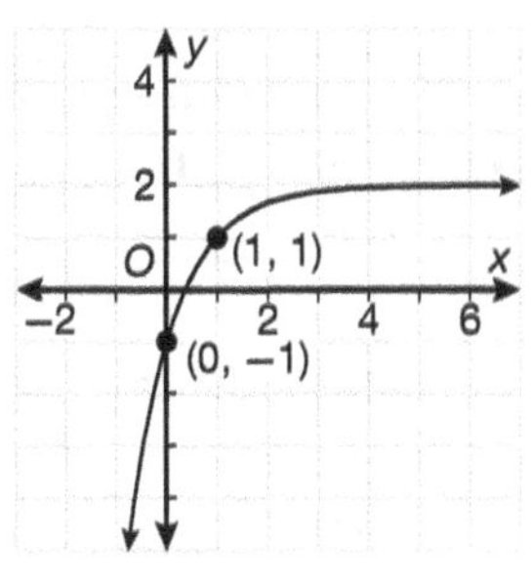

12. (59) Simliify the expression $2^{\frac{1}{3}} \cdot 4^{\frac{1}{6}} \cdot 8^{\frac{1}{9}}$.

13. (60) **Soccer** Of the 65 students going on the soccer trip, 43 are players and 12 are left-handed. Only 5 of the left-handed players are soccer players. What is the probability that one of the students on the trip is a soccer player or is left-handed?

© Saxon. All rights reserved.

14. Find the unknown lengths of the triangle shown.
(52)

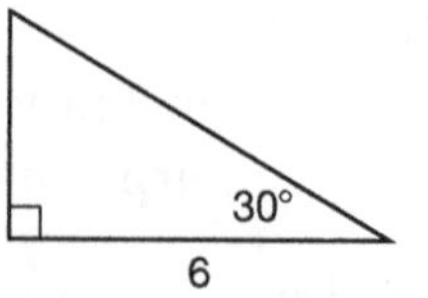

15. Given $f(x) = 3x - 5$ and $g(x) = x + 4$, find $(fg)(x)$.
(20)

*16. **Graphing Calculator** Solve $2x^2 + x - 4 = 0$ by using a graphing calculator.
(65)

17. **Error Analysis** Describe and correct the student's error in finding the area of a sector with a radius of 6 centimeters and a central angle of 40°.
(63)

$$A = \frac{1}{2}(6)^2(40) = 720 \text{ cm}^2$$

18. **Analyze** How is using a table of random digits to form a sample of 20 individuals different from using it to form a sample of 150 individuals?
(73)

19. **Probability** For i^a, if a is randomly chosen from the numbers 20 through 30 inclusive, what is the probability that the value of the expression is 1 or −1?
(69)

*20. **Justify** Explain why $f(x) = \begin{cases} x + 1, & \text{if } x < -2 \\ 3, & \text{if } -2 \leq x < 8 \\ 15, & \text{if } x \geq 8 \end{cases}$ is not a step function.
(79)

21. **Marketing** The logo for a new math product includes the graph of the polynomial $3x^3 + 5x^2 - 6x - 8 = 0$. What coordinates will the project manager give the art production team to be sure the curve crosses the x-axis at the correct locations?
(66)

*22. **Delivery Charges** A garden center delivers up to 10 items for a \$25 delivery charge. There is an additional charge of \$5 per item for each additional item delivered. Write a piecewise function for the cost having x items delivered.
(79)

23. **Analyze** Describe how the range of the inverse sine function and the range of the inverse tangent function are different. Explain why they are different.
(67)

Use the discriminant to find all values for which the equation has (a) two real solutions, (b) one real solution, and (c) two imaginary solutions.

*24. $x^2 - 4x - c = 0$
(74)

*25. $-4x^2 - 10x + c = 0$
(74)

26. **Multiple Choice** A coin purse contains 6 dimes, 2 nickels, and 10 pennies. When selecting three coins, one at a time, without replacement, what is the approximate probability of randomly selecting 3 pennies?
(68)

A 12.3% **B** 14.7% **C** 20.4% **D** 29.4%

27. **Formulate** Show how to derive the Law of Sines from the three expressions for the area of a triangle: $\frac{1}{2}bc \sin A = \frac{1}{2}ac \sin B = \frac{1}{2}ab \sin C$.
(71)

28. Find A^{-1} for $A = \begin{bmatrix} 1 & -1 \\ 4 & -6 \end{bmatrix}$.
(32)

© Saxon. All rights reserved.

29. (75) **Aviation** As an airplane is taking off from a runway, the force of lift on the plane can be calculated using the equation shown below. The plane begins to fly when the force of lift is equal to the weight of the plane. Find the radical function that can be used to find the minimum speed for flight.

Lift $= kv^2$, for constant k and velocity v

***30.** (79) Evaluate the piecewise function for $x = -3$ and $x = 4$.

$$f(x) = \begin{cases} 3x - 1 & \text{if } x < 0 \\ 2x^2 & \text{if } 0 \leq x < 4 \\ 1 - x & \text{if } 4 \leq x \end{cases}$$

© Saxon. All rights reserved.

Name ______________________ Date ____________ Class ____________

Finding the Normal Distribution

LESSON 80

1. Find an equation for the inverse of $y = x^2 - 7$. Determine whether each relation is a function.
(50)

*2. A set of results are normally distributed with a mean of 88 and a standard deviation of 4. Find the percent of results between 80 and 96.
(80)

3. Given a deck of cards, what is the probability of randomly drawing two ace cards without replacing the first card?
(60)

4. The number of lemmings grew exponentially. At first there were 400,000. Three weeks later there were 1,200,000. How many would there be after 8 weeks?
(57)

*5. A set of scores have a mean of 43 and a standard deviation of 2. Find the z-score for an outcome of 37.
(80)

6. **(Astronomy)** The binary star system 12 Bootis consists of two stars with nearly equal mass, and therefore a nearly equal gravitational pull. The distance between the two stars changes slightly over time, but is on average about 18.7 million kilometers. Suppose a spaceship crew wants to position their spaceship at a point equidistant from both stars, and so that the gravitational pulls were perpendicular to each other. How far from each star would the spaceship have to be?
(52)

7. P is a point on the terminal side of θ in standard position. Find the exact value of the six trigonometric functions for θ where $P(2, 9)$.
(56)

8. **Analyze** What are the values of a and b in the imaginary unit i?
(62)

9. Simplify $\dfrac{13^{\frac{1}{3}} \cdot 13^{\frac{1}{4}}}{13^{\frac{1}{12}} \cdot 13^{\frac{1}{2}}}$.
(59)

10. **Multiple Choice** What is the radian measure of a 90° angle?
(63)

A $-\frac{\pi}{2}$ radian **B** -1 radian **C** $\frac{\pi}{2}$ radian **D** 1 radian

11. **(Biology)** The formula $SA = \sqrt{\frac{mk}{36}}$ approximates the surface area SA in square meters of a human being with a height of m meters and a mass of k kilograms. Approximate the mass of a person who has a surface area of 1.64 square meters and a height of 1.7 meters.
(70)

12. **Multi-Step** **a.** Write the equation $y = \log_3 \frac{1}{9}$ in exponential form. What value of y makes both equations true?
(64)

b. Complete the table of values for the function $y = \log_3 x$.

x	$\frac{1}{9}$	$\frac{1}{3}$	1	3	9
$y = \log_3 x$					

c. Plot the points and sketch the graph of the function.

© Saxon. All rights reserved.

13. **Geometry** The length of the hypotenuse of a right triangle is 75 inches. Find the lengths of the legs given that the perimeter is 168 inches.
(65)

*14. **Write** Explain why the equation $16x^4 - 16 = 0$ can be solved by factoring the difference of two squares.
(78)

15. **Error Analysis** Find and correct the error a student made in determining the possible rational roots of $2x^3 + 7x^2 - 5x - 4 = 0$.
(66)

$$\frac{\pm1, \pm2}{\pm1, \pm2, \pm4} = \pm1, \pm\frac{1}{2}, \pm\frac{1}{4}, \pm2$$

16. **Navigation** "Lines" of longitude are actually circles that get closer together as you travel north or south from the equator. The formula for the approximate length l of a 1° arc of longitude in miles is $l \approx 69.033 \cos \theta$, where θ is the latitude in degrees at some point on the 1° arc of longitude.
(67)

a. At what latitude, to the nearest degree, is the length of a 1° arc of longitude approximately 53.6 miles?

b. The latitude at the equator is 0° and the latitude at the Arctic Circle is about 66°N. To the nearest mile, how much longer is the length of a 1° arc of longitude at the equator than at the Arctic Circle?

17. **Error Analysis** A student said that a cluster sample is a type of simple random sample because every cluster has an equal chance of being chosen. Explain the error in the student's thinking.
(73)

18. A box of colored pencils only holds primary colors. It has 5 red, 8 yellow, and 3 blue. Find the probability that a student will randomly grab 2 yellow pencils without replacement.
(68)

19. **Probability** Given that the discriminant is nonnegative and chosen randomly from the following list, find the probability that the equation it was derived from has exactly one real solution.
(74)

$$7, 0, -1, 4, -3, 5$$

20. **Electrical Engineering** The flow of a current, I, the resistance to the flow, Z, and the voltage, E, are related by $E = I(Z)$. Find the voltage of a circuit if the current is $40 - 36i$ amps and the resistance is $8 + 3i$ ohms.
(69)

21. **Geography** On a map, line segments connecting three southwest Virginia cities form a triangle as shown below. To the nearest tenth of a mile, what is the distance from Danville to South Boston if 1 inch = 13.5 miles?
(71)

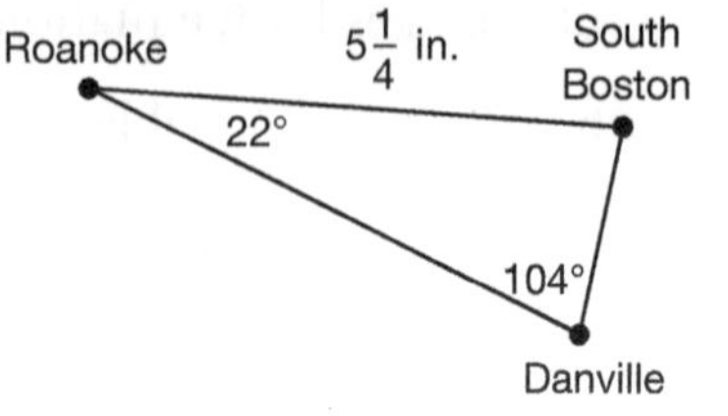

© Saxon. All rights reserved.

22. (75) **Write** What happens to the graph of $y = \sqrt{x^2 + 200}$ for very large values of x? What can you conclude about functions of the form $y = \sqrt[n]{x^n + c}$, for constants n and c?

***23.** (76) **Graphing Calculator** Use a graphing calculator to test this hypothesis: If a cubic function has two roots, one of the roots must have a multiplicity of 2.

***24.** (80) **Multiple Choice** Which z-score is closest to the mean of a standardized normal distribution?

A -2.36 **B** -0.45 **C** 0.78 **D** 2.9

25. (72) **Analyze** What pair of inverse functions contain the ordered pairs $(1.5, 3^{1.5})$ and $(3^{1.5}, 1.5)$?

***26.** (80) **Generalize** Write <, =, or >.

When standardizing a data value selected from a normally distributed set of data, $z \bigcirc 0$ when the mean is greater than the data value.

$z \bigcirc 0$ when the mean is less than the data value.

***27.** (77) **Estimate** In $\triangle PQR$, $p = 7.8935$, $q = 3.456$, and $r = \sqrt{37}$. Estimate the area of the triangle.

***28.** (79) **Comparison Shopping** At a party shop, balloons cost \$2 each if you buy fewer than 12, \$1.75 each if you buy between 12 and 24, inclusive, and \$1.50 each if you buy more than 24. Write a piecewise function for the cost of buying x balloons.

Evaluate each piecewise function for $x = \frac{1}{2}$ and $x = -10$.

***29.** (79) $f(x) = \begin{cases} 7, & \text{if } x < 0 \\ x^2, & \text{if } 0 \leq x < 10 \\ -x^2, & \text{if } x \geq 10 \end{cases}$

***30.** (79) $f(x) = \begin{cases} \frac{1}{2}, & \text{if } x < 1 \\ x - 4, & \text{if } 1 \leq x < 10 \\ -x - 9, & \text{if } x \geq 10 \end{cases}$

© Saxon. All rights reserved.

Name ______________________ Date __________ Class __________

Using Natural Logarithms

LESSON 81

1. (50) Find an equation for the inverse of $y = x^2 + 3$. Determine whether each relation is a function.

***2.** (80) Weights have a mean of 35 lbs and a standard deviation of 0.5 lbs. Find the z-score for a weight of 36.8 lbs.

Determine the domain and range.

3. (75) $y = -4\sqrt{x + 2}$

4. (75) $y = \frac{1}{2}\sqrt{x}$

***5.** (81) Rewrite ln 14e as a sum or difference of terms if possible. Then simplify.

6. (52) **Geometry** The lengths of the three sides of a right triangle ABC are 7.9 cm, 15.8 cm and $\sqrt{187.23}$ cm respectively. Find the measure of the angle C.

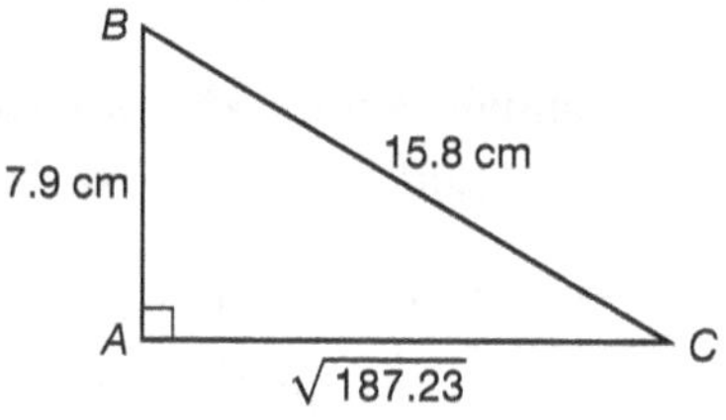

7. (72) **Write** Explain why $e^{\ln x} = x$.

8. (53) Let $p(u) = 2u + 5$ with domain {1, 3, 5, 7} and $r(u) = u - 3$ with domain {6, 8}. What are the domain and range of $p(r(u))$?

9. (61) **Verify** Show by synthetic division that $x + 9$ is a factor of $6x^3 + 51x^2 - 27x$.

10. (69) **Fractals** Some fractals are produced using the formula $Z_{n+1} = (Z_n)^2 + c$. Find Z_2 if $Z_1 = 0.3 + 0.8i$ and $Z_2 = (Z_1)^2 + 0.5$.

11. (60) **Error Analysis** A box contains 16 red balls numbered 1–16, 10 green balls numbered 27–36, and 14 yellow balls numbered 47–60. A ball is randomly selected from the box. The work below is used to find the probability that the ball selected is yellow or a one-digit number. Explain why the work is incorrect.

Y = event of yellow ball selected

D = event of one-digit number selected

$P(Y) = \frac{14}{40} = \frac{7}{20}$

$P(D) = \frac{9}{60} = \frac{3}{20}$

$P(Y \text{ or } D) = P(Y) \cdot P(D) = \frac{7}{20} \cdot \frac{3}{20} = 0.0525$

12. (65) **Multi-Step** A 5 inch by 7 inch photo is framed and the total area of the photo and the frame is 50 square inches.

a. Write a quadratic expression in standard form to represent the situation.

b. Find the width of the frame to the nearest hundredth of an inch.

Solve by completing the square.

13. (78) $2d^2 = 8 + 10d$

14. (78) $-3x^2 + 18x = -30$

© Saxon. All rights reserved.

15. **Housing** The table shows estimated housing occupancy for three states for the year 2006. Find the probability that a randomly selected house from one of these states is vacant given that the house is in Idaho. Write the probability as a percent rounded to the nearest hundredth.
(68)

	Occupied Houses	Vacant Houses
Idaho	548,555	67,148
Florida	7,106,042	1,425,818
Illinois	4,724,252	475,491

16. **Running** The expression representing a runner's speed is $120x^2 - 60x - 240$ feet per minute. Find the expression for the runner's speed in feet per second.
(23)

*17. **Multiple Choice** What are the roots of the equation $2x^2 = 50$?
(78)
A 0 and 50 **B** 0 and 25 **C** 5 and −5 **D** 25 and −25

18. **Multi-Step** Explain why the question below leads the reader to vote *no*. Then rewrite the question in a way that leads the reader to vote *yes*.
(73)

"A new shopping mall will bring more traffic to our already congested streets, increasing the noise and pollution levels and the time it takes to drive anywhere. Do you want a new shopping mall in our area?"

19. **Multiple Choice** Solve $\sqrt{3x} + 7 = 9$.
(70)
A $\frac{3}{4}$ **B** $\frac{4}{3}$ **C** $\frac{16}{3}$ **D** $\frac{256}{3}$

*20. **Analyze** What pair of inverse functions contain the ordered pairs $\left(e^{\frac{1}{2}}, \frac{1}{2}\right)$ and $\left(\frac{1}{2}, e^{\frac{1}{2}}\right)$?
(81)

21. **Ranching** A rancher has 380 feet of fencing material to enclose a rectangular area for her llamas. She wants the fenced-in area to be 9025 square feet. The equation $w(190 - w) = 9025$ gives the width of a rectangle that meets these requirements. Use the discriminant to explain if the rancher has enough material to build a fence that meets these requirements.
(74)

*22. **Paleontology** Carbon 14 is an isotope that is used to determine ages of fossils. It has a half–life of about 5730 years, which means that 50% of an initial amount will decay in 5730 years. To the nearest year, how long will it take for 51% of an initial amount to decay? (Use the natural decay function $N(t) = N_0e^{-kt}$.)
(81)

23. **Write** Explain why the inverses of the trigonometric functions are not functions.
(67)

*24. Given $N(t) = 0.3$, $N_0 = 1$, $k = 0.0974$, write the decay function and solve for t.
(81)

© Saxon. All rights reserved.

25. (76) **Construction** Concrete is going to be poured into a container in the shape of a rectangular prism. The container is constructed from the form shown. If the volume of concrete is 300, what are the actual dimensions of the container to the nearest hundredth?

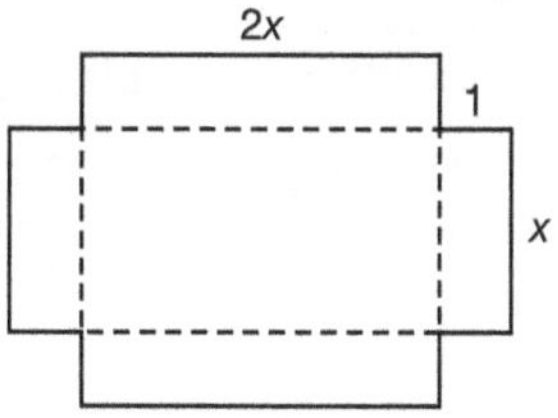

*26. (81) **Probability** An experiment consists of choosing a random integer from the integers 1 through 10 inclusive. Five trials are conducted. What is the probability that an integer greater than 2 is chosen on every trial?

*27. (77) **Graphing Calculator** Find c in $\triangle BCD$ given $b = 34.729$, $d = 21.65$, and $m\angle C = 125.37°$. Round to the nearest thousandth.

*28. (80) **Model** The heights of a group of children are normally distributed with a mean of 42 inches and a standard deviation of 2.2 inches. Draw a bell curve and label 3 standard deviations above and below the mean.

29. (67) Evaluate the inverse trigonometric function $\text{Cos}^{-1}\left(\frac{\sqrt{3}}{2}\right)$. Give your answer in both radians and degrees.

*30. (80) A set of results are normally distributed with a mean of 26 and a standard deviation of 2. Find the percent of results > 22.

© Saxon. All rights reserved.

25. [illegible] container [illegible] dimensions [illegible] is constructed from the [illegible]. If the volume of concrete is [illegible], what are the actual dimensions of the container to the nearest hundredth?

26. **Probability** An experiment consists of [illegible] through [illegible]. The trials are conducted. What is the probability [illegible] on every trial?

27. **Graphing Calculator** [illegible] $12^\circ 18'$. Round to the nearest thousandth.

28. **Make** [illegible] of a group of children are normally distributed [illegible] inches and a standard deviation of [illegible] inches. Draw a bell curve and [illegible] standard deviations above and below the mean.

29. Evaluate the inverse trigonometric function [illegible]. Give your answer in both radians and degrees.

30. A set of [illegible] normally distributed with a mean of [illegible] and a standard deviation of [illegible]. Find the percent of [illegible].

Name ______________________ Date ____________ Class ____________

Graphing the Sine and Cosine Functions

LESSON 82

1. (76) Which of the following is not a factor of $x^3 - 15x^2 + 74x - 120$?

A $(x - 6)$ **B** $(x - 5)$ **C** $(x - 4)$ **D** $(x - 3)$

2. (57) **Bacteria** A colony of bacteria begins with a population of 28, and after 45 minutes the population is 572. How long will it take the colony to grow to 1,200 bacteria?

***3.** (82) Given $h(x) = -2\sin(x)$, identify the amplitude and period. Graph the function.

***4.** (65) **Graphing Calculator** Solve $x^2 + 2x + 1 = 0$ by using a graphing calculator.

5. (76) Find the roots and give the multiplicity of each root: $x^3 + 2x^2 - 3x = 0$.

6. (52) Find the exact values of x and y in an isosceles right triangle with a hypotenuse 21 units long and legs x and y.

***7.** (81) Write $\ln\left(\frac{4x^2}{e^3}\right)^3$ as a sum or difference of terms if possible. Then simplify.

Find the area of $\triangle ABC$ with the given side lengths and included angle.

8. (71) $B = 124°$, $a = 9$, $c = 11$

9. (71) $A = 68°$ and $b = 13$, $c = 7$

10. (66) **Geometry** The volume of a pyramid is given by the formula $V = \frac{1}{3}Bh$, where B is the area of the base and h is the height of the pyramid. A pyramid with a square base has a volume of 108 cubic units.

a. Write a polynomial equation in standard form that can be used to find the length of one side of the base if the height is 3 units longer than the base.

b. Solve the polynomial equation to find the length of one side. (Hint: The length is less than 10 units.)

***11.** (80) In a study of 748 subjects, the mean height was 168.8 centimeters and the standard deviation was 8.9 centimeters. Assuming the distribution is normal, what is the range of heights that the middle 68% of the subjects fell into?

12. (72) **Aquarium** The recommended range for the pH of aquarium water for most fish is from 6 to 8. Use the formula $\text{pH} = -\log[\text{H}^+]$, and write the equivalent range for $[\text{H}^+]$, the concentration of hydrogen ions in moles per liter. Write your answer without exponents.

13. (67) **Error Analysis** A student incorrectly solved the equation $\cos\theta = 0.8$, for $0 \leq \theta \leq \pi$, as shown. $\cos\theta = 0.8 \longrightarrow \theta = \text{Cos}^{-1}(0.8) \longrightarrow \theta = \frac{1}{\cos(0.8)} \longrightarrow \theta \approx 1.44$. What is the error? Find the correct solution.

Find the roots of the polynomial function.

14. (76) $f(x) = 12x^3 + 4x^2 - 2x$

15. (76) $f(x) = (x - 2)(x^2 + 6) - (x - 2)(7x + 4)$

© Saxon. All rights reserved.

16. **Probability** A used car lot contains 16 red cars, 14 gold cars, 9 black cars, and 6 blue cars. A customer needs 5 cars for their new company. Find the probability that they will randomly choose 5 gold cars.
(68)

*17. Graph $y = 2 \cos 3x$.
(82)

18. **Multiple Choice** Choose the answer that best represents the probability of flipping two coins five times and always showing tails.
(60)

A 0.5 **B** 0.0005 **C** 0.0001 **D** 0.01

19. **Verify** Show that the product of two imaginary numbers (*bi* and *ci*) can be either positive or negative.
(69)

20. **Generalize** Suppose a researcher captures and tags *n* animals, goes back, captures $n - 1$ animals, and finds that all of the $n - 1$ animals are tagged. What is the estimated animal population?
(73)

Multiply. Write the result in the form $a + bi$.

21. $2(3i)$
(69)

22. $-4(5i)$
(69)

*23. **Write** Explain why $e^{\ln(x-3)} = x - 3$.
(81)

24. **Surveying** A surveyor stands on the south end of a roof and finds that the angle formed by the roof and the line of sight with a flagpole is 33°. The surveyor then walks to the north end of the roof and finds the angle formed by the roof and the flagpole to be 61°. Estimate the distance from the roof to the flagpole, given that the roof has a length of 50 feet.
(71)

25. **Vertical Motion** The height of a free-falling object (neglecting air resistance) is given by the function $h(t) = -16t^2 + v_0t + h_0$, where h_0 is the initial height in feet, v_0 is the initial velocity in feet per second, and $h(t)$ is the height in feet at time t seconds. How long does it take for an object to hit the ground after it is dropped from a height of 49 feet?
(78)

26. **Multi-Step** **a.** Write $5x - 3x^2 = 10$ in standard form.
(74)

b. Find the discriminant of the equation in part a.

c. Use the discriminant to describe the solutions of the equation in part a.

27. **Pendulum** The period of a pendulum, *T*, is the time it takes for the pendulum to make one back-and-forth swing, and is given by $T = 2\pi\sqrt{\frac{L}{9.8}}$, where *L* is the length of the pendulum in meters. Find the length of a pendulum whose period is 4 seconds.
(70)

© Saxon. All rights reserved.

***28.** *(82)* How many cycles of the function $y = 3\cos(2x)$ are in the interval 0 to 2π.

29. *(77)* **Write** Without writing a formula, explain how to find the area of a triangle given its three side lengths.

***30.** *(81)* **Radioisotopes** Thallium, a radioisotope used to track blood flow, has a half-life of about 73.1 hours. How long will it take for 1 mg of thallium to decay to 0.7 mg? Use the natural decay function $N(t) = N_0e^{-kt}$.

© Saxon. All rights reserved.

1. [illegible]

2. [illegible] their true length.

3. (Radioisotopes) Thallium, a radioisotope used to [illegible], has a half-life of about 73 hours [uncertain reading]. How long will it take for [illegible] of thallium to decay to [illegible]? Use the natural decay function [illegible: likely $N(t) = N_0 e^{-kt}$].

Name ______________________ Date __________ Class __________

Writing Quadratic Equations from Roots

LESSON 83

Simplify each expression.

1. (59) $(8 \cdot 216)^{\frac{1}{3}}$

2. (59) $\dfrac{6^{\frac{14}{9}}}{6^{\frac{6}{9}}}$

3. (68) A box of crayons has 3 purples, 5 reds, 8 greens, and 2 oranges. Find the probability that a student will randomly choose 1 purple, 2 red, and 1 green crayon in that order without replacement.

Factor each expression completely.

4. (61) $32z^5 - 2z$

5. (61) $a^5b^2 - a^2b^4 + 2a^4b - 2ab^3 + a^3 - b^2$

***6.** (60) **Multi-Step** A doctor organized data about her patients' ages and genders in the chart below.

a. Are the events male client under 36 or male client over 75 mutually exclusive or inclusive? Explain why.

b. Find the probability that a patient is male under 36 or male over 75. Round to the hundredths place.

c. Use the probability found in part b to find the probability that three clients, selected randomly with replacement, are male under 36 or male over 75. Round to the hundredths place.

Gender of Client

Age	Male	Female
18–35	39	41
36–55	45	52
56–75	54	40
76+	47	56

7. (53) Let $f(x) = 2x + 5$ and $g(x) = 3x$. Evaluate the composition $(f \circ g)(4)$ using two different methods.

8. (65) **Generalize** The Quadratic Formula can be written as $x = -\frac{b}{2a} \pm \frac{\sqrt{b^2 - 4ac}}{2a}$. How does this form show the symmetry of a parabola?

9. (72) **Multiple Choice** Which is equal to $\log_{20} 20^{a-b}$?

A $a - b$ **B** $20(a - b)$ **C** $\frac{a}{b}$ **D** $\frac{20^a}{20^b}$

***10.** (66) **Graphing Calculator** Solve $2x^3 + 4x^2 - 39x - 45 = 0$ by using a graphing calculator.

11. (75) **Analyze** Suppose that $f(x) = \sqrt[m]{g(x)} + \sqrt[n]{h(x)}$. If mn is an odd number, what can you conclude about the domain and range of $f(x)$? Why?

***12.** (83) **National Parks** The Landscape Arch, in Arches National Park, is the longest natural stone arch in the world. Its length is about 290 feet and its height is about 78 feet. Write a quadratic function to approximate the arch.

13. (67) **Estimate** Use what you know about the unit circle and special angles to estimate $\text{Sin}^{-1}(0.02)$ in degrees. Do not use a calculator. Explain your method.

© Saxon. All rights reserved.

14. (69) **Electrical Engineering** The flow of a current, I, the resistance to the flow, Z, and the voltage, E, are related by $E = I(Z)$. Find the voltage if the current is $24 - 28i$ amps and the resistance is $5 + i$ ohms.

15. (78) **Write** Explain why the equation $x^4 - 625 = 0$ can be solved by factoring the difference of two squares.

16. (70) **Geometry** The formula $d = \sqrt{l^2 + w^2 + h^2}$ gives the length of a diagonal d of a $l \times w \times h$ rectangular prism. Prism A has a width of 3 inches, a length of 7 inches, and a diagonal whose length is about 9.1 inches. Prism B has a width of 2 inches, a length of 8 inches, and a diagonal whose length is about 10.2 inches. Which prism has the greater height and by how much?

17. (71) **Analyze** When can you find the area of a triangle without knowing the height of the triangle?

18. (73) **Government** Suppose a politician must visit 4 states on the East Coast. His human resource personnel form a simple random sample by listing each state on the East Coast and numbering it as shown below. If they use the line of random digits shown below, which 4 states will the politician visit?

10: ME	11: NH	12: MA	13: RI	14: CT	15: NY	16: NJ
17: DE	18: MD	19: VA	20: NC	21: SC	22: GA	23: FL

63157	48257	29223	66713	89022	43069	91349	33111	63682	48864	53097

19. (74) **Multi-Step** **a.** Write $-18x^2 - 84x = 98$ in standard form.

b. Factor the left side of the equation in part a.

c. Find and use the discriminant to describe the solutions of the equation in part A.

20. (76) **Physics** A satellite in orbit accelerates according to the equation below, for orbital speed v and distance from the Earth's center r. Two satellites are in orbit, one at a speed of v and the other at a speed of $5v$. How far from Earth's center is the faster satellite compared to the slower one if they both have the same acceleration?

$$\text{acceleration} = \frac{v^2}{r}$$

21. (77) **Error Analysis** Explain and correct the error a student made in finding $m\angle C$.

$$7.5^2 = 4^2 + 10^2 - 2(4)(10)\cos C$$
$$56.25 = 116 - 80\cos C$$
$$56.25 = 36\cos C$$
$$1.5625 = \cos C$$

Error

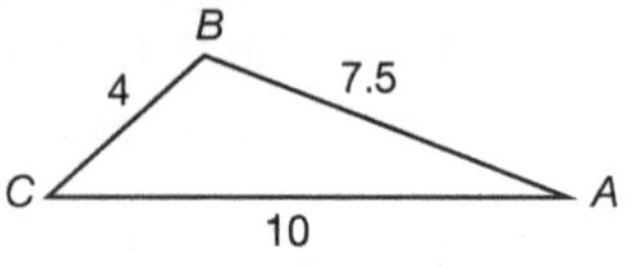

© Saxon. All rights reserved.

***22.** (83) **Multiple Choice** Which equation is a quadratic equation with a single root of 7?
A $x(x + 7) = 0$ **B** $x^2 - 7 = 0$ **C** $(x - 7)(x - 7) = 0$ **D** $(x + 7)(x + 7) = 0$

***23.** (82) **Error Analysis** Two students are finding the period of $y = 4\sin\left(\frac{1}{\pi}x\right)$ but get different results. Which student made the mistake?

Student A	Student B
The period is where $y = 0$ $\frac{1}{\pi}x = 2\pi$ $x = 2\pi^2$ ← Period	The period is where $y = 0$ $\frac{1}{\pi}x = \pi$ $x = \pi^2$ ← Period

24. (71) Find the area of ΔABC with the given side lengths and included angle. $a = 19$, $c = 8$, $B = 75°$

***25.** (81) **Economics** The formula for continuously compounded interest is $A = Pe^{rt}$, where A is the total amount, P is the principal, r is the annual interest rate, and t is the time in years. To the nearest hundredth of a percent, what annual interest rate would be necessary for the value of an investment to double in 10 years if the interest is compounded continuously?

Evaluate each piecewise function for $x = 0$ and $x = 2$.

26. (79) $f(x) = \begin{cases} 5, \text{ if } x < 0 \\ x + 2, \text{ if } 0 \le x \le 8 \\ 2x^2 + 1, \text{ if } x > 8 \end{cases}$

27. (79) $f(x) = \begin{cases} 9, \text{ if } x < -1 \\ 12, \text{ if } -1 \le x \le 0 \\ 20, \text{ if } x > 0 \end{cases}$

***28.** (82) **Multiple Choice** Which of the following has a period of π?
A $y = \sin(2\pi x)$ **B** $y = \sin(\pi x)$ **C** $y = \sin(x)$ **D** $y = \sin(2x)$

***29.** (83) **Probability** The roots of a quadratic equation are $4 \pm 5i$.

a. What is the probability that the related function crosses the x-axis?

b. What is the probability that the related function has a minimum or maximum at $x = 4$?

***30.** (83) Write a quadratic equation whose roots are 6 and -2.

© Saxon. All rights reserved.

Name ______________________ Date __________ Class __________

Solving Rational Equations

LESSON 84

1. (56) Given $\theta = 504°$, find the measure of the reference angle.

Find all the possible values.

2. (67) $\cos^{-1}\left(\frac{1}{2}\right)$

3. (67) $\tan^{-1}(1)$

4. (64) **Coordinate Geometry** The graph of the logarithmic function $y = \log_3 x$ is shown. Estimate the shaded area.

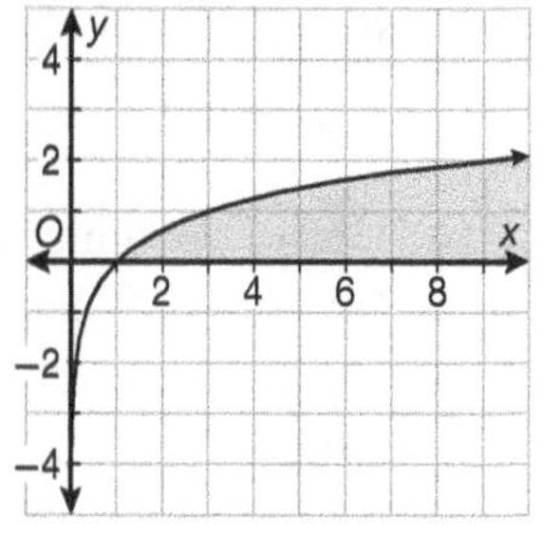

5. (74) Use the discriminant to find all values of c for which $x^2 - x + c = 0$ has (a) two real solutions, (b) one real solution, and (c) two complex solutions.

6. (58) Complete the square and factor the resulting perfect square trinomial: $x^2 - 24x$.

7. (80) **Analyze** The z-score of an unknown data value is -1.4. Find the data value given that the mean of the data is 60 and the standard deviation is 12.

8. (77) **Geography** A map of southwest Illinois shows that Waterloo is 34 miles from Chester and 44 miles from Pinckneyville. Pinckneyville is 27 miles from Chester. Find the number of square miles enclosed in the triangle formed by the lines connecting these three cities. Round to the nearest square mile.

***9.** (65) **Graphing Calculator** Solve $2x^2 + 4x - 3 = 0$ by using a graphing calculator.

***10.** (81) **Multiple Choice** Which is equal to $e^{\ln 4x^2}$?

A $8x$ **B** $\ln 8x$ **C** $2 \ln 4x$ **D** $4x^2$

11. (68) **Housing** The table shows estimated housing occupancy for three states for the year 2006.

Find the probability that a randomly selected house from one of these states is in Texas given that it is occupied. Write the probability as a percent rounded to the nearest hundredth.

	Occupied Houses	Vacant Houses
Virginia	2,905,071	325,750
Texas	8,109,388	1,115,532
Utah	814,028	87,294

12. (78) **Analyze** Describe how to solve the equation $\frac{1}{2}x^2 - 2 = 0$ by factoring the difference of two squares.

© Saxon. All rights reserved.

13. **Error Analysis** Which student made an error in finding $|2 - i|$? Describe the error.
(69)

Student A: $\sqrt{2^2 + 0^2} \rightarrow \sqrt{4} \rightarrow 2$ Student B: $\sqrt{2^2 + (-1)^2} \rightarrow \sqrt{4+1} \rightarrow \sqrt{5}$

***14.** Write a quadratic equation whose root is 7.
(83)

15. **Diameter** The formula $d = \frac{\sqrt{15w}}{\pi}$ gives the diameter in inches of the rope needed to lift w tons. How much more weight can be lifted with a rope of diameter 3 inches than with a rope of diameter 2.5 inches?
(70)

16. **Sound** Two measures of sound are loudness and intensity. They are related by the function $L(I) = 10\log\frac{I}{I_0}$, where $L(I)$ is loudness in decibels, I is intensity in watts per square meter, and $I_0 \approx 10^{-12}$ watt per square meter, the intensity of a barely audible sound. The sound intensity near a speaker is 0.01 watt per square meter. What is the loudness in decibels?
(72)

***17.** **Multi-Step** Write a quadratic equation with roots of $5 + 3i$ and $5 - 3i$ so that the parabola of the related function opens up. Then write one so that the parabola opens down and is wider than the one that opens up.
(83)

18. **Multiple Choice** Which type of sampling is *not* a type of probability sampling?
(73)

A simple random sampling **B** voluntary response sampling

C cluster sampling **D** systematic sampling

Solve.

***19.** $2 + \frac{1}{x} = 4$
(84)

***20.** $\frac{2}{x+2} + \frac{8}{x-2} = \frac{14}{x^2 - 4}$
(84)

***21.** $\frac{-6}{x-3} = 1$
(84)

22. **Generalize** What will be the value of the discriminant of an equation if the vertex of the related function is located in Quadrant III and the parabola opens upward? Why?
(74)

***23.** Write a quadratic equation whose roots are 6 and -1.
(83)

24. **Students** Of the 70 students going on the soccer trip, 58 are players and 8 are left-handed. Six of the left-handed students are soccer players. What is the probability that one of the students on the trip is a soccer player or is left-handed?
(60)

25. **Analyze** The graph of a radical function $f(x) = \sqrt[n]{g(x)}$ is shown. What can you conclude about n?
(75)

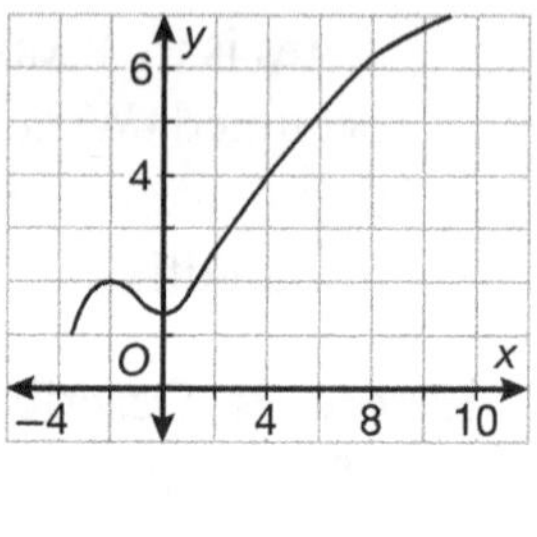

© Saxon. All rights reserved.

***26.** (82) **Formulate** Suppose that $f(x) = \sin(ax)$ and $g(x) = \sin(bx)$. If $f(x)$ completes four periods when $g(x)$ completes one, what is the relationship between a and b?

27. (76) **Geometry** The volume of a rectangular prism is $3x^3 + 5x^2 - 12x$. What are the dimensions of the rectangular prism?

28. (79) **Multi-Step** At a florist shop, roses cost \$3.50 each if you buy fewer than 12, \$3.00 each if you buy between 12 and 24, and \$2.50 each if you buy more than 24. Write a piecewise function for the cost per rose when buying x roses. Then, graph the function.

29. (77) In $\triangle RST$, $ST = 8.9$, $RT = 12.2$, and the $m\angle T = 78°$. Find $m\angle S$.

***30.** (84) **Error Analysis** A student said that the equation $\frac{3}{x^2 + 7x + 10} + \frac{1}{x^2 + 10x + 25} = 24$ can be solved by multiplying both sides of the equation by $(x + 2)(x + 5)$. Why is this not true?

© Saxon. All rights reserved.

Name ______________________ Date __________ Class __________

Finding Polynomial Roots II

LESSON 85

Find the roots of the given equations.

1. (76) $y = 6x^2 + 7x - 1$

2. (76) $y = x^4 - 27x$

***3.** (85) Which of the following is not a root of $f(x) = 3x^3 - 19x^2 + 22x + 24$?

A $-\frac{2}{3}$ **B** $\frac{2}{3}$ **C** 3 **D** 4

Determine whether each of the following are step functions.

4. (79) $f(x) = \begin{cases} 12, \text{ if } x < 1 \\ x + 12, \text{ if } x \geq 1 \end{cases}$

5. (79) $f(x) = \begin{cases} 0, \text{ if } x < 0 \\ 5, \text{ if } x \geq 0 \end{cases}$

6. (63) **Geometry** $\overline{AB}$ is tangent to the circle at point A and $\overline{BC}$ is tangent to the circle at point C. What is the length of $\widehat{AC}$? Give the answer in exact form and to the nearest tenth of a centimeter.

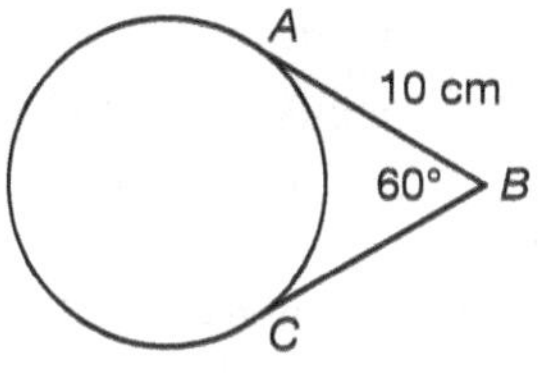

7. (78) **Gravity on the Moon** The height of a free-falling object on the moon (neglecting air resistance) is given by the function $h(t) = -0.8t^2 + v_0t + h_0$, where h_0 is the initial height in meters, v_0 is the initial velocity in meters per second, and $h(t)$ is the height in meters at time t seconds. How long does it take for an object to hit the surface of the moon after it is dropped from a height of 125 meters? (*Hint*: Multiply both sides of a quadratic equation by a number so that the coefficient of the quadratic term is a perfect square.)

8. (68) **Error Analysis** Find and correct the error a student made in finding $P(\text{AM}|\text{Female})$.

$$P(\text{AM}|\text{Female}) = \frac{4}{12} = \frac{1}{3} = 33\frac{1}{3}\%$$

	Male	Female
AM	16	4
PM	8	12

9. (70) **Pendulum** The period of a pendulum, T, is the time it takes for the pendulum to make one back-and-forth swing, and is given by $T = 2\pi\sqrt{\frac{L}{9.8}}$, where L is the length of the pendulum in meters. Find the length of a pendulum whose period is 1.5 seconds.

10. (55) Ty tosses a quarter three times. What is the probability that the quarter will land on tails all three times?

***11.** (83) **Write** How is deriving a quadratic equation from two complex roots different from deriving a quadratic equation from two real roots?

© Saxon. All rights reserved.

12. (Navigation) Two ships 320 yards apart spot the same lighthouse, as shown in the diagram. How much farther is ship B from the lighthouse than ship A?
(71)

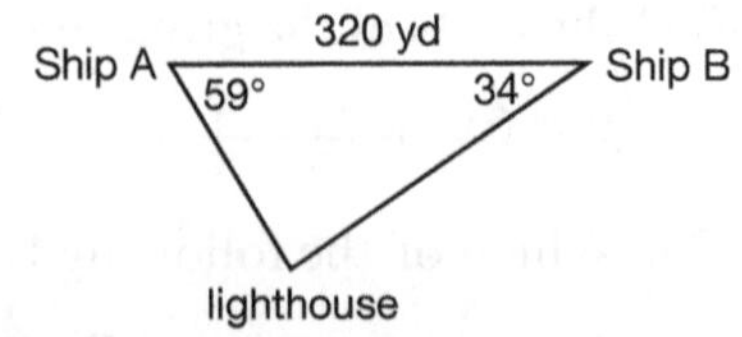

13. **Error Analysis** A student solved the equation $2x^3 - 72x = 0$ as shown below. What is the error?
(78)

$2x^3 - 72x = 0 \rightarrow 2x(x^2 - 36) = 0 \rightarrow 2x(x + 6)(x - 6) = 0 \rightarrow x = -6$ or $x = 6$

14. (Geology) The Richter magnitude M of an earthquake is expressed by $M = \frac{2}{3}\log\left(\frac{E}{10^{11.8}}\right)$, where E is the energy released in ergs. The earthquake of greatest magnitude, 9.5, occurred in 1960 in the Pacific, near the coast of Chile. Find the energy released by that earthquake.
(72)

*15. **Graphing Calculator** Use a graphing calculator to estimate the solution(s) of $\frac{x^4}{2} + \frac{1}{x^2 + 1} = x + 3$.
(84)

16. **Write** Explain what is meant by voluntary response sampling and why it is not a form of probability sampling.
(73)

17. **Multi-Step** The scores on a test are normally distributed with a mean of 86 and a standard deviation of 3.
(80)

a. What percent of the scores are between 83 and 89?

b. Tell how you can use the answer in part a to find the percent of scores that are either less than 83 or greater than 89. Then find the percent.

c. Tell how you can use the answer in part b to find the percent of scores that are less than 83. Then find the percent.

Find the restricted values for the rational equations.

*18. $\frac{1}{5} - \frac{1}{x + 5} = \frac{4}{3x^2}$
(84)

*19. $\frac{x}{3} + \frac{x + 3}{x - 1} = \frac{4}{x - 1}$
(84)

20. **Estimate** Estimate the discriminant of $43.876x^2 + \frac{4}{5}x - 4.128 = 0$.
(74)

*21. Let $f(x) = x^3 - 27$ and $g(x) = x + 2$. Find the roots of $f(g(x))$.
(85)

22. (Physics) The equation $h = -4.9t^2 + v_o t + h_o$ can be used to find the distance from the ground at time t for a ball thrown from a height h_o at an initial speed of v_o. Use the technique of completing the square to derive the function that can be used to calculate t.
(75)

© Saxon. All rights reserved.

23. Let $f(x) = 3x$, $g(x) = x - 5$, and $h(x) = x^2 - 2$. Find the composite function $f(g(h(x)))$.
(52)

24. **Analyze** In $\triangle ABC$, $m\angle A = 63°$, $b = 15$, and $c = 8$. To find $m\angle A$, which should be used, the Law of Sines or the Law of Cosines. Why?
(77)

*25. **Probability** A machine on an assembly line makes an acceptable product 90% of the time.
(81)

a. Ten samples are chosen at random. What is the probability that all 10 samples are acceptable?

b. At what number of samples is the probability 10% or less? Let n represent the number of samples. Write an equation and use natural logarithms to solve it.

*26. **Write** A radio station asks for listeners to call in and vote for their favorite high school football team. Identify the type of sample and determine whether it is biased. Explain your answer.
(Inv 7)

27. **Multiple Choice** Which is the graph of the function $f(x) = \begin{cases} -x, \text{ if } x < 0 \\ 3, \text{ if } x \geq 0 \end{cases}$?
(79)

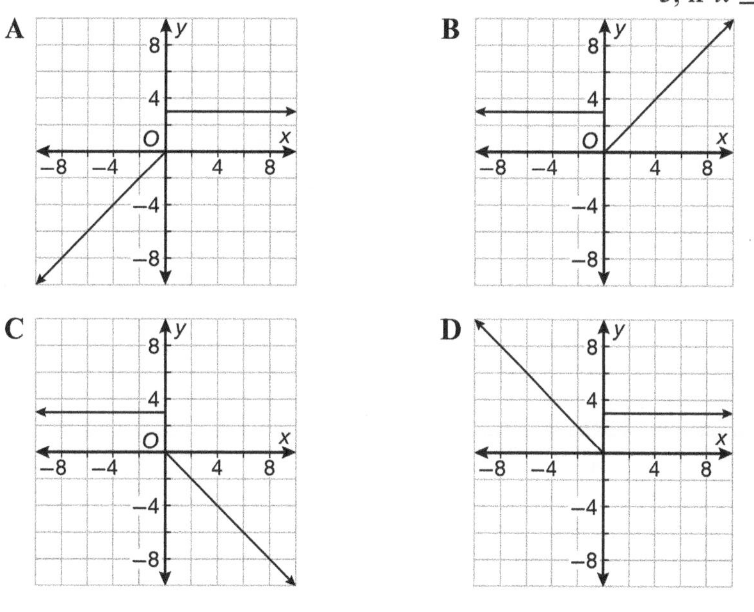

Identify all the real roots.

*28. $x^3 - 729 = 0$
(85)

*29. $x^4 - 13x^3 + 55x^2 - 81x + 18 = 0$
(85)

*30. Graph $y = -2 \sin\left(\frac{1}{4}x\right)$
(82)

© Saxon. All rights reserved.

Name ______________________ Date __________ Class __________

Translating Sine and Cosine Functions

LESSON 86

1. (60) Given a deck of cards, what is the probability of randomly drawing a face card, and then a number card without replacement of the first card? (The ace is not a face or number card)

Solve.

2. (70) $\sqrt[3]{8x^3 - 1} = 2x - 1$

3. (70) $\sqrt[3]{12x - 5} - \sqrt[3]{8x + 15} = 0$

4. (66) Find the roots and give the multiplicity of each root: $x^3 + 12x^2 + 36x = 0$

***5.** (8) Determine the period of the function $y = 3\cos\left(\frac{\pi}{2}x\right)$.

6. (67) **Jewelry** A jeweler is about to finish his sales for the year. He has 8 diamonds, 6 tanzanite stones, 9 opal stones, and 3 sapphires. A customer comes in needing three stones for a ring setting. Find the probability that the customer will choose 2 tanzanite stones and 1 sapphire.

7. (25) Find the range and standard deviation for the following set of data;

$$\{35, 67, 21, 16, 24, 51, 18, 32\}.$$

***8.** (86) Consider the function $f(x) = 3\cos(2x)$. Determine the period and amplitude of the function.

***9.** (71) **Multiple Choice** Which triangle cannot be solved by using the Law of Sines?

A

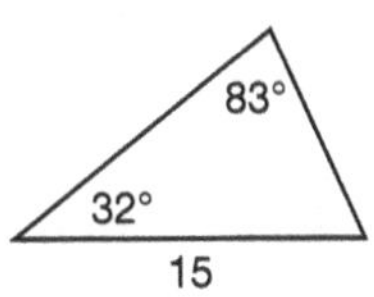

B

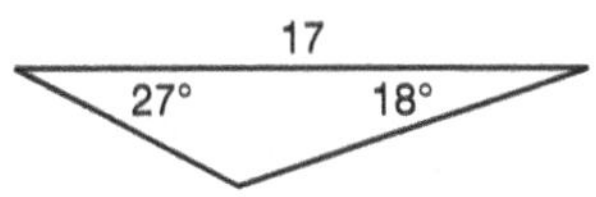

C

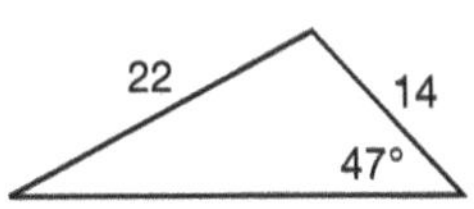

D

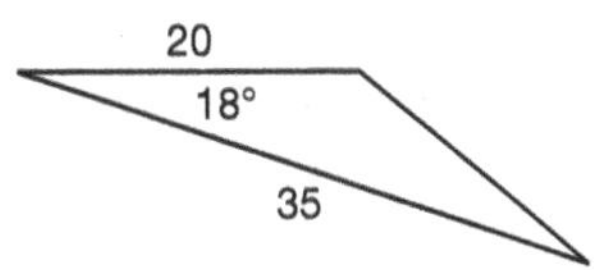

10. (80) **Generalize** Given a data value that is to be standardized and the mean of the data set, how can you tell if the z-score will be positive or negative without performing any calculations?

11. (77) An equilateral triangle has a side length of 12.7 centimeters. Find the area of the triangle by using Heron's formula.

***12.** (86) Which of the following has a vertical shift of 2 up?

A $y = \cos(2x) + 2$

B $y = \cos(2\pi x) - 2$

C $y = 2\cos(x)$

D $y = \cos\left(\frac{x}{2}\right)$

© Saxon. All rights reserved.

13. *(74)* **Geometry** The perimeter of a rectangle is 52 units.

a. Write an expression for the length if the width is represented by w.

b. Write a quadratic equation in standard form to show that the product of the length and width is 169 square units.

c. Find the discriminant of the equation. Explain what it means in terms of the rectangle.

***14.** *(85)* **Graphing Calculator** Use a graphing calculator to test this hypothesis: If a cubic function has only one rational root, then the other roots are complex.

15. *(75)* Determine the domain and range of the function $f(x) = \sqrt{x-4} + 3$ and its inverse.

16. *(58)* Complete the square and factor the resulting perfect square trinomial: $x^2 + 30x$.

***17.** *(76)* **Physics** Acceleration due to gravity is different on different planets. The equation below can be used to find the distance from the ground at time t for a ball thrown from a height h_o at an initial speed of v_o. Use the table to determine how long it will take a ball thrown with an initial speed of 20 at a height of 35 to hit the ground on Mars.

$$h = -\frac{1}{2}at^2 + v_o t + h_o$$

Planet	Acceleration (a)
Mercury	3.59
Venus	8.87
Mars	3.77
Jupiter	25.95
Saturn	11.08
Uranus	10.67
Neptune	14.07

18. *(84)* **Data Analysis** The harmonic mean x of y and z is given by the formula $\frac{2}{x} = \frac{1}{y} + \frac{1}{z}$. Find z when $x = 7.5$ and $y = 6$.

19. *(81)* A radioactive material has a half life of 46 hours. Find the decay constant.

20. *(78)* **Multi-Step** Complete parts a-b to help graph the quadratic function $y = \frac{1}{4}x^2 - \frac{9}{4}$.

a. Find the points in which the graph intersects the x-axis.

b. Find the vertex.

c. Graph the function.

21. *(79)* **Error Analysis** Jake graphed the piecewise function

$f(x) = \begin{cases} x, & \text{if } x < 0 \\ 3, & \text{if } x \geq 0 \end{cases}$ incorrectly. Explain Jake's error.

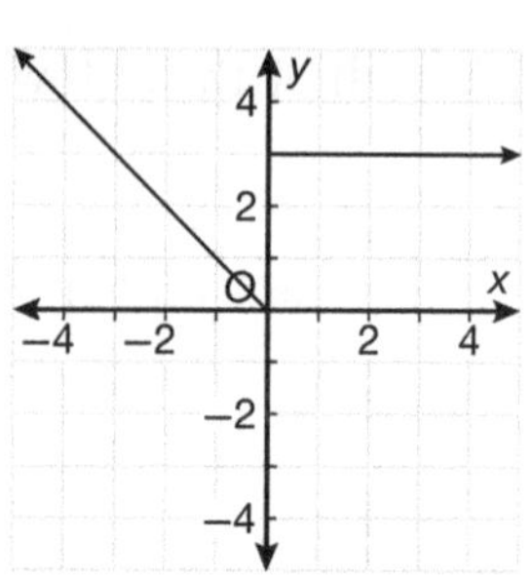

© Saxon. All rights reserved.

22. **Multi-Step** Suppose that the population of a certain species decreases at the rate
(57) of 5% per year and that the current population of that species in a certain habitat is 150.

a. Write an exponential function that gives the population as a function of x, the number of elapsed years. (Hint: $0 < b < 1$).

b. Write a logarithmic function that gives the number of elapsed years as a function of x, the population.

c. To the nearest tenth, how many years will it take for the population to drop below 100?

*23. **(Physics)** Two wheels spin in opposite directions. The
(86) larger wheel completes a cycle in 4 seconds and the smaller wheel completes a cycle in 9 seconds. The two squares attached to the wheels are facing each other at time $t = 0$. How many seconds elapse before they are back in sync?

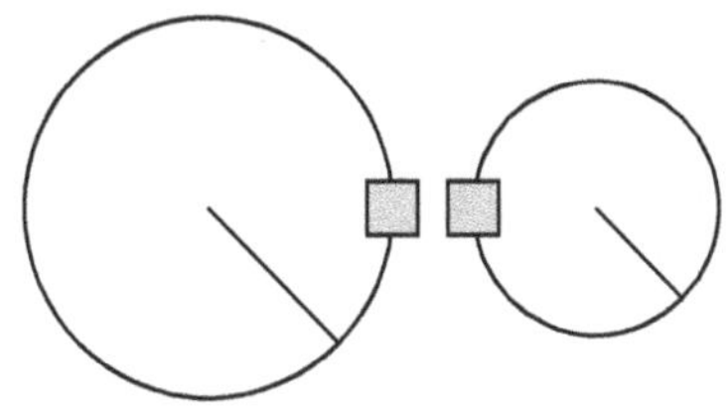

24. P is a point on the terminal side of θ in standard position. Find the exact value
(56) of the six trigonometric functions for θ where $P(-2, -1)$.

25. **Write** What is the converse of the Zero-Product Property? What can it be used for?
(83)

26. **(Government)** Suppose a politician must visit 6 counties in Massachusetts. Her
(73) human resource personnel form a simple random sample by listing each county and numbering it as shown below. If they use the line of random digits shown below, which 6 counties will the politician visit?

01: Barnstable	02: Berkshire	03: Bristol	04: Dukes	05: Essex
06: Franklin	07: Hampden	08: Hampshire	09: Middlesex	10: Nantucket
11: Norfolk	12: Plymouth	13: Suffolk	14: Worcester	

62010	60482	89824	08705	57913	46815	76221	25650	89337	53603	73597

27. **Analyze** Why is the amplitude of $\sin(\sin(x))$ 0.84 and not 1?
(82)

Identify all the real roots:

*28. $x^3 - 216$
(85)

*29. $x^9 + 125 = 0$
(85)

30. Find the distance between the points $(2, -1)$ and $(5, 4)$.
(41)

© Saxon. All rights reserved.

Name ______________________ Date __________ Class __________

Evaluating Logarithmic Expressions

LESSON 87

1. *(60)* A cabinet contains 12 blue cups, 12 red cups, and 20 green cups. What is the probability that a green cup and a blue cup are chosen at random in that order with replacement?

Simplify.

2. *(69)* $\frac{8 + 2i}{1 + 3i}$

3. *(69)* $i^{22} + i^{15}$

4. *(53)* Let $f(x) = x^2 + 1$ and $g(x) = 7 - x$. What are the domain and range of $(f \circ g)(x)$?

5. *(75)* Which of the following is equivalent to $y = \left(\sqrt{x^2 + 3x + 2}\right)^{\frac{1}{3}}$?

A $y = \sqrt[3]{x^2 + 3x + 2}$

B $\sqrt{\sqrt[3]{x^2 + 3x + 2}}$

C $y = \sqrt[3]{\sqrt{x^2 + 3x + 2}}$

D $y = \sqrt[3]{(x + 2)(x + 1)}$

6. *(59)* **Multi-Step** Use $\frac{13^{\frac{2}{3}} \cdot 13^{\frac{1}{4}}}{13^{\frac{1}{12}} \cdot 13^{\frac{1}{2}}}$.

a. Which property of rational exponents should be applied first to simplify the expression, explain?

b. Which property of rational exponents should be applied next?

c. Simplify the expression.

***7.** *(86)* **Model** Graph $y = 2\cos(2x) - 3$

Find the sine, cosine, and tangent of the given angle.

8. *(52)*

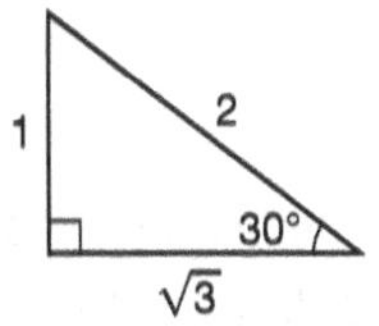

9. *(52)*

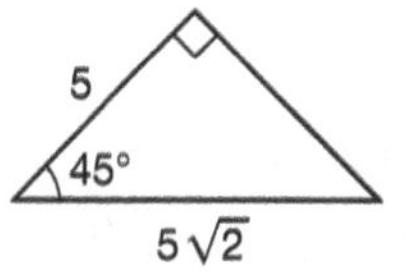

10. *(83)* **Multiple Choice** Which equation does *not* have the exact same roots as the others?

A $(x + 1)(x - 7) = 0$

B $2(x + 1)(x - 7) = 0$

C $4(x + 1)3(x - 7) = 0$

D $x(x + 1)(x - 7) = 0$

11. *(68)* **(Radio)** A radio station needs 4 different songs to complete the song set for the end of their show. They can a pick of 16 eighties hits, 20 nineties hits, and 18 current top hits. Find the probability that the DJ will select 2 current hits and 2 eighties hits in that order for his show.

***12.** *(87)* **(Earthquakes)** Solve $R = \log\frac{I}{I_0}$ for I and then determine the intensity of an earthquake with a magnitude, R, of 7. Your answer should be in terms of I_0.

© Saxon. All rights reserved.

13. **Probability** The right triangle is inscribed in the circle. Suppose a point is chosen at random inside the circle. What is the probability that the chosen point is inside the triangle?
(78)

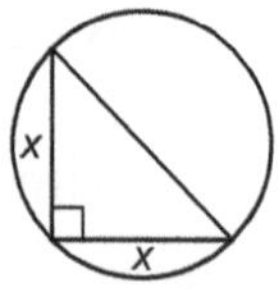

*14. **Justify** The solution of $100^{2x} = 1000$ is $x = \frac{3}{4}$.
(87)

15. **Postal Rates** The rates for first-class mail (retail letters and cards) are shown in the table. Write a piecewise function that represents the cost of mailing a first-class letter.
(79)

Fee	Weight
\$0.41	up to 1 ounce
\$0.58	greater than 1 ounce and up to 2 ounces
\$0.75	greater than 2 ounces and up to 3 ounces
\$0.92	greater than 3 ounces and up to 3.5 ounces

16. **Error Analysis** To rewrite $\ln\frac{5e}{x^2}$, a student wrote $\ln\frac{5e}{x^2} = \frac{\ln 5e}{\ln x^2} = \frac{\ln 5 + \ln e}{2\ln x} = \frac{\ln 5 + 1}{2\ln x}$. What is the error? Rewrite $\ln\frac{5e}{x^2}$ as a sum or difference of terms correctly.
(81)

*17. **Generalize** Suppose there are two cubic functions: $f(x) = x^3 - a^3$ and $g(x) = x^3 - b^3$. If $f(x) \cdot g(x)$ crosses the x-axis at only one point, what can you conclude about a and b?
(85)

*18. **Graphing Calculator** The weights of bridge tokens are normally distributed with a weight of 4.85 g and a standard deviation of 0.068 g. Find the range of weights for the middle 99.7% of bridge tokens.
(80)

19. Find the equation of the line perpendicular to the graph of $y = 2x - 4$ that crosses $(2, -8)$.
(36)

20. **Farming** A farmer has 820 feet of fencing material to enclose a rectangular grazing area for his livestock. He wants the area to be at least 50,000 square feet. The equation $w(410 - w) = 50{,}000$ gives the width of a rectangle that meets these requirements. Use the discriminant to explain if the farmer has enough material to build a fence that meets these requirements.
(74)

*21. **Error Analysis** A student rewrote the expression $\log_7(2x)^4$ as $4\log_7 2 + \log_7 x$.
(87)

a. Describe the student's error.

b. Rewrite the original expression.

Simplify.

22. $\ln e^{7x}$
(81)

23. $\ln e^{x+4}$
(81)

© Saxon. All rights reserved.

24. (70) **Geometry** The formula $r = \sqrt{\frac{S}{4\pi}}$ gives the radius of a sphere with a surface area S. How much greater is the surface area of a sphere with a radius of 20 inches than a radius of 15 inches? Give your answer in terms of π.

***25.** (86) **Physics** Every two seconds a radio beacon emits a signal. If the magnitude of the signal is 10, write the periodic function that models the signal using the form $y = a\cos(bx)$.

***26.** (84) **Analyze** What are the steps to solving a rational equation algebraically?

Solve for x.

***27.** (87) $1000^{6x} = 10$

***28.** $100^{3x} = 10$

29. (81) **Write** Explain why $\ln e^{x^2+3} = x^2 + 3$.

30. (82) Given $g(x) = 4\sin(3x)$, identify the period.

© Saxon. All rights reserved.

Name ______________________ Date __________ Class __________

Solving Abstract Equations

LESSON 88

Write the exponential equation in logarithmic form.

1. (63) $5^3 = 125$

2. (63) $20^3 = 8000$

Identify all the real roots.

3. (85) $x^3 + 8x^2 - 23x - 30 = 0$

4. (85) $6x^3 + 12x^2 - 18x = 0$

Write the expression as a complex number in standard form.

5. (62) $(1 - 9i)(1 - 4i)(4 - 3i)$

6. (62) $(3 + 2i) + (5 - i) + 6i$

7. (81) **Analyze** What pair of inverse functions contain the ordered pairs $(3, e^3)$ and $(e^3, 3)$?

8. (72) **Chemistry** Hydrochloric acid is classified as a strong acid, with a pH of 1. The pH of a solution is given by the formula $\text{pH} = -\log [H^+]$, where $[H^+]$ represents the concentration of hydrogen ions in moles per liter. What is the hydrogen ion concentration in hydrochloric acid?

***9.** (87) **Multiple Choice** The expression $\log_2(8x)^2$ when $x = 16$ is equivalent to:

A 7 **B** 12 **C** 14 **D** 16

10. (73) **Probability** A researcher visits a pond and captures and tags 75 fish. On a return visit, the researcher captures 130 fish, and 68 of them are found to be tagged. What is the probability that a randomly chosen fish in the pond was marked on the first day?

***11.** (88) **Write** Explain why $A = \frac{1}{2}h(b_1 + b_2)$ and $h = \frac{2A}{b_1 + b_2}$ describe the same relationship among the variables A, h, b_1, and b_2.

12. (74) **Write** How can finding the discriminant of a quadratic equation help you decide which method you will use to solve the equation?

Solve each formula for the indicated variable.

***13.** (88) Given $S = 2\pi r^2 + 2\pi rh$, solve for r.

***14.** (88) Given $\frac{5}{9}(F - 32) = C$, solve for F.

15. (75) **Physics** According to Einstein's theory of relativity, as an object moves faster, it appears shorter in length to a stationary observer. The equation below shows the relationship between the original length of the object and the new length, where v is the speed of the object and c is the speed of light. Suppose the ratio of the original length to the new length is 2:1. How fast is the object going as a factor of c?

$$\text{New length} = (\text{Original length})\sqrt{1 - \frac{v^2}{c^2}}$$

© Saxon. All rights reserved.

16. Multiple Choice Solve $\frac{2}{3x + 15} + \frac{1}{3} + \frac{x}{x + 5} = \frac{4}{9}$.
(84)

A -0.125 B 1 C -6.625 D no solution

17. Geometry An isosceles triangle with base angles of 45° and base measuring $x + 1$ has the same area as a square with sides x. What integer value of x is a solution to this problem?
(76)

***18. Multi-Step** **a.** Use the change of base formula to convert $\log_2(6x)^2$ to base e.
(87)

b. Evaluate when $x = 1$.

19. Error Analysis Explain and correct the error a student made in using Heron's formula to find the area of a triangle with side lengths of 3, 10, and 11.
(77)

$$A = \sqrt{24(21)(14)(13)} \approx 302.9 \text{ sq. units}$$

Identify the period and amplitude.

***20.** $y = \frac{1}{2}\cos(2x)$
(82)

***21.** $y = \frac{2}{3}\cos 4x$
(82)

22. Estimate Without using a calculator, estimate the root(s) of the equation $x^2 - 62 = 0$ to the nearest integer(s). Explain your answer by discussing x-intercepts.
(78)

***23.** Use the change of base formula to solve $\log_6 \frac{24}{5}$.
(87)

24. Delivery Charges An appliance store delivers up to 4 items for a $50 delivery charge. There is an additional charge of $15 per item for each additional item delivered. Write a piecewise function for the cost having x items delivered.
(79)

***25.** Describe the phase shift of the function $y = 2\sin\left(x - \frac{\pi}{2}\right) + 7$
(86)

26. Multi-Step IQ test scores are often adjusted to have a mean of 100 and a standard deviation of 15.
(80)

a. What percent of people have an IQ between 70 and 130?

b. Suppose a person scores 150 on an IQ test. How many standard deviations is their score above the mean?

27. Radio A radio signal generates the following data. Use the data to model the periodic function.
(82)

x	0	$\frac{\pi}{4}$	$\frac{2\pi}{5}$	$\frac{\pi}{2}$
y	0	-0.707	0	1

© Saxon. All rights reserved.

*28. **Graphing Calculator** Write a quadratic equation with roots of −2.58 and 1.002. Check your work by graphing the related function and finding the zeros.
(83)

29. **Error Analysis** Describe and correct the error in solving the equation.
(70)

*30. **Statistics** In a normal distribution a z-score is the number of standard deviations a particular data value lies above or below the mean. In a normal distribution with mean $\overline{x}$ and standard deviation σ, the z-score of a data value x is given by $z = \frac{x - \overline{x}}{\sigma}$.
(88)

a. Solve the formula for x.

b. A data value in a certain normal distribution is 2 standard deviations below the mean of 76. The standard deviation is 5.5. What is the data value?

© Saxon. All rights reserved.

Name ______________________________ Date ____________ Class ____________

Solving Quadratic Inequalities

LESSON 89

1. Evaluate the inverse trigonometric function $\text{Tan}^{-1}\left(\sqrt{3}\right)$. Give your answer in both radians and degrees.
(67)

Solve algebraically.

*2. $3x^2 - 13x > 10$
(89)

*3. $5x^2 - 6x - 2 < 0$
(89)

4. Find the arc length and area of a sector with the given radius r and central angle θ. $r = 12$ ft, $\theta = 150°$
(63)

5. A prize box contains 5 stickers, 13 erasers, 20 pencils and 2 highlighters. Find the probability that a student randomly chooses a sticker and a pencil when choosing 2 prizes.
(68)

6. **Error Analysis** Explain and correct the error a student made in writing a quadratic equation with a root of 9.
(83)

$$x = 9$$
$$x - 9 = 0$$

7. **Write** Explain how to write a piecewise function rule from a graph.
(79)

8. **Multiple Choice** A quadratic equation has 1 real solution. Which could be the discriminant of the equation?
(74)

A −6 **B** −4 **C** 0 **D** 4

*9. **Formulate** Consider the function $f(x) = \cos(x - \theta)$. For what value of θ is the graph of $f(x)$ the same as the graph of $y = \sin(x)$?
(86)

10. Graph the cube root function and its inverse. $y = -2\sqrt[3]{x+5} + 5$
(75)

*11. **Justify** Explain why the solution of $x^2 - 4x + 7 > -5$ is the set of all real numbers.
(89)

12. **(Physics)** Acceleration due to gravity is different on different planets. The equation below can be used to find the distance from the ground at time t for a ball thrown from a height h_o at an initial speed of v_o. Use the table to determine how long it will take a ball thrown with an initial speed of 35 at a height of 100 to hit the ground on Mercury.
(76)

$$h = -\frac{1}{2}at^2 + v_ot + h_o$$

Planet	Acceleration (a)
Mercury	3.59
Venus	8.87
Mars	3.77
Jupiter	25.95
Saturn	11.08
Uranus	10.67
Neptune	14.07

*13. **Analyze** Solve the equation $A = \pi r^2$ for r. Determine whether the solutions represent possible values for the radius of a circle. Explain.
(88)

© Saxon. All rights reserved.

14. (77) **Geometry** Three sides of a triangle measure 46 inches, 22 inches, and 50 inches. Classify the triangle by its side and angle measures.

15. (80) **Multiple Choice** The weights of a group of children are normally distributed with a mean of 68 pounds and a standard deviation of 3 pounds. What is the range of the middle 95% of the weights?

A 59 lbs to 77 lbs **B** 62 lbs to 74 lbs **C** 65 lbs to 71 lbs **D** 68 lbs to 77 lbs

16. (71) Solve $\triangle MAP$ given that $m\angle A = 12°$, $m\angle P = 93°$, and $m = 16$.

17. (82) **Physics** Two springs have two different weights attached at the ends. The movement of each weight is modeled by the periodic functions shown, where t is the time in seconds. How often will the weights be at the top of their movement at the same time?

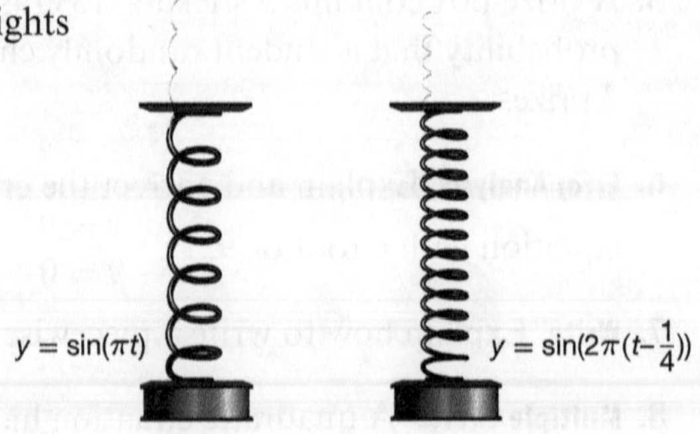

18. (84) **Multi-Step** Worker A can paint a room in 3 hours and Worker B can paint the same size room in 4 hours.

a. If it takes x hours to complete a job, the work rate is $\frac{1}{x}$ because $\frac{1}{x}$ of the job can be completed in one hour. Write a work rate for each worker.

b. Workers A and B worked together and painted a room (same size as above) in h hours. Write expressions to show the amount of work done by each worker.

c. Add the expressions in part b together and set them equal to 1 to represent one room. Solve the equation for h. How long did it take the workers to paint the room working together?

19. (81) **Economics** The formula for continuously compounded interest is $A = Pe^{rt}$, where A is the total amount, P is the principal, r is the annual interest rate, and t is the time in years. To the nearest tenth, how many years would it take for the value of an investment to double at an annual interest rate of 6%, compounded continuously?

20. (57) A savings account earns interest at an annual rate of 4.5%, compounded continuously. If the account begins with a principal amount of $3000, what will its value be after 5 years?

© Saxon. All rights reserved.

21. *(85)* **Error Analysis** Two students are solving for the roots of $y = x^{12} - 1$ but get different results. Which student made the mistake?

Student A	Student B
$x^{12} - 1 = (x^4)^3 - 1$ $= (x^4 - 1)((x^4)^2 + x^4 + 1)$ $= (x^2 + 1)(x^2 - 1)(x^8 + x^4 + 1)$ $= (x + 1)(x - 1)(x^2 + 1)(x^8 + x^4 + 1)$ The roots of $y = x^{12} - 1$ are ± 1.	$x^{12} - 1 = (x^4)^3 - 1$ $= (x - 1)((x^4)^2 + x^4 + 1)$ $= (x - 1)(x^8 + x^4 + 1)$ The root of $y = x^{12} - 1$ is 1.

*22. *(87)* **Data Analysis** The Ehrenberg relation $\log(w) = 0.8h + 0.4 \pm 0.04$ shows the relationship between height h and weight w in young children ages 5 through 13. Complete the table for the range of weight values.

h (m)	0.91	0.93	0.96	0.99	1.01
w (kg)					

23. *(73)* **Write** Tell if the sampling method performed was a probability sample. If not, explain why not. If so, state the type of probability sample.

A person running for local office asks drivers in a local gas/convenience station if they agree with the new gas tax being proposed. He asks every other driver who pulls into the station.

Solve.

*24. *(88)* $5 - \sqrt{x + 7} = 3$

*25. *(88)* $\sqrt{x + 2} = 2 - \sqrt{x}$

*26. *(89)* **Graphing Calculator** Use a graphing calculator to estimate the solutions of $-23.4 < x^2 + 7.56x - 40$. Round to the nearest hundredth.

27. *(78)* **Vertical Motion and Gravity** The height of a free-falling object (neglecting air resistance) is given by the function $h(t) = -4.9t^2 + v_0t + h_0$, where h_0 is the initial height in meters, v_0 is the initial velocity in meters per second, and $h(t)$ is the height in meters at time t seconds. How long does it take for an object to hit the ground after it is dropped from a height of 44.1 meters?

*28. *(88)* **Cliff Height** The Cliffs of Moher at Hag's Head offer one of the most spectacular views on the Atlantic coast of Ireland. If a boat is 90 meters from the base of the cliff, then it is 150 meters from an observer at the top of the cliff. Solve the equation $a^2 + b^2 = c^2$ for b. Then find the height of the cliff.

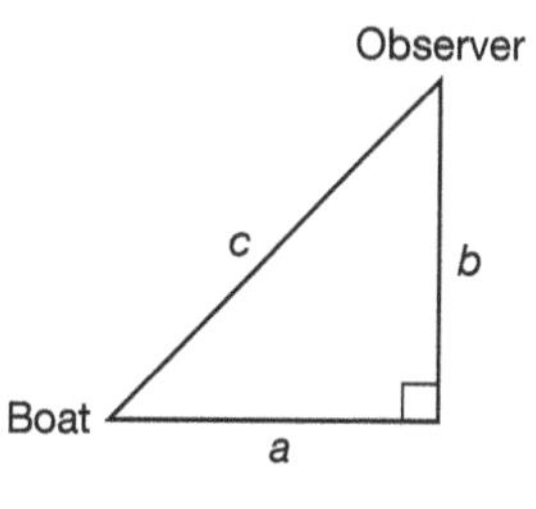

© Saxon. All rights reserved.

29. Solve $\triangle ABC$ given that $m\angle C = 114°$, $a = 8$, and $b = 6$.
(77)

30. Rewrite $\ln\left(\frac{e^5}{x^7}\right)^4$ as a sum or difference of terms if possible. Then simplify.
(81)

© Saxon. All rights reserved.

Name ______________________ Date __________ Class __________

Graphing the Tangent Function

LESSON 90

1. **Geography** On a map, line segments connecting three southeast Texas cities form a triangle as shown. About how many square miles are within the triangle?
(71)

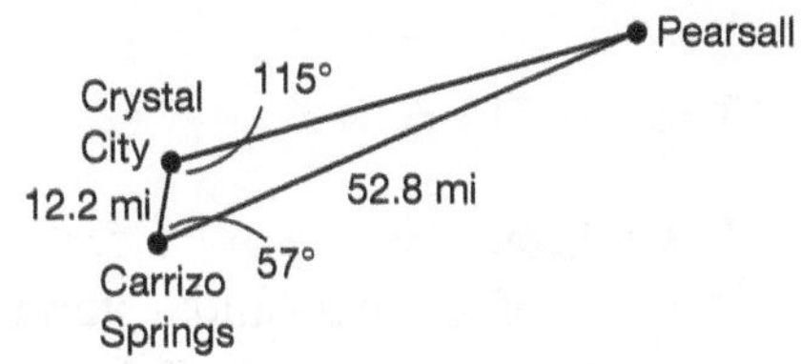

2. **Construction** The sheet of metal shown is rolled into a cylinder along the longer side. The area of the sheet is 6 square units. Find the radius of the cylinder.
(85)

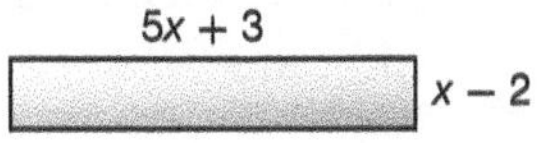

*3. **Jewelry Making** A jeweler is changing the angle of a facet for a diamond ring from θ to φ. The vertical distances change as shown in the diagram, while the value of w remains constant. Derive the function that the jeweler can use to find values of θ when the other values are known.
(90)

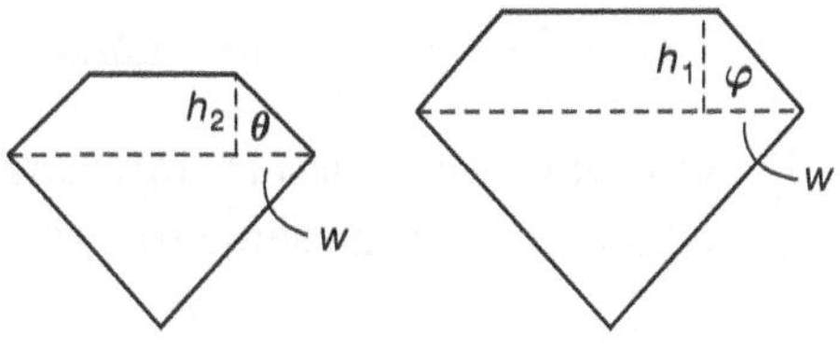

4. A bin has 3 apples and 5 oranges. What is the probability of selecting two apples chosen at random without replacement?
(55)

Write each expression as a radical.

5. $13^{\frac{3}{11}}$
(59)

6. $22^{\frac{5}{9}}$
(59)

7. **Geometry** The volume of a rectangular solid with a length of $x + 10$ feet has a volume of $x^3 + 18x^2 + 95x + 150$ cubic feet. Factor the expression for the volume completely.
(61)

8. Solve for the roots of the polynomial: $7x(x^2 + 4x - 12) = 0$.
(66)

9. **Geology** The Richter magnitude M of an earthquake is expressed by $M = \frac{2}{3}\log\left(\frac{E}{10^{11.8}}\right)$, where E is the energy released in ergs. In 2007 an earthquake of magnitude 8.0 occurred near the coast of Central Peru. Find the energy released by that earthquake.
(72)

10. **Error Analysis** A student said that a systematic sampling method is biased because the first individual on the list will always be chosen. Explain the error in the student's thinking.
(73)

11. **Soccer** A player standing on a 15-foot hill kicks a ball straight up at a velocity of 45 feet per second. She wants it to go above the roof of a nearby shed which is about 40 feet above the ground. The function that gives the height of the ball after x seconds is given by $y = -16x^2 + 45x + 15$. Use the discriminant to explain whether the ball will/will not reach the desired height.
(74)

12. **Analyze** Why is systematic sampling a probability sample but not a simple random sample?
(73)

© Saxon. All rights reserved.

Solve.

13. $2x^4 - 512 = 0$ *(78)*

14. $3x^4 + 4x - 4 = 0$ *(78)*

15. *(80)* **Multi-Step** The ages of a certain group of people are normally distributed with a mean of 42 years and a standard deviation of 6.5 years. What percent of the ages are between 29 and 55? How you can use that answer to find the percent of scores that are between 42 and 55? Find that percent.

16. *(81)* **Justify** Explain why $x = e^y$ and $y = \ln x$ are equivalent equations.

17. *(86)* Using $f(x) = \sin(x)$ as a guide, find the phase shift in $h(x) = \sin\left(x + \frac{\pi}{4}\right)$.

18. *(83)* **Generalize** Given a quadratic equation, how can you write another quadratic equation with the same roots?

19. *(84)* Gene can paint a room in 8 hours and Chandra and Gene working together can paint the room in 5 hours. How long would it take Chandra to paint the room by herself?

***20.** *(90)* **Analyze** Is $y = \tan(\theta)$ an odd or an even function? Explain.

***21.** *(90)* **Coordinate Geometry** Write the version of the slope formula that can be used to find the tangent function.

***22.** *(89)* **Write** Describe how to solve a quadratic inequality algebraically.

***23.** *(88)* **Multiple Choice** Solve $A = \frac{1}{2}bh$ for b. Which equation shows the correct solution?

A $b = \dfrac{2A}{h}$ **B** $b = \dfrac{A}{2h}$ **C** $b = A - \dfrac{1}{2}h$ **D** $b = \dfrac{1}{2}Ah$

***24.** *(87)* Use the change of base formula to convert $\log_2(x)^3$ to base e. Then evaluate when $x = 1$.

***25.** *(85)* **Graphing Calculator** A portion of a roller coaster is modeled by the polynomial function $y = 0.000013x^4 - 0.00255x^3 + 0.13505x^2 - 0.51x + 0.5$. Use a graphing calculator to find the roots of the polynomial.

Solve using a table.

***26.** $x^2 - 2x \geq 8$ *(89)*

***27.** $x^2 - 15x + 50 < 0$ *(89)*

***28.** *(86)* Find the period of $y = \cos\left(\frac{1}{\sqrt{5} - 1}x\right)$.

29. *(82)* Given $q(x) = -\sin\left(\frac{\pi}{2}x\right)$, identify the amplitude and period.

30. *(83)* Write a quadratic equation whose roots are $8 \pm 5i$.

© Saxon. All rights reserved.

Name ______________________ Date __________ Class __________

Making Graphs and Solving Equations of Circles

LESSON 91

1. (70) **Geometry** The radius of a sphere is given by $r = \sqrt[3]{\frac{3V}{4\pi}}$, where V is the volume of the sphere. Approximate the volume of a sphere with a radius of 4.5 centimeters.

*2. (91) **Multi-Step** The map of a town is placed on a coordinate grid. A radio station's transmitter is located at (0, 2), and the signal can be picked up by anyone within 95 miles of the transmitter. Write the equation of the circle that represents the broadcast area for the station's signal. Show how to use the equation to prove that a person located at (94, 6) can pick up the signal.

3. (58) Given that $x^2 - 5x + 2 = 0$, what needs to be added to both sides of the equation to get a perfect square on the left side?

4. (71) Solve $\triangle ABC$.

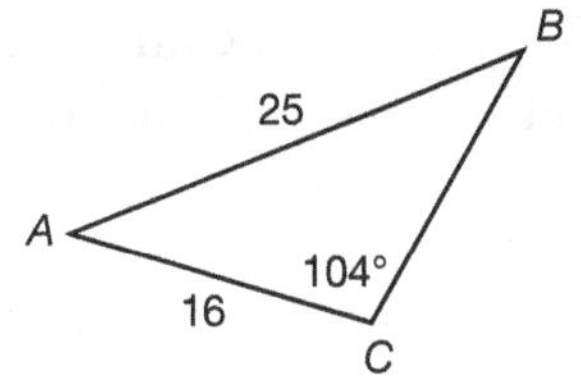

5. (63) A spiral staircase has 15 steps. Each step is a sector with a radius of 42 inches and a central angle of $\frac{\pi}{8}$. What is the length of the arc formed by the outer edge of a step?

*6. (90) **Error Analysis** Two students are finding the period of $y = \tan\left(\frac{3}{5}x\right)$ but get different results. Which student made the mistake?

Student A	Student B
$\text{Period} = \frac{2\pi}{b} = \frac{2\pi}{\frac{3}{5}} = \frac{10\pi}{3}$	$\text{Period} = \frac{\pi}{b} = \frac{\pi}{\frac{3}{5}} = \frac{5\pi}{3}$

7. (78) **Multi-Step** For each value of the leading coefficient a, write the quadratic function in the form $y = ax^2 + c$ that has zeros -2 and 2. (Hint: The value of c can be positive or negative.)

   a. $a = 1$ **b.** $a = \frac{1}{2}$ **c.** $a = -1$

   d. Graph the functions on the same coordinate system.

   e. How many quadratic functions exist that have two given zeros?

8. (55) A random number generator will output integers from 1 to 100. What is P(multiple of 5) with the generation of the first number?

9. (63) Find the arc length of a sector with a radius of 8 inches and a central angle of 110°.

*10. (91) **Generalize** What must be true about the values of h and k for a circle whose center is located in Quadrant II?

© Saxon. All rights reserved.

11. Explain why $f(x) = \sqrt{3x} + 5$ is a radical function.
(75)

*12. The endpoints of a diameter are located at $(-2, -1)$ and $(4, -1)$. Write an equation for this circle.
(91)

13. **(Optics)** The focal length of a lens, f, the distance from the lens to the object, o, and the distance from the lens to the image, i, are related by the formula $\frac{1}{f} = \frac{1}{o} + \frac{1}{i}$. Find f if o is 12 inches and i is 8 inches.
(84)

14. **Analyze** How is deriving a quadratic equation from two identical roots different from deriving a quadratic equation from two unique roots?
(83)

15. **(Sports)** A sports columnist wants to survey college basketball coaches about whether they think women's basketball nets should be raised to the same measure as in men's basketball. The writer mails out surveys to all the coaches and uses only the surveys that are returned. Identify the type of sample described.
(73)

*16. Write a quadratic equation whose roots are $7 + 3i$ and $7 - 3i$.
(83)

Find the roots of the polynomial function.

17. $f(x) = 15x^3 + 3x^2 - 6x$
(76)

18. $f(x) = (x + 1)(4x^2 + 4) - (x + 1)(2x - 3)$
(76)

*19. **Verify** Let $f(x) = \cos(x)$ and $g(x) = \tan(x)$. Compare the graph of $f(x)\,g(x)$ and $h(x) = \sin(x)$.
(90)

*20. Identify the period and undefined values of $y = \tan(12x) + 3$.
(90)

21. **(Surveying)** A surveyor stands on the east end of a boardwalk and finds that the angle formed by the boardwalk and the line of sight with a lighthouse is 76°. The surveyor then walks to the west end and finds the angle formed by the boardwalk and lighthouse to be 60°. Estimate the closest distance from the boardwalk to the lighthouse, given that the boardwalk has a length of 2700 feet.
(71)

*22. **Graphing Calculator** Graph $(x - 1)^2 + (y + 9)^2 = 7$ on a graphing calculator. Use the Trace feature to find the y-intercepts.
(91)

23. **(Geography)** A map of southeast Illinois shows that Flora is 44.4 miles from Carmi and 42.6 miles from Mt. Carmel. Mt. Carmel is 34.4 miles from Carmi. Find the number of square miles enclosed in the triangle that is formed when lines connecting these three cities are drawn. Round to the nearest square mile.
(77)

24. **(College Admissions)** In 2005, the mean score on the ACT reading test was 21.3 with a standard deviation of 6. The mean score on the mathematics test was 20.7 with a standard deviation of 5. Assume both distributions are normally distributed. Who would you say performed better: a student who got a score of 27 on the reading test or a student who got a score of 24 on the math test? Why?
(80)

© Saxon. All rights reserved.

25. (79) Evaluate the piecewise function $f(x) = \begin{cases} 8, & \text{if } x \le 0 \\ 3x - 1, & \text{if } x > 0 \end{cases}$ for $x = -0.4$, $x = 0$, and $x = 6$.

26. (81) **Multiple Choice** Which is equal to $\ln e^{x^2}$?
A $2x$ **B** x^2 **C** $2 \ln x$ **D** $\ln 2e^x$

***27.** (85) **Formulate** Find the roots of $(x^3)^3 - a^3$.

28. (78) **Probability** The right triangle is inscribed in the circle. Suppose a point is chosen at random inside the circle. What is the probability that the chosen point is NOT inside the triangle?

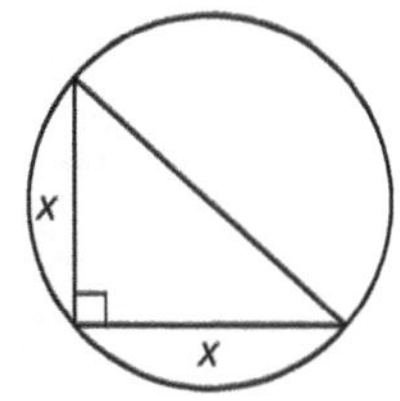

***29.** (88) **Write** Explain why $F = \frac{9}{5}C + 32$ and $C = \frac{5}{9}(F - 32)$ describe the same relationship between F and C.

30. (56) P is a point on the terminal side of θ in standard position. Find the exact value of the six trigonometric functions for θ where $P(-8, -8)$.

© Saxon. All rights reserved.

Name ______________________________ Date __________ Class __________

Finding Arithmetic Sequences

LESSON 92

***1.** (92) **Formulate** Give an example of a sequence that is formed by adding numbers in a pattern but is not arithmetic.

2. (84) **Home Maintenance** A homeowner can rake and bag the leaves in his yard in 5 hours. If he works with his children, the job can be done in 3 hours. How long would it take for just the children to rake and bag the leaves in the yard?

***3.** (92) **Multiple Choice** What is the 40th term of the arithmetic sequence whose first term is 13 and whose second term is 15.5?

A 97.5 **B** 100 **C** 110.5 **D** 123.5

4. (75) **Multi-Step** Find the radical function that is the inverse of $y = x^2 - 6x + 9$. Identify its domain and range.

5. (67) Evaluate the inverse trigonometric function $\text{Cos}^{-1}(-1)$. Give your answer in both radians and degrees.

6. (80) **Write** Describe the characteristics of a data set that is normally distributed.

***7.** (91) **Coordinate Geometry** If $A(5, 2)$ and $B(-4, -3)$ are the endpoints of a diameter of a circle, what is the equation of the circle?

***8.** (91) Write the equation for a circle centered at $(2, -9)$ with a radius of 3.

9. (73) **Geometry** A geometry teacher has a database with 400 problems about triangles. Can she choose a sample of questions by using a stratified sampling method where the strata are *right triangles, isosceles triangles,* and *scalene triangles*? Why or why not?

10. (76) **Physics** A satellite in orbit accelerates according to the equation acceleration $= \frac{v^2}{r}$, for orbital speed v and distance from Earth's center r. Two satellites are in orbit, one at a distance of r and the other at a distance of $2r$. How fast should the outer satellite travel to have the same acceleration as the inner satellite?

11. (69) Multiply $(3 + i)(1 - 4i)$. Write the result in the form $a + bi$.

12. (77) **Multiple Choice** Which triangle cannot be solved by using the Law of Cosines?

A

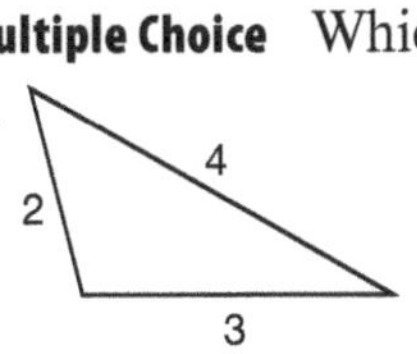

B

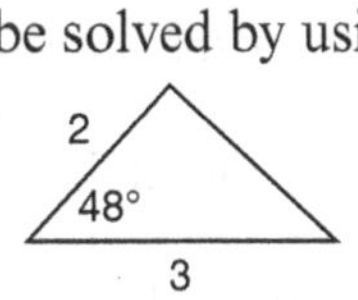

C

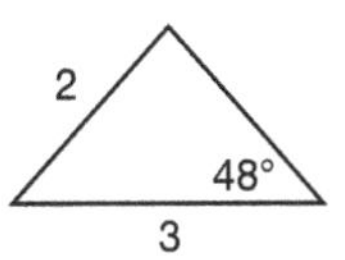

D

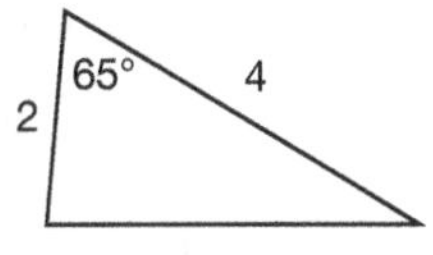

© Saxon. All rights reserved.

13. (81) **Multi-Step** Technetium-99m, a radioisotope used to image the skeleton and the heart muscle, has a half-life of about 6 hours.

   a. How long will it take for 1 mg of technetium-99m to decay to 0.2 mg? (Use the natural decay function $N(t) = N_0 e^{-kt}$.)

   b. On a calculator, graph the function $y_1 = 1 \cdot e^{-kx}$, using the value of k you found in part **a.** Also graph the functions $y_2 = 0.5$ and $y_3 = 0.2$. (suggested window values: x $[-1, 20]$ and y $[-0.1, 1.1]$)

   c. Describe what is represented by the relationships among the graphs of y_1, y_2, and y_3.

14. (79) **Delivery Charges** A furniture store delivers up to 4 items for a $75 delivery charge. There is an additional charge of $25 per item for each additional item delivered. Write a piecewise function for the cost of having x items delivered.

*15. (92) Find the 17th term of the arithmetic sequence 4, 21, 38, …

Find the roots of the polynomials.

16. (58) $y = 4x^2 + 5x - 1$

17. (76) $y = x^4 - 16$

18. (85) **Geometry** A rectangular prism has a volume of $3x^3 - 8x^2 + 3x + 2$. Find the linear dimensions.

*19. (92) **Travel** A driver on the Pennsylvania turnpike turned on the cruise control at milepost 30, Warrendale, and kept it on until milepost 359, the Delaware River Bridge, exactly 5 hours later. Show how to use an arithmetic sequence to find the speed at which the car traveled during those 5 hours.

*20. (86) **Graphing Calculator** Graph $y = 5 \cos 2(x - 3\pi)$ using a graphing calculator. Determine its period and phase shift.

*21. (87) **Verify** Show that $\log_5 (125x)^2$ equals 8 when $x = 5$.

22. (57) A principal amount of $1,500 earns interest at an annual rate of 2.7%, compounded monthly. What will its value be after 7 years?

*23. (89) **Write** When solving a quadratic inequality, what is meant by the *critical values*?

24. (62) Solve $6t^2 + 5 = 2t^2 + 1$. Write the solution in terms of i.

25. (83) **Analyze** Which equations have the same solutions as $x^2 - 8x + 7 = 0$?

$-x^2 + 8x - 7 = 0$ $\quad$ $-x^2 + 8x + 7 = 0$ $\quad$ $-2x^2 + 8x - 7 = 0$

$2x^2 - 8x + 14 = 0$ $\quad$ $2x^2 - 16x + 14 = 0$

© Saxon. All rights reserved.

Write the exponential equation in logarithmic form or vice versa.

26. (64) $11^4 = 14{,}641$

27. (64) $\log_9 729 = 3$

***28.** (91) **Basketball** A drafter is creating the plans for a sport and fitness center, which includes an official-size basketball court. On her grid, the units represent feet. The center of the basketball court's center circle is located at $(-14, -1)$, and another point on the center circle is located at $(-14, 2)$. Write an equation for this circle.

29. (74) **Error Analysis** A student found that the discriminant of a quadratic equation was 0 and therefore the number of solutions of the equation was also 0. Correct the student's reasoning.

30. (78) Solve by completing the square: $4x^2 = -12x + 4$.

© Saxon. All rights reserved.

Name ______________________________ Date ____________ Class ____________

Solving Exponential Equations and Inequalities

LESSON 93

1. (73) **Fast Food** At a fast food restaurant, each take-out order has a ticket in the bottom of the bag asking customers to call an 800 number to register for a prize drawing. Describe the individuals in the population and in the sample.

*2. (93) **Multiple Choice** Which equation is equivalent to $1.4 = 1.06^x$?

A $x = 1.4 - 1.06$ **B** $x = \log 1.4 - \log 1.06$ **C** $x = \dfrac{1.4}{1.06}$ **D** $x = \dfrac{\log 1.4}{\log 1.06}$

3. (78) **Gravity** The height of a free-falling object (neglecting air resistance) is given by the function $h(t) = -4.9t^2 + v_0t + h_0$, where h_0 is the initial height in meters, v_0 is the initial velocity in meters per second, and $h(t)$ is the height in meters at time t seconds. How long does it take for an object to hit the ground after it is dropped from a height of 14.4 meters?

*4. (92) **Verify** The first term of an arithmetic sequence is 19 and the common difference is 9. Show that the 13th term is 127.

*5. (92) **Geometry** A cube has 6 sides. When two cubes are joined together, the figure has 10 sides. When three cubes are joined together, to form a row, there are 14 sides. Show how to use an arithmetic sequence to find the number of sides in a row of 20 cubes joined together.

Determine the domain and range for each of the following.

6. (75) $y = -3\sqrt[3]{x}$

7. (75) $y = (x + 1)^{\frac{1}{2}} + 8$

*8. (92) Find the common difference and use it to find the next three terms. 4, 6.5, 9, ...

*9. (91) **Science** Vredefort is an impact crater located in South Africa. Given that its circumference is about 942.5 kilometers, write an equation for the circle that represents the rim of the crater, assuming the center is located at the origin of a coordinate plane.

*10. (93) Solve for x: $4^{3x-6} = 32^{x+4}$

11. (84) **Generalize** Describe two ways to find the solution(s) of $\frac{3}{3x+9} + \frac{2}{3} = x - 1$ on a graphing calculator.

*12. (90) **Graphing Calculator** Graph $y = \tan(2x + 3)$ on your graphing calculator. Identify its period, undefined values, and phase shift.

*13. (89) **Tourist Attractions** The world's largest pair of cowboy boots are located outside of a mall in San Antonio, Texas. The boots are 40 feet tall. Suppose a painter at the top of a boot drops a paintbrush. The height of the brush, in feet, after x seconds, is modeled by $y = -16x^2 + 40$. Write and solve a quadratic inequality that can be solved to find the time span for which the brush is above a second painter located 20 feet beneath the first painter. Round to the nearest hundredth of a second.

© Saxon. All rights reserved.

*14. (93) **Depreciation** A truck is purchased for \$18,500 on January 2, 2007. Its value decreases 16% each year. In what year will its value first be less than \$2,000?

15. (88) **Multi-Step** The formula for the area of a sector of a circle is $A = \frac{\theta r^2}{2}$, where θ is the central angle measure in radians and r is the radius.

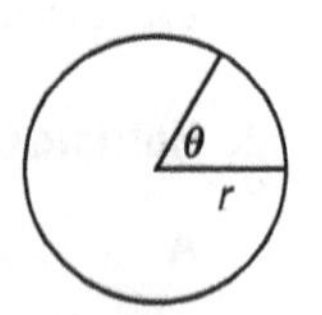

a. A landscape architect wants to create a flower bed in the shape of a sector of a circular ring, as shown by the shaded region. Write a formula for the area S of a sector of a circular ring.

b. Solve the formula you wrote in part **a** for θ.

c. The landscape architect wants the area S of the flower bed to be 200 square feet, with $R = 25$ feet and $r = 10$ feet. Determine the necessary angle measure θ and then convert it to the nearest degree.

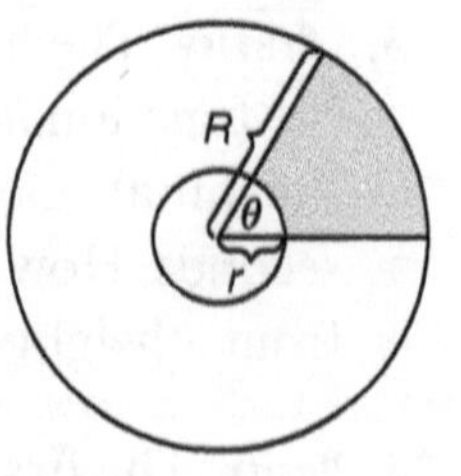

16. (87) **Error Analysis** A student rewrote the expression $\log_8(3x)$ as $\frac{\ln 8}{\ln 3 + \ln x}$.

a. Describe the student's error.

b. Rewrite the original expression correctly.

17. (85) **Analyze** Consider the polynomial function $f(x) = ax^2 + bx + cx$. Suppose that the polynomial is divisible by $\left(x - \frac{c}{a}\right)$. Use synthetic division to show that $a + b + c = 0$.

18. (82) Which of the following has a period of 2π?

A $y = \sin(2\pi x)$ **B** $y = \sin(\pi x)$ **C** $y = \sin(x)$ **D** $y = \sin\left(\frac{x}{2}\right)$

*19. (93) **Estimate** Thallium has a half-life of 73.1 hours. Estimate how long it will take for 1 gram of thallium to decay to 0.26 gram. Explain your method.

Solve to the nearest tenth using the given restrictions.

20. (67) $\sin\theta = 0.95$, for $-90° \le \theta \le 90°$

21. (67) $\cos\theta = -0.181$, for $180° \le \theta \le 360°$

Determine the domain and range of each function.

22. (79) $f(x) = \begin{cases} 0, & \text{if } x < 0 \\ 3, & \text{if } x \ge 0 \end{cases}$

23. (79) $f(x) = \begin{cases} x, & \text{if } 0 < x < 10 \\ 10, & \text{if } x \ge 10 \end{cases}$

Solve the following equations.

24. (76) $3x^4 = 12x^3 - 9x^2 + 6x$

25. (76) $x^3 = 2x^4 - 5x^2 + 4x$

26. (83) **Generalize** Given that a, b, c, and d are real numbers, explain why $(x - a)(x - b) = 0$ and $(cx - ca)(dx - db) = 0$ have the same roots. What are the roots?

27. (81) Given $N(t) = 0.6$, $N_o = 1$, $k = 0.6372$, write the decay function and solve for t.

28. (83) Write a quadratic equation whose roots are -5 and 4.

© Saxon. All rights reserved.

29. **Error Analysis** A student says that the roots of the equation $x^4 - 81 = 0$ are -3 and 3. What complex roots were left out?
(78)

30. **Probability** The area under a normal curve is the probability that a randomly selected data value from that data set falls within that interval. Suppose the weights of cereal boxes have a mean of 15.5 ounces with a standard deviation of 0.4 ounces. What is the probability that a randomly selected box of cereal weighs less than 14.7 ounces?
(80)

© Saxon. All rights reserved.

Name ______________________ Date __________ Class __________

Solving Rational Inequalities

LESSON 94

Solve using the quadratic formula. Write the solution as complex numbers in standard form.

1. (65) $f(x) = x^2 + 2x + 4$

2. (65) $f(x) = x^2 - x + 12$

3. (88) Given $P = 2l + 2w$, find l.

***4.** (94) **Multi-Step** **a.** Factor both the numerator and denominator of $\frac{x^2 - 3x - 18}{x^2 - 16} \leq 0$.

b. Determine the intervals created by the critical values.

c. The intervals for which test values are negative contain the solutions. What is the solution?

5. (80) The average height of giant sunflowers is 6 feet tall and the standard deviation is 3 inches. Find the z-score for a giant sunflower that is 5 feet 6 inches tall.

6. (78) **Multiple Choice** What are the roots of the equation $(4x^2 - 4x + 1) - (16x^2 - 24x + 9) = 0$?

A $\frac{2}{3}$ and -2 **B** $\frac{2}{3}$ and 1 **C** $\frac{1}{2}$ and $-\frac{3}{4}$ **D** $\frac{1}{2}$ and $\frac{3}{4}$

***7.** (94) **Government** Suppose the citizens of counties in the state of Texas had the option to donate an equal amount of money toward a one million dollar donation to be given to a charity. Write and solve an inequality to show the number of counties whose citizen participation would bring the cost per county to less than $6500. There are 254 counties in Texas.

8. (80) **Error Analysis** A student said if a number cube is rolled and the results are recorded in a histogram, a smooth curve drawn through the tops of the histogram would resemble a bell curve. Explain the error in the student's thinking.

***9.** (94) **Justify** Explain why there are four intervals when solving $\frac{(x + 2)}{(x - 3)(x + 1)}$ by using test points.

10. (77) **Geometry** The perimeter of an isosceles triangle is 200 inches. The base has a length of 92 inches. Find the measure of the vertex angle.

***11.** (93) **Analyze** If $500 is invested at 4% compounded monthly, then at the end of t years the investment will have the value A, where A is given by the expression $500\left(1 + \frac{0.04}{12}\right)^{12t}$. What expression gives the value A if the compounding is daily instead of monthly?

12. (71) What is the side length c in $\triangle ABC$ if $A = 32°$, $C = 67°$, and $b = 31$ ft?

© Saxon. All rights reserved.

*13. (93) **Error Analysis** While attempting to solve an inequality, a student performed the step shown below.

$$n \log (0.5) < \log 2 - \log 20$$

$$n < \frac{\log 2 - \log 20}{\log 0.5}$$

What is the error? What is the correct step?

14. (74) An object is thrown upward from a height of 15 feet at an initial velocity of 35 feet per second. How long will it take the object to hit the ground?

15. (89) **Business** The profit earned from selling tickets to a certain event is modeled by $y = -1.25x^2 + 66x - 720$. If the cost per ticket will be a whole number amount, what range of ticket prices will earn a profit of at least $100?

*16. (93) A school's enrollment increases 6.5% a year and is currently 1100. How long will it take to reach 1500 students?

17. (68) **Probability** A student has a spinner with four equal sections labeled 2, 4, 6, and 8. If he spins the spinner twice, find the probability that the first spin lands on 6 and the sum of the results is less than or equal to 10.

*18. (90) **Multiple Choice** Which of the following has a period of 2π?

A $y = \tan(2x)$ **B** $y = \tan(2\pi x)$ **C** $y = 2\tan(x)$ **D** $y = \tan\left(\frac{x}{2}\right)$

*19. (92) **Graphing Calculator** With the Table set to increase by 1, enter $15 + (x - 1)(-4)$ for Y1 to represent an arithmetic sequence whose first term is 15 and whose common difference is -4. Use the table to find the 6th and 15th terms.

20. (83) **Formulate** Write a quadratic equation with roots of -1 and 5 so that the parabola of the related function opens up. Then write one so that the parabola opens down.

*21. (92) **Analyze** When finding the nth term of an arithmetic sequence, when will the value added to the first term be positive and when will it be negative?

22. (82) Given $k(x) = 3\sin(x)$, identify the amplitude and period.

*23. (91) **Drafting** A computer-aided drafting technician is drawing a bicycle wheel such that the center is located at (6, 2) on the coordinate grid. Each unit on the grid represents one inch. What is the equation of the wheel given that it has a diameter of 28 inches?

© Saxon. All rights reserved.

24. (73) **Data Analysis** Twelve names already numbered are listed below. Three must be randomly chosen for a sample. What three names will be picked if numbers are chosen from the string of random numbers below?

15 Ann	16 Luke	17 Cassie	18 Finn	19 Jared	20 Tanela
21 Jude	22 Gunner	23 Drew	24 Halle	25 Colby	26 Anton

60201 60482 89824 08705 17913 46815 76221 25650 89337 53603 73597 04633

25. (88) Given $f = \frac{1}{\frac{1}{d_1} + \frac{1}{d_2}}$, find d_2.

26. (75) **Physics** The equation for finding the period of a pendulum is a radical function given by $T = 2\pi\sqrt{\frac{L}{9.8}}$. The period is the amount of time it takes for the pendulum to complete a back-and-forth sweep. How much shorter does a pendulum need to be to have half the period?

27. (81) **Chemistry** Uranium-238 is a naturally abundant isotope because of its long half-life. Its half-life is about 4.5 billion years. About how long would it take for just 1% of an initial amount to decay? (Use the natural decay function $N(t) = N_0e^{-kt}$.)

28. (87) Using the change of base formula, solve for y when $x = 2$ and $x = 4$ given that $y = \frac{\log x}{\log 2}$.

Find the zeros of the polynomial function.

29. (76) $f(x) = 4x(7x - 3)(6x + 1)$

30. (76) $f(x) = 16x^3 - 24x^2 + 6x$

© Saxon. All rights reserved.

Name ______________________ Date __________ Class __________

Factoring Higher-Order Polynomials

LESSON 95

Solve.

1. (84) $x - \frac{6}{x} = 1$

2. (84) $\frac{x^2 + x - 6}{x + 1} = 0$

3. (84) $\frac{7x}{3x + 2} = 2$

4. (57) Does the graph of $y = b^x + k$, through the points $(3, -3)$ and $(5, 0)$, model exponential growth or decay?

***5.** (94) Solve $\frac{1}{x^3} \geq 5$. Round to the nearest thousandth.

6. (8) In a certain recipe, the amount of sugar is directly proportional to the amount of flour. If 3 cups of sugar are used with 8 cups of flour, how many cups of sugar are used with 12 cups of flour?

***7.** (95) **Error Analysis** Two students were evaluating $P(-4)$ for the polynomial $P(x)$, but they got different results. Which student made the mistake?

$$P(x) = x^6 + 4x^5 - x^4 - 6x^3 - 8x^2 + 2x + 8$$

Student A

$$\begin{array}{r|rrrrrrr} -4 & 1 & 4 & -1 & -6 & -8 & 2 & 8 \\ & & -4 & 0 & 4 & 8 & 0 & -8 \\ \hline & 1 & 0 & -1 & -2 & 0 & 2 & 0 \end{array}$$

$P(-4) = 0$

Student B

$$\begin{array}{r|rrrrrrr} 4 & 1 & 4 & -1 & -6 & -8 & 2 & 8 \\ & & 4 & 32 & 124 & 472 & 1856 & 7432 \\ \hline & 1 & 8 & 31 & 118 & 464 & 1858 & 7440 \end{array}$$

$P(-4) = 7440$

***8.** (94) **Analyze** When solving $\frac{(x-4)(x+6)}{(x+2)(x-3)} \geq 0$, which intervals will use strict inequalities ($<$ or $>$) and why?

***9.** (64) **Multi-Step** As of the 2000 U.S. census, Nevada had the fastest growing population of all the states, and Connecticut had nearly the slowest (47th out of 50). The table below is based on U.S. census statistics.

	Nevada	Connecticut
Population in 2000 (to nearest thousand)	1,998,000	3,406,000
Average annual increase (1990–2000)	5.21%	0.36%

a. Write a function ($y1 = abt$), where $y1$ represents Nevada's population t years after 2000.

b. Write a function ($y2 = abt$), where $y2$ represents Connecticut's population t years after 2000.

c. Write and solve an equation to predict the year in which Nevada's population will overtake Connecticut's population.

Simplify each of the following.

10. (81) $2 \ln e^x$

11. (81) $x \cdot \ln e^3$

© Saxon. All rights reserved.

12. **Estimate** A researcher visits a wildlife preserve and marks endangered African elephants. He marks 6 elephants and releases them. On a return visit several months later, he comes across 16 elephants, and 4 of them are marked from the previous visit. Estimate the elephant population in the preserve.
(73)

13. **Surveying** A surveyor finds that the lengths between three stakes on the ground are 125 feet, 182 feet, and 211 feet. He connects the stakes with string, forming a triangle. To the nearest tenth, what is the measure of the largest angle in this triangle?
(77)

14. Determine the domain and range of the function $f(x) = \begin{cases} -x, & \text{if } x < 0 \\ 4, & \text{if } 0 \le x < 10. \\ 18, & \text{if } x \ge 10 \end{cases}$
(79)

15. **Research** In a study of 413 men, the mean height was 174.1 centimeters and the standard deviation was 7 centimeters. Assuming that the distribution is normal, approximate the z-score of a man whose height is 182 centimeters.
(80)

16. A set of values has a mean of 13 and a standard deviation of 0.625. Find the z-score of a value of 10.25.
(80)

17. **Justify** Formulate a conjecture (statement) about the degree of a polynomial that is a sum or difference of polynomials compared to the degree of the polynomials that are added or subtracted to get that sum or difference. Give examples to justify your conjecture. (Hint: Name the polynomials P_1, P_2, P_3, etc. to make it easy to refer to them.)
(11)

18. **Geometry** The area of a rectangular field is 100 meters. The field is 15 meters longer than it is wide. Find the length and width of the field.
(23)

*19. **Multiple Choice** Which of the following polynomials has $P(5) = 0$?
(95)

A $P(x) = 48x^6 + 212x^5 - 1098x^4 - 5298x^3 + 1174x^2 + 22{,}350x + 18{,}900$

B $P(x) = 48x^6 + 644x^5 + 2754x^4 + 2154x^3 - 12{,}974x^2 - 30{,}750x - 18{,}900$

C $P(x) = 48x^6 + 868x^5 + 6282x^4 + 23{,}238x^3 + 46{,}274x^2 + 46{,}950x + 18{,}900$

D $P(x) = 48x^6 - 268x^5 - 818x^4 + 4282x^3 + 6254x^2 - 14{,}790x - 18{,}900$

20. **Multiple Choice** Identify which property or properties of real numbers are being demonstrated.
(1)

$$(2 \cdot 9) \cdot 5 = (2 \cdot 5) \cdot 9$$

A Commutative Property of Multiplication

B Associative Property of Multiplication

C Distributive Property

D Both A and B

© Saxon. All rights reserved.

***21.** (95) Write a possible polynomial $P(x)$ that fits the parameters $P(0) = 0$, $P(2) = 20$, and $P(-4) = 0$.

***22.** (87) Use the properties of logarithms to expand the expression $\ln (8x)^3 + \ln e\left(\frac{2x}{3}\right)$.

23. (13) **Predict** The table below shows the sales in dollars, y, made by a gift shop x years after it opened.

Years	2	5	8
Sales	\$30,000	\$75,000	\$120,000

a. Plot the data on a coordinate grid and draw a line that fits the data.

b. Use the line to predict the total sales 15 years after the shop opened.

24. (76) **Error Analysis** A student performs the following steps while finding the roots of $y = (x^2 - 7)(3x^2 + 4) - (x^2 - 7)(8x - 3)$. What is his mistake?

$$(x^2 - 7)(3x^2 + 4) - (x^2 - 7)(8x - 3) = (x^2 - 7)(3x^2 - 8x + 1)$$

***25.** (92) **Travel** A driver on the Pennsylvania turnpike turned on the cruise control at milepost 30, Warrendale, and kept it on until milepost 242, Harrisburg West, exactly 4 hours later. Show how to use an arithmetic sequence to find the speed at which the car traveled during those 4 hours.

26. (71) Solve $\triangle ABC$.

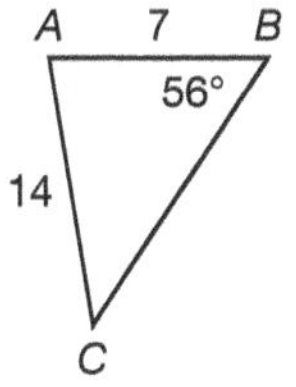

***27.** (91) Write the equation for the circle centered at (3, 8) with a radius of 4.

28. (1) John saves \$125 each month. Use the Distributive Property to mentally calculate the amount of money that he will save in 18 months.

***29.** (90) **Graphing Calculator** Use a graphing calculator to graph the function $y = 3\tan(2x - 2\pi) - 4$. Identify its period, undefined values, and phase shift.

***30.** (83) Write a quadratic equation whose root is -3.

© Saxon. All rights reserved.

Name ______________________ Date ____________ Class ____________

Using Polar Coordinates

LESSON 96

1. **Multi-Step** **a.** Use the change of base formula to convert $\log_{1000}(10x)^2$ to base 10.
(87)
b. Evaluate when $x = 100$.

2. **Geography** The city of Madera, California, is 95 miles due southeast of Stockton, which is 95 miles due southwest of South Lake Tahoe. How far would you have to fly from Madera to South Lake Tahoe, and in what direction?
(52)

*3. Convert $\left(-3, \frac{\pi}{2}\right)$ to Cartesian coordinates.
(96)

4. A taxicab company that wants to know if customers are satisfied has each driver survey three customers during the day. Is the sample biased? Explain.
(73)

*5. **Justify** Suppose that for polynomials $P_1(x)$ and $P_2(x)$, there are constants a and b such that $P_1(a) = P_2(b) = 0$. Is it correct to conclude that b is a root of $P_1(x)$ and a is a root of $P_2(x)$? Explain.
(95)

Solve and graph the following compound inequalities.

6. $3t > 18$ or $t - 3 < 0$
(10)

7. $-(h - 2) > 7$ or $-8 \geq -2h$
(10)

8. **Statistics** The table shows the number of home runs hit by a softball player over a three-year period. Use properties of real numbers to mentally calculate the average annual home runs that she hit during this period.
(1)

	Year 1	Year 2	Year 3
Home runs	8	15	17

Determine the domain and range.

9. $y = \frac{3}{4}x^{\frac{1}{3}} - 1$
(75)

10. $f(x) = \sqrt{x + 2} + \sqrt[3]{x - 1}$
(75)

*10. If $1,000 is invested at 7% compounded continuously, how long would it take for the value of the investment to reach $3,000?
(93)

11. **Juggling** A juggler tosses a ball into the air. The ball leaves the juggler's hand 4 feet above the ground and has an initial velocity of 40 feet per second. The juggler catches the ball when it falls back to a height of 3 feet. How long is the ball in the air?
(74)

12. In $\triangle LMN$, $LM = 14$, $MN = 8$, and $m\angle M = 84°$. Find LN.
(77)

13. **Simple Interest** The simple interest formula is $A = P + Prt$, where P is the principal, or original amount invested, r is the annual simple interest rate, and A is the value of the investment at the end of t years. Solve the formula for t. Then determine how many years it will take for an investment to double in value at a 5% annual simple interest rate.
(88)

© Saxon. All rights reserved.

14. (82) **Geometry** Derive the function that can be used to find the area of an isosceles triangle with base a and congruent sides measuring b. Each base angle measures θ. Express in simplified form.

***15.** (91) **Multiple Choice** Which equation represents a circle centered at (–5, 4) with a radius of 3?

A $(x - 5)^2 + (y + 4)^2 = 3$ **B** $(x - 5)^2 + (y + 4)^2 = 9$

C $(x + 5)^2 + (y - 4)^2 = 3$ **D** $(x + 5)^2 + (y - 4)^2 = 9$

16. (83) **National Parks** The Surprise Arch, in Arches National Park, has a span of about 60 feet and a height of about 50 feet. Write a quadratic function to approximate the arch.

***17.** (95) Find the roots of $y = x^9 - x^7 - 8x^6 - 16x^5 + 8x^4 + 16x^3 + 128x^2 - 128$.

18. (84) **Formulate** Solve $\frac{1}{a} + \frac{1}{b} = \frac{1}{c}$ for c.

19. (85) Find the roots of $f(x) = 0.15x^3 - 2.85x^2 + 14.85x - 12.15$ using the Rational Root Theorem.

***20.** (86) **Graphing Calculator** Use a graphing calculator to graph $y = \cos(7x)$ and compare its period to that of the parent function.

21. (89) **Multiple Choice** Which is not a solution of $\begin{matrix} y \le -x^2 + 4x + 8 \\ y < -3x + 1 \end{matrix}$?

A (0, 0) **B** (0, –3) **C** (1, –6) **D** (2, –2)

22. (90) Let $f(x) = \tan(5x + 5)$ and $g(x) = 3x + 5$. Find the period of $f(g(x))$.

***23.** (84) A kayaker paddles with the current for 7 miles, turns around, and paddles against the current for 7 miles. The average paddling rate is 3 miles per hour. Write an inequality to represent the speed of the current if the total time is less than 7 hours.

24. (81) **Error Analysis** To rewrite $\ln(ex)^3$, a student wrote $\ln (ex)^3 = \ln(3 \cdot (ex)) = \ln 3 + \ln (ex) = \ln 3 + \ln e + \ln x = \ln 3 + \ln x + 1$. What is the error? Rewrite $\ln (ex)^3$ as a sum or difference of terms correctly.

***25.** (96) **Write** Explain why every point in a polar coordinate system has more than one set of polar coordinates.

***26.** (92) **Savings** During week 1, a customer opened a bank account with \$450. Each week thereafter, the customer deposits \$50. How much will the customer have in the account after the deposit is made during week 52?

27. (78) **Error Analysis** A student says that the roots of the equation $4x^3 - 36x = 0$ are -3 and 0. What is the error?

28. (23) **Verify** Use FOIL to verify the difference of two squares formula $a^2 - b^2 = (a + b)(a - b)$.

© Saxon. All rights reserved.

29. (80) **Analyze** How are z-scores of –0.5 and 0.5 alike? How are they different?

*30. (96) **Cell Phone Tower** A planned cell phone tower will service an area with a 6 mile radius. It is to be located 6 miles west of a small town. Write a polar equation of the boundary of the region that will be serviced. Place the location of the town at the pole. Graph the equation on a calculator.

© Saxon. All rights reserved.

Name ______________________________ Date __________ Class __________

Finding Geometric Sequences

LESSON 97

*1. Given $V = \pi r^2 h$, find h.
(88)

2. **Write** A survey asks students, “Who would you vote for in the next school election, the relatively unknown sophomore Eileen Johnson, or the popular Zack Jennings?” Explain the bias in the question.
(73)

Simplify the following expressions.

3. $8^{\log_8 x}$
(72)

4. $\log_3 81^x$
(72)

*5. **Multi-Step** The value of a car in its first year was $18,900. Each year thereafter, the value was 85% of what it was the previous year. The values each year form a geometric sequence.
(97)

a. Write a formula to find the value of the car in the nth year.

b. Find the value of the car in year 6.

6. What number can be added to both sides of the equation $x^2 + 18x + 36 = 0$ to make it a perfect square?
(Inv 6)

7. **Analyze** How can you tell that $4 + \sqrt{x} = 1$ will have no solutions?
(70)

Find each of the following matrix operations for $A = \begin{bmatrix} -6 & 2 \\ -1 & -3 \end{bmatrix}$ **and** $D = \begin{bmatrix} 11 & 2 \\ 8 & 3 \end{bmatrix}$.

8. Find $A + D$.
(5)

9. Find $D - 3A$.
(5)

*10. Find the fifteenth term of the geometric sequence 2, 6, 18, …
(97)

11. **Error Analysis** Which student made an error in determining the number of solutions of $-3x^2 + 6x = 4$? What was the error?
(74)

	Student A:		Student B:
	$b^2 - 4ac$		$b^2 - 4ac$
	$6^2 - 4(-3)(4)$		$6^2 - 4(-3)(-4)$
Student A:	$36 + 48$	**Student B:**	$36 - 48$
	84		-12
	2 real solutions		2 complex solutions

*12. **Estimate** Write approximate polar coordinates for the point with Cartesian coordinates (6, 6.2). Explain your method.
(96)

13. **Geometry** A student is told to draw a rectangle so that the perimeter is 48 units and the area is 150 square units. The equation $24x - x^2 = 150$ gives the values of x that meet these criteria where x is the length of the rectangle. Solve the equation. Describe your findings.
(62)

© Saxon. All rights reserved.

*14. (96) **City Planning** A park lawn is a square. A diagonal sidewalk is planned, shown as $\overline{AB}$ in the diagram. Using point A as the pole and $\overrightarrow{AC}$ as the polar axis, write a polar equation of the line that contains $\overline{AB}$.

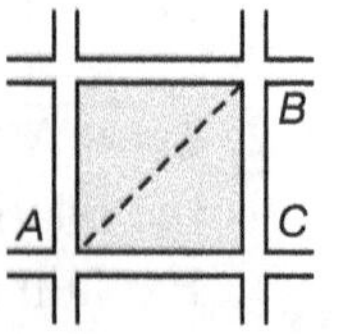

15. (22) **Coordinate Geometry** Graph {(2, 4), (5, 6), (–1, 0), (7, 10)}. Determine if this relation is a function. Determine if the graph is continuous, discontinuous, and/or discrete.

16. (75) **Model** Graph the square root function and its inverse. $y = \frac{1}{3}\sqrt{x} - 4$

17. (84) **National Highways** In Texas, the speed limit on state highways at night is 5 miles per hour less than what it is during the day. A driver drove 350 miles during the day and 195 miles at night, with the cruise control set to the appropriate speed limit. The total driving time was 8 hours. Write and solve a rational equation to find the speed limit during the day.

*18. (97) **Multiple Choice** The second term of a geometric sequence is 16 and the fourth term is 1. What is the common ratio?

A $\frac{1}{16}$ **B** $\pm\frac{1}{16}$ **C** $\frac{1}{4}$ **D** $\pm\frac{1}{4}$

19. (85) **Analyze** Consider the polynomial function $f(x) = ax^4 + bx^3 + cx^2 + dx + e$. Suppose that the polynomial is divisible by $(x - 1)$. Use synthetic division to show that $a + b + c + d + e = 0$.

20. (86) **Physics** Two wheels spin in the same direction. The larger wheel completes a cycle in 3 seconds and the smaller wheel completes a cycle in 5 seconds. The two squares attached to the wheels are facing each other at time $t = 0$. How many seconds elapse before they are back in sync?

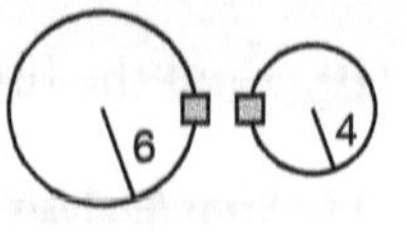

21. (92) Find the common difference of the arithmetic sequence –62, –67, –72, –77, ...

*22. (89) **Graphing Calculator** Graph $\begin{matrix} 4y + 12 > x^2 \\ -\frac{1}{2}x \geq y \\ y \geq -2 \end{matrix}$ on your graphing calculator. Name two points in the solution set.

23. (82) **Multiple Choice** Which of the following has a period of 7π?

A $y = \cos(7x)$ **B** $y = \cos\left(\frac{2}{7}x\right)$ **C** $y = \cos(3.5x)$ **D** $y = \cos\left(\frac{x}{7}\right)$

24. (82) Given $g(x) = 0.5\sin(2x)$, identify the amplitude and period.

25. (80) A set of values has a mean of 15 and a standard deviation of 1.5. Find the percent of values above 18.

© Saxon. All rights reserved.

26. (79) Evaluate the piecewise function $f(x) = \begin{cases} 9 - 5x, & \text{if } x < -0.1 \\ 2, & \text{if } -0.1 \le x \le 2 \\ x^3 - x, & \text{if } 2 < x \le 6 \\ 3 - x^2, & \text{if } x > 6 \end{cases}$ for $x = -0.4$, $x = 0$, and $x = 6$.

***27.** (93) **Medicine** Cobalt-60 is an isotope that is used in radiation therapy for cancer patients. It has a half-life of about 5.3 years. How long will it take for 1 gram of cobalt-60 to decay to 0.9 gram? (Use the natural decay function $N(t) = N_0e^{-kt}$.)

28. (77) **Boating** A boat leaves a dock and travels in a straight path for 6 miles at an angle 15° north of east. Another boat leaves the same dock and travels in a straight path for 11 miles at an angle 65° south of east. If the second boat puts down an anchor and the first boat travels directly toward the second, estimate the time it will take the first boat to reach the second boat if the first boat travels at a constant rate of 8 miles per hour.

***29.** (91) The endpoints of a diameter of a circle are located at $(-10, -2)$ and $(2, -2)$. Write an equation for this circle.

30. (87) Convert $\log_6 (5x)^4$ to base e. Then evaluate when $x = 3$.

© Saxon. All rights reserved.

Name ______________________________ Date ____________ Class ____________

Making Graphs and Using Equations of Ellipses

LESSON 98

***1.** (14) **Graphing Calculator** Calculate the determinant of $\begin{bmatrix} -5 & 2 & 11 \\ 4 & -1 & 0 \\ 19 & 1 & 1 \end{bmatrix}$ using a graphing calculator.

***2.** (98) **Generalize** How many ellipses have an eccentricity of 0.5 and cross the minor axis at (0, 2)?

***3.** (98) **Optics** An elliptical mirror is modeled by the equation $\frac{x^2}{15^2} + \frac{y^2}{10^2} = 1$. The property of an elliptical mirror is that if you shine a beam of light from a focal point to the mirror, the light is reflected toward the other focal point. What is the length of the two light beams?

4. (71) Find the missing side lengths of $\triangle ABC$. $A = 73°$; $a = 18$; $b = 11$

***5.** (98) Write the equation of the ellipse given by $2x^2 + 3y^2 = 6$ in standard form.

6. (66) **Packaging** The manager of a company that sells pasta is looking into a new container shape of a rectangular prism whose base is square and whose height is 5 inches greater than the length of one side of the base. If the volume is 28 cubic inches, what is the length of one side of the base? What is the height?

7. (2) **Geometry** A rectangle has length $4c$ and width d. Another rectangle has length 16 and width $(2 + 5c)$. Write a simplified expression of their combined area.

***8.** (97) **Population** The estimated population of the District of Columbia from 2005 to 2006 decreased by about −0.089%. Assuming that the percent of decrease stays the same, the populations each year form a geometric sequence. Show how to use the formula for the nth term of a geometric sequence to find the population of DC in 2012 given that the estimated population in 2005 was 582,049. (Hint: Call 2005 year 1.)

9. (87) **The Ehrenberg Relation** The Ehrenberg relation $\log(w) = 0.8h + 0.4 \pm 0.04$ shows the relationship between height h and weight w in young children ages 5 through 13. Solve for h and determine the height, in meters, of a child who weighs 40 kilograms.

10. (13) **Write** Explain how to graph $3x + 5y = -35$ using slope and intercept. Be sure to show each step.

***11.** (97) **Error Analysis** Explain and correct the error a student made in finding the common ratio of the geometric sequence 270, 90, 30, 10, ...

$$r = \frac{30}{10} = 3$$

12. (82) Given $h(x) = 6\sin(8x - 9)$, identify the amplitude and period.

© Saxon. All rights reserved.

13. (76) Find the roots of the polynomial function.
$f(x) = (x + 8)(3x^2 - 6) - (x + 8)(11x - 4)$

***14.** (95) **Justify** Suppose that for polynomials $P_1(x)$ and $P_2(x)$ there are constants a and b such that $P_1(a) \neq 0$ and $P_2(b) \neq 0$. Is it correct to conclude that b is *not* a root of $P_1(x)$ and a is *not* a root of $P_2(x)$? Explain.

15. (86) **Acoustics** A guitar string is strummed twice, which creates two waves along the string. The first wave is reflected back and meets the second wave. If the waves are modeled by the equations below, what happens when the waves meet? (Hint: When one wave's crest coincides with another wave's trough, they tend to cancel each other out. This called destructive interference.)

$y = \cos\left(x - \frac{\pi}{2}\right)$ $\qquad$ $y = \cos\left(x + \frac{\pi}{2}\right)$

16. (88) **Error Analysis** A student attempted to solve the formula $V = \frac{1}{3}\pi r^3$ for r and wrote $r = \sqrt[3]{\frac{V}{3\pi}}$. What is the error? Solve the formula for r correctly.

Simplify.

17. (3) $\dfrac{(x^{-2}yp)^{-3}(x^0yp)^2}{(2x^2)^{-2}}$

18. (3) $-\dfrac{3x^2y}{xx} + \dfrac{2x^{-2}x^4}{y^{-1}x^2} - \dfrac{5xy^2}{xy}$

19. (89) **Multi-Step** A rectangular window has dimensions of 9 feet by 12 feet. The homeowner wants to increase the window size by lengthening two sides by the same amount as shown. The area of the window is to remain less than 300 square feet.

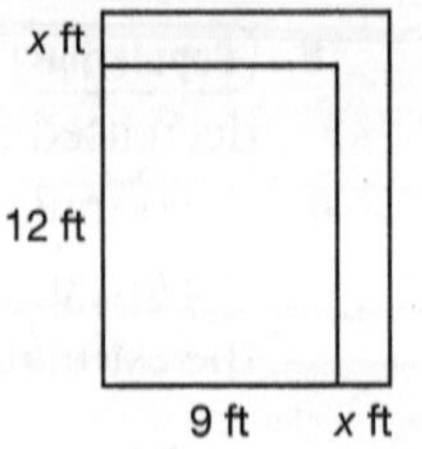

a. Write an inequality to find the range of the amounts that can be added to the two sides.

b. Solve the inequality.

20. (90) **Model** For what values of θ is $y = \dfrac{\sin(x)}{\cos(x - \theta)}$ the equivalent of $y = \tan(\theta)$?

Evaluate each piecewise function for $x = 3$ and $x = 0$.

21. (79) $f(x) = \begin{cases} x^2 - 5, & \text{if } x \leq 0 \\ x^2, & \text{if } 0 < x < 3 \end{cases}$

22. (79) $f(x) = \begin{cases} \frac{1}{2}, & \text{if } x < 1 \\ x, & \text{if } 1 \leq x < 10 \\ -x, & \text{if } x \geq 10 \end{cases}$

23. (83) Write a quadratic equation whose roots are $5i$ and $-5i$.

Identify all the real roots.

24. (85) $x^3 + 10x^2 + 17x = 28$

25. (85) $x^3 - 343 = 0$

© Saxon. All rights reserved.

***26.** (94) **Multiple Choice** When solving $\frac{x^2 + 5x - 6}{x^2 - 12x + 32} > 0$ by using a sign table, for how many intervals will a test point need to be chosen?

A 3 **B** 4 **C** 5 **D** 6

Simplify.

27. (48) $\dfrac{\frac{1}{2} - \frac{4}{15}}{\frac{5}{6} + \frac{1}{9}}$

28. (48) $\dfrac{\frac{1}{x+1} - \frac{1}{x-1}}{\frac{x}{x^2 - 1}}$

29. (84) **Write** How and why is the LCD used to solve a rational equation?

***30.** (96) **Probability** A point is randomly chosen inside the graph of the polar equation $r = 3$. What is the probability that the chosen point is at least 1 unit away from the pole?

© Saxon. All rights reserved.

Name ______________________ Date __________ Class __________

Using Vectors

LESSON 99

1. **Error Analysis** Explain the error a student made below.
(70)
$5 + \sqrt{x} = 3 \rightarrow \sqrt{x} = -2 \rightarrow (\sqrt{x})^2 = (-2)^2 \rightarrow x = 4$ The solution is 4.

*2. **Generalize** How many ellipses have an eccentricity of 0? Explain.
(98)

3. **Write** Explain why $\ln e^{x^2+3} = x^2 + 3$.
(81)

4. **Engines** Two-stroke engines require a premix of gas and oil. The amount of gas used varies directly with the amount of oil used. In some two-stroke engines, 5 gal of gas requires 20 oz of oil.
(8)
   a. Write the proportion that can be used to find how many ounces of oil to use with 9 gal of gas.
   b. Solve the proportion in part **a.**
   c. Check the answer from part **b** with the proportion from part **a.**

5. **Geometry** Write a polynomial in standard form that represents the total area formed by the rectangle and trapezoid. (Hint: The formula for the area of a trapezoid is $A = \frac{1}{2}(b_1 + b_2)h$).
(11)

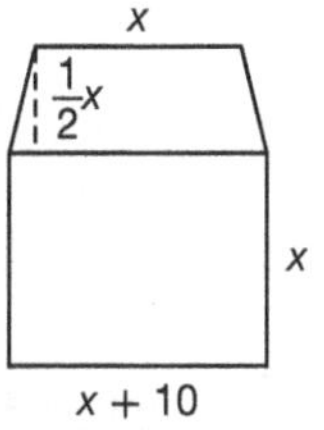

6. **Probability** A student has a spinner with four equal sections labeled 2, 4, 6, and 8. If the student spins the spinner two times, find the probability that the first spin lands on a 4 and the sum of the results is greater than or equal to 10.
(68)

7. Evaluate the piecewise function $f(x) = \begin{cases} x - x^2, \text{ if } x \leq 1 \\ 12, \quad \text{if } 1 < x \leq 2 \\ -6, \quad \text{if } 2 < x < 4 \\ -x - 8, \text{ if } x \geq 4 \end{cases}$ for $x = -0.4$, $x = 0$, and $x = 6$.
(79)

8. **Error Analysis** Explain and correct the error a student made in finding the z-score for a data value of 15, taken from a normally distributed set of data, where the mean is 20 and the standard deviation is 4.
(80)

$$z = \frac{20 - 15}{4} = \frac{5}{4} = 1.25$$

9. In $\triangle RST$, $ST = 17$, $RT = 20$, and $m\angle T = 38°$. Find $m\angle S$.
(77)

10. **Write** If two quintic polynomials are added, what are all the possible types of the resulting polynomial (classified by degree)?
(11)

© Saxon. All rights reserved.

11. (75) The graph of $y = \sqrt[4]{x+1} + \sqrt[3]{x+1}$ is shown to the right. Use the axis of symmetry to draw the inverse function.

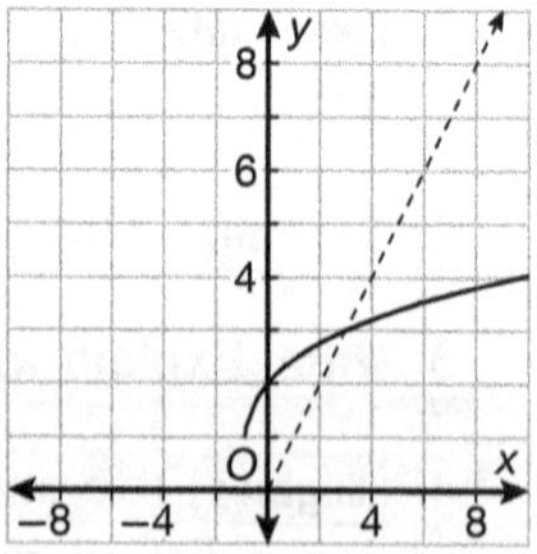

12. (91) **Seismology** To locate the epicenter of an earthquake, a seismologist graphs the circles created from three seismographs in different locations and finds their point of intersection.

a. The equations below were created from the readings of three seismographs where each unit represents one mile. Sketch the circles on the same coordinate plane.

$$(x+4)^2 + (y-4)^2 = 25$$
$$(x-1)^2 + (y+3)^2 = 49$$
$$(x-5)^2 + (y-4)^2 = 16$$

b. Estimate the location of the epicenter.

13. (73) **Prom** A member of the prom committee polls 40 random seniors from the senior class meeting to ask about possible locations for the prom. Describe the individuals in the population and in the sample.

14. (83) **National Parks** Kolob Arch in Zion National Park is one of the longest arches in the world with a span of about 288 feet and a height of about 105 feet. Write a quadratic function to approximate the arch.

15. (87) **Sound Intensity** The loudness of a given sound is represented by $d = 10\log\frac{I}{I_o}$ where d is decibels, I is intensity of the sound, and I_o is the intensity of a sound that can just be heard by humans. Determine the decibel level of a sound with an intensity of $(2.3 \times 10^9)I_o$.

16. (84) Use cross multiplying to show that $\frac{3}{x+5} = \frac{2}{x+5}$ has no solution.

17. (73) **Write** An English teacher needs to pick 5 students to present book reports to the class. The teacher writes the names of all students in the class on pieces of paper, puts the pieces in a hat, and chooses 5 names without looking. Determine what type of sample is used and whether it is biased or unbiased. Explain your answer.

***18.** (89) **Analyze** Can a quadratic inequality have no critical values? Explain.

***19.** (92) **Coordinate Geometry** The points (1, −5), (2, −11), (3, −17), (4, −23), and (5, −29) represent the first five terms of an arithmetic sequence. What is the common difference? What is the y-coordinate when the x-coordinate is 12?

***20.** (32) **Graphing Calculator** Use a graphing calculator to find the inverse of the matrix, if it exists. $H = \begin{bmatrix} 2 & 1 & 3 \\ 1 & 1 & 2 \\ 1 & 4 & 6 \end{bmatrix}$

© Saxon. All rights reserved.

***21.** Find the dot product between the vectors $\begin{bmatrix}6\\8\end{bmatrix}$ and $\begin{bmatrix}2\\7\end{bmatrix}$.
(99)

***22.** **Multiple Choice** Which are polar coordinates for the point with Cartesian coordinates $\left(-3, -3\sqrt{3}\right)$?
(96)

A $\left(3, \frac{7\pi}{6}\right)$ **B** $\left(3, \frac{4\pi}{3}\right)$ **C** $\left(6, \frac{7\pi}{6}\right)$ **D** $\left(6, \frac{4\pi}{3}\right)$

***23.** Write an equation in standard form for the ellipse with center (0, 0), vertex (6, 0), and covertex (0, −5).
(98)

Solve.

24. $3\frac{2}{5}x - 4\frac{1}{10}x = 2\frac{1}{4}$
(2)

25. $0.02(p - 2) = 0.03(2p - 6)$
(2)

***26.** Use the Rational Root Theorem to find the roots of $y = 2x^3 - 3x^2 - 8x + 12$.
(85)

Add.

27. $3xy^2m + \frac{4}{x}$
(37)

28. $\frac{5x^2}{pm} - 4 + \frac{c}{p^2m}$
(37)

***29.** **Multi-Step** Find the magnitude of vectors $\begin{bmatrix}-3\\7\end{bmatrix}$ and $\begin{bmatrix}3\\7\end{bmatrix}$. Calculate the angle between the two vectors. Then calculate the dot product.
(99)

30. Find the distance between (−3, 7) and (4, −2).
(41)

© Saxon. All rights reserved.

Name ______________________ Date __________ Class __________

Graphing Rational Functions I

LESSON 100

Solve.

1. (84) $x = 4 + \frac{5}{x}$

2. (84) $-x^2 - 2x - 1 > 2$

***3.** (99) **Error Analysis** Two students calculated the angle between vectors $\vec{A} = \begin{bmatrix} 12 \\ 9 \end{bmatrix}$ and $\vec{B} = \begin{bmatrix} 17 \\ 8 \end{bmatrix}$ but their results were different. Which student made the mistake?

Student A	Student B
$\theta = \arccos\left(\frac{(12 \cdot 17) + (9 \cdot 8)}{\sqrt{12^2 + 9^2}\sqrt{17^2 + 8^2}}\right)$ $= 11.67°$	$\theta = \arccos\left(\frac{(12 \cdot 9) + (17 \cdot 8)}{\sqrt{12^2 + 9^2}\sqrt{17^2 + 8^2}}\right)$ $= 30.03°$

4. (36) Find the equation of the line parallel to $y = 7x + 6$ that crosses (6, 10).

***5.** (96) **Phone Service** A planned cell phone tower will service an area with a 13-mile radius. It is to be located 5 miles east and 12 miles south of a radio tower. Write a polar equation of the boundary of the region that will be serviced. Place the location of the radio tower at the pole. Graph the equation on a calculator.

6. (56) **Multi-Step** The formula $\theta = \frac{180°(n - 2)}{n}$ gives the measure of each interior angle of an n-sided regular polygon.

a. Use the formula to find the measure of an interior angle of a regular decagon.

b. Find the reference angle for the interior angle.

***7.** (95) **Geometry** A rectangular prism has the dimensions shown. The volume $V(x)$ is the product of the linear dimensions. Use the Remainder Theorem to evaluate $V(20)$.

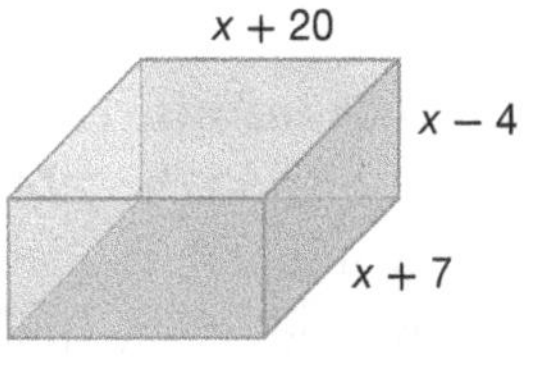

Write a piecewise function rule for each graph.

8. (79)

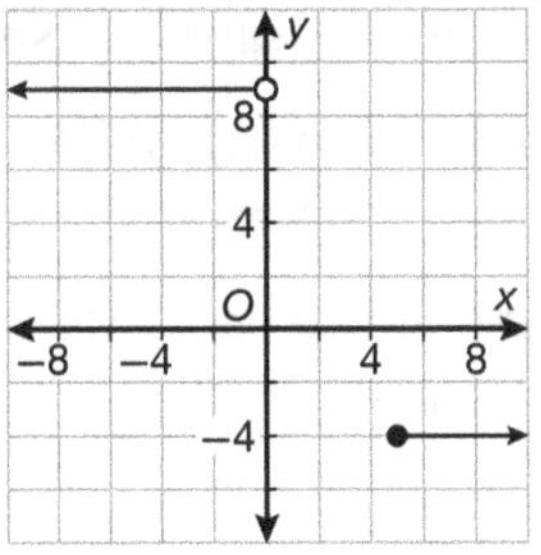

9. (79)

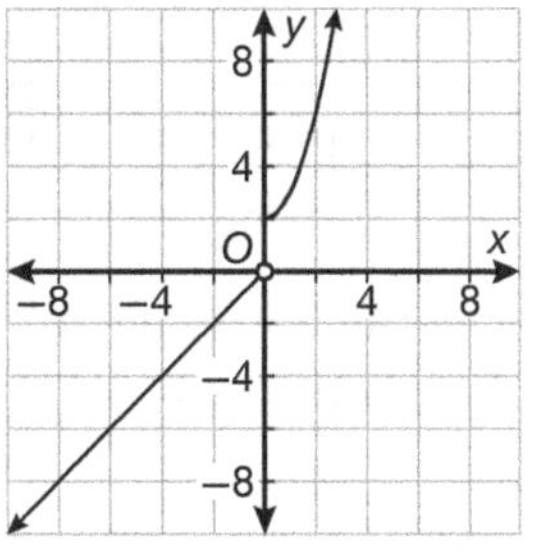

***10.** (100) **Multiple Choice** Which of the following rational functions includes a vertical asymptote at $x = 7$?

A $y = \frac{x - 7}{x^2 - 49}$

B $y = \frac{x - 7}{x^2 + 12x + 35}$

C $y = \frac{x^2 - 16}{x^2 + 11x + 28}$

D $y = \frac{x^2 - 16}{x^2 - 11x + 28}$

© Saxon. All rights reserved.

11. **Analyze** Use the table of values for $y = \log_2 x^2$ to answer the questions.
(87)

x	−4	−3	−2	−1	0	1	2	3	4
y	4	3.17	2	0	–	0	2	3.17	4

a. As the negative x values increase to 0, what happens to the y values?

b. As the positive x values increase, what happens to the y values?

12. **Justify** Can the difference of two polynomials have a greater degree than the sum of the same two polynomials? Justify your answer with an example.
(11)

***13.** **Graphing Calculator** Use a graphing calculator to evaluate $y = 2x + 3$ for the given domain: −2, −1, 0, 1, 2. Identify the range of the function and classify the function.
(22)

14. **(Parking)** An airport parking garage costs $38 per day for the first week. After that, the cost decreases to $35 per day. Write a piecewise function for the cost of parking x days.
(79)

15. **Analyze** Suppose that for polynomials $P_1(x)$ and $P_2(x)$ there is a constant a such that $P_1(a) = P_2(a) = 0$. What can you conclude about the graphs of $P_1(x)$ and $P_2(x)$?
(95)

16. **(Research)** In a study of 413 men and 335 women, the mean height of men was 174.1 centimeters with a standard deviation of 7 centimeters. The mean height of women was 162.3 centimeters with a standard deviation of 6.2 centimeters. Assume both distributions are normal. Compare the actual height of a man with a z-score of 2 to the actual height of a woman whose z-score is 2.
(80)

17. **Data Analysis** The number of days it takes to complete a year for different planets is shown in the table. Let Earth's yearly motion be modeled by $y = \sin(0.017x)$. How would you model Jupiter's motion? (*Hint*: The days in a year corresponds to the period of the function.)
(82)

Planet	Mercury	Venus	Earth	Mars	Jupiter	Saturn	Uranus	Neptune
Days in a Year	88.03	224.63	365.25	686.67	4331.87	10,760.27	30,681.00	60,193.20

***18.** **Error Analysis** Which student made an error in determining intervals to check for solutions and nonsolutions of $\frac{x-2}{(x+7)(x-5)} \geq 0$? What is the error?
(94)

Student A
$x \leq -7$
$-7 \leq x \leq 2$
$2 \leq x \leq 5$
$x \geq 5$

Student B
$x < -7$
$-7 < x \leq 2$
$2 \leq x < 5$
$x > 5$

© Saxon. All rights reserved.

19. (1) **Analyze** Identify which property of real numbers is being demonstrated by $(4 \cdot 6) \cdot 5 = 4 \cdot (6 \cdot 5) = 4 \cdot 30 = 120$. Explain why this property might be helpful in solving this problem without a calculator.

20. (89) **Multi-Step** The perimeter of a rectangular garden will be 100 feet. Write an inequality to find the widths that will give an area of at least 450 square feet. Solve the inequality and round to the nearest tenth.

21. (90) For what values of θ is $y = \frac{\sin(x)}{\cos(x - \theta)}$ no longer a periodic function?

22. (82) **Physics** Every millisecond a radio beacon emits a signal. If the magnitude of the signal is 100, write the periodic function that models the signal using the form $y = a\cos(bx)$.

Simplify.

23. (40) $2\sqrt{3}\left(5\sqrt{3} - 2\sqrt{6}\right)$

24. (40) $2\sqrt{3} \cdot 3\sqrt{6} \cdot 5\sqrt{12}$

25. (91) **Write** A student wants to graph a circle whose equation is $(x - 5)^2 + (y - 5)^2 = 2$ on a graphing calculator. How would you explain to the student how this can be done?

26. (100) **Physics** In a parallel circuit, the total resistance, R_T, is found using $R_T = \frac{1}{R_1} + \frac{1}{R_2} + \frac{1}{R_3} \ldots$. Suppose that a parallel circuit has two resistors of magnitude R and $2R + 1$. Solve for R_T.

Divide.

27. (38) $x^4 + 5x^3 - 6x^2$ by $(x - 1)$

28. (38) $x^4 - 20x^3 + 123x^2 - 216x$ by $(x - 3)$

29. (99) Add vectors $\begin{bmatrix} 10 \\ 6 \end{bmatrix}$ and $\begin{bmatrix} 4 \\ 5 \end{bmatrix}$.

***30.** (99) Subtract vectors $\begin{bmatrix} 10 \\ 4 \end{bmatrix}$ and $\begin{bmatrix} 3 \\ 14 \end{bmatrix}$.

© Saxon. All rights reserved.

Name ______________________ Date __________ Class __________

Making Graphs of Polynomial Functions

LESSON 101

1. Determine whether the matrices are inverses.
(32)

$$A = \begin{bmatrix} 2 & 7 \\ -1 & -2 \end{bmatrix} \text{ and } L = \begin{bmatrix} -\frac{2}{3} & -\frac{7}{3} \\ \frac{1}{3} & \frac{2}{3} \end{bmatrix}$$

*2. **Furniture Design** A table top is to consist of a rectangular region with a semicircle on each end. The perimeter is to be 200 inches. Find the maximum possible area of the rectangular region.
(101)

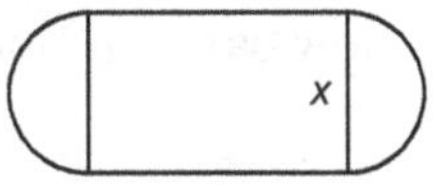

*3. **Graphing Calculator** Use a graphing calculator to determine how long it will take an investment of \$1000 to grow to \$1800 at 6% interest compounded monthly.
(93)

4. **Error Analysis** Explain and correct the error a student made in solving $x^2 + 4x > 12$ algebraically.
(89)

$$x^2 + 4x - 12 > 0$$
$$(x - 2)(x + 6) > 0$$

critical values: 2, −6
solutions: $-6 < x < 2$

5. Find the roots of $f(x) = 0.1x^3 - 1.4x^2 + 6.0x - 7.2$ using the Rational Root Theorem.
(85)

*6. The product of two variables is a constant. Show that this describes a rational function.
(100)

Factor.

7. $6x^3 - 12x^2 - 18x + 6$
(23)

8. $x^2 - 64$
(23)

*9. **Physics** Work is defined as the dot product of the force, $\vec{F}$, on an object and the displacement, $\vec{d}$. If $\theta = 45°$, $|\vec{F}| = 25$, and $|\vec{d}| = 10$, how much work is exerted on the wooden block?
(99)

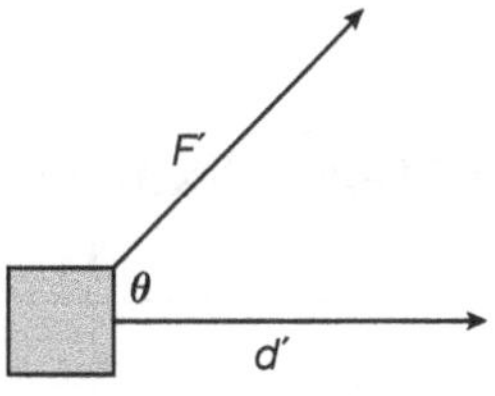

10. Solve for x, y, and z: $\begin{bmatrix} 1 & x^2 \\ y + 4 & \frac{y}{2} \end{bmatrix} = \begin{bmatrix} z + 2 & 25 \\ 16 & x + 1 \end{bmatrix}$.
(5)

© Saxon. All rights reserved.

11. Evaluate the piecewise function $f(x) = \begin{cases} -12 \text{ if } x < 1 \\ 7x \text{ if } 1 \le x \le 4 \\ 2x - x^2 \text{ if } 4 < x \end{cases}$ for $x = -3$ and $x = 4$.
(79)

12. **(Ice Cream)** A store has 31 flavors of ice cream. They also have a choice of chocolate or rainbow sprinkles and chocolate or caramel syrup. Assume a child picks one flavor ice cream, one type of sprinkle, and one type of syrup. How many different desserts could the child make?
(33)

*13. **Predict** Without using a formula, how can you find the 100th term of the geometric sequence, 3, −3, 3, −3, ...?
(97)

14. **(National Parks)** The Black Arch, in Arches National Park, has a span of about 65 feet and a height of about 45 feet. Write a quadratic function to approximate the arch.
(83)

15. A set of data is normally distributed with a mean of 34 and a standard deviation of 2.7. Find the percent of data that is less than 25.9.
(80)

16. **Geometry** A triangle has side lengths of 14 meters, 19 meters, and 21 meters. Use Heron's formula to find the area of the triangle.
(77)

*17. **Multi-Step** Complete parts a–d to graph a polar equation and analyze the graph.
(96)

a. Graph the polar equation $r = \frac{\cos\theta}{\sin^2\theta}$ on a calculator, using these window settings: $\theta\min = 0$, $\theta\max = \pi$, $\theta\text{step} = \frac{\pi}{24}$, $X\min = -1$, $X\max = 11$, $Y\min = -4$, $Y\max = 4$.

b. What shape does the graph appear to be?

c. Convert the polar equation to a Cartesian equation. (Hint: Multiply both sides by $\sin^2\theta$, then multiply both sides by r, and then substitute x for $r\cos\theta$ and y for $r\sin\theta$.)

d. The equation obtained in part c is the inverse of what function?

18. **(Football)** The first table below shows the scoring plays made in three games by the Philadelphia Eagles. The second table shows the point value of each play. Use matrix multiplication to find out in which game the team scored the most points.
(9)

Plays Made

Game	Touchdown	Field Goal	Extra Point
#9	3	2	3
#15	2	3	2
#16	3	1	3

Point Value

Touchdown	6
Field Goal	3
Extra Point	1

19. Expand the expression $\log 3x^4$.
(72)

© Saxon. All rights reserved.

20. (12) **Multiple Choice** Based on the data set below, what is the relationship between x and y?

x	1	2	3	4
y	4	2	$1\frac{1}{3}$	1

A Joint Variation **B** Direct Variation
C Inverse Variation **D** None of the above

21. (98) **Multiple Choice** Which of the following points is not on the ellipse $\frac{x^2}{4^2} + \frac{y^2}{7^2} = 1$?
A $(-7, 0)$ **B** $(4, 0)$ **C** $(0, -7)$ **D** $(-4, 0)$

22. (82) **Error Analysis** Two students are finding the period of $y = 5 \sin\left(\frac{1}{\sqrt{2}+1} x\right)$ but get different results. Which student made the mistake?

Student A	Student B
The period is $\frac{2\pi}{b}$.	The period is $\frac{2\pi}{b}$.
Period $= \frac{2\pi}{\sqrt{2}+1}$	Period $= 2\pi\left(\sqrt{2} + 1\right)$

23. (84) **Analyze** How can a rational equation with all linear polynomials form a quadratic equation after the fractions are cleared? Give a simple example.

24. (87) **Write** Explain the steps used to apply the change of base formula.

25. (90) **Generalize** Find the period and phase shift of $y = a \tan(bx + c)$.

***26.** (100) Let $f(x) = x - 1$ and $g(x) = x^2 - 1$. Find the vertical asymptotes and holes for $\frac{f(x)}{f(g(x))}$.

Use $P(x) = x^3 - 10x^2 + 19x + 30$.

***27.** (95) Determine if $x - 6$ is a factor of $P(x)$.

***28.** (95) Factor $P(x)$.

29. (39) Determine if $(1, 1)$ is a solution of the inequality $y < -5x + 3$.

***30.** (101) **Analyze** Which function has end behavior that is different from the end behavior of the others? Explain.

$f(x) = 4x^3 - x^2 - 2x$ $g(x) = x^7 - 1$ $h(x) = -3x^3 - 3x^4 + x^5$ $k(x) = -5x^3 + x^2 + x$

© Saxon. All rights reserved.

Name ______________________ Date __________ Class __________

Solving Logarithmic Equations and Inequalities

LESSON 102

1. (80) A set of scores have a mean of 74 and a standard deviation of 5. Find the percent of scores between 69 and 84.

Find the roots of each equation.

2. (85) $y = 4x^2 + 5x - 1$

3. (85) Find the roots of $y = x^4 - 16$.

***4.** (102) **Union Membership** Beginning in the 1930s, labor union membership in the U.S. grew dramatically. During the years 1935–1955, labor union membership in the U.S. can be modeled by the equation $y = -4.4 + 12.6\ln t$, where $5 \le t \le 25$, $t = 5$ represents 1935, and y is the percent of the U.S. labor force that were union members. Use the model to approximate the year in which union membership in the U.S. reached 30%.

***5.** (101) **Analyze** A cubic polynomial function $f(x)$ has exactly three real zeros; they are 1, 3, and 4. It has a relative maximum at an x-value between 3 and 4. Describe the end behavior of $f(x)$.

6. (84) **National Highways** In Rhode Island, the speed limit outside a business or residential district is twice the speed limit inside a business or residential district. A driver drove 12.5 miles inside business and residential districts and 75 miles outside of business and residential districts for a total driving time of 2 hours. Suppose the driver kept a constant speed at the posted speed limits. Write and solve a rational equation to find the speed limit inside a business or residential district.

***7.** (98) **Probability** Use the equation for the area of an ellipse, πab, to find the probability of a point randomly landing within the ellipse but outside the circle.

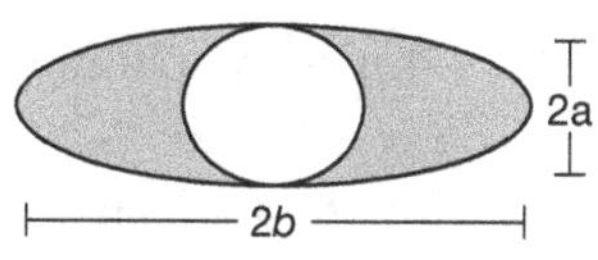

8. (96) **Construction** The diagram represents a plan for a deck in the shape of an isosceles trapezoid. Write polar coordinates for points A, B, C, and D. Use point A as the pole and $\overrightarrow{AD}$ as the polar axis.

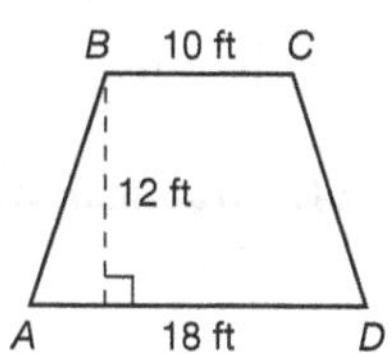

***9.** (99) **Generalize** For two nonzero vectors $\vec{A}$ and $\vec{B}$, what must be true for $\vec{A} + \vec{B} = 0$?

10. (32) Find the inverse of the matrix $T = \begin{bmatrix} -6 & -2 \\ 11 & -3 \end{bmatrix}$, if it exists.

***11.** (100) **Geometry** Write the rational function that shows the ratio of the surface area to the volume for a right circular cylinder. Identify any asymptotes.

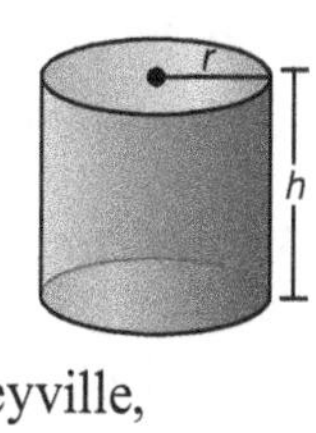

12. (77) **Geography** On a map of southwest Illinois, line segments connect Jerseyville, Carlinville, and Litchfield. The angle formed at Jerseyville measures 18°. The distance from Jerseyville to Carlinville is 28 miles and the distance from Jerseyville to Litchfield is 37 miles. To the nearest tenth of a mile, what is the distance from Carlinville to Litchfield?

© Saxon. All rights reserved.

13. (88) **Analyze** The formula for the surface area of a sphere is $S = 4\pi r^2$. The formula for the volume of a sphere is $V = \frac{4}{3}\pi r^3$. Solve each equation for r. Explain why the first equation has a solution that cannot represent a possible value for the radius. Then tell why this is not true of the second equation.

14. (93) **Write** Explain why the equations $4^x = 100$ and $x \log 4 = 2$ are equivalent.

15. (73) **(Town Government)** A town council wants to know if residents support having an off-leash area for dogs in the town park. Eighty dog owners are surveyed at the park. Describe the individuals in the population and in the sample.

***16.** (102) **Multiple Choice** What is the solution to $\log 5x + \log 2 = 4$?
A $x = 1000$ **B** $x = 1428.6$ **C** $x = 1999.6$ **D** $x = 9990$

***17.** (102) Solve $\log_4(4x + 7) = \log_4 11x$.

***18.** (97) **Graphing Calculator** The first term of a geometric sequence is 9 and the common ratio is $\frac{2}{3}$.

a. Explain how to use the Table function to find the value of the 14th term.

b. Explain how to use the Graph function to find the value of the 14th term.

c. Rounded to the nearest ten-thousandth, what is the value of the 14th term?

19. (82) Given $g(x) = 3 \sin \frac{1}{2}(x)$, identify the amplitude and period.

20. (85) **(Physics)** A spaceship is coming in for a landing on Mars. The equation $h = -1.885t^2 + v_o t + h_o$ can be used to find the distance h from the ground at time t based on an initial height h_o and an initial speed of v_o. To the nearest hundredth of a second, how long it will take the ship to land from an initial height of 2000 and an initial speed of 200?

***21.** (101) **Error Analysis** A student identified the degree of $P(x) = 2x^3 + 3x^2 - x^4$ as 3. What is the error?

22. (91) **Multi-Step** The map of a town is placed on a coordinate grid. The center of a small earthquake is located at $(-1, -3)$ and can be felt up to 12 miles away.

a. Write the equation of the circle that represents the border of the affected area.

b. Justify Show how to use the equation in part **a** to prove that people in a building located at $(11, -2)$ did not feel the earthquake.

23. (9) **Multi-Step** Use $A = \begin{bmatrix} 10 & 1 \\ 4 & 10 \end{bmatrix}$ and $B = \begin{bmatrix} 11 & 4 \\ 16 & 11 \end{bmatrix}$.

a. Find AB. **b.** Find BA. **c.** Is AB = BA?

24. (83) Write a quadratic equation whose roots are $6 \pm 2i$.

© Saxon. All rights reserved.

Solving Logarithmic Equations and Inequalities

***25.** Factor the terms of the rational function $y = \frac{x^2 + 3x - 4}{x - 2}$ to identify vertical asymptotes.
(100)

***26.** Write an equation in standard form for the ellipse with center (0, 0), $a = 4$ and $b = 6$.
(98)

Divide using synthetic division.

27. $x^3 - 6$ by $x - 2$
(51)

28. $x^3 + 3x^2 + 7x + 5$ by $x + 1$
(51)

29. Find the distance between (–2, 5) and (3, 4).
(41)

30. Solve $4\begin{bmatrix} 2 & 1 \\ -6 & 3.5 \end{bmatrix} - 3\begin{bmatrix} 0 & 0.4 \\ 8 & -2 \end{bmatrix}$.
(5)

© Saxon. All rights reserved.

Name ______________________ Date ____________ Class ____________

Graphing Reciprocal Trigonometric Functions

LESSON 103

*1. **Graphing Calculator** Use a graphing calculator to graph $y = 3\sec(2x)$ from 0 to 2π.
(103)

2. **Multi-Step** A drinking glass is to be in the shape of a frustum of a right circular cone. The formula for the volume of a frustum of a right circular cone is $V = \frac{\pi(r^2 + rR + R^2)h}{3}$.
(88)

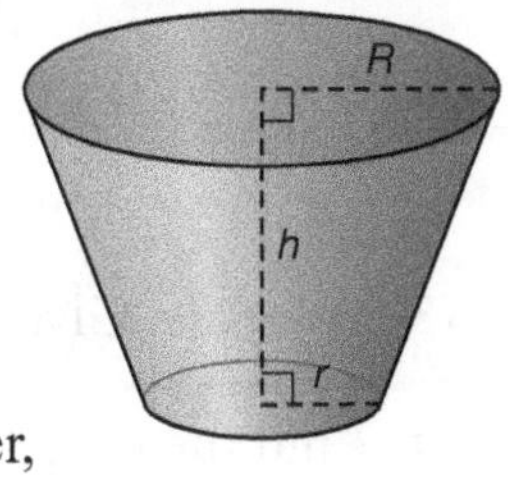

a. Solve the formula for h.

b. If $R = 5$ centimeters and $r = 4$ centimeters, what is the minimum height necessary, to the nearest tenth of a centimeter, so that the glass will hold at least 500 cubic centimeters?

*3. **Landscape Design** A landscape architect has 96 feet of landscape timber to enclose a garden, using an existing wall for one side as shown. The area of the garden can be modeled by $A(x) = 96x - 3x^2$, where x is in feet. Find the maximum area of the garden.
(101)

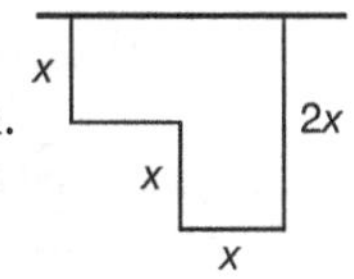

4. **Multiple Choice** What are the Cartesian coordinates for the point with polar coordinates $(5, -\frac{\pi}{4})$?
(96)

A $\left(5\sqrt{2}, -5\sqrt{2}\right)$ **B** $\left(-5\sqrt{2}, 5\sqrt{2}\right)$ **C** $\left(\frac{5\sqrt{2}}{2}, -\frac{5\sqrt{2}}{2}\right)$ **D** $\left(-\frac{5\sqrt{2}}{2}, \frac{5\sqrt{2}}{2}\right)$

*5. **Population** The estimated population of Illinois from 2005 to 2006 increased by about 0.52%. Assuming that the percent of increase stays the same, the populations each year form a geometric sequence. Show how to use the formula for the nth term of a geometric sequence to find the population of Illinois in 2010 given that the estimated population in 2005 was 12,765,427.
(97)

6. How many 4-digit pass codes can be made using the numbers 1–5, if numbers may be repeated?
(33)

7. **Business** The profit earned from selling tickets to a certain event is modeled by $y = -1.5x^2 + 80x - 600$. If the cost per ticket will be a whole number amount, what range of ticket prices will earn a profit? What range of ticket values will earn a profit of at least \$200?
(89)

8. Solve the system by substitution. $\begin{array}{l} 2x + 5y = 7 \\ x + 4y = 2 \end{array}$
(21)

9. **Geometry** For any two vectors expressed as complex numbers, find the dot product from the components of the complex numbers.
(99)

10. **Justify** When the ordered pairs (n, a_n) for the sequence $\{3, 7, 11, 15, 19\}$ are graphed, the points form a straight line. Show algebraically why the slope is equal to the common difference.
(92)

*11. **Model** The graph of a rational function has vertical asymptotes at $x = 7$ and -3 and holes at $x = -2$ and 0. Write an equation of a function that can be used to model these data points.
(100)

© Saxon. All rights reserved.

12. *(84)* **Multiple Choice** To solve the equation, what should both sides of $\frac{1}{x^2-4} + \frac{3}{4x+8} = \frac{6}{x}$ be multiplied by?

A $(x+2)(x-2)$ **B** $4(x+2)(x-2)$

C $4x(x+2)(x-2)$ **D** $4x(x+2)^2$

13. *(11)* **Formulate** Give an example of two trinomials whose sum has 6 terms.

14. *(25)* Find the range and standard deviation of the data set 10, 12, 7, 11, 20, 7, 8, 6, 9.

***15.** *(98)* **Formulate** The eccentricity of an ellipse centered at the origin is 0.92. The graph of the ellipse crosses the minor axis at (0, 2). Write the equation of the ellipse.

16. *(83)* **(National Monuments)** The height and span of the arch legs of the St. Louis Gateway Arch are both 630 feet. Write a quadratic function to approximate the arch.

Identify all the real roots.

17. *(85)* $x^9 + 1331 = 0$ **18.** *(85)* $x^3 + 10x^2 + 17x = 28$

19. *(90)* **(Physics)** Derive an equation that an air traffic controller can use to find the angle an airplane makes with the horizon, given the plane's altitude h and its horizontal distance from the airport d.

20. *(95)* Evaluate the polynomial $P(x)$ for $x = 4$. $P(x) = 2x^3 - 3x^2 + x - 5$

***21.** *(103)* Find the period and asymptotes for $y = 3 \cot \frac{2}{3}x$.

22. *(93)* **Multi-Step** Iron-62 has a half-life of 68 seconds.

a. Use the natural decay function $N(t) = N_0e^{-kt}$ to find the decay constant k for iron-62.

b. Write the natural decay function for iron-62 and solve for t to find how long it would take 10 grams to decay to 7 grams.

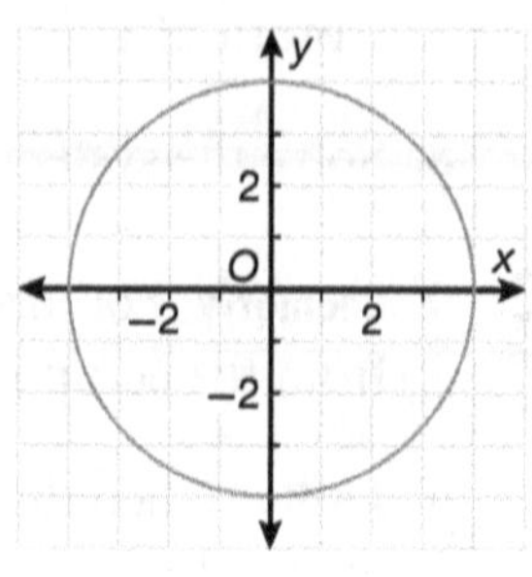

23. *(91)* **Error Analysis** Explain and correct the error a student made in graphing $x^2 + y^2 = 4$.

***24.** *(102)* **Error Analysis** A student solved $\log x + 5 = 4$ incorrectly, obtaining 9,995 as the solution. What error did the student likely make?

***25.** *(102)* **Write** Can a logarithmic equation have a negative number as a solution? Justify your answer. Give an example, if possible.

Simplify the expression.

26. *(40)* $\frac{48}{\sqrt{3}}$ **27.** *(40)* $\sqrt{108} + \sqrt{12} + \sqrt{112}$

© Saxon. All rights reserved.

Graphing Reciprocal Trigonometric Functions

LESSON 103

28. (79) Write a piecewise function for a hardware store that will deliver up to 6 items for a $35 delivery charge. There is a $7 charge for each additional item.

***29.** (94) Solve $\frac{x^2 - 3x + 2}{x - 3} < x$ by finding the values of test points.

***30.** (103) A traffic helicopter is flying at an altitude of 8,000 feet. The driver spots an accident at angle of elevation, x. Let y be the distance from the accident to a point directly below the helicopter. Write y as a function of x.

© Saxon. All rights reserved.

Name ______________________________ Date ____________ Class ____________

Finding Transformations

LESSON 104

1. (94) **Multiple Choice** When solving $\frac{x^2 + 5x - 6}{x^2 - 12x + 32}$ by using a sign table, for how many intervals will a test point need to be chosen?

A 3 **B** 4 **C** 5 **D** 6

2. (77) A triangle has side lengths of 7.5 meters, 11 meters, and 13 meters. Use Heron's formula to find the area of the triangle.

***3.** (103) Graph $y = 4\cot\left(\frac{1}{2}x\right)$. Determine its period and asymptotes.

***4.** (90) **Graphing Calculator** Use a graphing calculator to graph $y = \tan(x + 6)$. Identify the period and undefined values of the function.

***5.** (104) **Error Analysis** In the coordinate plane shown, functions $f(x) = \sqrt{x}$ and $g(x) = 3\sqrt{x - 5} - 5$ are graphed. Is the graph of g correct? If not, find and explain the error and sketch the correct graph of g.

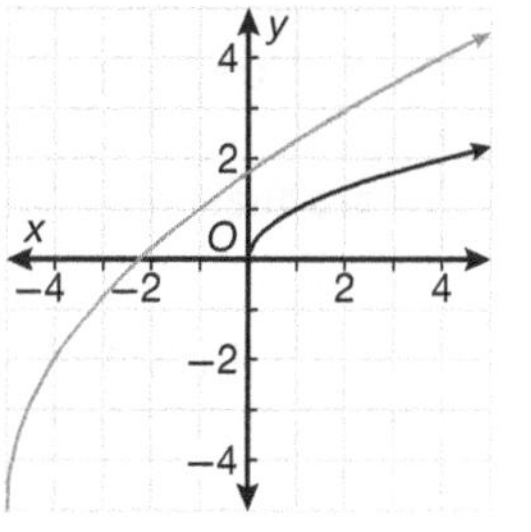

***6.** (101) **Finance** The NASDAQ Composite is an indicator of stock prices. The monthly low NASDAQ Composite for the year 2002 can be modeled by $f(x) = 2.229x^3 - 34.667x^2 + 60.339x + 1787$, where $x = 1$ represents January, $x = 2$ represents February, and so on, with $x = 12$ representing December. Use the model to approximate the lowest monthly NASDAQ Composite during 2002. Based on the model, in which month did it occur?

7. (95) **Analyze** Suppose that for polynomial $P(x)$, $P(a) = 0$ for constant a. What can you conclude about the graph of rational function $f(x) = \frac{1}{P(x)}$?

8. (96) **Error Analysis** A student incorrectly converted the polar coordinates $(-1, \pi)$ to the Cartesian coordinates $(-1, 0)$. What is the error? Find the correct Cartesian coordinates.

9. (87) **Radioactive Decay** A radioactive substance decays based on $d = d_0e^{-0.0063t}$. The time, in days, is represented by t, and d_0 represents the initial amount of the radioactive substance. Solve for t.

10. (97) **Chemistry** The half-life of Barium-131 is 12 days. The amounts of Barium-131 after every half-life (every 12th day) form a geometric sequence. What is the common ratio of this sequence?

11. (80) **Geometry** The students in a geometry class each chose a polygon that has between 3 and 12 sides and wrote a paragraph about its side and angle measures. The table shows how many students chose each type of polygon. Tell if the data is normally distributed. Explain your answer.

Number of Sides in Polygon	3	4	5	6	7	8	9	10	11	12
Number of Students Who Chose Polygon	2	5	7	6	2	5	6	8	4	1

© Saxon. All rights reserved.

12. (98) **Formulate** The eccentricity of an ellipse centered at $(-3, 5)$ is 0.9682. The graph of the ellipse crosses the major axis at $(-3, 21)$. Write the equation of the ellipse.

13. (28) Identify any excluded values for the expression $\frac{12m^7}{3m^9}$, then simplify.

***14.** (99) **Multiple Choice** In what quadrant is the vector $22 + (-33)i$?

A I **B** II **C** III **D** IV

15. (34) **Formulate** Rewrite the following equation in slope-intercept form: $6x - 8y = 24$.

***16.** (100) **Model** The graph of a rational function has vertical asymptotes at $x = 0, -1$, and 3 and a hole at $x = 5$. Write an equation of a function that can be used to model these data points.

17. (79) **Data Analysis** The rates for media mail are shown in the table. Write a piecewise function that represents the cost of mailing a first-class letter.

Fee	Weight
\$1.30	up to 1 ounce
\$1.64	greater than 1 ounce and up to 2 ounces
\$1.98	greater than 2 ounces and up to 3 ounces

***18.** (103) **Error Analysis** Describe and correct the error in finding $\csc\theta$, given that θ is an acute angle of a right triangle and $\cos\theta = \frac{7}{11}$.

$$\csc\theta = \frac{1}{\cos\theta} = \frac{11}{7}$$

19. (92) **Salaries** An employee's salary is structured so that after the first year, the employee receives an annual raise of a set amount. What was the employee's starting salary if the salary in the eighth year was \$42,710 and the salary in the 17th year was \$50,135?

***20.** (102) **Multi-Step** The Richter magnitude M of an earthquake is expressed by $M = \frac{2}{3}\log\left(\frac{E}{10^{11.8}}\right)$, where E is the energy released in ergs.

a. Find the energy released by an earthquake of magnitude 6.

b. Find the energy released by an earthquake of magnitude 7.

c. By what factor is the energy multiplied when the magnitude is increased by 1?

21. (88) **Simple Interest** The simple interest formula is $A = P + Prt$, where P is the principal, or original amount invested, r is the annual simple interest rate, and A is the value of the investment at the end of t years. Solve the formula for P. Then determine the amount P that must be invested at 5% annual simple interest to have a value of \$10,000 at the end of 2 years.

22. (10) Darryl lives 2 miles from the mall and Taylor lives 8 miles from the same mall. Write an inequality to determine how far Darryl and Taylor live from each other.

© Saxon. All rights reserved.

*23. (104) **Write** Explain in complete sentences what must be done to an equation to vertically shift a graph down.

Use matrices $B = \begin{bmatrix} 3\frac{1}{2} & -\frac{1}{2} & -\frac{1}{4} \end{bmatrix}$ **and** $C = \begin{bmatrix} 2\frac{1}{2} & \frac{1}{2} & -3 \end{bmatrix}$.

24. (5) Find $-C$.

25. (5) Find $\frac{1}{2}C + 4B$.

26. (31) Divide, and identify all values of x that make the expression $\frac{x^2 + 6x + 9}{x^2 - 9} \div (x - 7)$ undefined.

Solve and classify each of the following systems.

27. (24) $4x - 3y = 10$
$8x - 6y = 20$

28. (24) $7x + 2y = 11$
$-2x + 3y = 29$

29. (82) Using $\sin(x)$ as a guide, find the phase shift in $g(x) = 2 \sin 3(x - 8) + 5$.

*30. (103) Find the period and asymptotes of $y = -\sec 4x$.

© Saxon. All rights reserved.

Name ______________________ Date __________ Class __________

Finding Arithmetic Series

LESSON 105

***1.** Let $f(x) = x^4$ and $g(x) = x^2 - 5x + 6$. Find $P(3)$ for $P(x) = f(g(x))$.
(95)

***2.** **Verify** The first and second terms of an arithmetic sequence are 48 and 30 respectively. Show that the sum of the first 16 terms is -1392.
(105)

***3.** **Multiple Choice** The graph is a translation of the graph of $f(x) = \sqrt{x}$. Choose the letter of the equation that best represents the graph.
(104)

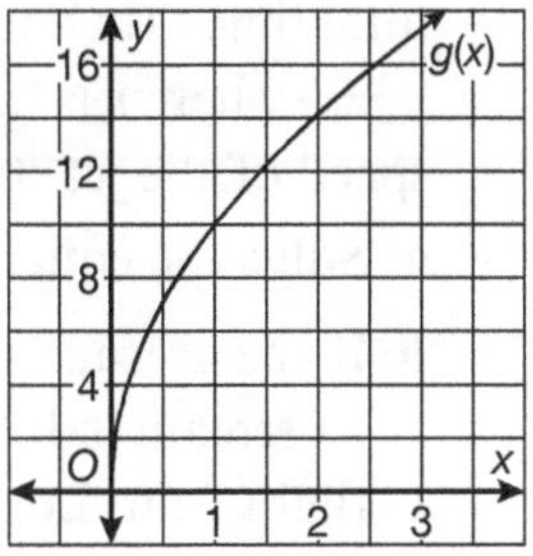

A $g(x) = \sqrt{x + 10}$　　**B** $g(x) = \frac{1}{10}\sqrt{x}$

C $g(x) = \sqrt{x} + 10$　　**D** $g(x) = 10\sqrt{x}$

***4.** **Retirement Funds** A Teachers Retirement System paid out an interest rate of 4% compounded annually from 1920 to 1955. The function $A(x) = P \cdot 1.04^x$ can be used to calculate the amount in the account, $A(x)$, after x years with the original amount placed in the account, P. Use the function $f(x) = 1.04^x$ to sketch a graph of the equation $A(x) = P \cdot 1.04^x$ if the original amount in the account is \$1,000.
(104)

5. Write a quadratic equation whose root is 7.
(83)

***6.** **Coordinate Geometry** A rectangle has a side on the x-axis, a side on the y-axis, and a vertex in Quadrant I on the graph of $y = -\frac{1}{4}x^2 + 6$. Find the maximum possible area of the rectangle and the corresponding vertex (x, y).
(101)

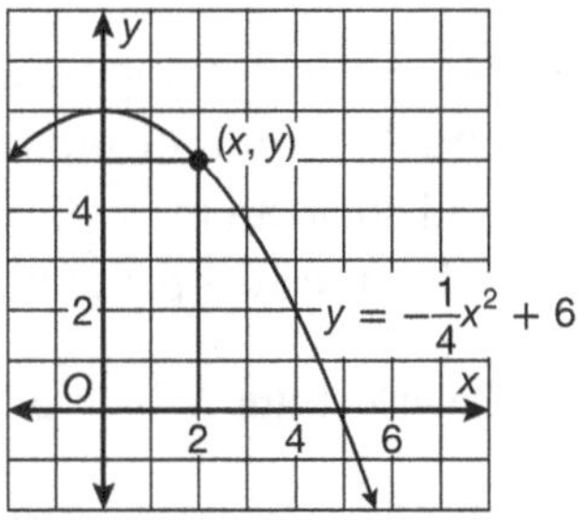

7. **Geometry** A triangle has a base of 10 cm and a height of x cm. Write and solve an inequality for all the values of x that will result in a triangle with an area of at least 95 cm.
(10)

8. Graph each of the complex numbers on the same coordinate plane.
(69)
a. $2i$　　**b.** $-4i$　　**c.** $3 + i$

9. Find the 4th term of an arithmetic sequence if the first term is 6.2 and the 19th term is 33.2.
(92)

10. **Cafeteria** C.J., Lyle, and Avery had lunch together. C.J. bought 1 drink, 3 sandwiches, and 3 snacks. Lyle bought 2 drinks, 1 sandwich, and 4 snacks. Avery bought 2 drinks, 2 sandwiches, and 5 snacks. The cost of a drink is \$1.00, a sandwich is \$3.50, and a snack is \$1.50. Use matrices to determine how much each person spent and who spent the most money.
(9)

© Saxon. All rights reserved.

11. (32) Use an inverse matrix to solve the linear system given by $\begin{aligned} -3x + y - 8z &= 18 \\ x - 2y + z &= 11 \\ 2x - 2y + 5z &= -17 \end{aligned}$.

12. (88) **Jet Stream** The jet stream is a wind pattern. Between London and New York the jet stream generally blows west to east, sometimes at hundreds of miles per hour. The total time t (in hours) of a round-trip flight is modeled by the equation $t = \frac{d}{r-w} + \frac{d}{r+w}$, where r is the average speed of the plane in miles per hour, w is the average speed of the jet stream in miles per hour, and d is the one-way distance in miles.

a. Solve the equation for d.

b. If the average speed of a plane is 500 miles per hour and the average speed of the jet stream is 100 miles per hour, then it would take 14.4 hours for a round-trip flight from London to New York. Find the distance from London to New York.

***13.** (105) **Graphing Calculator** Use the **sum(seq(** commands to find the sum of $\sum_{k=1}^{100} 4.25k$.

***14.** (105) Evaluate the series $\sum_{k=1}^{10}(8 - 3k)$.

15. (84) **Error Analysis** Explain and correct the error made in the steps shown below.

$$\frac{2}{3x+6} + 4 = \frac{1}{2} \rightarrow {}^{2}\cancel{6}\cancel{(x+2)}\left(\frac{2}{\cancel{3}\cancel{(x+2)}} + 4\right) = {}^{3}\cancel{6}(x+2)\left(\frac{1}{\cancel{2}}\right) \rightarrow 4 + 8 = 3x + 6$$

***16.** (94) **Government** Suppose counties in the state of California had the option to donate an equal amount of money towards a \$500,000 donation to be given to a charity. Write and solve an inequality to show the number of counties whose participation would bring the cost per county to less than \$14,000. There are 58 counties in California.

17. (85) **Multiple Choice** Which of the following is not a root of $f(x) = 8x^3 - 18x^2 + 3x + 2$?

A -3 **B** $-\frac{1}{4}$ **C** $\frac{1}{2}$ **D** 2

18. (87) **Multi-Step** Use the properties of logarithms to rewrite the expression $\log_3(9x)^5$. Evaluate the expression when $x = 81$.

19. (90) **Surveying** Derive an equation that a surveyor can use to find the height (h) of a mountain given the angle of elevation (θ) and the distance from the mountain (d).

20. (21) Solve the system $\begin{aligned} 3x - y &= 2 \\ 6x + 3y &= 14 \end{aligned}$ by substitution.

21. (91) **Analyze** Is a circle a function? Why or why not? Sample:

***22.** (93) **Write** Explain why the inequalities $2(3)^x < 310$ and $\log 2 + x \log 3 < \log 310$ are equivalent.

23. (10) Solve the compound inequality $4 < 3x + 1 \leq 10$ by writing and solving two inequalities. Show the steps you followed to reach your answers.

© Saxon. All rights reserved.

24. A line has slope 5 and crosses the y-axis at (0, 3). What is the equation of the line written in slope-intercept form?
(26)

25. **Write** Explain how to simplify this problem: 12.65 in. + 30.1 in. + 15.843 in.
(18)

26. Determine if (7, 19) is a solution of the inequality $y > 4x + 8$.
(39)

Evaluate each piecewise function for $x = -2$ and $x = 0$.

27. $f(x) = \begin{cases} 7x, & \text{if } x < -2 \\ 0, & \text{if } x \geq -2 \end{cases}$
(79)

28. $f(x) = \begin{cases} 15, & \text{if } x \leq -2 \\ -x^2, & \text{if } -2 < x \leq 0 \\ 2 + x, & \text{if } x > 0 \end{cases}$
(79)

***29.** **Estimate** Estimate the solution to $1 + \log x = 3.998$. Explain your method.
(102)

30. Convert $\log_8 (9x)^2$ to base 10. Then evaluate when $x = 4$.
(87)

© Saxon. All rights reserved.

Name ______________________ Date __________ Class __________

Using the Fundamental Theorem of Algebra

LESSON 106

*1. (106) **Medicine** A vitamin is shaped like a cylinder with congruent hemispheres on either end. If the volume of the vitamin is 22.5π cubic millimeters, and the height of the cylindrical part is 8 millimeters, what is the radius of the vitamin?

*2. (102) **Population Growth** Based on U.S. Census statistics, the population of Maryland for the years 1950–1990 can be modeled by the equation $y = -1202 + 1495\ln t$, where $10 \leq t \leq 50$, $t = 10$ represents 1950, and y is the population in thousands. Use the model to approximate the year in which the population of Maryland reached 3,000,000.

3. (94) **Generalize** How is solving a quadratic inequality similar to and different from solving a rational inequality?

*4. (105) **Analyze** Explain the difference between S_9 and a_9 for an arithmetic series.

*5. (105) **Error Analysis** Explain and correct the error a student made in writing the arithmetic series {9 + 13 + 17 + 21 + 25} in summation notation.

$$\sum_{k=1}^{5} 9 + 4k$$

6. (87) **Multiple Choice** Using the change of base formula, $\log_{12} 5$ is equivalent to:

A $\dfrac{\log 12}{\log 5}$ **B** $\dfrac{\log 5}{\log 12}$ **C** $\dfrac{\log_5 10}{\log_{12} 10}$ **D** $\dfrac{\ln 12}{\ln 5}$

7. (103) Graph $y = \frac{2}{3}\csc(x)$. Determine its period and asymptotes.

8. (49) Use the Binomial Theorem to expand $(x + 3y)^3$

*9. (104) **Retirement Funds** A teachers' retirement program paid out an interest rate of 3% compounded annually from 1955 to 1963. The function $A(x) = P \cdot 1.03^x$ can be used to calculate the amount in the account, $A(x)$, after x years with the original amount placed in the account, P. Use the function $f(x) = 1.03^x$ to sketch a graph of the equation $A(x) = P \cdot 1.03^x$ if the original amount in the account is $10,000.

10. (91) The endpoints of a diameter of a circle are located at (−8, 4) and (2, 4). Write an equation for this circle.

*11. (101) **Analyze** A polynomial function $f(x)$ of degree 4 has exactly four real zeros; they are −1, 2, 3, and 6. It also has a negative y-intercept. Describe the end behavior of $f(x)$.

12. (98) **Geometry** For the equation to calculate eccentricity, $e = \sqrt{1 - \frac{b^2}{a^2}}$, what is the value of e as a approaches infinity? For this limiting value, is the figure still an ellipse?

13. (97) **Multiple Choice** What is the 11th term of a geometric sequence that starts −4, 4, ...?

A −4,194,304 **B** −4 **C** 4 **D** 4,194,304

14. (27) Convert $f(x) = (x - 3)^2 + 6$ into standard form.

© Saxon. All rights reserved.

Simplify the expression.

15. (87) $\log_6 36^x$

16. (87) $\log_5 125^x$

***17.** (100) **Multi-Step** Let $f(x) = x^2 - 9$ and $g(x) = x + 4$. Find $\frac{f(x)}{f(g(x))}$ and then determine the vertical asymptotes and holes for it.

***18.** (30) **Graphing Calculator** Graph $f(x) = -x^2 + 2$ using a graphing calculator. Compare with the graph of x^2, and explain how the graph is shifted.

19. (85) **Physics** A spaceship is coming in for a landing on Jupiter. The equation $h = -12.95t^2 + v_0t + h_0$ can be used to find the distance h from the ground at time t based on an initial height h_0 and an initial speed of v_0. To the nearest hundredth of a second, how long it will take the ship to land from a height of 2000 and an initial speed of 200?

Simplify.

20. (48) $\frac{6}{x} + \frac{2x}{x+2}$

21. (48) $\frac{\frac{1}{x+5}}{\frac{x}{2}}$

22. (96) **Athletic Field** The diagram represents a soccer field. Write polar coordinates for points A, B, C, and D. Use point A as the pole and $\overrightarrow{AD}$ as the polar axis.

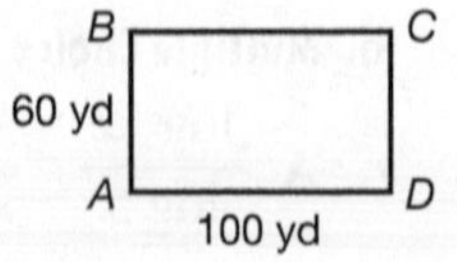

23. (42) Find the number of permutations of 9 objects taken 6 at a time.

24. (Inv 8) Estimate the area under the curve $y = -x^2 + 5x + 5$ from $0 \le x \le 5$. Use 5 partitions.

25. (33) A teacher needs 3 volunteers to go to the cafeteria to get ice for the next chemistry lab. With a class of 26 students, how many different ways can the teacher choose the volunteers for the task?

26. (80) **Statistics** A set of results are normally distributed with a mean of 50 and a standard deviation of 4. Find the percent of results between 46 and 54.

***27.** (106) **Multi-Step** Consider the polynomial equation $x^3 + x = 0$.

a. How many roots must it have and why?

b. Factor the polynomial. Name a real root.

c. Find the remaining two roots.

d. Graph the polynomial on a graphing calculator and tell how the graph supports your answer.

© Saxon. All rights reserved.

Using the Fundamental Theorem of Algebra

LESSON 106

28. **Write** Explain how to write the equation of a circle given the endpoints of a diameter of the circle.
(91)

*29. Write the simplest polynomial function given the following roots: $-\frac{3}{4}$, 6, -1
(106)

30. **Formulate** For two nonzero vectors $\vec{A}$ and $\vec{B}$ what must be true for $\vec{A} \cdot \vec{B} = 0$?
(99)

© Saxon. All rights reserved.

Name ______________________ Date __________ Class __________

Graphing Rational Functions II

LESSON **107**

1. (31) Multiply and then evaluate for $t = 2$, $k = 5$: $\frac{4t^3k^7}{8t} \cdot \frac{3k^3}{6t^4k^9}$.

***2.** (105) Find S_{30} for $101 + 95 + 89 + 83 + \ldots$

3. (96) **Estimate** Write approximate Cartesian coordinates for the point with polar coordinates $\left(2, \frac{1}{2}\right)$. Explain your method.

***4.** (107) **Multiple Choice** Which of the following rational functions has a slant asymptote of $y = 2x - 4$?

A $y = \frac{2x^2 + 1}{2x + 1}$ **B** $y = \frac{x^3 - 8}{0.5x^2 + x + 5}$

C $y = \frac{(2x - 4)^2}{x + 8}$ **D** $y = \frac{2x^2 - 1}{x + 2}$

5. (49) 1 in 6 cars sold on a lot are silver. Today, 4 cars were sold. What is the probability that 2 of the cars sold were silver?

***6.** (97) If the 1st term of a geometric sequence is 5 and the common ratio is −4, what is the 6th term?

***7.** (47) **Graphing Calculator** Graph $y = 6^x$ and $y = \left(\frac{1}{6}\right)^x$ on a graphing calculator and describe the graphs.

8. (92) **Error Analysis** A student said that the finite sequence {5, 10, 20, 35, 55, 80} is arithmetic because it is formed by adding numbers in a pattern. Explain and correct the student's reasoning.

9. (2) **Multiple Choice** Evaluate $-5x^2 + 2y$ if $x = 1$ and $y = -1$.

A −7 **B** −3 **C** 3 **D** 7

10. (71) **Geometry** Derive the function that can be used to find the area of the parallelogram. Express in simplified form.

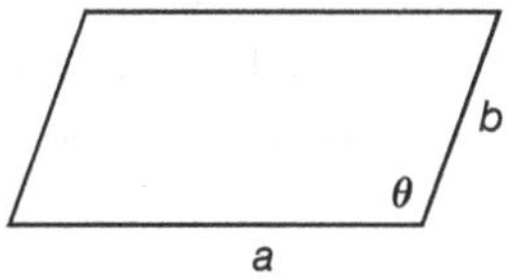

Divide.

11. (38) $5x^4 - 2x^3 - 7x^2 - 39$ by $2x$

12. (38) $3x^2 - 11x - 26$ by $(x - 5)$

13. (85) **Error Analysis** A student solves for the roots of $y = x^3 - 3x + 2$; what was his mistake?

Factors of 1: ± 1 ← Values of q Factors of 2: ± 1, 2 ← Values of p $\frac{p}{q} = \{\pm 1, 2\}$

$$\begin{array}{r|rrr} 1 & 1 & -3 & 2 \\ & & 1 & -2 \\ \hline & 1 & -2 & 0 \end{array} \checkmark$$

$y = (x - 1)(x^2 - 2)$ The roots of $y = x^3 - 3x + 2$ are $x = 1$ and $\pm\sqrt{2}$.

© Saxon. All rights reserved.

14. (106) **Error Analysis** A student said that a polynomial equation with roots of 4 and $6 + i$ will have exactly four roots because each has a conjugate pair, -4 and $6 - i$. Explain the error in the student's thinking.

15. (Inv 9) **Multi-Step** To join the local gym, there is a $60 initial sign-up fee and an additional monthly fee. If you join the gym for 6 months, it is $50 per month. If you join the gym for 1 year, the monthly fee is $45 per month. There is a $5 monthly discount for each year added to your membership, up to 5 years.

a. If you join the gym for 6 months, and then sign up for an additional year, what will be the total cost?

b. What will the total cost be if you later add an additional 6 months?

c. If you join the gym for 2 years, what will be the total cost?

d. How much money will you save by joining the gym for 2 years initially?

16. (91) **Analyze** How is the graph of $x^2 + (y - 7)^2 = 20$ similar to, and different from, the graph of $x^2 + (y - 7)^2 = 24$?

***17.** (100) **Generalize** Show that rational functions of the form $f(x) = \frac{1}{x^2n}$, for positive integers n, are even functions.

18. (94) **Write** Describe two ways to use a sign table to solve rational inequalities. When should each be used?

19. (95) **Space Science** If you throw a ball in the air, the height (h) it travels is based on the acceleration due to gravity (g), the initial height (h_o) the object is thrown from, its initial speed (v_o), and the time (t) that the object is in the air. The table shows different values of g for different planets. Use the Remainder Theorem to compare $h(10)$ for Earth and Saturn, assuming that $h_o = 100$ and $v_o = 100$. Account for any differences.

$$h(t) = -\frac{1}{2}gt^2 + v_ot + h_o$$

Planet	Gravity, g(m/s^2)
Mercury	3.59
Venus	8.87
Earth	9.81
Mars	3.77
Jupiter	25.95
Saturn	11.08
Uranus	10.67
Neptune	14.07

20. (87) **Commodities** P represents the selling price, in dollars, of a commodity and x represents the demand, in number sold per day. This relationship is indicated by the equation $p = p_0e^{-ax}$. Solve the equation for x.

21. (93) **Population Growth** The population of Japan grew at an average annual rate of approximately 0.26% from 1990 to 2000, and the population in 2000 was 127,000,000 (rounded to the nearest million). If the population continues to increase at the same rate, in what year will it reach 150,000,000?

© Saxon. All rights reserved.

*22. (107) **Consumer Finance** You want to compare the cost of buying a more expensive car that has a higher miles per gallon (mpg) rating to a less expensive car with low mpg. Use the data in the table to generate two rational functions. Assume that the number of miles traveled is 30,000 and the cost of fuel is $4.50 per gallon. Use the graph of both functions to determine the number of years it takes for the car with 40 mpg to be a better deal than the car with 20 mpg.

MPG	Car Price
20	$20,000
40	$40,000

$$\text{Yearly cost} = \frac{\text{Price} + \dfrac{\text{Miles traveled}}{\text{MPG}} \times \text{Cost of Fuel per Gallon} \times \text{Number of Years}}{\text{Number of Years}}$$

23. (99) **Multi-Step** Find the magnitude of vectors $\begin{bmatrix}3\\6\end{bmatrix}$ and $\begin{bmatrix}2\\-5\end{bmatrix}$. Calculate the dot product and then calculate the angle between the two vectors.

*24. (104) **Probability** The probability that a single coin tossed in the air will not land tails up until the nth toss can be found using the equation $P(n) = 0.5(0.5)^{n-1}$, where $P(x)$ is the probability and n is the number of times the coin is tossed. Use the graph of $f(n) = 0.5^n$ to sketch a graph of $P(n)$. Use the graph of $P(n)$ to estimate the probability that the coin will not land tails up until the third toss.

*25. (107) **Formulate** Write a possible rational function that fits these parameters: Vertical asymptotes $x = \pm 1$; slant asymptote $y = 3x + 1$.

Find the zeros of the quadratic function.

26. (35) $f(x) = x^2 + 21x - 46$

27. (35) $f(x) = x^2 + \frac{5}{12}x - \frac{1}{6}$

Simplify.

28. (44) $\dfrac{1}{5 + \sqrt{6}} =$

29. (44) $\dfrac{3 + \sqrt{7}}{2 - \sqrt{10}} =$

30. (89) **Tourist Attractions** The world's tallest thermometer is located in Baker, California, with a height of 134 feet. Suppose a maintenance worker at the top drops a nail. The height of the nail, in feet, after x seconds, is modeled by $y = -16x^2 + 134$. Write and solve a quadratic inequality that can be solved to find the time span for which the nail remains at least 50 feet above the ground. Round to the nearest hundredth of a second.

© Saxon. All rights reserved.

Name ______________________ Date __________ Class __________

Using Fundamental Trigonometric Identities

LESSON 108

Write the exponential equations in logarithmic form.

1. $6^5 = 7776$ (64)

2. $x^3 = 6859$ (64)

***3.** Let $f(x) = \sin(x)$ and $g(x) = (x - 1)(x + 1)$. Find $g(f(x)) + 1$. (108)

4. **Construction** A construction team has 230 feet of fencing material for which to fence in a rectangular play area. They were told that the play area should be at least 3000 square feet. Find the range of possible widths they could use. (89)

***5.** **Write** Explain in complete sentences what must be done to an equation to vertically stretch the graph. (104)

6. **Lockbox** A homeowner is choosing a combination to the lockbox for the house.Four digits (1–9) can be chosen. How many combinations can be made if a digit cannot be repeated? (33)

***7.** **Generalize** Use the trig ratios $\cos(\theta) = \frac{x}{r}$ and $\sin(\theta) = \frac{y}{r}$ to show that $\frac{1}{1 - \frac{1}{1 + \tan^2(\theta)}} = \csc^2(\theta)$. (108)

8. **Analyze** A quadratic trinomial in standard form is added to another quadratic trinomial in standard form and the result is written in standard form. The leading coefficients of the two trinomials are opposites. What are all the possible types of the resulting polynomial (classified by degree)? (11)

9. **Multiple Choice** Solve $S = B + \frac{1}{2}pl$ for l. Which equation shows the correct solution? (88)

A $l = \frac{1}{2}(S - B)p$ **B** $l = S - B - \frac{1}{2}p$ **C** $l = \frac{2S - B}{p}$ **D** $l = \frac{2S - 2B}{p}$

10. Write a function that has zeros −6, −2, and 1. (35)

***11.** **Formulate** Write a possible rational function that fits these parameters: Vertical asymptotes $x = \pm 2$; slant asymptote $y = -2x + 3$. (107)

12. Use the Binomial Theorem to expand $(2x + y)^2$. (49)

13. **Multiple Choice** Which ordered pair contains a local maximum of $g(x) = 2x^3 - 3x^2 - 12x$? (101)

A (−1, 7) **B** (0, 0) **C** (4, 32) **D** (5, 115)

14. **Analyze** Is the sequence {5, 5, 5, 5} an arithmetic sequence? Why or why not? (92)

15. Use synthetic substitution to find $f(4)$ for $f(x) = 3x^4 + 6x^2 - x - 22$. (51)

16. **Soccer** A drafter is creating the plans for a sport and fitness center, which includes an official size soccer field. On her grid, the units represent yards and the endpoints of a diameter of the center circle are located at (23, −4) and (29, −4). Write an equation for this circle. (91)

© Saxon. All rights reserved.

***17.** Find the real zeros of $y = x^5 - 4x^3 - x^2 + 4$.
(107)

18. Solve $\frac{x+3}{x-6} > 0$ by finding the sign of the numerator and denominator.
(94)

***19.** **Multi-Step** A polynomial equation has roots of 6 and $7i$.
(106)

a. What is the minimum degree of the polynomial? Name the other roots if there are any.

b. What is the simplest polynomial equation with these roots?

c. Give another polynomial equation with these roots.

20. **Coordinate Geometry** Use a table of values to graph $f(x) = |x - 4| + 2$.
(17)

21. Given $a^2 + b^2 = c^2$. Solve for b.
(88)

22. **Physics** Two springs have two different weights attached at the ends. The movement of each weight is modeled by the periodic functions shown, where t is the time in seconds. How often will both weights be at their lowest point at the same time.
(82)

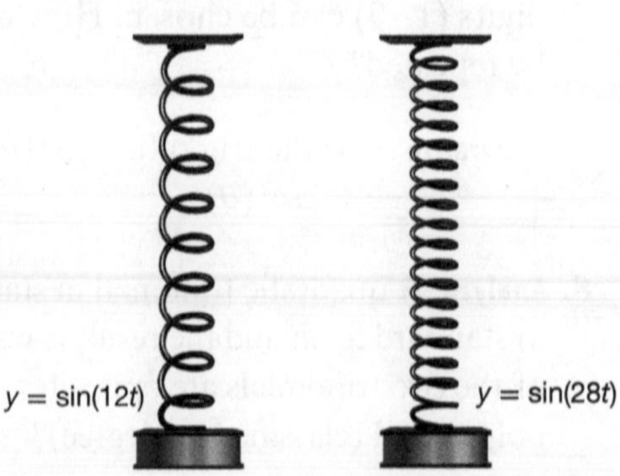

23. **Error Analysis** Two students are subtracting two vectors written as complex numbers but they get different results. Which student made the mistake?
(99)

Student A	Student B
$(3 + 4i) - (-5 + 3i)$ $= (3 - 5) + (4 - 3)i$ $= -2 + i$	$(3 + 4i) - (-5 + 3i)$ $= (3 + 5) + (4 - 3)i$ $= 8 + i$

***24.** **Sound** Two measures of sound are loudness and intensity. They are related by the function $L(I) = 10 \log \frac{I}{I_0}$, where $L(I)$ is loudness in decibels, I is intensity in watts per square meter, and $I_0 \approx 10^{-12}$ watt per square meter, the intensity of a barely audible sound. The loudness of a quiet library is about 40 decibels. Find the intensity that corresponds to a loudness of 40 decibels.
(102)

25. **Geometry** The length of $\overline{BC}$ is four times the length of $\overline{AB}$, and $\frac{1}{AB} + \frac{1}{BC} = \frac{5}{32}$. Find the length of $\overline{AB}$.
(84)

*26. (108) **Error Analysis** A student is simplifying the expression below using trigonometric identities. What mistake did the student make?

$$\frac{1-\cos^2(x)}{1-\dfrac{1}{1+\cot^2(x)}}=\frac{\sin^2(x)}{1-\dfrac{1}{\csc^2(x)}}=\frac{\sin^2(x)}{1-\cos^2(x)}=\frac{\sin^2(x)}{\sin^2(x)}=1$$

Solve.

27. (78) $63x^3 - 7x = 0$

28. (78) $4x^3 + 6x^2 - 40x = 0$

29. (26) A line passes through points $(-2, 4)$ and $(0, 5)$. Write the equation of the line in slope-intercept form.

*30. (103) **Graphing Calculator** Graph $y = 2\sec(x)$ on your graphing calculator. Determine its period and asymptotes.

© Saxon. All rights reserved.

Name ______________________ Date __________ Class __________

Making Graphs and Using Equations of Hyperbolas

LESSON 109

Simplify.

1. (48) $\frac{x+4}{x^2-x-12}+\frac{2x}{x+3}$

2. (48) $\frac{\frac{x-1}{x+5}}{\frac{x+6}{x-3}}$

Convert from Cartesian to polar coordinates.

3. (96) $(-5, -5)$

4. (96) $(0, -4)$

***5.** (109) **Formulate** A hyperbola has asymptotes with equations $y = \pm x$. The graph of the hyperbola crosses the x-axis at $(5, 0)$. Write the equation of the hyperbola.

6. (32) Determine whether the matrices are inverses.

$M = \begin{bmatrix} 10 & -3 \\ 3 & -1 \end{bmatrix}$ $N = \begin{bmatrix} 1 & -3 \\ 3 & -10 \end{bmatrix}$

7. (Inv 9) **Data Analysis** The general sizing chart for infant/toddler shoe sizes is shown to the right. Lana is buying shoes for her 9-month-old brother. What shoe size(s) can she buy? Does this table form a function? Explain.

Age (in months)	Size
$3 \leq x \leq 6$	2
$6 \leq x \leq 9$	3
$9 \leq x \leq 12$	4

8. (101) **Analyze** Explain why the leading coefficient and degree of the highest-degree term of a polynomial function are the only characteristics that determine end behavior.

9. (93) **Error Analysis** To evaluate $\frac{\log 2}{12 \log 1.05}$ with a calculator, a student entered $\log(2) \div 12\log(1.05)$. What is the error? What is a correct expression to enter on a calculator?

***10.** (109) **(Space Science)** A satellite is following a hyperbolic path, and there are two monitoring stations located at the foci of the hyperbola. What data can be used to ensure that the satellite is maintaining its hyperbolic trajectory?

11. (96) **Analyze** Point P has polar coordinates (r, θ). Describe all the polar coordinates of point P that have r as the first coordinate.

Solve.

12. (5) $\frac{1}{4}\begin{bmatrix} 2 & 4 \\ 6 & 8 \end{bmatrix} + \begin{bmatrix} -2 & 1 \\ -\frac{1}{2} & 5 \end{bmatrix}$

13. (84) $\frac{x^2-x-12}{x-2} = 0$

***14.** (108) **Graphing Calculator** Graph $y_1 = \cot^2(x)$ and $y_2 = \csc^2(x)$. Use the information in the graphs to prove the trigonometric identity $1 + \cot^2(x) = \csc^2(x)$.

© Saxon. All rights reserved.

Making Graphs and Using Equations of Hyperbolas

LESSON 109

15. (85) **Construction** The sheet of metal shown is rolled into a cylinder along the longer side. The area of the sheet is 22 square units. Find the radius of the cylinder.

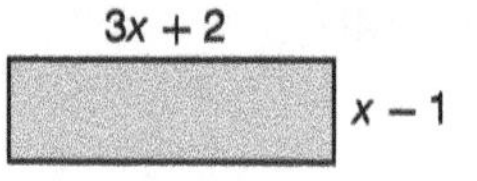

16. (36) Find the equation of the line perpendicular to the graph of $y = 19$ that passes through the point $(6, -5)$.

17. (79) Evaluate the piecewise function $f(x) = \begin{cases} 2 - x \text{ if } x \leq 5 \\ -x^2 \text{ if } 5 < x < 8 \\ 6 \text{ if } 8 \leq x \end{cases}$ for $x = -8$ and $x = 5$.

18. (88) **Error Analysis** A student solved the formula $A = P + Prt$ for P as shown below. What is the error? Solve the formula for P correctly.

$$A = P + Prt$$
$$A - P = Prt$$
$$A - \frac{P}{rt} = P$$

***19.** (108) **Multiple Choice** Which expression is equivalent to $\frac{1}{1 + \tan^2(\theta)}$?

A $\tan^2(\theta)$ **B** $\csc^2(\theta)$ **C** $\sin^2(\theta)$ **D** $\cos^2(\theta)$

20. (46) **Geometry** A wall casts a shadow depending on the angle of the sun. Derive the equation that can be used to find the length of the shadow, L.

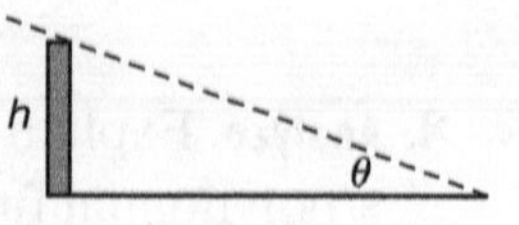

21. (91) **Multiple Choice** Concentric circles have the same center but different radii. Which pair of equations represents a pair of concentric circles?

A $(x - 1)^2 + (y + 2)^2 = 6$ and $(x - 1)^2 + (y + 2)^2 = 6$

B $(x - 1)^2 + (y + 2)^2 = 6$ and $(x - 1)^2 + (y + 2)^2 = 8$

C $(x - 1)^2 + (y + 2)^2 = 6$ and $(x - 2)^2 + (y + 1)^2 = 6$

D $(x - 1)^2 + (y + 2)^2 = 6$ and $(x - 2)^2 + (y + 8)^2 = 12$

***22.** (102) **Population Growth** Based on U.S. Census statistics, the population of New Jersey for the years 1950–1990 can be modeled by the equation $y = 628 + 1842 \ln t$, where $10 \leq t \leq 50$, $t = 10$ represents 1950, and y is the population in thousands. Use the model to approximate the year in which the population of New Jersey reached 7,000,000.

© Saxon. All rights reserved.

23. (93) **Multi-Step** The table below is based on census statistics from India and China.

	China	India
Population in 2000 (to nearest million)	1,267,000,000	1,005,000,000
Average annual increase (1990–2000)	1.04%	1.83%

a. Write a function of the form $y_1 = ab^t$, where y_1 represents China's population t years after 2000.

b. Write a function of the form $y_2 = ab^t$, where y_2 represents India's population t years after 2000.

c. Write and solve an equation to predict the year in which India's population will overtake China's population.

***24.** (107) **Physics** If you throw a ball in the air, the vertical distance d that it travels over time t is found using the equation $d(t) = -4.9t^2 + v_0t + d_0$. The term v_o is the initial speed that the object is thrown, and d_o is the initial height the object is thrown from. The rational function $y = \frac{d(t)}{t}$ is the average speed the object has traveled. Find the slant asymptotes of this equation for the function that has $v_o = 65$ and $d_o = 25$.

***25.** (97) **Write** How is a geometric sequence similar to an arithmetic sequence?

26. (100) **Generalize** An odd function is a function with a graph that is symmetric with respect to the origin. A function is odd if and only if $f(-x) = -f(x)$. Show that rational functions of the form $f(x) = \frac{1}{x(2n + 1)}$, for positive integers n, are odd functions.

***27.** (105) **Physics** The number of feet an object falls during each second after it is dropped is given by the sequence 16, 48, 80, 112, ... It takes between 8 and 9 seconds for an object that falls off the top of the John Hancock Center in Chicago to hit the ground. Show how to use an arithmetic series to estimate the height of the John Hancock Center.

28. (28) Identify any excluded values and then simplify the expression $\frac{4x + 28}{x^2 - 49}$.

***29.** (106) Determine where the graph of $y = (x + 4)(x + 4)(x + 4)(x - 2)(x - 6)(x - 6)$ passes through the x-axis and where it just touches the x-axis.

***30.** (109) The distance between the two foci of a hyperbola is 10. The slopes of the asymptotes are $\pm\frac{3}{4}$. Write one possible equation for such a hyperbola.

© Saxon. All rights reserved.

Name ______________________________ Date ____________ Class ____________

Graphing Logarithmic Funons

LESSON 110

***1.** (85) Use the Rational Root Theorem to find the roots of
$y = 12x^{11} - 23x^{10} + 10x^9 - 12x^8 + 23x^7 - 10x^6 - 12x^5 + 23x^4 - 10x^3 + 12x^2 - 23x + 10.$

2. (92) **Multiple Choice** The first term of an arithmetic sequence is -12 and the fifteenth term is -54. What is the common difference?

A -4.4 **B** -3 **C** 3 **D** 4.4

Write the polynomials in standard form.

3. (27) $16x = 2 - x^2 + y$

4. (27) $-9 + 13x = 4x^2 - y$

5. (37) For what values of x is the denominator of the expression $\frac{3}{x^2 + x - 30}$ zero?

6. (106) **Multi-Step** A shipping crate has dimensions of x, $x - 1$, and $x - 2$.

a. What is the simplest polynomial function that represents the volume of the crate?

b. Describe the possible zeros of the function.

c. What are the dimensions of the crate if the volume is 120 cubic units?

***7.** (110) **Analyze** A chemical process goes at a logarithmic pace to create a chemical by-product. How long will it take to go from 1 unit of by-product to 2 units? Express your answer as a function of the base of the logarithm.

8. (14) **Analyze** Find the determinant of the multiplicative identity matrix $\begin{bmatrix} 1 & 0 \\ 0 & 1 \end{bmatrix}$.

***9.** (84) **Optics** The focal length of a lens, f, the distance from the lens to the object, o, and the distance from the lens to the image, i, are related by the formula $\frac{1}{f} = \frac{1}{o} + \frac{1}{i}$. Find i if f is 4 cm and o is 48 cm.

***10.** (32) **Graphing Calculator** Solve the system using a graphing calculator.

$$\begin{aligned} x + y + z &= -2 \\ 3x + 3y + z &= -18 \\ 4x + 2y + z &= -20 \end{aligned}$$

11. (42) Find the number of outfits possible using 2 of 4 shirts and 2 of 3 pants.

***12.** (102) **Motor Vehicle Ownership** The number of motor vehicles owned in U.S. households during the years 1970–2000 can be modeled by the equation $y = -82{,}110 + 70{,}059 \ln t$, $10 \leq t \leq 40$, where $t = 10$ represents 1970, and y is the number of motor vehicles owned in households, in thousands. Use the model to approximate the year in which the number of motor vehicles owned in U.S. households reached 100 million.

***13.** (109) **Generalize** A hyperbola has the form $ax^2 + by^2 + cx + dy + e = 0$. Complete the square for the x-term.

14. (53) Let $f(x) = 12\log(4x)$ and $g(x) = \frac{1}{\sqrt{x}}$. Find the x-intercept for $f(g(x))$.

© Saxon. All rights reserved.

15. **Analyze** How can the equation of a circle located at the origin be derived from the equation of a circle located at any point?
(91)

16. A club's membership increases 4% each year. There are 800 members. How long until it reaches 1000?
(93)

Divide using synthetic division.

17. $x^4 - 1$ by $x + 1$
(51)

18. $x^3 - 7$ by $x - 5$
(51)

***19.** **Error Analysis** A student is finding the equations of the asymptotes for the hyperbola with following equation: $\frac{(x-15)^2}{9^2} - \frac{(y+5)^2}{7^2} = 1$. What is her mistake?
(109)

Calculate the slopes: $m = \pm\frac{7}{9}$

Use the slope formula:

$\frac{7}{9} = \frac{y-5}{x-15}$ $\quad y = \frac{7}{9}x - \frac{20}{3}$ $\quad\Big|\quad$ $-\frac{7}{9} = \frac{y-5}{x-15}$ $\quad y = -\frac{7}{9}x - \frac{50}{3}$

Use the triangle to solve problems 20 and 21.

20. Find the cosecant of $\angle A$.
(46)

21. Find the secant of $\angle A$.
(46)

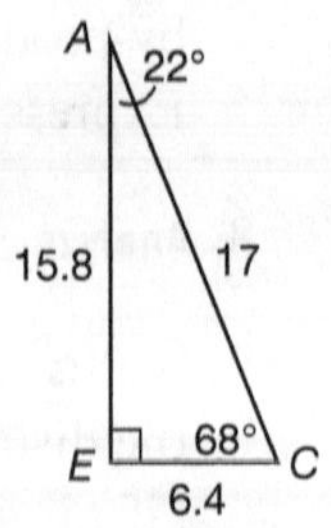

22. **Multiple Choice** What are the solutions of $x^2 + 4x < 5$?
(89)
A $-5 < x < 1$ **B** $-1 < x < 5$ **C** $x < -5$ or $x > 1$ **D** $x < -1$ or $x > 5$

***23.** **Model** Do the trigonometric identities hold true even if each function is phase shifted by angle θ? Provide examples to support your claim.
(108)

24. **Geometry** A pyramid with a square base has a height of $3x$ and a volume of $x^3 + 4x^2 + 4x$. Find the dimensions of the square base.
(85)

***25.** **Algebra** The sum of the first n consecutive integers can be found by using the function $f(n) = \frac{1}{2}n(n + 1)$. The sum of the first n consecutive odd integers can be found by using the function $f(n) = n^2$. Write the rational function that is the ratio of the sum of the first n consecutive integers to the sum of the first n consecutive odd integers. Graph the function to find the horizontal asymptote. Explain the significance of the asymptote.
(107)

© Saxon. All rights reserved.

26. **Error Analysis** Two students are finding the period of $y = \cos\left(\frac{2}{3}x\right)$ but get different results. Which student made the mistake?
(86)

Student A	Student B
$\text{Period} = \frac{2\pi}{b} = \frac{2\pi}{\frac{2}{3}} = \frac{6\pi}{2} = 3\pi$	$\text{Period} = \frac{2\pi}{b} = \frac{2\pi}{\frac{2}{3}} = \frac{4\pi}{3}$

27. **Jewelry Making** A jeweler is changing the angle of a facet for a diamond ring from θ to φ. The vertical distances change as shown in the diagram, while the width remains constant. Derive the function that the jeweler can use to find values of θ when the other values are known.
(90)

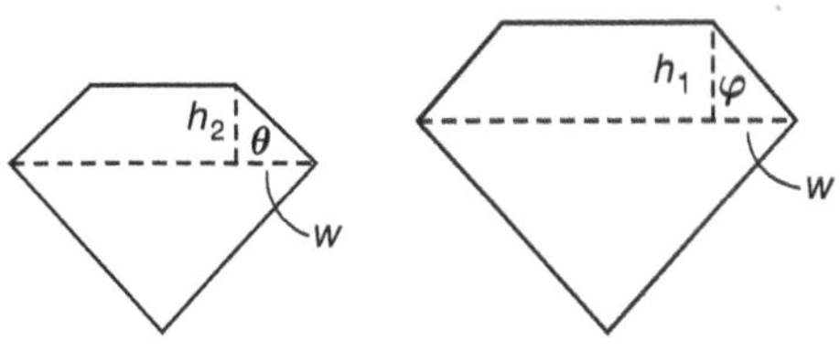

28. **Finance** The Dow Jones Industrial Average (DJIA) is an indicator of stock prices. The quarterly high DJIA for 1999–2003 can be modeled by $f(x) = 0.195x^4 - 5.035x^3 + 6.205x^2 + 338.331x + 10219$, where $x = 1$ represents the first quarter (January–March 1999), $x = 2$ represents the second quarter (April–June 1999), and so on, with $x = 20$ representing the last quarter (October–December 2003). Use the model to approximate the highest quarterly Dow Jones Industrial Average during 1999–2003. Based on the model, in which quarter did it occur?
(101)

Solve by factoring.

29. $0 = x^2 + 4x - 21$
(35)

30. $x^2 - 16 = 0$
(35)

© Saxon. All rights reserved.

Name ______________________ Date __________ Class __________

Transforming Polynomial Functions

LESSON 111

1. (26) A line has slope -4 and passes through $(6, 8)$. What is the equation of the line written in slope intercept form?

*2. (111) **Baseball Attendance** The *cumulative* attendance at home baseball games for the years 1996–2005 can be modeled by $f(x) = 1.922x^4 - 36.769x^3 + 132.212x^2 + 3558.615x - 11$, where x is the number of years since 1995 and $f(x)$ is in thousands. (Cumulative means the statistic for each year is the sum of that year's attendance and all the previous years' attendances.) Describe the transformation $g(x) = f(x - 1)$ by writing the rule for $g(x)$ and explaining the change in the context of the problem.

*3. (99) Use matrix multiplication to show that the dot product of two vectors that are perpendicular to each other is zero.

*4. (110) **Multiple Choice** Which of the following functions has a graph with greater y-values?
A $y = \ln(x)$ **B** $y = \log_2(x)$ **C** $y = \log_{20}(x)$ **D** $y = \log_{15}(x)$

*5. (Inv 11) Given the complex number $8 + 24i$ written in $a + bi$ form, convert it to the trigonometric and polar forms.

6. (10) Solve and graph the compound inequality $-8 < 4(x + 1)$ and $12 > 4x$.

7. (89) **Error Analysis** Explain the error or errors a student made in graphing $x^2 + 1 > y$.

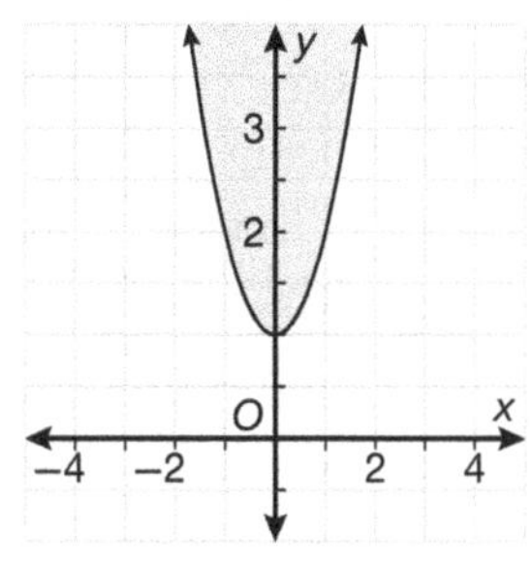

8. (90) **Multiple Choice** Which of the following has a period of $\frac{1}{5}\pi$?
A $y = 5\tan(x)$ **B** $y = \tan(x - 5)$ **C** $y = \tan(5x)$ **D** $y = \tan\left(\frac{x}{5}\right)$

*9. (109) **Geometry** In hyperbolic geometry, $\tanh(x) = \frac{\sinh(x)}{\cosh(x)}$. Show that $1 - \tanh^2(x) = \frac{1}{\cosh^2(x)}$.

10. (92) **Theater** The number of seats in the first 14 rows of the center orchestra aisle of the Marquis Theater in New York City form an arithmetic sequence. The third row has 13 seats and the last row has 24 seats. Find the number of seats in the 7th row.

11. (50) **Temperature** The formula $C = \frac{5}{9}(F - 32)$ relates Celsius temperature C and Fahrenheit temperature F. Solve the formula for F. Then write and solve a new equation to find the number that represents the same temperature on both scales. (Hint: Substitute x for both C and F.)

12. (93) **Analyze** Cobalt-58ml has a half-life of 9.04 hours. Calculate mentally how long it would take for 4 grams of cobalt-58ml to decay to 1 gram. Explain your method.

© Saxon. All rights reserved.

13. (95) **Construction** Use the Remainder Theorem to determine the volume of the box if $x = 3$.

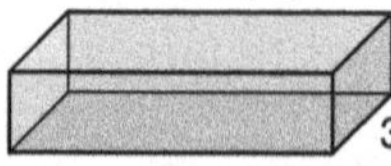

14. (29) How many solutions does the system of equations have, and what type of solution is it?

$$x + 5y - 2z = 1$$
$$-x - 2y + z = 6$$
$$-2x - 7y + 3z = 7$$

15. (97) **Write** Describe how to find the nth term of a geometric sequence, given the first and second terms.

*16. (110) **Predict** Which function has the greater x-intercept, $f(x) = \log_b(x)$ or $g(x) = \log_b(\log_b(x))$? What can you conclude about the function with the greater x-intercept.

17. (96) **Multi-Step** Complete parts a–c to graph a polar equation and analyze the graph.

a. Convert the Cartesian equation $y = x^2$ to a polar equation by using $x = r\cos\theta$ and $y = r\sin\theta$. (*Hint*: Factor and then eliminate the case $r = 0$.)

b. Graph the polar equation on a calculator, using these window settings: $\theta\text{min} = 0$, $\theta\text{max} = \frac{\pi}{2}$, $\theta\text{step} = \frac{\pi}{24}$, $X\text{min} = -6$, $X\text{max} = 6$, $Y\text{min} = -1$, $Y\text{max} = 7$. Do you get the same graph as the graph of $y = x^2$? Explain why or why not.

c. If $\theta\text{min} = 0$ is used as a window setting, what is the least value of θmax needed to get the same graph as the graph of $y = x^2$? Explain.

*18. (98) Write the equation $5x^2 + 2y^2 = 10$ as an ellipse in standard form.

*19. (100) **Graphing Calculator** Graph the function $y = \frac{x^2 - 7x - 60}{x + 3}$ on a graphing calculator. Identify any vertical asymptote(s).

20. (102) **Analyze** Without graphing, determine the point in which the graphs of $y = \log x$ and $y = 3\log x$ intersect. Explain your reasoning.

21. (61) Determine whether the linear binomial $x + 3$ is a factor of the polynomial $P(x) = x^3 + 19x^2 + 79x - 35$.

*22. (111) **Justify** Give an example of a polynomial function of degree 3 or higher whose reflection across the x-axis is the same as its reflection across the y-axis. Justify your answer.

23. (35) Write a quadratic function that has zeros 18 and 3.

24. (85) Let $f(x) = x^3 - 125$ and $g(x) = 2x - 1$. Find the roots of $f(g(x))$.

© Saxon. All rights reserved.

Find the roots of the equations.

25. (90) $0 = 3x^3 + 2x^2 + 1$

26. (90) $0 = 5x^4 + 2x^3 + x^2$

Solve the equations.

***27.** (102) $\log(12x - 11) = \log(3x + 13)$

***28.** (102) $\log_2(x - 4) = 6$

29. (80) Scores from a test have a mean of 87 and a standard deviation of 4.3. A randomly selected test has a score of 82.5. Find the z-score for this test.

30. (33) **Probability** Five folded pieces of paper are in a hat. Three are to be chosen at random. Is it a dependent or independent event if the papers are not returned to the hat once they are chosen?

© Saxon. All rights reserved.

Name ______________________ Date ____________ Class ____________

Using Sum and Difference Identities

LESSON 112

Write the expression in simplest form.

1. (40) $\frac{3}{\sqrt[4]{144}}$

2. (40) $\frac{\sqrt[3]{9}}{\sqrt[5]{27}}$

3. (82) **Data Analysis** The number of days it takes to complete a year for different planets is shown in the table. Let Earth's yearly motion be modeled by $y = \sin(0.017x)$. How would you model Venus' motion?

Planet	Days in a Year
Mercury	88.03
Venus	224.63
Earth	365.25
Mars	686.67
Jupiter	4331.87
Saturn	10760.27
Uranus	30681.00
Neptune	60193.20

4. (18) Convert 30 hours into seconds.

***5.** (112) Find the exact value of sin 75°.

***6.** (106) **Graphing Calculator** Graph $y = x^7 - 3x^4 - 2$ and describe the solutions of $x^7 - 3x^4 - 2 = 0$. Round real solutions to the nearest thousandth if needed.

7. (11) **Geometry** Write a polynomial in standard form that represents the shaded area formed by the two rectangles.

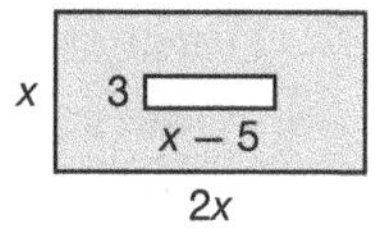

8. (95) **Multiple Choice** Which of the following polynomials has $P(3) = 533{,}386$?

A $P(x) = x^{12} + 3x^6 + 5x^2 - 100x + 13$

B $P(x) = x^{14} + 3x^7 + 5x^2 - 100x + 13$

C $P(x) = x^{11} + 3x^5 + 5x^2 - 100x + 13$

D $P(x) = x^9 + 3x^5 + 5x^4 - 100x + 13$

***9.** (109) **Formulate** A hyperbola with vertical orientation has asymptotes with equations $y = \frac{4}{3}x - \frac{11}{3}$ and $y = -\frac{4}{3}x + \frac{29}{3}$. Write the equation of the hyperbola.

10. (94) **Error Analysis** Find the error(s) in the sign chart for $\frac{x+4}{(x-5)(x-1)} < 0$. What is the solution of the inequality?

	$x < -4$	$-4 < x < 1$	$1 < x < 5$	$x > 5$
	-5	0	3	8
$x + 4$	–	+	+	+
$x - 5$	–	–	–	+
$x - 1$	+	–	+	+
Value of expression	+	–	–	+

© Saxon. All rights reserved.

11. (98) **Analyze** Describe a method for converting a polynomial of the form $ax^2 + by^2 + cx + dy + e = 0$ to an ellipse in standard form, assuming the graph is an ellipse. Use this method with the polynomial $x^2 + 9y^2 - 10x - 18y + 7 = 0$.

***12.** (111) **Multi-Step** $f(x) = x^3 - 6x^2 + 4$ has turning points at (0, 4) and (4, −28). Identify the turning points of each function and justify your answers.

a. $\frac{1}{4}f(x)$ **b.** $f\left(\frac{1}{4}x\right)$ **c.** $f\left(x - \frac{1}{4}\right)$

13. (31) Multiply, then evaluate for $a = 2$, $b = 3$. $\frac{6a^2b}{4ab} \cdot \frac{3ab^3}{5a^2b^2}$

14. (99) **Navigation** An airplane travels 225 mph 30° south of due west for two hours. The pilot makes an adjustment so that the plane then flies for another three hours at 268 mph 20° north of due west. What is the distance and direction of the plane from its original position?

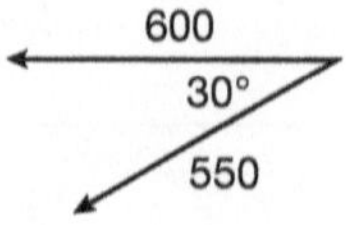

***15.** (111) **Error Analysis** To graph $g(x) = (x + 4)^3 + 1$, a student shifted the graph of $f(x) = x^3 + 1$ right 4 units. What is the error?

16. (100) **Generalize** Show that for rational functions $y = \frac{1}{x} + n$, with constant n, the horizontal asymptote is $y = n$.

17. (102) **Unions** From the 1930s on, labor union membership in the U.S. grew dramatically. During the years 1935–1955, labor union membership in the U.S. can be modeled by the equation $y = -4.4 + 12.6 \ln t$, where $5 \le t \le 25$, $t = 5$ represents 1935, and y is the percent of the U.S. labor force that were union members. Use the model to approximate the year in which union membership in the U.S. reached 30%.

***18.** (104) **Savings Accounts** A share certificate pays 5% interest, compounded yearly. The function $A(x) = P \cdot 1.05^x$ can be used to calculate the amount in the account, $A(x)$, after x years with the original amount, placed in the account, P. Use the function $f(x) = 1.05^x$ to sketch a graph of the equation $A(x) = P \cdot 1.05^x$ if the original amount in the account is $50,000.

19. (96) **Analyze** P has polar coordinates (r, θ). Write polar coordinates for P that have a different 1st coordinate.

***20.** (112) **Multiple Choice** Given that $\tan A = \frac{1}{2}$ and $\tan B = \frac{1}{4}$, what is the value of $\tan(A + B)$?

A $\frac{2}{9}$ **B** $\frac{2}{7}$ **C** $\frac{2}{3}$ **D** $\frac{6}{7}$

***21.** (106) **Farming** A grain silo is shaped like a cylinder with a hemisphere on top. The height of the cylindrical part is 28 feet. The radius of the hemisphere is x feet. The volume of the entire silo is 8550π cubic feet. Find the radius of the silo.

22. (37) Find any values of x for which the following expression is undefined: $\frac{1}{x^3 + 4x^2 - 21x}$.

© Saxon. All rights reserved.

*23. (112) **Write** What is the value of $\cos\frac{2\pi}{5}\cos\frac{3\pi}{5} - \sin\frac{2\pi}{5}\sin\frac{3\pi}{5}$? Explain how to answer without a calculator.

*24. (105) **Organizing** A homeowner organized wooden planks in his backyard into 12 rows where each row has 2 more planks than the row above it. How many planks are there if the bottom row has 32 planks?

25. (88) Given $d = \sqrt{l^2 + w^2 + h^2}$, find l.

26. (77) In $\triangle LMN$, $LM = 24$, $MN = 29$, and $m\angle M = 65°$. Find LN.

27. (35) Write a cubic function that has zeros 0, 16, and −9.

28. (97) **Salaries** An employee's salary is structured so that he earns $25,925 in the first year and a 2.75% raise each year thereafter. How much can the employee expect to earn in his 10th year?

29. (32) Solve the system. $\begin{aligned} y + z + w &= 6 \\ -y + 3z - w &= 2 \\ 2y - z + w &= 5 \end{aligned}$

30. (87) Evaluate $\log_{10}(15x)^2$ when $x = 1$.

© Saxon. All rights reserved.

[illegible]

23. Why [illegible] without a calculator.

24. [illegible] A homeowner organized wooden planks in his backyard into 12 rows where each row has [illegible] than the row above it. How many planks are there if the bottom row has [illegible] planks?

25. Given [illegible]

26. In $\triangle MNP$, [illegible] and [illegible] Find [illegible]

27. Write a cubic function that [illegible] and [illegible]

28. Salaries An employee's salary is [illegible] so that he earns [illegible] in the first year and a [illegible] each year thereafter. How much can the employee expect to earn in his 10th year?

29. Solve the system: [illegible]

30. Evaluate [illegible] when [illegible]

Name ______________________ Date __________ Class __________

Using Geometric Series

LESSON **113**

***1.** (113) **Verify** Show numerically that a convergent geometric series has a sum of 125 if the first term is 25 and the common ratio is $\frac{4}{5}$.

2. (28) Identify any excluded values, then simplify the expression $\frac{x^2 + 4x - 12}{x^2 + 6x}$.

***3.** (111) **Baseball Attendance** The season attendance at Baltimore Orioles home games for the years 1996-2005 can be modeled by $f(x) = 7.300x^3 - 116.411x^2 + 363.122x + 3400$, where x is the number of years since 1995 and $f(x)$ is in thousands. Describe the transformation $g(x) = f(x) + 100$ by writing the rule for $g(x)$ and explaining the change in the context of the problem.

4. (48) Simplify: $\dfrac{\dfrac{x}{x+2}}{2x + \dfrac{x}{5}}$.

5. (37) Add: $\frac{5}{2x^8} + \frac{7}{2x^8}$.

6. (31) Simplify: $\frac{x(y^3 + 6)}{4x + 8} \cdot \frac{x + 2}{x^2y^2} \div \frac{y}{x}$.

***7.** (112) **Travel** The London Eye is a Ferris wheel with an approximate diameter of 440 feet, making one full rotation in 30 minutes. The diagram represents the London Eye centered on a coordinate grid. From this view, the Ferris wheel rotates counterclockwise. To the nearest tenth, what will be the coordinates of point P in one minute? Assume a constant rate. Show how you arrived at your answer.

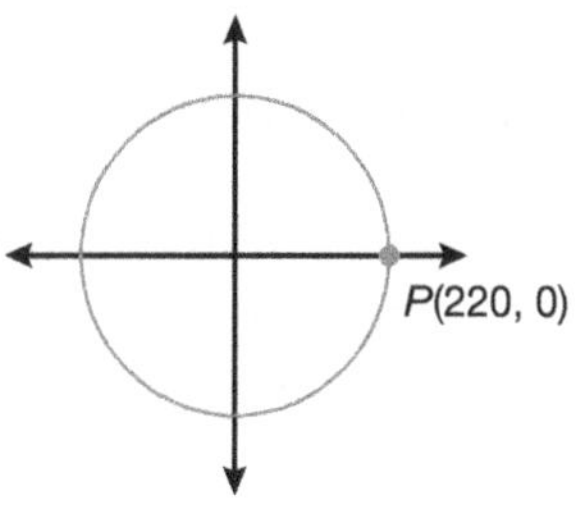

8. (88) Given $A = \frac{1}{2}(b_1 + b_2)h$, find b_1.

***9.** (112) **Error Analysis** Given that $\sin A = \frac{4}{5}$ and $90° < A < 270°$, a student found $\cos A$ as shown below. What is the error? What is the correct value of $\cos A$?

$$x^2 + y^2 = r^2$$
$$x^2 + y^2 = 52$$
$$x = \sqrt{25 - 16} = 3$$
$$\cos A = \frac{x}{r} = \frac{3}{5}$$

10. (12) **Geometry** Write the equation for the area of a triangle as a joint variation.

11. (83) **Write** Write a quadratic equation whose roots are 4 and 1.

12. (89) **Model** Sketch a system of inequalities, which includes at least one quadratic inequality, such that the system has no solutions.

Find the mean, median, and mode for the following sets of data.

13. (25) 18, 20, 14, 15, 20, 17, 16

14. (25) 21, 23, 22, 25, 28, 31, 28

© Saxon. All rights reserved.

***15.** (30) **Graphing Calculator** Graph the function $y = -2x^2 - 6x + 3$ using your graphing calculator. Determine the vertex and axis of symmetry.

16. (37) Find the LCM. $\frac{1}{2x^2 - 3x - 2} - \frac{1}{x^2 - 4}$

***17.** (102) **Estimate** Estimate the solution to $\log_2 25x = \log_2 151$. Explain your method.

***18.** (107) **Multi-Step** Let $f(x) = x^2 - 1$ and $g(x) = x^2 - 1$.

a. Find $\frac{x^5}{f(g(x))}$.

b. Find all asymptotes and holes for $\frac{x^5}{f(g(x))}$.

19. (Inv 8) Estimate the area under the curve $y = \frac{1}{2}x^2 + 4x + 1$ from $0 \le x \le 4$. Use 4 partitions.

***20.** (113) **Multi-Step** A job-seeker has offers from two companies. Job A offers a first-year salary of \$31,225 with a 1.85% raise every year thereafter. Job B offers a first-year salary of \$28,995 with a 2.25% raise each year thereafter. With which job will he make more money all together after 15 years? What is the difference?

21. (49) Use the Binomial Theorem to expand $(n + 2m)^4$.

***22.** (105) **Exercise** An athlete is on a 12-day jogging plan. On the plan, the athlete is to jog 3 miles on the first day, and on each day thereafter, jog 0.75 miles longer than the previous day. How many total miles will the athlete have jogged while on the plan?

23. (21) Solve the system $\begin{matrix} 10x - 2y = 16 \\ 5x + 3y = -12 \end{matrix}$ by substitution.

***24.** (113) **Salaries** A salary is structured so that the employee earns a 1.5% raise each year after the first year. How much did the employee earn in the first year if his total after 10 years was \$393,967.18?

25. (90) Determine the period of $y = 3\tan(2x) + 6$.

26. (93) **Multiple Choice** A substance has a half-life of 16 years. Which equation can be solved to find the approximate number of years t that it will take for 2 grams of the substance to decay to 0.5 gram?

A $2 = e^{-0.5t}$

B $2 - 0.5 = e^{-16t}$

C $0.25 = e^{-0.04332t}$

D $0.5 = e^{-0.04332t}$

27. (94) **Probability** **a.** Write a simplified rational expression to represent the probability of a randomly selected point in the larger circle also being in the smaller circle.

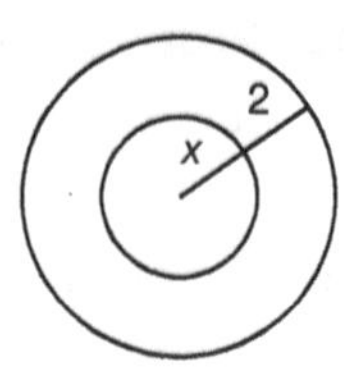

b. Write and solve a rational inequality to represent the values of x for which the probability is less than or equal to 0.25.

© Saxon. All rights reserved.

***28.** (113) **Multiple Choice** Which series converges?

A $2 + 4 + 8 + 16 + \ldots$ B $16 + 8 + 4 + 2 + \ldots$

C $3 + 15 + 75 + 375 + \ldots$ D $3 + (-15) + 75 + (-375) + \ldots$

29. (97) **Analyze** When finding the *n*th term of a geometric sequence, given any two terms, what must be true about the given terms in order for there to be two possible values for the common ratio? Why?

30. (99) **Analyze** Describe geometrically what the matrix equation below shows.

$$\begin{bmatrix} |\vec{A}|\cos(60) \\ |\vec{A}|\sin(60) \end{bmatrix} + \begin{bmatrix} |\vec{B}|\cos(30) \\ |\vec{B}|\sin(30) \end{bmatrix} = \begin{bmatrix} |\vec{A}|\cos(60) + |\vec{B}|\cos(30) \\ |\vec{A}|\sin(60) + |\vec{B}|\sin(30) \end{bmatrix}$$

© Saxon. All rights reserved.

Name ______________________________ Date __________ Class __________

Identifying Conic Sections

LESSON 114

1. Solve for matrix X. $\begin{bmatrix} 1 & 5 \\ 0 & -2 \end{bmatrix} X = \begin{bmatrix} 3 & -1 & 0 \\ 6 & 8 & 4 \end{bmatrix}$
(32)

2. Identify the values for which $y = \frac{1}{2}\tan(2x)$ is undefined.
(90)

Simplify each expression.

3. $\sqrt[3]{-125}$
(40)

4. $\sqrt[3]{12} \cdot \sqrt[3]{18}$
(40)

*5. **Baseball Salaries** The total payroll of a baseball team for the years 1996–2005 can be modeled by $f(x) = 0.048x^3 + 0.605x^2 + 5.649x + 45$, where x is the number of years since 1995 and $f(x)$ is in millions of dollars. Describe the transformation $g(x) = f(x) - 20$ by writing the rule for $g(x)$ and explaining the change in the context of the problem.
(111)

6. **Multi-Step** A line passed through points $(-2, 4)$ and $(0, 5)$. Write the equation of the line in slope-intercept form. Then, determine the x and y-intercepts.
(26)

7. **Write** Explain what must be done to an equation to horizontally shift the graph to the right.
(104)

8. **Physics** A satellite in circular orbit moving at speed v has an acceleration a of $\frac{v^2}{r}$, where r is the radius of the circular orbit. Write and graph the family of functions for calculating the acceleration for $v = 1, 2, 3, 4$, and 5. At what radius does the acceleration range from $a = 0.5$ to 12.5?
(100)

*9. **Write** An equation of a conic section written in general form has $B^2 - 4AC < 0$. Explain why you need more information to identify the conic section.
(114)

*10. **Carousel** A carousel's path can be modeled by the equation $x^2 + y^2 - 10x - 10y - 575 = 0$. Write the equation in standard form.
(114)

Evaluate.

11. $\sum_{k=1}^{20}(0.75k - 5)$
(105)

12. $\sum_{k=2}^{7}(8 + 5k)$
(105)

*13. **Graphing Calculator** Graph $y = 6\cot(x)$ on a calculator. Determine its period and asymptotes.
(103)

14. **Analyze** For what values of x is the equation $\log x^2 = 2\log x$ true? Explain why the equations $\log x^2 = 2$ and $2\log x = 2$ are not equivalent.
(102)

15. **Coordinate Geometry** The points $(1, -5)$, $(2, -10)$, $(3, -20)$, and $(4, -40)$ represent the first four terms of a geometric sequence. What is the common ratio? What is the y-coordinate when the x-coordinate is 6?
(97)

© Saxon. All rights reserved.

*16. **Multiple Choice** Which is the standard form of the equation $x^2 - 4x - 8y - 84 = 0$?
(114)

A $(x-2)^2 = 8(y+11)$ **B** $\frac{1}{8}(x-2)^2 = y+11$

C $8(x-2)^2 = y+11$ **D** $(x-2)^2 = \frac{1}{8}(y+11)$

17. Solve the system of equations: $\begin{matrix} 4x - 8y + 2z = 10 \\ -3x + y - 2z = 6 \\ -2x + 4y - z = 8 \end{matrix}$.
(29)

18. **Business** The profits in thousands of dollars for a business over x years can be approximated by $f(x) = x^4 - 37x^3 + 406x^2 - 1068x - 1512$. The company broke even in the 18th year of business. What other years did they break even?
(106)

19. **Multi-Step** Silver-101 has a half-life of 11.1 minutes.
(93)

a. Use the natural decay function $N(t) = N_0e^{-kt}$ to find the decay constant k for silver-101.

b. Write the natural decay function for silver-101 and solve for t to find how long it would take 5 grams to decay to 1 gram.

20. **Write** Explain why a polynomial function that has exactly n distinct real zeros must have exactly $n - 1$ turning points.
(101)

21. Let $f(x) = \frac{1}{x^2 - 1}$ and $g(x) = \csc(x)$. Find $f(g(x)) + 1$.
(108)

*22. Find a_1 of an arithmetic sequence that $a_9 = 60$ and $a_{13} = 8$.
(92)

*23. **International Landmarks** The first level of the Eiffel Tower is about 57 meters above the ground. Suppose a ball is dropped from this level and rebounds 30% of its previous height after each bounce.
(113)

a. Use summation notation to write an infinite geometric series to represent the total distance the ball travels after it initially hits the ground. Keep in mind the ball travels both down and up on each bounce.

b. Find the sum of the series from part a. Round to the nearest tenth.

24. The distance between the two foci of a hyperbola is 26. The equations of the asymptotes are $y = \frac{5}{12}x - \frac{20}{3}$ and $y = -\frac{5}{12}x - \frac{10}{3}$. Write the equation of the hyperbola.
(109)

25. **Geometry** The area of a circle is given by $A = \pi r^2$. Solve the formula for r. If the ratio of areas of two circles is 2:1, what is the ratio of the radii?
(88)

*26. **Error Analysis** Explain and correct the error a student made finding the sum of the infinite geometric series $5 + \frac{15}{2} + \frac{45}{4} + \ldots$.
(113)

Student's work: $S = \frac{5}{1 - \frac{3}{2}} = \frac{5}{-\frac{1}{2}} = -10$

© Saxon. All rights reserved.

27. (105) **Multiple Choice** Which series is not an arithmetic series?

A $\sum_{k=1}^{5} 16k$ **B** $\sum_{k=1}^{5} 16k + 2$ **C** $\sum_{k=1}^{5} 16^k$ **D** $\sum_{k=1}^{5} \frac{1}{16}k$

28. (49) 1 in 3 people that enter a post office wears glasses. At noon, 4 people enter. What is the probability that 2 of the 4 people are wearing glasses?

29. (98) **Error Analysis** A student writes the equation $16x^2 + 9y^2 = 144$ in standard form. What is his mistake?

$$16x^2 + 9y^2 = 144 \longrightarrow \frac{16}{144}x^2 + \frac{9}{144}y^2 = 1 \longrightarrow \frac{x^2}{16} + \frac{y^2}{9} = 1 \longrightarrow \frac{x^2}{4^2} + \frac{y^2}{3^2} = 1$$

***30.** (112) **Estimate** Without using a calculator, estimate the coordinates of the image point that results when the point (1, 1) is rotated 47° counterclockwise about the origin. Explain your reasoning.

© Saxon. All rights reserved.

Name ______________________ Date ___________ Class ___________

Finding Double-Angle and Half-Angle Identities

LESSON 115

1. (107) **Analyze** In the rational function $f(x) = \frac{g(x)}{h(x)}$, if polynomial $g(x)$ is of degree $3m + 1$, what must the degree of $h(x)$ be for $f(x)$ to have a slant asymptote?

Factor completely.

2. (23) $x^2 - 9x - 10$

3. (23) $4ax + ax^2 - 5a$

4. (Inv 10) **Model** Write and graph the polar equation of a rose with 5 petals, each of length 4.

***5.** (115) **Soccer** The horizontal distance x traveled by an object kicked from ground level with an initial speed v and angle θ is given by $x = \frac{1}{32}v^2 \sin 2\theta$. A soccer player would like to determine the maximum distance her ball will travel depending on the angle of the ball leaving the ground. She knows she can kick with an initial velocity of 80 feet per second.

a. Find the distance traveled for an angle of 30°, 45°, 70°, and 90°.

b. Which angle maximizes the distance? Use the value of $\sin 2\theta$ to explain.

***6.** (108) **Coordinate Geometry** Graph $y_1 = 1 + \sec^2(x)\sin^2(x)$ and $y_2 = \tan^2(x)$. Use the information in the graphs to prove the following: $\sec^2(x)\sin^2(x) = \tan^2(x)$.

7. (55) Gisella spins a spinner with equal-sized sections numbered 1–6. In one spin, what is the likelihood that the spinner will stop on an even number?

Write the exponential equation in logarithmic form.

8. (64) $16^4 = 65536$

9. (64) $3^{14} = 4782969$

10. (96) **Geometry** Describe the geometric figure represented by the polar equation $r = 4$.

***11.** (114) **Recreation** A bungee jumper's path can be modeled by the equation $x^2 - 10x - 12y - 95 = 0$.

a. What conic section models the situation?

b. Write the equation in standard form.

Divide using long division.

12. (38) $4x^4 + 5x - 4$ by $x^2 - 3x + 2$

13. (38) $x^3 - 2$ by $x - 5$

14. (97) **Error Analysis** Explain and correct the error a student made in finding the 8th term of the geometric sequence 2, −10, 50, −250, …

$$a_8 = 2(-5)^8$$
$$a_8 = 2(390{,}625) = 781{,}250$$

***15.** (115) **Justify** Use half-angle identities to find the exact value of cos 112.5°. Show your work.

© Saxon. All rights reserved.

16. Use an inverse matrix to solve the linear system. $\begin{aligned} 4x - y &= 10 \\ -7x - 2y &= -25 \end{aligned}$
(32)

17. **Multiple Choice** A polynomial equation has roots of $1 + 2i$, 0, and $3i$. What is the minimum degree of the polynomial?
(106)

A 3 **B** 4 **C** 5 **D** 6

***18.** Which of the following are the equations for the asymptotes of $\frac{(x-9)^2}{12^2} - \frac{(y-13)^2}{7^2} = 1$?
(109)

A $y = \frac{12}{7}x - \frac{17}{7}$; $y = -\frac{12}{7}x + \frac{199}{7}$ **B** $y = \frac{7}{12}x + \frac{31}{4}$; $y = -\frac{7}{12}x + \frac{73}{4}$

C $y = \frac{12}{7}x + \frac{17}{7}$; $y = -\frac{12}{7}x - \frac{199}{7}$ **D** $y = \frac{7}{12}x - \frac{31}{4}$; $y = -\frac{7}{12}x - \frac{73}{4}$

***19.** **Analyze** Without dividing, how can you tell if the common ratio of a geometric sequence is positive or negative?
(97)

20. Convert $\log_8 (32x)^4$ to base e. Then evaluate when $x = 5$.
(87)

21. Solve $4x^2 + 8x - 21 \geq 0$ algebraically.
(89)

22. **Retirement Funds** A retirement system paid out an interest rate of 2.25% compounded annually from 1963 to 1965. The function $A(x) = P \cdot 1.0225^x$ can be used to calculate the amount in the account, $A(x)$, after x years with the original amount placed in the account, P. Use the function $f(x) = 1.0225^x$ to sketch a graph of the equation $A(x) = P \cdot 1.0225^x$ if the original amount in the account is \$15,000.
(104)

23. **Population Growth** Based on census statistics, the population of the United States grew at an average annual rate of approximately 1.24% from 1990 to 2000, and the population in 2000 was 281,000,000 (rounded to the nearest million). If the population continues to increase at the same rate, in what year will it reach 400,000,000?
(93)

***24.** **Multi-Step** **a.** Identify the conic section for the equation $x^2 + (y-2)^2 = 36$.
(114)

b. Write an equivalent equation in general form.

***25.** **Graphing Calculator** Use a graphing calculator to solve the system of equations.
(29)

$$\begin{aligned} 4x + 5y + 3z &= 15 \\ x - 3y + 2z &= -6 \\ -x + 2y - z &= 3 \end{aligned}$$

© Saxon. All rights reserved.

Finding Double-Angle and Half-Angle Identities

LESSON 115

26. (108) **Algebra** Using the information in the figure below show algebraically that $1 + \cot^2(\theta) = \csc^2(\theta)$.

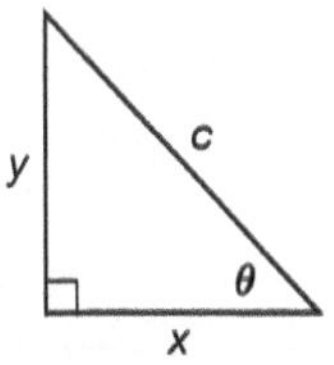

27. (91) **Error Analysis** Explain and correct the error a student made in graphing $(x - 2)^2 + (y + 9)^2 = 25$.

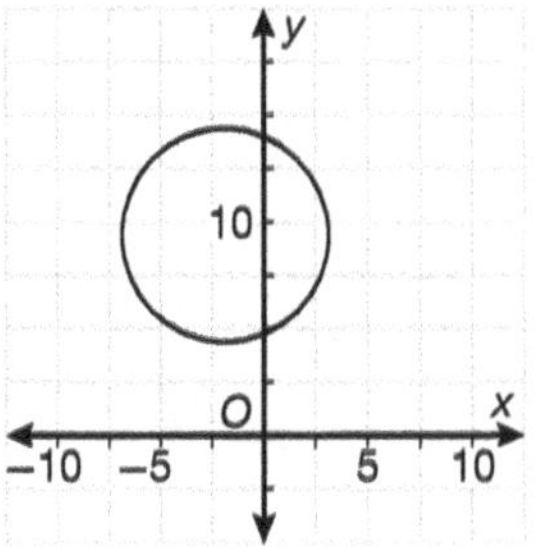

28. (33) **Editors** A publishing company needs 4 editors for the next big assignment. How many ways can the editors be chosen from a pool of 13 editors?

***29.** (110) **Generalize** The function $y = a\log_b(cx)$ has an x-intercept at $x = \frac{1}{c}$. What is the x-intercept for $y = a\log_b(cx - d)$?

30. (47) Identify the domain, range, and asymptote(s) of $y = \left(\frac{7}{11}\right)^x + 3$.

© Saxon. All rights reserved.

Name ______________________ Date __________ Class __________

Finding Best Fit Models

LESSON 116

***1.** (116) **Multi-Step** Write a cubic function to model the data in the table. Then estimate the value of y when x is 3. How does the estimate change when a quartic function is used instead?

x	−10	−5	0	5	10
y	1996	263	−12	−245	−2010

***2.** (113) **International Landmarks** The Santa Justa Elevator (Elevador de Santa Justa) in Lisbon, Portugal is 45 meters tall. Suppose a ball is dropped from the top of the elevator and rebounds 25% of its previous height after each bounce.

a. Use summation notation to write an infinite geometric series to represent the total distance the ball travels after it initially hits the ground. Keep in mind that the ball travels both down and up on each bounce.

b. Find the sum of the series from part a.

c. Find the total distance the ball travels by adding the distance traveled before the ball initially hit the ground.

3. (33) Determine the number of outcomes if you choose an even number or an odd number greater than 25 between the numbers 1 through 50.

4. (107) Find the roots of $y = x^9 - 8x^6 - x^3 + 8$.

***5.** (116) **Population** The table shows the approximate populations of the United States for certain decades.

Year	1930	1940	1960	1980	1990	2000
Population (millions)	1.23	1.32	1.79	2.27	2.49	2.81

a. List the following types of regressions in order from those of best fit to worst fit for the data: linear, quadratic, cubic, quartic, logarithmic, and exponential.

b. Use the first model listed for the answer in part a to estimate the population of the United States in 1950.

Simplify the expressions. (40)

6. $\sqrt{15} \cdot \sqrt{5}$

7. $\sqrt{175} - \sqrt{63} + \sqrt{20}$

8. (92) The last term of a finite arithmetic sequence is 33 and the common difference is −9. Find the 5th term of the sequence given that there are 21 terms in all.

***9.** (115) **Error Analysis** A student claims that $\cot\theta\cos\theta - \sin\theta = \cos 2\theta \csc\theta$ is NOT an identity based on the work shown below. What is the student's error?

$$\cot\theta\cos\theta - \sin\theta \stackrel{?}{=} \cos 2\theta\csc\theta$$
$$\stackrel{?}{=} \cos^2\theta - \sin^2\theta\left(\frac{1}{\sin\theta}\right)$$
$$\stackrel{?}{=} \cos^2\theta - \sin\theta$$

© Saxon. All rights reserved.

10. (31) Divide and then evaluate for $x = 7$: $\frac{x+9}{3x} \div \frac{3x+27}{x}$.

***11.** (112) **Coordinate Geometry** Find the coordinates of the images of points A, B, and C after a 25° rotation counterclockwise about the origin. Round answers to the nearest hundredth. Show how you arrived at your answers.

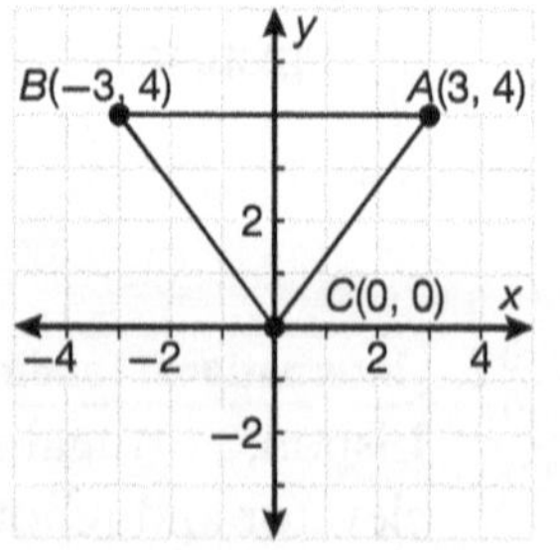

Determine if the given points are solutions of the inequalities.

12. (39) $(3, -3)$; $y \le \frac{2}{3}x - 5$

13. (39) $(-2, -6)$; $y < 9x - 3$

***14.** (111) **Analyze** Choosing from translations, stretches, compressions, and reflections, which transformation(s) can result in a polynomial function which has a different description of end behavior than that of the original polynomial function? Justify your answer.

15. (109) **Optics** A diagram of a hyperbolic mirror is shown. The property of a hyperbolic mirror is that if you shine a beam of light from the mirror, the light is reflected toward the focal point. For this mirror, where should you place a view lens to see the converging light?

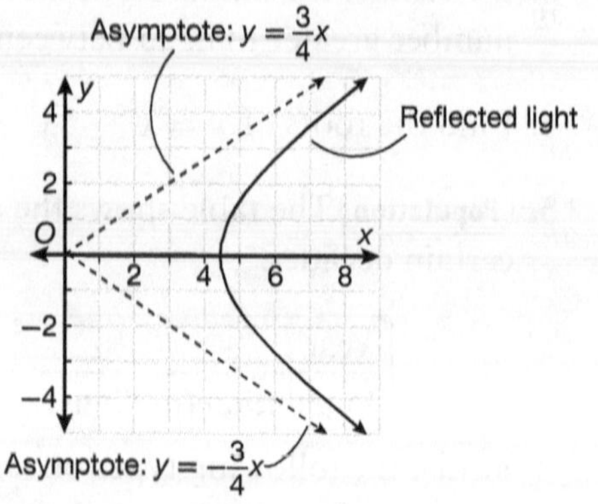

***16.** (114) **Write** Tell why the graph of the equation $4x^2 + 4xy + y^2 - 12x + 8y + 36 = 0$ is not a parabola.

Find the roots of the equations.

17. (106) $y = 12x^5 - 49x^4 + 49x^3 - 96x^2 + 392x - 392$

18. (106) $y = x^{14} - x^{12} - x^{11} + x^9 - x^5 + x^3 + x^2 - 1$

19. (100) **Multiple Choice** Which of the following rational functions includes a hole at $x = -5$?

A $y = \frac{x^2 - 25}{x^2 - 12x + 35}$

B $y = \frac{x^2 - 25}{x^2 - 14x + 48}$

C $y = \frac{x^2 - 25}{x^2 - x - 30}$

D $y = \frac{x^2 - 25}{x^2 + x - 30}$

20. (91) **Geometry** Write the equation of a circle if its center is located at $(5, -1)$ and its circumference is 20π units.

© Saxon. All rights reserved.

21. **Error Analysis** A student described the end behavior of $f(x) = -x^2 + 2x^3 + x^4$ as shown below. What error did the student likely make? Describe the end behavior correctly.
(101)

$$\text{As } x \longrightarrow +\infty, f(x) \longrightarrow -\infty, \text{ and as } x \longrightarrow -\infty, f(x) \longrightarrow -\infty.$$

***22.** **Graphing Calculator** Perform a quadratic regression for the data in the table. Give the R^2 value. Use the function to predict the y-value when x is 6.
(116)

x	1.5	2.6	3.5	4.5	8
y	−4.3	−3.05	−2.11	−0.95	0

23. **Forestry** The volume of a giant sequoia, in cubic feet, can be approximated by the function $y = 0.485x^3 - 362x^2 + 89{,}889x - 7{,}379{,}874$, where x is the height of the tree, between 220 feet and 280 feet inclusive. What are the possible heights of a tree whose volume is 45,000 cubic feet? Hint: Set the Window of your graphing calculator to the range of heights for which the function is given.
(106)

***24.** **Multiple Choice** Which of the following is the exact value of $\sin\frac{\theta}{2}$ if $\cos\theta = -\frac{1}{4}$ and $90° < \theta < 180°$.
(115)

A $-\frac{\sqrt{10}}{4}$ **B** $\frac{\sqrt{10}}{4}$ **C** $-\frac{\sqrt{6}}{4}$ **D** $\frac{\sqrt{6}}{4}$

25. **Money** The members of a bowling team are sharing the cost of a $125 gift for their team leader. Write and solve an inequality to show the numbers of members whose participation would bring the cost per member to less than $7.50.
(94)

26. **Write** Explain in complete sentences what must be done to an equation to vertically compress the graph.
(104)

27. Find an equation for the inverse of $y = 4x^2 + 24$.
(50)

Factor completely.
(61)

28. $x^3 + 7x^2 + 7x - 15$ **29.** $x^4 + 3x^3 - 25x^2 + 9x - 84$

***30.** **Formulate** Substitute the formula for the nth term of an arithmetic sequence into the formula for the sum of the first n terms of an arithmetic series. In what situation could this new formula be used?
(105)

© Saxon. All rights reserved.

Name ______________________ Date __________ Class __________

Solving Systems of Nonlinear Equations

LESSON **117**

*1. (109) **Generalize** For a hyperbola of the form $ax^2 + by^2 + cx + dy + e = 0$, what must be true about a and b if the orientation of the hyperbola is vertical.

2. (88) Given $A = \frac{1}{2}d_1d_2$ find d_1.

3. (47) **Savings** \$2,000 is deposited into a savings account. How much money will be in the account in 30 years if there is an 8% interest rate compounded quarterly?

*4. (111) **Multiple Choice** The graph of $g(x)$ is the graph of $f(x) = 3x^4 - 4$ shifted 2 units left. Which is the correct rule for $g(x)$?

A $g(x) = 3(x + 2)^4 - 4$ **B** $g(x) = 3(x - 2)^4 - 4$

C $g(x) = 3x^4 - 2$ **D** $g(x) = 3x^4 - 6$

5. (106) **Probability** A function is randomly selected from the list below and graphed.

$P(x) = x^3 + 2x^2 - 13x + 10$, $Q(x) = x^3 - 2x^2 + x$, $R(x) = 3x^3 + 48x$,
$S(x) = 2x^3 - 32x$, $T(x) = x^3 - 7x^2 + 4x - 28$

What is the probability that the graph has exactly one x-intercept? What are the odds in favor?

Simplify the logarithms.

6. (72) $\log_7 5^3$

7. (72) $\log_5 42 - \log_5 7$

*8. (116) **Justify** Tell why it is incorrect to call the R^2 value the *correlation coefficient.*

9. (95) Determine if $P(x) = 3x^3 - 4x^2 - 28x - 16$ has a zero remainder when divided by $x + 2$. Determine $Q(x)$.

*10. (22) **Graphing Calculator** Graph $y = -x^2 + 3$ on your calculator. Classify the function as discrete or continuous and identify the range.

11. (92) Find a_6 of an arithmetic sequence given that $a_3 = 55$ and $a_{20} = 140$.

*12. (117) **Recreation** A boy's remote-controlled airplane is making loops in a park and the path can be modeled by $4x^2 + y^2 = 25$. A girl's remote-controlled plane is making a straight line that can be modeled by $2x + y = 7$. Is there any chance that the two planes will collide? If so, where?

13. (94) **Analyze** Explain why you must consider two cases when solving a rational inequality by using the LCD.

14. (63) **Physics** As an airplane comes in for a landing, the pilot wants to maintain a constant angle relative to the ground. If the pilot wants to maintain an angle between 30 and 40 degrees, define the bounds on x for the tangent function $y = \tan x$ in radians that monitor the plane's orientation.

© Saxon. All rights reserved.

15. (105) **Coordinate Geometry** For the sequence {2, 4, 6, 8, 10}, graph the ordered pairs (n, a_n) and (n, S_n). How do the graphs compare?

16. (98) **Multiple Choice** Which of the following points is not on the ellipse $\frac{x^2}{2^2} + \frac{y^2}{5^2} = 1$?

A (0, 5) **B** (2, 0) **C** (5, 0) **D** (−2, 0)

17. (101) **Multi-Step** A manufacturer wants to design an open box with a square base and a total surface area of 200 square inches.

a. Write an equation that relates x, h, and 200. Solve it for h.

b. Write a function $V(x)$ for the volume of the box.

c. Graph $V(x)$ on a graphing calculator. Find the maximum possible volume of the box and the corresponding dimensions.

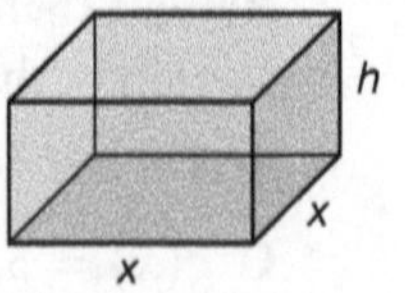

***18.** (117) **Analyze** What is the maximum number of intersection points that a circle and a line can have?

19. (104) **Formulate** In the coordinate plane, functions f and g are graphed. If g is a translation of $f = \sqrt{x}$, find an equation for g.

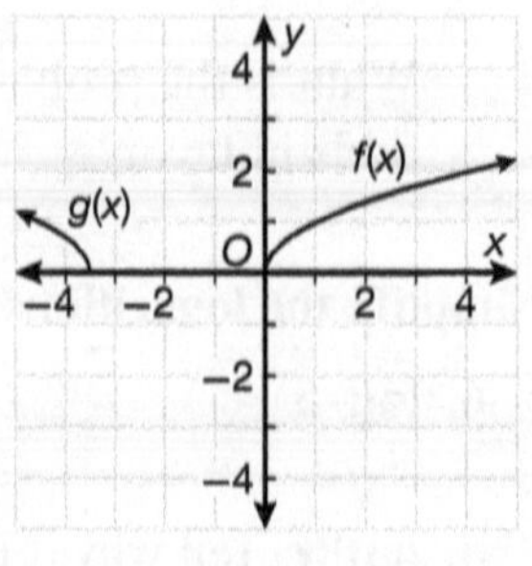

***20.** (117) **Multi-Step** Consider the system $\begin{matrix} x^2 - y^2 = 15 \\ 9x^2 + 16y^2 = 160 \end{matrix}$.

a. What figures do the graphs of each equation make?

b. At most, how many solutions could there be?

c. Solve the system by elimination.

d. **Verify** If you were to verify your solutions by using a graphing calculator, what would be the equations you would enter?

21. (36) Find the equation of the line that passes through the point (1, 7) and is perpendicular to the line $y = -\frac{1}{2}x + 4$.

22. (Inv 10) Describe the graph of a conic section whose eccentricity is 2 and vertical distance from its focus or center is 2 and write the general equation in polar form.

23. (45) Use the data in the table to write the equation for the line of best fit.

Level	2	3	4	5	6
Cars Sold	8	10	13	18	25

© Saxon. All rights reserved.

*24. (115) **Entertainment** The horizontal distance x traveled by an object launched from ground level with an initial speed v and angle θ is given by $x = \frac{1}{32}v^2 \sin 2\theta$. A firework with a shell size of 36 inches has an initial velocity of 481 feet per second. What horizontal distance will a firework travel if it is launched from ground level at an angle of 85°?

Solve.

25. (102) $\log_5 625$

26. (102) $\log_5 (5x + 9) = \log_5 6x$

27. (110) **Error Analysis** Two students are simplifying the logarithmic function below, but they get different results. Which student made the mistake?

$$y = \log(9x^2 + 30x + 25)$$

Student A	Student B
$y = \log(9x^2 + 30x + 25)$ $= \log((3x + 5)(3x + 6))$ $= \log(3x + 5) + \log(3x + 6)$	$y = \log(9x^2 + 30x + 25)$ $= \log(9x^2 + 2 \cdot 3 \cdot 5x + 5^2)$ $= \log(3x + 5)^2$ $= 2\log(3x + 5)$

28. (101) Describe the end behavior of the graph of the polynomial function $f(x) = -2x^3 + 7x - 4$.

*29. (116) **Finance** The table shows stock values of a certain stock for 5 different days.

Day	3	6	8	14	16
Value of Stock	\$38	\$21	\$15	\$34	\$52

Use a sketch of the scatter plot to determine if a quartic or logarithmic model would better fit the data. Then write the function of the chosen regression model.

*30. (105) Find S_{18} for 2, 9, 16, 23, 30, …

© Saxon. All rights reserved.

Name ______________________ Date __________ Class __________

Recognizing Misleading Data

LESSON 118

1. (105) **(Savings)** A teen deposits money into a savings account. The first week she deposits \$20. Each week thereafter, she deposits \$10 more than the previous week. Show how to use an arithmetic series to find the total amount of money in the account after 16 weeks.

Find the zeros of the functions.

2. (99) $y = 36x^4 - 27x^3 - 13x^2 + 3x + 1$

3. (99) $y = 80x^4 - 64x^3 - 21x^2 + 4x + 1$

***4.** (118) **(Automobiles)** Explain why the graph is misleading. Who might have made the graph and why?

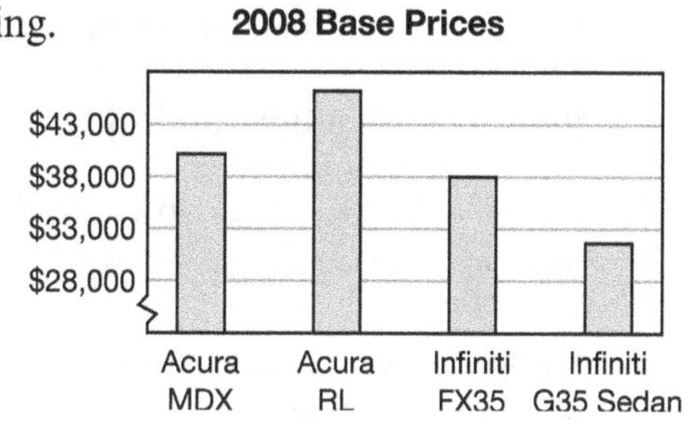

5. (115) **Multi-Step** If $\tan\theta = \frac{5}{12}$ and $0° < \theta < 90°$.

a. What is $\cos\theta$?

b. What is the exact value of $\sin\frac{\theta}{2}$?

6. (89) **Geometry** The perimeter of a rectangle is 82 feet. Write and solve an inequality to find the width, rounded to the nearest tenth, for which the rectangle has an area less than 250 square feet.

7. (39) Determine if $(-6, 10)$ is a solution of the inequality $y > \frac{4}{3}x + 11$.

8. (107) **Analyze** The graph of the rational function $f(x) = \frac{g(x)}{h(x)}$ has holes at $x = \pm c$, for constant c. Define a new polynomial using $j(x)$ that is equivalent to $h(x)$ and takes the values of c into account.

***9.** (116) **Probability** Suppose for the data set $\{(1, 4), (4, 10), (6, 11), (10, 12), (12, 13)\}$ that one of the following regression models is randomly chosen to predict a value: linear, quadratic, cubic, quartic, exponential, and logarithmic. What is the probability that the R^2 value for the chosen model is less than 0.95?

10. (106) **Analyze** Can a sixth-degree polynomial function have exactly six irrational roots? Why or why not?

11. (115) **Write** Find $\sin 2\theta$ and $\cos 2\theta$ if $\cos\theta = -\frac{1}{4}$ and $90° < \theta < 180°$. Did you need to find the value of $\sin\theta$ to find these values? Explain.

***12.** (116) **(Postage)** The cost of a US first class stamp for given years are shown in the table.

Year	1895	1914	1947	1966	1973	1980	1982	1991	2001	2006	2007
Cost, in cents	2	2	3	5	8	15	20	29	34	39	41

a. Find an exponential function to model the data. Use the number of years before or after 1900 for x. Use the model to predict the cost of a stamp in 2025.

b. Predict the cost of a stamp in 2025 when a quartic model is used instead.

c. Justify Which price do you think is more reliable? Why?

© Saxon. All rights reserved.

13. **Error Analysis** Find and correct the error a student made in stating that the graph of the equation $\frac{(x-4)^2}{25} + \frac{(y-1)^2}{8} = 1$ is a hyperbola.
(114)

*14. **Multiple Choice** A data set has an outlier. Which statement is false?
(118)

A Reporting the mean is likely to be misleading.

B Reporting the median is likely to be misleading.

C Reporting the range is likely to be misleading.

D Reporting either the mean or range is likely to be misleading.

15. **Write** What is a limit and when does a geometric series have a limit?
(113)

16. Identify the leading coefficient, degree, and describe the end behavior of $f(x) = x^4 - x^3 - 4x^2 + 4$.
(101)

*17. **Multiple Choice** Which could not have three points of intersection?
(117)

A circle and line **B** hyperbola and circle

C circle and ellipse **D** two parabolas

18. **Furniture** The diagram represents a table top in the shape of a regular hexagon centered on a coordinate grid. To the nearest hundredth, what are the coordinates of point P'? Show how you arrived at your answer. (*Hint*: Use a rotation matrix.)
(112)

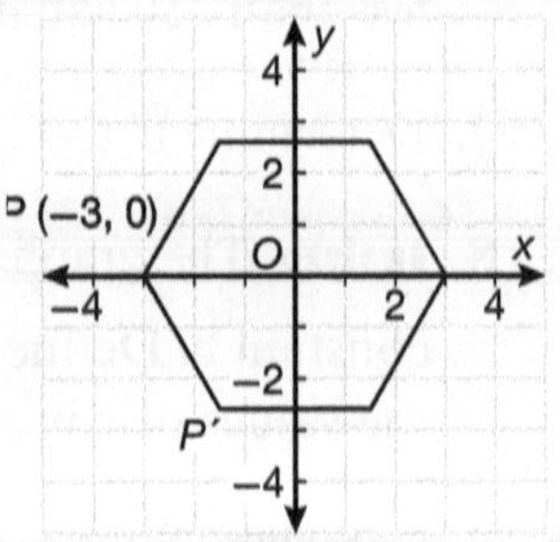

*19. **Justify** A pollster suggests the following question to be on a ballot. 'Do you support a new traffic light on First Street and Walnut Street which engineers claim will reduce accidents by up to 65%?' Another pollster says that this question is biased and must be changed. Explain why this pollster is correct in saying the question is biased.
(118)

*20. **Multi-Step** This conical container has a radius of 6 feet and a height of 8 feet.
(111)

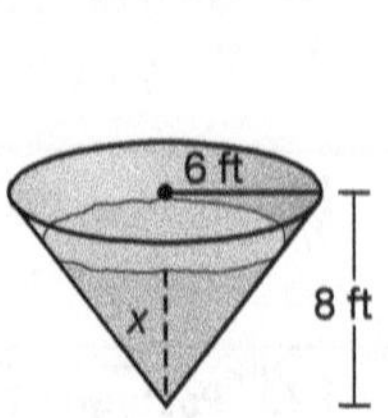

a. Write a function $V(x)$ that gives the volume of water in the container when the height of the water is x feet.

b. Describe the transformation $g(x) = V(2x)$ by writing the rule for $g(x)$ and explaining the change in the context of the problem.

Divide using synthetic division.

21. $x^4 - 11x^3 + 14x^2 + 80x$ by $x + 2$
(51)

22. $x^3 - 57x + 56$ by $x - 1$
(51)

23. Solve the equation by finding all the roots: $x^4 - 2x^3 - 14x^2 - 2x - 15 = 0$.
(106)

© Saxon. All rights reserved.

24. Let $f(x) = \tan(x)$ and $g(x) = 3x - 2$. Find the period of $f(g(x))$.
(90)

***25.** **Graphing Calculator** Graph the function $y = -4x^2 + 8x + 2$. Determine the vertex and axis of symmetry.
(30)

***26.** **Error Analysis** Explain and correct the error(s) a student made in solving the system $\begin{matrix} x = y + 2 \\ x^2 - y^2 = 16 \end{matrix}$.
(117)

$(y + 2)^2 - y^2 = 16$	$x = y + 2$
$y^2 + 4y + 4 - y^2 = 16$	$x = 3 + 2$
$4y + 4 = 16$	$x = 5$
$y = 3$	The solution is (3, 5).

***27.** Use the Rational Root Theorem to find the roots of
(110)
$y = 2x^7 - x^6 - 15x^5 + 18x^4 - 2x^3 + x^2 + 15x - 18$.

28. **Coordinate Geometry** The graphs of $y_1 = \tan^2(x)$ and $y_2 = \sec^2(x)$ are shown at right. The graph of y_1 has a y-intercept of 0, and the graph of y_2 has a y-intercept of 1. Use the graphs to prove the trigonometric identity, $1 + \tan^2(x) = \sec^2(x)$.
(108)

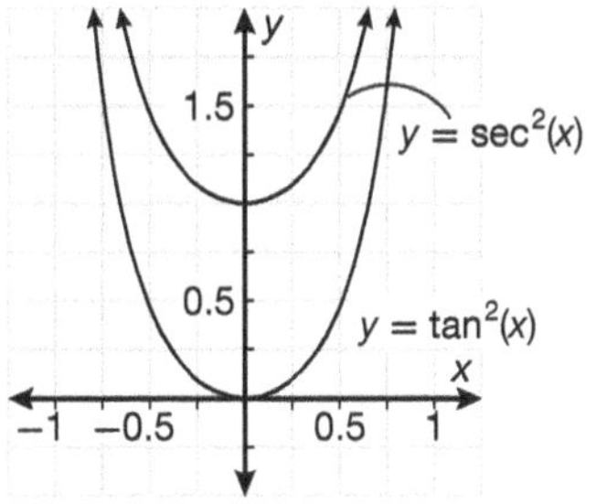

29. A card is drawn at random from a standard deck. How many outcomes are in the event of drawing a diamond or a 4?
(33)

30. Evaluate 4! • 6!
(42)

© Saxon. All rights reserved.

Name ______________________ Date __________ Class __________

Solving Trigonometric Equations

LESSON 119

1. (106) **Analyze** A polynomial equation has a root of $2 + 3i$ and this root has a multiplicity of 2. What is the least degree that the polynomial can be? Why?

***2.** (119) **Write** Describe the difference between an equation and an identity.

3. (93) If a private school's enrollment is 600 students and it increases 5% each year, how long will it take to get 800 students?

4. (114) **Multi-Step** The boundary of the set of possible points for the epicenter of an earthquake recorded at an observation station can be represented by the equation $x^2 + y^2 - 8x - 40y - 209 = 0$.

a. What conic section represents the situation?

b. Write the equation in standard form.

5. (42) Find the number of combinations of 16 objects taken 12 at a time.

***6.** (117) **Graphing Calculator** Solve $\begin{matrix} 25x^2 + 4.3y^2 = 89 \\ x^2 + y^2 = 9.8 \end{matrix}$. Round to the nearest hundredth.

***7.** (119) **Solar Eclipses** For a solar eclipse to be possible, the moon must be near the line between the earth and the sun within 3 days of a new moon. Suppose the cycle of the moon can be modeled by $M(t) = \cos\left(\frac{\pi}{14}t\right)$, where t is the number of days from now. The minimum value of $M(t)$ represents a new moon. How many days from now is the next new moon? When $P(t) = 2\sin^2\left(\frac{\pi}{14}t\right) + \cos\left(\frac{\pi}{14}t\right) - \frac{1}{2}$ equals $M(t)$, the moon is on the line between earth and the sun. Is a solar eclipse possible before the next new moon? Why or why not? Explain.

***8.** (118) **Write** When surveying, what are the pros and cons of open questions and closed questions?

9. (97) Find the common ratio of the geometric sequence and use it to find the next three terms. $14, 2, \frac{2}{7}\ldots$

***10.** (118) **Data Analysis** What could be misleading about the graph shown?

Population

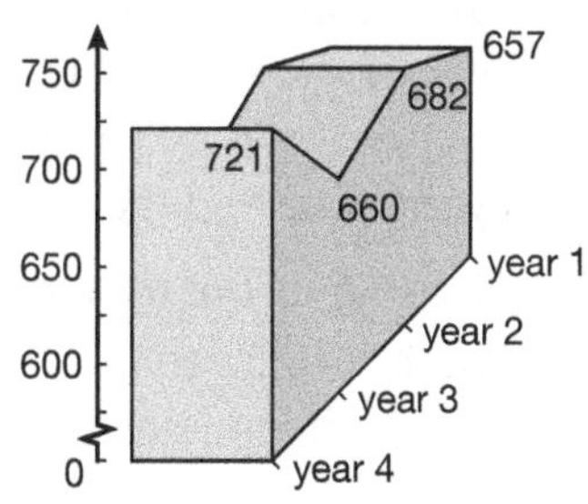

11. (Inv 11) Use De Moivre's Theorem to evaluate the complex number $(6 - 7i)^3$ to express the result in trigonometric form.

***12.** (117) **Model** Sketch diagrams to show how two parabolas can intersect in 0, 1, 2, 3, or 4 points.

© Saxon. All rights reserved.

***13. Multiple Choice** For what values $0 \leq \theta < 2\pi$ does $\sin 2\theta = \sin \theta$?
(119)

A $\theta = \frac{1}{2}$ **B** $\theta = 0, \frac{1}{2}$ **C** $\theta = 0, \frac{\pi}{3}, \pi, \frac{5\pi}{3}$ **D** $\theta = \frac{\pi}{3}, \frac{5\pi}{3}$

14. Population The year when the world population reached each billion mark is shown in the table.
(116)

Population (billions)	1	2	3	4	5	6
Year	1800	1927	1960	1974	1987	1999

Find a logarithmic function to model the data and use it to predict when the world population will reach 8 billion.

15. Finance The monthly rent for an apartment is \$850 the first year. Every year thereafter, the rent increases by 2%. Write a geometric series in summation notation to represent the total rent paid after 10 years. Then find the sum.
(113)

***16. Multiple Choice** Which data set is best modeled by an exponential function?
(116)

A {(1, −16), (2, −12), (3, −8), (4, −4), (5, 0)}

B {(1, −16), (2, −8), (3, −4), (4, −2), (5, −1)}

C {(1, −16), (2, 0), (3, 16), (4, 32), (5, 48)}

D {(1, −16), (2, −64), (3, −144), (4, −256), (5, −400)}

17. Manufacturing The horizontal distance x traveled by a golf ball struck from ground level with an initial speed v and angle θ is given by $x = \frac{1}{32}v^2 \sin 2\theta$. The rule determined by the United States Golf Association states that the initial velocity of a golf ball cannot exceed 255 feet per second when tested under specified conditions. If a ball is manufactured with the highest allowed initial velocity, use the equation to determine the horizontal distance of the ball if it is hit at an angle of 45°.
(115)

18. Geometry The Pythagorean Theorem states that the length of the hypotenuse of a right triangle is equal to the square root of the sum of the squared lengths of the legs of the triangle. The equation $h(x) = \sqrt{x + 16}$ can be used to model the possible lengths of the hypotenuse and the square of the other leg for the right triangle shown.
(104)

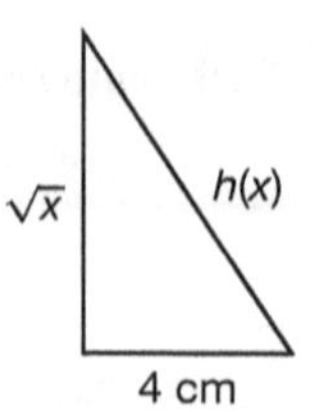

Use $f(x) = \sqrt{x}$ to find the graph of $h(x) = \sqrt{x + 16}$. Then use the graph of $h(x)$ to find two possibilities for the lengths of the other leg and the hypotenuse.

© Saxon. All rights reserved.

Solving Trigonometric Equations

19. (107) **Formulate** The graph of a rational function includes the asymptote shown to the right. Write an equation that fits these parameters.

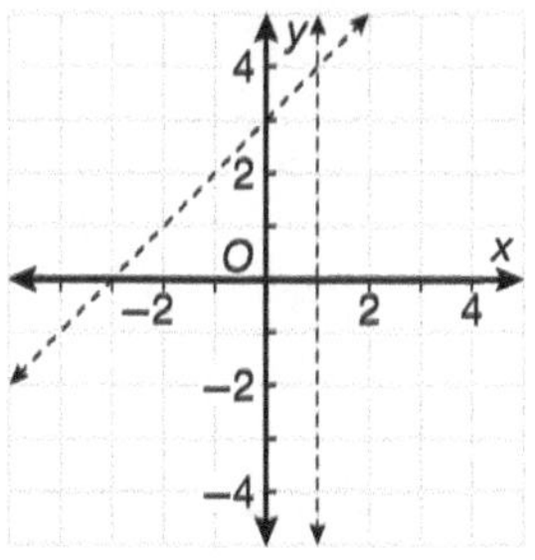

20. (110) **Multi-Step** Let $f(x) = 12\log(4x)$ and $g(x) = \frac{x+2}{(x^4-1)}$. Find the x-intercepts of $f(g(x))$.

21. (87) **Temperature** Using Newton's Law of Cooling $T = e^{(kt+C)} + R$, determine the amount of time needed to cool a cup of water (80°C) to 50°C in a room temperature of 30°C.Use k = −0.200064 and C = 4.0073.

22. (102) **Error Analysis** A student solved $\log 2x + \log 4 = 3$ as shown. What is the error? What is the correct solution?

$$\log 2x + \log 4 = 3 \rightarrow \log(2x + 4) = 3 \rightarrow 2x + 4 = 1000 \rightarrow x = 498$$

23. (105) The common difference in an arithmetic series is 8 and the first term is −160. Find the sum of the first 40 terms.

Find the roots of the equations.

24. (100) $y = 6x^4 - 4x^3 - 8x^2 + 4x + 2$

25. (100) $y = 15x^4 - 16x^3 - 56x^2 + 64x - 16$

Write the expression in simplest form.

26. (40) $5\sqrt[3]{48} - \sqrt[3]{750}$

27. (40) $\frac{\sqrt[4]{36} \cdot \sqrt[4]{9}}{\sqrt[4]{4}}$

***28.** (119) **Multi-Step** Consider the equation $3\tan^2 z + 2\tan z - 1 = 0$.

a. What values of $-90° \le z \le 90°$ satisfy the equation?

b. For how many of the values of z that satisfy the equation does $\sin z = \cos z$?

***29.** (118) **Error Analysis** A student with a part-time job at a movie theater uses ticket stubs he found on the floor to collect data about the types of movies people watch on different days. He says that he takes a simple random sample of the stubs he finds, so his sample cannot be biased. Find the error in the student's reasoning.

30. (45) The data in the table is represented by an exponential function.Use the data to solve for the correlation coefficient, r.

Time (in years)	1	2	3	4	5
Bunnies	30	100	335	1100	3650

© Saxon. All rights reserved.